African Freedom

The push for independence in African nations was ultimately an incomplete process, with the people often left to wrestle with a partial, imperfect legacy. Rather than settle for liberation in name alone, the people engaged in an ongoing struggle for meaningful freedom. Phyllis Taoua shows how the idea of freedom in Africa today evolved from this complex history. With a pan-African, interdisciplinary approach, she synthesizes the most significant issues into a clear narrative. Tracing the evolution of a conversation about freedom since the 1960s, she defines three types and shows how they are interdependent. Taoua investigates their importance in key areas of narrative interest: the intimate self, gender identity, the nation, global capital, and the spiritual realm. Allowing us to hear the voices of African artists and activists, this compelling study makes sense of their struggle and the broad importance of the idea of freedom in contemporary African culture.

Phyllis Taoua is Professor at the University of Arizona in Francophone Studies where she teaches courses on Africa and the French-speaking world. She is affiliated with Africana Studies, World Literature and the Human Rights program.

African Freedom

How Africa Responded to Independence

Phyllis Taoua
University of Arizona

CAMBRIDGE
UNIVERSITY PRESS

University Printing House, Cambridge CB2 8BS, United Kingdom

One Liberty Plaza, 20th Floor, New York, NY 10006, USA

477 Williamstown Road, Port Melbourne, VIC 3207, Australia

314–321, 3rd Floor, Plot 3, Splendor Forum, Jasola District Centre, New Delhi – 110025, India

79 Anson Road, #06-04/06, Singapore 079906

Cambridge University Press is part of the University of Cambridge.

It furthers the University's mission by disseminating knowledge in the pursuit of education, learning, and research at the highest international levels of excellence.

www.cambridge.org
Information on this title: www.cambridge.org/9781108427418
DOI: 10.1017/9781108551700

First published 2018
Printed and bound in Great Britain by Clays Ltd, Elcograf S.p.A.

A catalogue record for this publication is available from the British Library.

Library of Congress Cataloging-in-Publication Data

Names: Taoua, Phyllis, author.
Title: African freedom : how Africa responded to independence / Phyllis Taoua.
Description: New York : Cambridge University Press, 2018. | Includes index.
Identifiers: LCCN 2018011060| ISBN 9781108427418 (hardback : alk. paper) | ISBN 9781108446167 (pbk. : alk. paper)
Subjects: LCSH: Human rights—Africa. | Human rights in literature. | Human rights in motion pictures. | African literature--20th century—History and criticism. | Motion pictures, African—History and criticism. | Self-realization—Africa. | Liberty. | Africa—Social conditions—20th century. | Africa—Social conditions—21st century.
Classification: LCC HN773.5 .T36 2018 | DDC 306.096—dc23
LC record available at https://lccn.loc.gov/2018011060

ISBN 978-1-108-42741-8 Hardback

ISBN 978-1-108-44616-7 Paperback

For Bitti, my dear
And in memory of Alain Ricard

Contents

Figures

Acknowledgments

This book has been a long time in the making, and over the years many people have supported my efforts. There have been senior colleagues who provided indispensable institutional support, mentors who gave me honest guidance, and intellectual friends who talked about ideas with me over dinner. Other people on campus and at conferences around the world suggested books to read, commented on drafts of individual chapters, and dissected with me every aspect of this book from its conceptual organization to the titles I have chosen.

I would first like to thank Susan Suleiman and Kwame Anthony Appiah, who codirected my dissertation and whose support since then has meant a lot to me. I am grateful to my editor Maria Marsh who had confidence in this project and to Natasha Whelan who kindly helped it come to fruition. I would like to express my sincere gratitude to the anonymous reader who gave me expert advice for revision. I felt gifted to have received such thoughtful guidance, which has made the final version so much better than it would have been otherwise. I could not have sustained my work on this book without the encouragement and support of many intellectual friends to whom I express my heartfelt thanks. I benefited from advice, conversation, and suggested revisions from the late Alain Ricard and Abiola Irele, and from Anita and Orlando Patterson, Irène d'Almeida, Moradewun Adejunmobi, Tejumola Olaniyan, Ato Quayson, Harry Garuba, Cilas Kemedjio, Praise Zenenga, Juliana Makuchi Nfah-Abbenyi, Nicolas Martin-Granel, Xavier Garnier, Suzi Dovi, Adam Ewing, Jacot Allant, Bernard de Meyer, Wayne Decker, Valerie Orlando, Claire Griffiths, and Alan Smith. Those whose names I have left out, please forgive me. I would like to thank Toyin Falola and Carina Rey for introducing me to Maria Marsh at Cambridge University Press. I would like to thank the faculty and students at the African Studies Centre at the University of Cape Town who inspired me to completely rewrite Chapter 3 and rekindled my interest in decolonial theory in the final stages of writing. I would like to thank Elizabeth Ault who took my work seriously and encouraged me to step into the strength of my argument with bold confidence. I am indebted to Laura Hunter in the Provost's office for her program to help writers become more productive and to Suzi Dovi who has been a faithful, brilliant, and inspiring interlocutor about the writing process. I have benefited from the competent research assistance of Ronnie Uribe in the preparation of the list of works cited and Danielle Eastin in securing copyright permissions. I would like to thank Maggie Smith for her carefully considered editorial advice. Many thanks to David Huber for his assistance preparing the photographs in this book for publication. I have also benefited from the friendly, efficient assistance of the SILLC business team at the University of Arizona who handled so many requests and reservations as I traveled around the world talking to colleagues about ideas in this book.

In 2006, I received an award from the Sheila Biddle Ford Foundation to spend a semester in residence at the DuBois Institute for African and African American Research at Harvard University. Over the years, the Department of French and Italian, the College of Humanities, and the division on Global Initiatives at the University of Arizona have funded my research and travel. I would like to thank the Humanities Center at Harvard University and the African Studies Centre at the University of Cape Town for invitations to lecture and exchange ideas. Laura Berry invited me to teach at the Honors College at the University of Arizona, and those encounters, inside and outside the classroom, have been stimulating and inspiring. I would also like to thank my students who have engaged in debate with me, pushing me to refine and rethink over the years. Finally, I would like to express my deepest gratitude and love to my friends, family, and daughter, Bitti, who have lived through the writing of this book with me.

Caveat: The autobiographical stories that I share in this book are based on true events in which I participated, but the impressions they convey are my own. I do not claim to represent the views or experiences of others.

Note
W. S. Merwin

Remember how the naked soul
comes to language and at once knows
loss and distance and believing

then for a time it will not run
with its old freedom
like a light innocent of measure
but will hearken to how
one story becomes another
and will try to tell where
they have emerged from
and where they are heading
as though they were its own legend
running before the words and beyond them
naked and never looking back

through the noise of the questions

Introduction

The Meaning of Freedom in Africa

> Seated in his armchair, his coat unbuttoned, his straw hat pulled down to his ears, slowly scratching his bare belly, Ti Noël issued orders to the wind. But they were the edicts of a peaceable government, inasmuch as no tyranny of whites or Negroes seemed to offer a threat to his liberty.
>
> *Alejo Carpentier, The Kingdom of This World*

The ideal of meaningful freedom in Africa today evolved from a complex history. For better or for worse, many people around the world came to associate the struggle for freedom in Africa during much of the twentieth century with the fate of the South African people. Several factors, from the duration and brutality of the apartheid regime, to the global campaign to end its oppression, made this a reality. On February 11, 1990, when Nelson Mandela was released from prison, he walked onto the balcony of City Hall in Cape Town and addressed the restless crowd that had gathered, evoking, once again, the cause of freedom: "Friends, comrades and fellow South Africans. I greet you all in the name of peace, democracy, and freedom for all!"[1] Indeed, it was this inclusive ideal of freedom for all South Africans that he had defended in his statement from the dock while on trial in 1963 and 1964. On April 20, 1964, he proclaimed, "I have cherished the ideal of a democratic and free society in which all persons live together in harmony and with equal opportunities. It is an ideal which I hope to live for and to achieve. But if needs be, it is an ideal for which I am prepared to die."[2] That Mandela repeated the word "ideal" three times in the dramatic conclusion to what was a carefully crafted statement signals the vital importance of his vision for a free and democratic society – a vision he believed was worthy of both a collective armed struggle and his own ultimate sacrifice. This powerful ideal of freedom, which had brought Mandela and his codefendants sharply up against the repressive authority of the apartheid state, was more than an idea but not yet a collectively shared value among all South Africans.[3] For our purposes, the specific way Mandela performed the discourse of national liberation to advance the cause of freedom, which embraced the armed struggle as a means of attaining an inclusive ideal of freedom based on the principles of democracy, serves as a point of departure for articulating the relationship between national liberation and the idea of freedom in Africa.

Even as the National Party in South Africa brutally supplanted antiapartheid protest led by Mandela, Oliver Tambo, Robert Sobukwe, Ahmed Kathrada, Walter and Albertina Sisulu, and many others during the 1950s and 1960s, "new" African nations had begun to emerge elsewhere on the continent. The West African nation of Ghana played a pioneering role in this transition as the first to gain independence and as a crucible of pan-Africanism. Kwame Nkrumah, the first prime minister of an independent Ghana, was an ardent defender of national liberation and had been a participant in pan-African congresses since the 1940s, which "had the cause of African freedom at heart" and whose "moving spirit" had been W. E. B. DuBois, a leading US civil rights activist, pan-Africanist, author, and editor. We see the defining importance of Nkrumah's pan-African perspective in the speech he delivered on March 6, 1957, on the eve of independence: "At long last, the battle has ended! And thus, Ghana, your beloved country is free forever!" He also added a broader appeal to his fellow citizens: "We have won the battle and we again re-dedicate ourselves ... Our independence is meaningless unless it is linked up with the total liberation of Africa."[4] For Nkrumah, Ghana's achievement of national sovereignty was a partial triumph that could only be completed through the realization of his pan-African project to liberate every nation on the continent from foreign domination. The following year, Nkrumah rearticulated these goals in his address to his "fellow African Freedom Fighters" at the first All-African People's Conference on December 8, 1958. Whereas his conceptual repertoire in this historic speech included "emancipation," "liberation," "sovereignty," and "independence" in addition to "unity" and "struggle," Nkrumah most often evoked the cause of freedom with no fewer than thirty-five references to "freedom," "free," and "freely." The centrality of freedom in Nkrumah's pan-African project is equally evident in his enumeration of the four stages of liberation that was the subject of their collective deliberations:

1. The attainment of freedom and independence.
2. The consolidation of that freedom and independence.
3. The creation of unity and community between free African states.
4. The economic and social reconstruction of Africa.

Nkrumah goes on to articulate the need for freedom *and* independence in a discussion where freedom is associated with the potential for the culturally and spiritually liberating effects created by political independence in terms that echo both W. E. B. DuBois's *The Souls of Black Folk* (1903) and Alioune Diop's editorial vision in *Présence Africaine*. The comprehensive scope of Nkrumah's project was anti-imperial, calling for the consolidation of political power in the hands of African leaders, as well as the social and economic reconstruction of new nations. In his speeches at this conference, and at the United Nations two years later, Nkrumah promoted his ideal of pan-African freedom with passion and in explicit solidarity with southern Africa and demanded that European imperial powers decolonize the entire continent.[5] Nkrumah stands out as an important example for the way he assumed his responsibility as a pioneer, convening emerging leaders in Accra and articulating the relationship between the "Political Kingdom," which is to say "the complete independence and self-determination of national territories," and the broader goals of unity, reconstruction, and shared prosperity.

Of the icons of national liberation in Africa, Patrice Lumumba is remembered for his painful frankness and its tragic consequences. While I will consider the complexities of decolonization in the Democratic Republic of Congo (DRC) in some detail later, for now I would like to take another look at the language of freedom that Lumumba deployed in his speeches at the time of independence. Lumumba had the strongest national platform in the DRC and shared Nkrumah's dreams of unfettered sovereignty and African reconstruction in what Lumumba imagined would be a partnership among equals with former Belgian colonials. In fact, he attended the All-African People's Conference in Accra, and his participation in these deliberations transformed him.[6] In his infamous Independence Day speech on June 30, 1960, Lumumba opened with a tone that echoed Nkrumah's candor and self-confidence: "For this independence of the Congo, even as it is celebrated today with Belgium, a friendly country with whom we deal as equal to equal ..."[7] Yet with the wounds of Belgian domination so "fresh and painful," Lumumba continued by listing the offenses he and his compatriots suffered, including exploitation, insult, dispossession of land and rights, social injustice, racial inequality, harassing work, brutal subjugation, and deprivations worse than death itself. In this respect, Lumumba was the least conciliatory of leaders. He boldly presented Congolese independence as a decisive step in the liberation of the entire continent:

> Together, my brothers, my sisters, we are going to begin a new struggle, a sublime struggle, which will lead our country to peace, prosperity and greatness.
>
> Together, we are going to establish social justice and make sure everyone has just remuneration for his labour.
>
> We are going to show the world what the black man can do when he works in freedom, and we are going to make of the Congo the center of the sun's radiance for all of Africa.[8]

Lumumba clearly lays the fruits of freedom on the line. And the speech was interpreted differently in different quarters. Malcolm X effusively praised it as the "greatest speech" by the "greatest black man who ever walked the African continent."[9] King Baudouin of Belgium and his imperial partners received Lumumba's independence speech as an unpardonable affront. What Lumumba brought back with him from Accra, where he also met Frantz Fanon, was a "mature nationalism" that included "national unity, economic independence, and pan-African solidarity."[10] The popular support Nkrumah amassed for his party, the Mouvement National Congolais, was unique insofar as it was not based on regional or ethnic identities, and with this, Georges Nzongola-Ntalaja claims in *The Congo from Leopold to Kabila: A People's History* that, "a veritable democracy movement was born as the nationalist awakening in the Congo found a positive articulation with the fight for expanded rights by the *évolués* and the working people's aspirations for freedom and material prosperity."[11]

I would argue that the way these and other leaders of African national liberation deployed the language of freedom to advance their cause was so pervasive as to be taken for granted. This equation of liberation with freedom persisted across the continent for much of the twentieth century from the mobilization of independence movements during the postwar era through to Mandela's election in 1994. Looking back on these important historical junctures in modern African history, one may be tempted to say that the pioneers of African national liberation were too idealistic, but evidence suggests they were quite aware of the imperial forces arrayed against them as a result of Cold War divisions and competition.[12] One might also be tempted to say that they were foolish to put faith in fellow Africans to choose solidarity and unity over rivalry; yet, here again, the archive reveals that they were cognizant of the colonial tools used to divide communities into weaker, manageable units, and they worked actively to overcome the threat of these divisions. We see this in the speeches and writings of Nkrumah and Black Consciousness Leader Steve Biko, to cite only two of the most well-known examples.[13] Thus, in my view, to advance criticism in a retrospective manner that emphasizes primarily the limited, insufficient nature of the discourse of national liberation or a given leader's naïveté about the gritty, unpleasant reality of the struggle tends to capture only part of a more complex set of dynamics at work.

It is also important to note that national liberation was seen as instrumental to changing daily life for ordinary people in the nations that were to emerge. While there are notable differences in style and sensibilities among Mandela, Nkrumah, and Lumumba – the three leaders I have cited as examples of nationalists who deployed the language of freedom to advance their cause of liberation – it is instructive to note from the outset how each of these leaders made a claim for national liberation that was embedded in a broader set of concepts. In *Africa since 1940: The Past of the Present* (2002), Frederick Cooper interprets Nkrumah's often quoted phrase, "Seek ye first the political kingdom" as not "just a call for Ghanaians to demand a voice in the affairs of the state, but a plea for leaders and ordinary citizens to use power for a purpose – to transform a colonized society into a dynamic and prosperous land of opportunity."[14] The way leaders connected the promise of achieving political sovereignty with the potential for meaningful social transformation was explicit, and their performance of this discourse of nationalism appealed to the imagination of ordinary people. Yet, while critics have devoted substantial attention to the pitfalls of national liberation both as a discourse and as a process, the meaning of freedom deserves more careful consideration as an integral part of the cultural narrative of independence and renewal in Africa.

James Ferguson warned more than a decade ago that, "At the end of a century dominated by anticolonial nationalist struggles for sovereignty and independence, we can hardly help but see national independence as almost synonymous with dignity, freedom, and empowerment. This … may be in some respects a trap."[15] His observation in *Global Shadows: Africa in the Neoliberal World Order* (2006) was directed at scholars in the field of African cultural studies and asked for a widening of the scope of analysis through disentangling national liberation and the ideas of "dignity," "freedom," and "empowerment." The distinction between liberation and freedom is especially useful and will be important for my definition of meaningful freedom as involving more than just the political achievement of national sovereignty. Other critics of African decolonization in the West, such as Basil Davidson in *The Black Man's Burden: Africa and the Curse of the Nation-State* (1992), have argued with the cultural history of nationalism itself, claiming that the European idea of the nation became, in effect, the black man's "burden." Yet in *Imagined Communities: Reflections on the Origin and Spread of Nationalism* (1983), Benedict Anderson has shown that the way independence leaders in Africa appropriated the European language of nationalism and the way their communities engaged in an imaginative process of belonging left behind a significant, enduring legacy – much more than simply a burden. I will argue that understanding the history of the idea of the nation is indispensable to coming to terms with how decolonization unfolded, but the foreignness of the concept itself proved less problematic than how departing colonials took advantage of the structures and institutions within the nation-states that emerged.

When we expand our focus beyond these academic debates to include the perspectives of activists at work after decolonization another kind of recalibration becomes possible. Citing her personal experience as a scholar, project director, activist, and teacher who travels extensively, Françoise Vergès remarked how working for change in practice shifted her critical thinking about narratives of emancipation:

> All this has transformed my theoretical approach and made me wary of grand claims, suspicious of grand narratives, particularly of the narrative of emancipation as a total rupture, as an erasure of the past, as the dawn of a "new" world. Instead, emancipation is a long process in which any victory opens up a terrain for new struggles (see, for instance, the abolition of slavery followed by struggles against new forms of economic exploitations and post-slavery colonialism).[16]

Like Vergès, I view progressive change – whether we call it *emancipation* or *liberation* – as incremental, involving a series of shifts over time, and necessarily limited to what Alejo Carpentier has called "The Kingdom of This World."

In order to explore further the idea of recalibrating our analytical perspective in relation to facts on the ground, let us return to the example of Mandela in South Africa – the hope he represented after he was elected in the first multiracial democratic presidential election, and what life is like for the majority of South Africans today. Unfortunately, we find that South Africa remains one of the most unequal societies in the world; wealth is still concentrated in the hands of the white minority, while the vast majority of blacks do not enjoy a comparable standard of living.[17] In terms of statistics, the data show that there is persistent inequality in access to resources and land, as well as income distribution and indicators used to measure quality of life (see Appendix). In terms of a collective conversation, the Truth and Reconciliation Commission (TRC) documented cases of individual abuse, but passed up the opportunity to frame a narrative of social justice in terms of the institutional oppression of groups.[18] As a result, a bitter sense of disaffection remains more widespread than some outside the country might imagine.

While it is fair to say that national liberation did not deliver meaningful freedom to a majority of South Africans, significant achievements have been made and are deserving of recognition. We may begin with the establishment of a multiracial democracy, the drafting of a new constitution, and averting civil war under exceedingly difficult circumstances during the tumultuous transition. Yet, in 2014, I had a conversation with a graduate student in political science at the University of Cape Town, who told me that having a civil war may have been better because, maybe then, fewer blacks would be stuck in grinding poverty. Although I disagree with this statement, because I believe that digging out from

Figure I.1 Cape Town seen from Robben Island, South Africa, 2014
Source: Photo by Phyllis Taoua

civil war would have made the situation worse, I find it hard to dismiss the sentiment expressed. In addition to recalibrating our expectations and setting aside a narrative of triumphant nationalism, we must also broaden the scope of our analysis as we search for explanations. Perhaps it is Mandela's fault for cutting the cards with the Nationalist Party while he was negotiating his release from prison.[19] Perhaps the problems today derive from the African National Congress's ideological incoherence, poor leadership, and inability to deliver results after national liberation.[20] Perhaps the unacceptably slow progress is best explained by the long and brutal history of how all that wealth came to be concentrated in the hands of the white minority.[21] Perhaps the underlying problem is the persistent legacy of the bifurcated state where whites were citizens with civil rights and blacks were native subjects under customary law.[22] Or perhaps ongoing inequality and injustice are best explained by the expansion of neoliberal capitalism, of which South Africa is just one of many examples.[23]

There can be no doubt that a confluence of these and other factors explains the current situation. To make sense of these multiple, interrelated factors – not only in South Africa, but also in other countries – my analysis will draw on scholarship in the social sciences and readings of complex narratives by major African writers and filmmakers, which will allow me to flesh out the full range of human responses to the ongoing struggle for meaningful freedom in Africa. The hunger for freedom cannot be adequately understood with charts and statistical data about human development alone; it also requires us to try to comprehend the world from the people's point of view and how they represent their experiences of it.

It has been fairly well established by now that the various transitions to independence from Ghana to South Africa produced uneven results that do not fit neatly into a narrative of "failure" or "success."[24] The process of decolonization in Africa unfolded as a tug-of-war between the leaders of protest movements and the defenders of European colonial rule. Because this history was shaped by the dynamic relationship between resistance and repression, what happened to leaders mattered immensely. Mandela was in jail for nearly three decades, but ultimately survived. Biko died in police custody. Chris Hani was assassinated. Lumumba, like Simon Kimbangou and André Matswa before him, was arrested and detained for political reasons and died in the custody of colonial collaborators. The list could be extended further with the names of participants in armed anticolonial conflicts in Algeria, Cameroon, and Kenya, among others. All of this matters because the effects of violent repression defined the landscape by deciding who would participate in charting the way forward, and forcing survivors to continue to hope while living with tremendous loss. The historical record shows that African leaders forced the limits of what was acceptable to those in power, and the custodians of imperial domination pushed back in ways that were violent and nonviolent, direct and indirect.[25] While it is undeniable that Mandela's vision and leadership were instrumental in shaping the antiapartheid movement in South Africa, it is also true that thousands of activists died in that same struggle, activists whose names are not well-known. As those of us who have visited the prison on Robben Island can attest, it is painful to discover, as I did, in the presence of a former prisoner, so many intimate details – handwritten letters and photographs – that document just how many lives were crushed by the systematic dehumanization of political prisoners, who were stripped of their clothes and issued numbers as soon as they arrived.

The central argument of this book is that national liberation did not deliver meaningful freedom to the majority of people in Africa. While a reassessment of African national liberation has been underway for more than a decade, articulating a conceptual language for the ongoing struggle

Figure I.2 Display inside the courtyard of Robben Island Prison, South Africa, 2014
Source: Photo by Phyllis Taoua

to achieve meaningful freedom has been missing from the debate. This is an unfortunate omission not only because leaders explicitly deployed the language of freedom to advance the cause of national liberation but also because writers and filmmakers have been wrestling with the meaning of their unfinished freedom in their creative works in such compelling ways since independence. To address these issues, we will examine facts on the ground as well as representations of life after national liberation, as writers and filmmakers were left to contend with the incompleteness of the process and a partial, imperfect legacy.

The argument I make in the pages that follow synthesizes the most significant issues into a single framing narrative and offers an in-depth exploration of how activists and leaders, as well as writers and filmmakers, engaged with the idea of freedom. This synthesis allows us to see connections and patterns that could not be accounted for in a more narrowly defined study. Whereas Orlando Patterson has argued that freedom is recognized as a cherished ideal and a widely shared value in the West, what freedom means in Africa today is not as well understood. For many, freedom may be thought of primarily in relation to slavery, but not necessarily as the objective of national liberation movements. However, the language of freedom has been explicitly used in the context of decolonization, and slavery is also frequently evoked, either as a political analogy for colonial subjugation in speeches by Nkrumah and Lumumba, or figuratively as a trope for the unfreedoms of motherhood by Buchi Emecheta in *The Joys of Motherhood*. Because the meaning of freedom after national liberation is multifaceted and evolves over time, I will make my case by tracking specific examples of how writers and filmmakers explore, interrogate, and refine the idea of freedom by expanding its parameters as part of their coming to terms with how much had actually not yet been achieved.

Before I say more about how I have approached the study of African freedom and organized my argument into chapters, let me step back for a moment and reflect more generally on how I have navigated this terrain.

Writing about Freedom

During the winter of 1998, I traveled to the West African nation of Niger for the first time. I arrived in this country that extends into the Saharan desert at a formative time in my intellectual life. I had already discovered Cameroon first-hand in the summer of 1996 after reading Mongo Beti, and had started a conversation with the author at his bookstore, Peuples Noirs. We corresponded until his death in 2001. I had also spent time that summer in Brazzaville after reading Sony Labou Tansi, but since my visit fell after he passed away, I only met his family and friends. As I prepared for Niamey in the winter of 1998, I packed lightly, taking only one carry-on bag for a month in Niger and that included my mosquito net. Yet I had some heavy questions on my mind. I brought Georg W. Hegel's *The Philosophy of History* and Robert Tucker's *The Marx-Engels Reader* with me, and every morning, with a pot of black coffee, I read these books, trying to decide whether I could consider myself a consciously committed Marxist or not.[26] A contemplation of Marx's definition of private property and Hegel's imaginative construction of others accompanied me around town as I tended to university business.

On my first evening in Niamey, I went down to have dinner on the terrace of the Grand Hotel overlooking the Niger River. I knew enough to request a safe, clean, local hotel, not a Sofitel where Western expatriates tend to gather. As I drank my cold Flag beer and ate my lamb brochettes, I started up a conversation with some men my age at a nearby table. In those days, I smoked on occasion, so I had asked to bum a cigarette. They were the leaders of UFRA (Union des Forces de la Résistance Armée), the last armed group involved in the Tuareg rebellion of the 1990s to lay down their weapons and negotiate a peace agreement. As fate would have it, the government was housing them in bungalows at the Grand Hotel. Our conversations progressed over the course of the month, and even as negotiations about the implementation of peace were underway, I traveled to Agadez as their guest, crossing into the previous zone of operations where I saw mass graves and slept in a room with a closet full of AK-47s. As it turned out, I fell in love with the État Major of UFRA, Sidi-Amar, and the following year we got married. Some years later, we had a beautiful daughter named Bitti, who lives with me now.

Although professional objectives motivated my early travels in Africa, these trips ended up becoming significant encounters for me both as a scholar and as a person; once I was there, I established life-defining relationships that continue to this day. These experiences accompanied me as I entered the field of francophone studies at the turn of the millennium when postcolonial theory was the dominant critical currency. But this, too, was an arena in flux, when leaders in my field were renegotiating the status of theory, challenging critical paradigms on the cusp of major conceptual realignments. In hindsight, I realize that the way I navigated this terrain shaped the scope of this book, which deserves some discussion to clarify both how and why, I decided to write about African freedom.

A debate about the status of theory in African cultural studies has been roiling over the past two decades. Alain Ricard made arguably the most consequential intervention with his review – published in *Research in African Literatures* – of Christopher Miller's *Theories of Africans* (1990). "Most of my irritation with the book," Ricard wrote in 1994, "stems from a long series of statements which are plainly false, outdated, or misleading. The ambition to theorize should be built on solid foundations and on a solid knowledge of Africa. Unfortunately, this is not the case here."[27] Ricard's frankly polemical review essay cites numerous examples and characterizes Miller's book as naïve in its discussion of African languages, pretentious in its theoretical claims – especially those that appropriate anthropology to elucidate "francophonie" in (West) Africa – and ambitious in its guise of mastery and authority. The core lesson from Ricard's incisive criticism is simple: a theoretical discourse is not *in itself* problematic, but it misses the mark if divorced from solid and thorough knowledge of the subject at hand. Six years later, Simon Gikandi, in his keynote address at the African Literature Association published in *Research in African Literatures* in 2001, was still wrestling with Miller's *Theories of Africans*, specifically the chapter on "Ethics and Ethnicity." Gikandi brought up for reexamination the relevance of Derridean *différance* for African studies and sought, in the shadow of the Rwandan genocide, to differentiate between the ethics of difference in theory and in the tangible effects of the use of power and violence in the real world.[28] That Gikandi's intervention subsequently inspired Kenneth Harrow to publish his own in *Research in African Literatures* in 2002 illustrates the breadth of what was a high-profile collective debate about the relevance of post-structuralist theory for African studies.[29]

Tejumola Olaniyan, in his keynote address at a conference on African cultural studies in 2010 published in *Rethinking African Cultural Production*, revisited an early polemical manifestation of this debate and proposed that two "accents" have come to characterize the scholarship of Africanists in the years since.[30] To create a context for considering both the tone and the evolution of these tensions within the field, Olaniyan reaches back to the 1980s and recounts a scene he witnessed first-hand at Cornell. In 1989, Omofolabo Ajayi-Soyinka, a visiting scholar of Nigerian origin, dared to say in public that she did not find deconstruction useful to her work. Gayatri Spivak, a participant at the conference, stood up and gave a lengthy monologue in defense of deconstruction and then left the packed lecture hall without waiting for a reply. Biodun Jeyifo wrote a widely circulated response entitled "'Race' and the Pitfalls of Ventriloquial Deconstruction: Gayatri Spivak's Regressive Monologue on Africa" ("African cultural studies," 95–6). What Olaniyan shows is that cultural critics who have invested in the mastery of a highly theoretical discourse have the most prestigious, well-paid positions in the United States and Europe, and they occasionally wield the leverage of their cultural capital with arrogance and hostility to those who question the relevance of their expertise for African studies. These dynamics help explain why the way Ricard – who was an accomplished philologist, translator, and scholar of both oral and written forms of African-language expression and their interface with European languages – performed his rigorous and substantive critique, making an example of an Ivy League star with tenure at Yale University, which had a wide-ranging and long-lasting effect across the field.

According to Olaniyan, we have two general tendencies in African cultural studies and the battle is still on between them. *Affirmative* African cultural studies – mostly based in Africa – are "more or less nationalist in character and affirmative of indigenous traditions and cultures against Euro-American cultural imperialism" ("African cultural studies," 100). This "formation's epistemology" is "overwhelmingly realist" and there is a "particular privileging of a self-authorizing personal and collective experience" ("African cultural studies," 100). *Interstitial* African cultural studies – originating in the powerful academic worlds of Europe and the United States – is characterized by a sustained critique of the notions of "center" and "periphery" and deconstructs given differences such as "race," "class," and "nation" to reveal how these concepts produce "disabling, identitarian positions" ("African cultural studies," 100–1). He adds that there are "starkly opposed ecologies of scholarly production" in the privileged and powerful world of European and American academe as opposed to life on African university campuses ("African cultural studies," 102). Scholars working in Africa must contend with the effects of a widening gap in economic inequality after decolonization, including slow Internet connections, electrical power outages, and the "mind-numbing scale of political corruption with impunity" that "sponsors" this unfortunate reality ("African cultural studies," 102). Olaniyan ironically laments the inequality that persists between Africanists whose work employs an affirmative accent who are disadvantaged in comparison to Africanists who have mastered the interstitial academic idiom. He admits that it is the gleam of institutional power that greases the wheels of this unequal system, rather than a growing awareness of the insight, appropriateness, and utility of a highly theoretical discourse.

The decision to write about African freedom is the result of a long, arduous process of searching for a way of reconciling tensions within myself; I was torn between the real, persistent effects of an Ivy League imprint and the equally important life lessons I gained from living with a Tuareg husband who had seen people starve to death and who resorted to a collective armed struggle as a last resort. I began work on this book in search of an explanation for postcolonial dispossession in Africa and wound up writing about an ongoing struggle for meaningful freedom. As I set aside unproductive aspects of French post-structuralism and postcolonial theory, the scope of my project shifted. My essay, "The Anti-Colonial Archive: France and Africa's Unfinished Business," published in *SubStance* in 2003, marked the beginning of this change in my writing.[31] The central element of postcolonial theory that I challenged was the proposition that a "grand narrative" of decolonization had been already established and simply needed fleshing out with micro narratives, as Ania Loomba and Peter Hulme had proposed ("The Anti-Colonial Archive," 146). In *Africa since 1940: The Past of the Present*, Frederick Cooper presents decolonization as a complex process that can appear uneven and rather contradictory, which he illustrates by juxtaposing the Rwandan genocide and Mandela's election which both took place during the spring of 1994. His analysis of African decolonization inspired me to rethink looking at Africa through the prism of postcolonial dispossession. Narratives that are either utopic or dystopic similarly advance incomplete claims about what was, or was not, accomplished. The second aspect of postcolonial theory that needed calling into question was the narcissistic impulse in French post-structuralism, which I had previously examined at some length in *Forms of Protest: Anti-Colonialism and Avant-Gardes in African, Caribbean and French Literatures* (2002). My criticism of this discourse included the Derridean notion of the critic-as-reader who is authorized – or self-authorized – to bracket off the real, to speculate about the absence of an *hors texte,* and to fend off the trauma of French, bourgeois loss – the loss of imperial status, the loss of central importance – in an endless refinement of ways to examine textual detail, nuance, and meaning outside of history, outside the time of Western thought.[32] As I advanced in this new direction, I became indebted to scholars who deliberately bridge Euro-American theory and Africa with purposeful engagement such as Mahmood Mamdani. In the end, this project has also been shaped by what I have called the "Formule Ricard," as I have taken inspiration from Ricard's example as a scholar who travelled in Africa, who cultivated dialogue with African artists and intellectuals over a lifetime, and who read extensively.[33]

The most difficult postcolonial habits of mind to set aside were those anchored in the temporality of disaffection and disillusionment. The backward-looking gaze in postcolonial theory creates the possibility for a potentially endless refinement of naming and renaming aspects of an existential hangover half a century later. I wrestled with this conceptual impasse at the turn of the new millennium, which coincided with mounting evidence of growing inequality across Africa, as documented by the United Nations Human Development Index (see Appendix), with failing states (Sierra Leone, Somalia); civil wars (Algeria, Congo); armed insurrections (Niger, South Africa); genocide (Rwanda, Darfur); and widespread repression of human rights. While I witnessed these events unfold with my husband who was not only an eyewitness but also a participant in an armed struggle, it was impossible to remain immune to the human toll of the ongoing struggle. Thus I brought this project to fruition believing that it is possible to be tuned into realities on the ground and to offer an analysis of creative storytelling that has been informed by theory and admittedly enabled by the privilege of an Ivy League education while, nonetheless, striving to be socially relevant and politically incisive.

Mamdani affirms the contribution that informed analysis and theory can make to achieving social justice in *Citizen and Subject: Contemporary Africa and the Legacy of Late Colonialism* (1996): "Although theory cannot by itself transform reality, without a theoretical illumination reality must appear a closed riddle."[34] In my view, it is entirely appropriate to continue to question, at the very least, the value of a highly theoretical postcolonial discourse on "Africa" steeped in French post-structuralism when faced with the tangible results of expanding neoliberal capitalism in a world where the largest influx of external capital investments went, at the end of the twentieth century, to African states with the weakest forms of national sovereignty such as Liberia, Sierra Leone, DRC, and Nigeria.[35] It is equally important to resist going down the rabbit hole of endless analytical refinement, as Geoff Eley recommends in his discussion of globalization:

> The point I want to make here is very straightforward: in a public environment defined so pervasively and aggressively – so noisily – by globalization talk of this kind [with reference to Thomas Friedman's interventions], in which the talk is so completely embedded in an expanding repertoire of process and policy, it becomes naïve and ineffectual to continue insisting primarily on the historical imprecisions of the term itself. Something is happening here, and as a matter of intellectual and political urgency we need to focus on trying to capture what that is.[36]

My book is an attempt to capture what is most essential in an evolving conversation about the ongoing struggle to achieve meaningful freedom in Africa after national liberation.

Articulating Meaningful Freedom

I came away from working on *Forms of Protest* looking for a way of explaining Sony Labou Tansi's unfulfilled longing for a restoration of wholeness. It seemed that he had lost something intangible and would never get it back. The dispossession he evoked was intimate and existential; we see this in his use of figurative language to convey a struggle for self-definition in a world that appears to conspire against him. Then there are the questions of sexuality and gender; his novels portray masculinity both in terms of a male appetite for sexual pleasure and as a gendered incarnation of power within Kongo culture. The Kongo people, also called Bakongo, are a Bantu ethnic group that speaks Kikongo; they live along the Atlantic coast of Central Africa. These various aspects of the experience he describes – the intimate self, gender identity, and existential wholeness – were always represented as entangled with the terrain of national politics in a vaguely defined country somewhere in Equatorial Africa. But, there is more: we also discover how global investors doing business with gatekeeping dictators in these African states, such as the DRC and Congo-Brazzaville, had deep pockets and insufficient incentives to desist from interfering with the people's struggle for democracy as long as the Cold War raged on. Thus, Tansi's novels creatively express a complex longing for meaningful freedom, and, since this aspiration was not realized during his lifetime, he began to interpret the world around him as forsaken by the gods.

I struggled with the idea of "dispossession" because it conveys the essence of Tansi's existential unfreedom, but not the creative and moral effort to overcome it. The answer to my questions about his sense of his place in the world would have to address the specificity of his situation and the unfreedom/freedom dialectic. First, I wanted to understand how the multiple spheres – intimate, gendered, national, global, and spiritual – in his comprehensive vision were related to one another. I started by looking for scenarios of interconnectedness and identified a number of them in similar narratives that involve the confluence of several factors at once. In the complex narratives that I consider in the chapters that follow, we have stories in which individual struggles are embedded within multiple spheres of experience. Conflicts between husbands and wives, dictators and activists, and workers and bosses are presented as clusters – thick with meaning and rich with ethical implications. Ultimately, it was through my critical engagement with primary sources – after extensive reading, viewing, and distilling over the course of a decade – that I derived the conceptual framework of my argument.

I propose that there are five significant areas of narrative interest in African novels and films that contribute to an evolving conversation about freedom as an increasingly inclusive ideal after national liberation. They are: (1) introspection and the intimate self; (2) gender relations; (3) the nation and national liberation; (4) the expansion of global capital; and, (5) the spiritual realm. Initially I thought of these areas as "dynamics," but discarded that term as it does not convey the central importance of complex storytelling. I chose not to speak of "discourse" or "discursive fields" because the primary issues at stake relate to how writers and filmmakers craft their stories and explain the world around them from their various perspectives. I do not think of these areas of narrative interest as "themes," "motifs," or "thematic clusters," because these terms would not adequately account for how an introspective gaze reveals the intimate self, as I argue in Chapter 1. Perhaps discussion of other areas not included here, or further refinements of the ones I am proposing, would help flesh out further the pan-African study of freedom as an area of critical and theoretical inquiry going forward.

My analysis of how the conversation about freedom unfolded after national liberation shows how artists contributed to the articulation of an increasingly inclusive and meaningful ideal with layered depictions of human experience. I do not present these areas of narrative interest in a linear or chronological sequence, but as a series of interconnected spheres from a variety of viewpoints. Different aspects of freedom are not only at work in each of the areas of narrative interest that I will consider, but also may work in concert within a single novel or film. I find these areas of narrative interest analytically useful because they are consistently present in the conversation. The same cannot be said, for instance, of ethnicity. Ethnic identity is far more important to Sony Labou Tansi than it is to Mongo Beti or Bessie Head. Some writers see ethnicity as a colonial tool used to divide and conquer, whereas Ahmadou Kourouma wrote fiction that was invested in an ethnocentric worldview. In fact, one could argue that affiliations to ethnic communities and kinship obligations negatively impact the emergence of freedom as a collectively held value at the national level. Although not every narrative I consider has an introspective gaze that reveals an intimate self, this was a sufficiently compelling innovation in narratives after decolonization to warrant a thorough discussion. The conceptual framework that I am proposing here offers a way of moving beyond the conjunction of national liberation and freedom by opening up new avenues for a more productive discussion that incorporates multiple realms of experience.

I considered many factors when deciding what to include, beginning with the geographical scope of this project. There was a time, not so long ago, when it was unfashionable to write about the situation in South Africa as one case among others within the field of African studies. The inclusion of South Africa is necessary for me here because any evaluation of an ongoing struggle for meaningful freedom in Africa after independence in the French and British colonies that neglects the subsequent entrenchment of apartheid after 1960 would miss an element of decisive importance. The persistence of white settler societies in southern Africa was an affront to the pan-African vision of a united and prosperous Africa that Nkrumah and other African leaders embraced during the 1950s. Once Mandela was in prison on Robben Island, Oliver Tambo and other ANC activists living in exile turned the cause of black liberation into a global issue that gained support for divestment, boycotts, sanctions, and South Africa's exclusion from the Olympic games. We see evidence of this international concern in the realm of African cultural expression in Wole Soyinka's Nobel lecture in 1986. It is remarkable that this Nigerian writer devoted much of his address, on such a momentous occasion, to the ongoing legacy of European racism in Africa and the persistence of apartheid in South Africa.[37] In his lecture "This Past Must Address Its Present," Soyinka's expression of solidarity with antiapartheid protest was potent and visceral and explicitly linked – conceptually, ethically, and rhetorically – the European colonial past to what was, then, the enduring presence of apartheid.

In the social sciences, Mamdani has arguably made the most decisive intervention, calling for the inclusion of South Africa in *Citizen and Subject*. His awareness of this necessity, although not without its own controversy, happened while he was in the country.[38] Of course, limited access to fieldwork in the country under apartheid represented an obstacle for Africanist scholars in the social sciences. Mamdani builds a persuasive case for an inclusive approach with his original and influential analysis of the state, and of the need to work for meaningful freedom by taking into account the specific mechanisms by which the oppressed were actually ruled. In the years since, social scientists routinely include South Africa, as we see in Cooper's *Africa since 1940: The Past of the Present*. It is also not uncommon, these days, in African literary and cultural studies to find both South Africa and the Maghreb on the map and up for discussion, as we see in Anne McClintock's *Imperial Leather: Race, Gender, and Sexuality in the Colonial Contest* (1995), Susan Andrade's *The Nation Writ Small: African Fictions and Feminisms, 1958–1988* (2011), and Anjali Prabhu's *Contemporary Cinema of Africa and the Diaspora* (2014). As I decided what to include, I balanced: (1) my interest in great writing and filmmaking; (2) my desire to select major contributions to significant areas of narrative interest; and, (3) my desire to identify patterns that help us understand the complexity of the struggle for meaningful freedom in Africa after national liberation. In the chapters that follow, I discuss many African countries and cover every region from North (Algeria), West (Mali, Mauritania, Ghana, Senegal, Nigeria), and Central (Cameroon, Congo) to South (South Africa, Botswana) and East (Somalia, Kenya).[39]

With this geographical scope, it would be impossible to offer an in-depth discussion that would be focused on a single ethno-linguistic sphere. However, I feel it is important to note that this is not an exclusively Europhone project either, since I discuss African-language films, and African languages play a vital role in much of the writing. While my discussion includes novels published in English and French, it is worth noting that Ngũgĩ wa Thiong'o translated *Wizard of the Crow* from Gikuyu into English. Tansi wrote in his native Kikongo as well as in French, which was, for him, a tainted colonial language. I would, therefore, like to draw the reader's attention to the multilingual palimpsest, to borrow a phrase from Chantal Zabus, operating in the background when European languages are used.[40] African languages are never sealed off from an author's creative expression when writing in French or English. Other artists whose works I consider have experimented with multilingual creativity across genres, including Nuruddin Farah, who wrote plays in Somali before switching to novels in English, which is actually his fourth language. Other writers' prose is inflected with their language of origin, as is the case with Akan in Ayi Kwei Armah's novels in English. This multilingual palimpsest not only contributes distinctive aesthetic qualities, but also nourishes the African imagination in terms of what Abiola Irele, in *The African Imagination: Literature in Africa and the Black Diaspora* (2001), called the oral matrix of creative expression.

When selecting individual works, I decided to focus on the modern narrative genres of novels and films because they tell compelling stories that make sense of complex issues in a changing world. In my readings, I return to major canonical works with broad appeal such as Armah's *The Beautyful Ones Are Not Yet Born* (1968) and *Afrique, je te plumerai* (1992; *Africa, I will fleece you*) to support my claims that the language of freedom is of central importance in canonical works and that the areas of narrative interest I consider are, indeed, significant. In some cases, artists explicitly employ a language of freedom, as in Armah's *The Beautyful Ones Are Not Yet Born*:

> The man had said something earnest about the connectedness of words and the freedom of enslaved men, but then Teacher had said one of the harshest things he had ever said. With a shrug he had said that men were all free to do what they chose to do, and would laugh with hate at the bringer of unwanted light if what they knew they needed was the dark. He had told a story he said meant more to him in his unhappiness than any other story, something he called the myth of Plato's cave. *(Beautyful Ones, 79)*

In addition to Armah's contemplation of the meaning of freedom in Ghana in the decade after independence, I also consider works where it is the narrative as a whole that takes up the question of what it means to be free as in Chieck Oumar Sissoko's film *Finzan* (1992), where women's issues of marriage and genital cutting are symbolically connected to the community's quest for democracy and freedom. Though I discuss many works in each chapter, I am confident readers who are familiar with the issues will be able to cite many more films and novels that have not been included for reasons of personal taste and limited space. While the chapters are not organized to trace a historical chronology, I have attempted to delineate a genealogy of narrative expression across different modes that coheres around the idea of freedom.

I have chosen to write about novels and films together, although this choice grows less unexpected every day. In *Contemporary Cinema in Africa and the Dispora*, Prabhu refers to African literature as a way of framing the decolonization of culture in relation to cinema, and engages with Ousmane Sembène's narratives in both their written and cinematographic forms. Similarly, Andrade, in *The Nation Writ Small*, discusses both the novella and film versions of Sembène's *Xala* as intertexts with Mariama Bâ's novel *So Long a Letter*, without feeling unduly obliged to justify her choice. In addition to Sembène adapting written narratives with audiovisual storytelling for African-language communities inside and outside Senegal, there is a vast network of intertexts between literature and cinema. Of the many instances of literary citation in filmmaking we may consider the opening sequence in *Africa, I Will Fleece You* where Teno cites Beti's *Ville cruelle* (1954). Finally, there are filmic adaptations of novels as in Stéphane Sauvaire's film based on Emmanuel Dongala's novel *Johnny Chien Méchant* (2002; *Johnny Mad Dog*) and other cases where cinema has been used to convey important writing, such as John Boorman's feature film *In My Country* (2004), inspired by Antjie Krog's memoir *Country of My Skull: Guilt, Sorrow, and the Limits of Forgiveness in the New South Africa* (1998). I selectively discuss narrative, discursive, and thematic overlap between the genres as well as these explicit intertexts as they relate to my areas of narrative interest.

The creative works with which I engage offer provocative and critical representations of life in Africa after national liberation. Moradewun Adejunmobi, in her essay "Provocations: African Societies and Theories of Creativity," in *Rethinking African Cultural Production* frames the longstanding issue of the relevance of high theory in African studies in terms of the status of humanities research on Africa.[41] Adejunmobi's argument is sanguine and her approach pragmatic as she urges Africanists to consider the *usefulness* of their research projects both within the Western academy and in Africa. In response to her call for relevant scholarship, we may ask: Why is it useful to understand the meaning of freedom in Africa after national liberation? It may be argued that many people in Africa carry on with their lives without perceiving themselves as unfree. Social scientists who study human development present metrics and data in comparative international contexts that conform to generally formulated standards with respect to literacy, life expectancy, and income (see Appendix). These experts may characterize the deprivations that come with extreme poverty as an impediment to freedom, whereas the people themselves may not necessarily describe their lives in the same way. The grassroots organization Tostan, in Senegal, is working to eliminate the practice of female genital cutting village by village because individuals are not considered to have the freedom to choose whether to conform or not. But women whose parents subjected them to genital cutting as girls may see their lives as normal and not as a betrayal of freedom. If a writer or filmmaker strives to document the negative effects of poverty or criticize genital cutting, it is by definition from a subjective point of view and often with the intention of provoking discussion, raising awareness, and challenging the status quo. As Adejunmobi argues, it is the role of artists to be provocative, to engage others in conversation, and to bring important issues up for reconsideration.

In each chapter, my argument engages the relationship between creative expression in films and novels as texts and their social, political, and historical contexts. While I do not have a purely textual interest in representations of ongoing struggles for meaningful freedom, I believe that attempts to understand statistical data about human development, as well as archival documentation about the process of decolonization and economic theories of capitalism, benefit from a serious engagement with complex narratives about these issues and with how to interpret them. Similarly, the multiplicity of creative voices that I contend with in each area of narrative interest cannot be reduced to one homogeneous narrative or single perspective. I hope this liberates individual artists from the burden of representing an "indigenous" point of view. I do not consider films and novels as "open" repositories that communicate "transparent" content about African social, political, and cultural life. They are works of creative expression that are very often innovative and experimental, and as such require interpretation. Thus, I do not wish to cede too much terrain to the social sciences, as I maintain that thoughtful consideration of artistic expression offers valuable insight into the complexity of African experience.

Once I had defined my areas of narrative interest, I sought a way to bring more definition to the idea of freedom. There is a striking absence of attention to freedom in postcolonial theory and African cultural studies. Fanon, arguably the most important theorist on liberation in this field, writes about the black man's existential alienation, the liberating potential of insurrectional violence, and the pitfalls of national consciousness. Yet, he does not offer a sustained, coherent discussion of freedom as an idea or an aspirational ideal, and this includes his writing published posthumously in *Écrits sur l'aliénation et la liberté* (2015). Given the lack of an available conceptual vocabulary, I had to derive my own definition of freedom – more specifically, meaningful freedom in an African context – from scholarship in the social sciences, including historical sociology and economics.

I started with Orlando Patterson's work on freedom as a value that emerged in Western culture from the experience of slavery. In *Freedom in the Making of Western Culture* (1991), Patterson presents freedom as an ideal of unique importance in the West and argues that the idea, while integral to the development of Western culture from the seeds of democracy in ancient Athens to the spread of Christianity in Europe, was significantly less important, if not nonexistent, elsewhere in the world. Patterson claims that it was through contact with the West that non-Western cultures adopted ideas of freedom over time. As a historical sociologist, he is interested in understanding how ideas come to be shared as collectively held values by members of society, from powerful elites to ordinary people. It is especially relevant to my discussion that Patterson observes an essential relationship between the existence of slavery and the formulation of freedom as a shared value in the Western world. "The basic argument of this work is that freedom was generated from the experience of slavery," he states in the preface. "People came to value freedom, to construct it as a powerful shared vision of life, as a result of their experience of, and response to, slavery or its recombinant form, serfdom, in their roles as masters, slaves, and nonslaves." He explains that, "Armed with the weapons of the historical sociologist, I had gone in search of a man-killing wolf called slavery; to my dismay I kept finding the tracks of a lamb called freedom." Thus, for Patterson, seeking to understand "the taken-for-granted tradition of slavery in the West" led him, in the end, to finding the "sociohistorical roots of freedom."[42] As Patterson defines his terms, he presents freedom as a tripartite value including personal, sovereignal, and civic freedoms, which are interrelated and referred to with the musical metaphor of a chord: each note is distinct, but may be played together.[43] The coexistence of multiple kinds of freedom and the unfreedom/freedom dialectic have been instrumental in my definition of freedom as well as the distinctions between "idea," "ideal," and "shared value" within a community. My study does not take up the sociological claim that freedom is, or is not, a shared value within specific African communities; instead, I propose that freedom is more than an idea, and I show how it evolved into an increasingly inclusive ideal after national liberation.

Let's briefly return to Mandela's ideas of freedom in light of Patterson's claims. In his autobiography *Long Walk to Freedom* (1995), Mandela says his values were first forged in his village in the Transkei among the amaXhosa and then refined into a vision of life over time as he came into contact with an urban way of life in Johannesburg, the brutality of the apartheid system, and Western ideas of democracy and Christianity while in school at Fort Hare. Many intellectuals of South African origin came to reflect on freedom and contribute to its formulation as an aspirational ideal under similar circumstances, from the writings and life story of Sol Plaatje to Peter Abrahams's *Tell Freedom* (1954). The question of how the Xhosa, Zulu, or Shona people may have conceptualized freedom prior to the arrival of Europeans in southern Africa, although inherently interesting, lies beyond the scope of my argument here. Yet that kind of project, taking, for instance, the Zulu word *ubuntu* and providing a discussion of its etymology and discursive uses in the context of culturally specific liberation struggles in southern Africa, with an approach along the lines of what Jan Vansina does in *Paths in the Rainforest: Toward a History of Political Tradition in Africa* (1990), would be very useful for fleshing out African concepts in each and every local context. That kind of inquiry dovetails with what Walter Mignolo calls for in *The Darker Side of Western Modernity: Global Futures, Decolonial Options* (2011) in terms of working with indigenous ideas as a means of articulating alternatives to Western modernity and delinking from the colonial matrix of power – to which I shall return in a moment. What I would like to emphasize in Patterson's work on freedom, for now, is his insight into how freedom as a shared value and cherished ideal emerged as a response to the experience of unfreedom in Western culture.

Next, I turned to Amartya Sen's definition of freedom in relationship to the concept of development that was of critical importance to the history of decolonization and the formulation of social and economic policies in what became known as the Third World. The pioneering work of this economist and Nobel Laureate in *Development as Freedom* (1999) radically challenges received ideas about development. The First World's claims to be "developing" the Third World constituted an essential rationale for the spread of neoliberal capitalism after decolonization and the spawning of an industry of international aid organizations. These First World claims are broadly considered to have failed in their objectives, since economic indicators show that inequality increased, poverty persisted, and quality of life indicators, especially for girls and women, were usually stagnant or in decline.[44] Yet Sen does more than simply spell out why bankers' policies were failing to accomplish their stated objectives. He demanded that they redefine the agenda of development with input from the people whose lives they claimed to be improving. Sen clearly articulated a conceptual language for freedom and presented it as the most meaningful measure of improving lives. He also provided metrics for measuring outcomes, and his research contributed to the establishment of the United Nations Human Development Index, where statistical data is made publicly available in order to ensure that accountability can be routinely included in our assessments of human development (see Appendix).[45] Thus both Sen's ideas and their implementation were transformative.

Sen sees development as a process that should enhance and expand the substantive freedoms of the people policy makers claim to be helping. This represented a shift in perspective away from focusing on economic indicators like growth of GNP or household incomes to an emphasis on the well-being of human agents and their freedoms. He claims that human freedom depends on social and political arrangements (facilities in health care and education) as well as political and civil rights (the liberty to participate in public debate and scrutiny). According to Sen, development should be measured by whether it removes unfreedoms or not; these include poverty and poor economic opportunities, as well as tyranny in the form of social deprivations and political repression. He proposes that: (1) development should be evaluated primarily in terms of whether people's freedoms have been enhanced; and (2) the effectiveness of development is dependent on the free agency of people. Sen defines different kinds of freedoms and argues persuasively that there are "mutually reinforcing connections" between them.[46] As an economist, he approaches freedom from an "instrumental" perspective and proposes that there are five distinct types: (1) political freedoms (voting, civil rights); (2) economic facilities (access to resources, income); (3) social opportunities (health care, education); (4) transparency guarantees (public trust, absence of corruption); and (5) protective securities (social security, famine relief).[47] He presents empirical studies of each of these types of freedom and states that: "While development analysis must, on the one hand, be concerned with objectives and aims that make these instrumental freedoms consequentially important, it must also take note of the empirical linkages that tie the distinct types of freedom together, strengthening their joint importance."[48] When working together, these instrumental freedoms can contribute to social justice by enhancing the substantive freedoms of people and ensuring that they have the capacity to live the kind of life they have reason to value.[49] In addition to the coexistence of multiple kinds of freedoms, Sen's claim that they are interrelated and mutually dependent has informed my thinking. While I do not take an "instrumental" perspective in economic terms, I have adapted his ideas of "instrumental" and "substantive" freedoms, also adding a third term, "existential" freedom, to capture a longing for wholeness in psychological and spiritual terms.

I explore meaningful freedom as a complex idea that is multifaceted and includes more than political self-determination or national sovereignty; it involves different kinds of freedoms that are interconnected and mutually dependent. I propose a preliminary discussion of three types of freedom: (1) *instrumental* freedoms pertain to tools that serve a purpose; political and civil rights and liberties such as voting, free speech, freedom of the press, the right to organize, and access to resources;(2) *substantive* freedoms are the ability to make choices, as in a spouse or one's faith, and the capacity to develop one's potential through education, work, and social opportunities in order to improve one's quality of life; and (3) *existential* freedoms are intangible; they relate to the spiritual realm, to ethical values, and to the psyche as in the absence of alienation.

The idea of freedom is occasionally evoked in studies devoted to decolonial theory. Mignolo, for instance, discusses the legacy of Western imperialism and possibilities for disentanglement from the "colonial matrix of power" in the future by pursuing indigenous priorities and epistemologies as a way of formulating new decolonial options. In *The Darker Side of Western Modernity: Global Futures, Decolonial Options,* reevaluating decolonial paradigms of the past necessarily raises questions about the possibilities for future freedoms. Mignolo's critique of modernity is categorically anti-Western and anticapitalist: he links the dark side of Western modernity with colonialism and proposes that we think of the colonial legacy in terms of a "colonial matrix of power" and resistance to it as "decolonial thinking and doing." Mignolo's project seeks to understand and unravel the confluence of many factors – he offers a list of twelve of them – from global race and class formations to gendered and spiritual hierarchies.[50] It is only in the final pages of his book that Mignolo explicitly challenges Sen's faith in "capitalism," "development," and "progress," three terms that Mignolo criticizes as the defining features in his cultural narrative of Western modernity. He presents Sen's project as a form of re-Westernization, or trying to do Western modernity differently, without addressing the psychological injury of the colonial imposition. Mignolo observes, "One of the key points in the dewesternizing argument is the concept of 'freedom.'" For Mignolo, "freedom" is a Western concept that has been imposed on non-Western people. He adds, "I bring Sen's argument into the conversation for two reasons. One is that Sen's argument may be confused with dewesternization, when in reality what he proposes falls in line with rewesternization. Not that Sen was supporting neoliberal projects at that time. His argument, parallel to those advanced by the philosopher and entrepreneur George Soros, looks for a form of capitalism with a good heart, which, of course, is a logical dead end."[51] Mignolo calls for a reengagement with the idea of freedom from outside Western culture: "It has to be engaged from the history of the non-Western world upon which the concept of freedom was impinged."[52] Mignolo is able to advocate delinking from the colonial matrix of power partly because he is convinced that Wall Street is on the verge of collapse and that Western gatekeepers are no longer needed in a polycentric capitalist world. If this is going to be true in the future, it has not been true in Africa during the last half of the twentieth century. Sen's project is a compelling anti-imperial corrective in my view because he calls for resetting the agenda with input from the people whose interests are at stake and for enhancing their capacity to live a life they have reason to value. The way I map out the terrain of an evolving conversation about African freedom and derive analytical tools from primary sources intersects with scholarship that looks to the areas or regions studied as sources of theory that can provide alternative critical paradigms as a means of resisting the perpetuation of Western standards and priorities.

Chapter Summaries

In Chapter 1, I focus on introspective narratives that reveal aspects of the intimate self, such as self-definition and identity formation, that are represented as being nested within broader social and political dynamics. This point of departure allows us to see how existential issues related to selfhood are interconnected with other kinds of freedoms (instrumental, substantive) with which they are mutually interdependent. I begin by considering how Fanon contributed to the emergence of this area of narrative interest and emphasize that the way he carved out a space for his autobiographical self in *Peau noire, masques blancs* (1952; *Black Skin, White Masks*, 2007) was analytically indispensable to his therapeutic project. I argue that this examination of Fanon's own lived experience, combined with his affective ability to narrate the effects of colonial alienation, opened up new possibilities that inspired artists and theorists for generations. For example, in *The Intimate Enemy: Loss and Recovery of Self Under Colonialism* (1983), theorist Ashis Nandy extended Fanon's analysis to include a recovery of the self in the aftermath of imperial domination in terms of "inner lives" and "cultural selves."

I develop my argument by looking at Ayi Kwei Armah's novel *Fragments* (1969), Djibril Diop Mambety's film *Touki Bouki* (1973), and Mariama Bâ's novel *Une si longue lettre* (1979; *So Long a Letter*, 1981). Armah employs a language of freedom and sets up a Fanonian intertext, which invites readers to reflect on the ideal of meaningful freedom in Ghana in the decade after national liberation.[53] I review the archive of criticism on his early novels to establish how a rigid over-reliance on the collective dimension of decolonization significantly delayed accepting the relevance of the intimate self and the private lives of individuals as part of a discourse of liberation.[54] Mambety's film is stylistically different, yet offers a similar reflection on the limits of freedom for young people after independence. My reading refreshes our appreciation of this canonical film by reconsidering how the signs of disaffection are critical elements that frame the protagonist's existential struggle to lead a meaningful life at home in Africa. Similarly, I return to Bâ's canonical novel to show how it expanded the parameters of what could be said about freedom to include women's perspectives and shows that meaningful freedom depends on mutually enriching kinds of freedoms that operate together within the narrative as an explicit critique of what national liberation failed to deliver. These complex narratives participate in a revision of the cultural narrative of triumphant nationalism from aesthetically innovative points of view.

In Chapter 2, I argue that when African women entered into the conversation, they had a more complex awareness of freedom than African men did because of their social and economic subordination within patriarchal society. Women were more keenly aware of how their private lives were influenced, constrained, and determined by networks of power that were not entirely, if it all, within their control. I argue that women developed an increasingly specific language of freedom that emerged from novels focused on marriage to more symbolic and metaphorical representations of freedom. I begin with South African novels – Nadine Gordimer's *Occasion for Loving* (1963) and *July's People* (1981), and Bessie Head's *When Rain Clouds Gather* (1969) – in which a central marriage plot links substantive freedoms in the private lives of individuals to questions of racism, political inequality, and social justice. Then I turn to Buchi Emecheta's novel *The Joys of Motherhood* (1980), which also employs the language of freedom by offering a sharply critical portrait of the socialization of girls to fulfill patriarchal expectations and represents motherhood as a joyless form of slavery. Finally, I look at more overtly symbolic engagements with the idea of freedom in Assia Djebar's *Vaste est la prison* (1995; *So Vast the Prison: A Novel,* 2001) and Chimamanda Ngozi Adichie's novel *Purple Hibiscus* (2007). Djebar offers a sustained reflection on gender and freedom where she proposes alternative cultural and historical references for women and uses prison as a trope for women's unfreedom within patriarchal societies. By contrast, *Purple Hibiscus* features a rare flower as a symbol for meaningful freedom; it includes both the existential freedom "to be" and the substantive freedoms "to do" as complements to political efforts to achieve the instrumental freedoms that democracy guarantees at the national level.

Chapter 3 fleshes out the historical context of national liberation and considers why it failed to deliver meaningful freedom for the majority. I trace the evolution of the idea of the nation along a trajectory from the expansion of empire and global capital, to postwar colonial development schemes. I argue that, with the hindsight that an expansion of global capitalism affords us, we can see how European colonials instrumentalized the structures of the nation-state and took planned steps to create enclaves for future capital investment that would be difficult to govern. I offer a fresh look at two canonical novels Armah's *The Beautyful Ones Are Not Yet Born* and Tansi's *La vie et demie* (1979; *Life and a Half, 2011*) and show how they represent people trying to survive in gatekeeper states in relation to the national historiographies. I draw attention to the fact that Armah's novel explicitly employs a language of freedom and reflects on its meaning as part of a critique of national liberation. Then I consider how Tansi represents the expanding hegemony of global capital in the last decade of the Cold War and the obstacles to political citizenship that this created within African nation-states. I go on to consider two works, Sissoko's film *Finzan* (1992) and Beti's *Trop de soleil tue l'amour* (1999), from the pivotal decade of the 1990s during the transition to democracy after the Cold War. We see how anxiety about change got expressed in gendered terms in works with a post-feminist awareness of how meaningful freedom is embedded within familial, social, national, and transnational contexts. Finally, I look at representations of South Africa's

Truth and Reconciliation Commission in film and fiction. I begin with Antjie Krog's memoir *Country of My Skull: Guilt, Sorrow and the Limits of Forgiveness in the New South Africa* (1998) and Steve Biko's *I Write What I Like* (1978), which anchors the discussion and serves as an intertext for other narratives, including Sindiwe Magona's novel *Mother to Mother* (1998), Tom Hooper's film *Red Dust* (2004), Suleman Ramadan's film *Zulu Love Letter* (2004), and Oliver Hermanus's film *Shirley Adams* (2009). We see how, in these narratives of national reconciliation, efforts to rearticulate the ideal of freedom after apartheid requires dealing with residual black anger and healing the wounds in South Africa that persist.

In Chapter 4, I extend and develop my discussion of freedom with a focus on the expansion of neoliberal capitalism and the effects of dispossession that can lead to armed conflict. As a counterpoint, I consider progressive, feminist alternatives to the perpetuation of poverty, injustice, and cycles of violence. I begin by considering the rationale for neoliberal banking policies and the assumption that remaking the world on the model of Western capitalism will improve lives. I contrast Jeffrey Sachs's theories of prosperity with Eley's and James Ferguson's work on the expansion of global capital in Africa. To place these issues in the historical context of African decolonization, I return to Cooper's analysis of gatekeepers and how they "sit astride the interface" between the territory of the nation-state and the rest of the world outside.[55] It is within this context that we can best appreciate Sen's radical proposition that the efficacy of development should be measured in terms of whether it enhances people's freedoms. I open my discussion of film and fiction with two precursor films, Sembène's *La noire de …* (1966; *Black Girl*) and Teno's documentary *Afrique, je te plumerai* (1992; *Africa, I Will Fleece You*), which identifies links between old-school criticism of national liberation and neoliberal capitalism. In the rest of the chapter, I focus on twenty-first century works and begin by looking at two documentaries about extractive industries, Idrissou Mora Kpai's *Arlit: Deuxième Paris* (2004; *Arlit: Second Paris*) and Robert Nugent's *End of the Rainbow* (2006). Then I discuss three works, Abderrahmane Sissako's film *Bamako* (2006), Chris Abani's novel *Graceland* (2004), Thiong'o's global epic *Wizard of the Crow* (2006), that represent the neoliberal world order and critically engage with what globalization looks like from African perspectives. I conclude by considering two novels about civil war Dongala's *Johnny chien méchant* (2002; *Johnny Mad Dog*, 2005) and Farah's novel *Knots* (2007). These narratives about armed conflict, prevalent in twenty-first century film and fiction, testifies to the consequences of persistent inequality and corruption.

Chapter 5 is something of an epilogue in which I reconsider issues related to the spiritual realm that have come up along the way and propose a few new examples to illustrate how there have been three major responses to what Chinua Achebe famously called "things falling apart." African responses to the colonial imposition of foreign faiths have been: resistance, disorientation, and synthesis. I begin with a discussion of the meaning of Okonkwo's suicide in *Things Fall Apart* and then track metaphors of things unravelling and falling apart in major works of African literature. This allows us to observe that it is in the spiritual realm that writers and filmmakers often grapple with the existential dimension of meaningful freedom and express a sense of intangible loss in their complex narratives, which were the seeds for the project as a whole.

In the Conclusion, I reflect on the scope of the project and what can be learned from the central argument. One important observation is how the legacy of national liberation in Africa cannot be adequately accounted for in a narrative of disillusionment or disaffection, just as it cannot be realistically understood as a narrative of settled accomplishments simply in need of fleshing out with details. Although our exploration has led us to examine historical aspects of the past and to grapple with contradictions in the present, ultimately our discussion of ongoing struggles for meaningful freedom looks to the future and projects imaginative, creative solutions that may be achieved in the years ahead.

Notes

1. Nelson Mandela, *Long Walk to Freedom: The Autobiography of Nelson Mandela* (Austin, TX: Holt, Rinehart and Winston, 1995), p. 404.
2. Ibid., p. 176.
3. Orlando Patterson differentiates between ideas, ideals, and collectively held values in *Freedom: Vol. 1: Freedom in the Making of Western Culture* (New York, NY: Basic Books, 1991).
4. For the text, an audio file and historical context of Kwame Nkrumah's speech, see www.bbc.co.uk/worldservice/focusonafrica/news/story/2007/02/070129_ghana50_independence_speech.shtml
5. For the text of Nkrumah's address to the General Assembly at the United Nations on September 23, 1960, see www.un.org/africarenewal/magazine/august-2010/visions-independence-then-and-now. For the text of Nkrumah's address at the opening session of the All-African People's Conference on December 8, 1958, see www.columbia.edu/itc/history/mann/w3005/nkrumba.html
6. Leo Zeilig, *Lumumba: Africa's Lost Leader* (London: Haus Publishing, 2015), pp. 67–9.

7. For the complete text of Lumumba's speech and historical context, see Zeilig, *Lumumba*, pp. 96–102.
8. Zeilig, *Lumumba*, p. 98.
9. Ibid., p. 100.
10. Georges Nzongola-Ntalaja, *The Congo from Leopold to Kabila: A People's History* (London and New York, NY: Zed Books, 2002), p. 84.
11. Ibid., pp. 84–5.
12. We see this, for instance, in the speeches by Nkrumah cited above.
13. In addition to Nkrumah's interventions on this topic cited here, see also Steve Biko, *I Write What I Like: Selected Writings* (Chicago, IL: Chicago University Press, 2002).
14. Frederick Cooper, *Africa since 1940: The Past of the Present* (Cambridge: Cambridge University Press, 2002), p. 161
15. James Ferguson, *Global Shadows: Africa in the Neoliberal World Order* (Durham, NC: Duke University Press, 2006), pp. 50–1.
16. Françoise Vergès, "Wandering Souls and Returning Ghosts: Writing the History of the Dispossessed," *Yale French Studies*, no. 118/119 (2010): 136–54. Quote from p. 137.
17. Cooper, *Africa since 1940.*
18. Mahmood Mamdani, "Beyond Nuremburg, the Historical Significance of the Post-Apartheid Transition in South Africa," *Politics & Society* vol. 43, no. 1 (March 2015): pp. 61–88.
19. Anne McClintock, *Imperial Leather: Race, Gender and Sexuality in the Colonial Contest* (New York, NY/London: Routledge, 1995).
20. Anthony Butler, *The Idea of the ANC* (Columbus: Ohio University Press, 2013).
21. Cooper, *Africa since 1940.*
22. Mahmood Mamdani, *Citizen and Subject: Contemporary Africa and the Legacy of Late Colonialism* (Princeton, NJ: Princeton University Press, 1996).
23. Geoff Eley, "Historicizing the Global, Politicizing Capital: Giving the Present a Name," *History Workshop Journal*, vol. 63, no. 63 (Spring, 2007): 154–88. Let me add, here, that it would be possible and useful to further differentiate how these issues of uneven progress and persistent poverty play out among black South Africans within the country in terms of different regions (i.e., the tradition of black protest can be felt more in the Cape Province and in the Eastern Cape than in the Rand).
24. Cooper, *Africa since 1940.*
25. Ibid.
26. An answer to this question is involved and would require an essay in itself. Let me just say, for now, that I felt unconvinced by some of Marx's discussion of private property. This would serve as my point of departure for writing an essay on the limited achievements of Marxism in practice. My obvious affinities with other aspects of Marxist criticism and historiography are expressed in the chapters that follow. Regarding Hegel, his armchair theorizing about places he never visited or hoped to visit still stands as a major point of reference in my writing and when I teach my graduate seminar on theory.

27. Alain Ricard, "Post-Colonial Reader Lost in a Bush of Ghosts: 'Theories of Africans' by Christopher L. Miller," *Research in African Literatures*, vol. 25, no. 1 (Spring, 1994): 101–6.
28. Simon Gikandi, "Theory, Literature and Moral Considerations," *Research in African Literatures*, vol. 32, no. 4, (Winter, 2001): 1–18.
29. Ken Harrow, "Ethics and Difference: A Response to Simon Gikandi's 'Theory, Literature and Moral Considerations'," *Research in African Literature*, vol. 33, no. 4 (Winter, 2002): 154–60.
30. Tejumola Olaniyan, "African Cultural Studies: Of Travels, Accents, and Epistemologies," *Rethinking African Cultural Production*, eds. Frieda Ekotto & Ken Harrow, (Bloomington, IN: Indiana University Press, 2015), pp. 94–108.
31. Phyllis Taoua, "The Anti-Colonial Archive: France and Africa's Unfinished Business," *SubStance*, Issue 102, vol. 32, no. 3 (Winter 2003): 146–64. Let me add to this footnote by telling a story. While I was visiting Alain Ricard at his home in Bordeaux during the summer of 2016, he suggested I read an essay by Jacques Derrida about Nelson Mandela that he has in his substantial personal library. I read Derrida's essay (along with many other things, including Antjie Krog's poetry) during the course of that day and we discussed it over dinner with friends. I cite Derrida's insightful essay in a footnote in Chapter 3. Among Derrida's less helpful contributions, in my view, is the implication in his early theoretical writing that textual analysis can be properly conducted without attending to (1) knowledge of the circumstances of production, and (2) the effects of the text in the world.
32. Phyllis Taoua, *Forms of Protest: Anti-Colonialism and Avant-Gardes in African, Caribbean and French Literatures* (Portsmouth, NH: Heinemann, Studies in African Literature, 2002).
33. Phyllis Taoua, "La Formule Ricard" in *Les littératures africaines. Homage à Alain Ricard* (Paris: Karthala, 2011), pp. 311–20.
34. Mamdani, *Citizen and Subject*, p. 299.
35. Ferguson, *Global Shadows*. In terms of capital investment, the top five destination for direct foreign investment according to *The Financial Times* in 2014 were: Egypt, Angola, Nigeria, Mozambique, and Morocco ("Foreign direct investment in Africa surges," source www.ft.com/content/79ee41b6-fd84–11e4-b824–00144feabdc0). These nations do not have the weakest national sovereignty in Africa. Africa, according to a World Bank study in 2015, is the second most attractive region for direct foreign investment in the world, reaching $60 billion in 2015 (source www.worldbank.org/en/news/opinion/2015/06/30/africa-still-poised-to-become-the-next-great-investment-destination). These investments are not exclusively in natural resource extraction; they also include real estate, agriculture, and infrastructure with growing prospects for manufacturing and financial services. A growing number of nongovernmental organizations have put pressure on African governments to be transparent about where profits from natural resources are going, with Niger being the worst case scenario and Botswana as the example to follow. The campaign to end "conflict diamonds" in Sierra Leone and to divest from South Africa companies during apartheid set the standard for initiatives related to corporate conflict prevention.

36. Eley, "Historicizing the Global, Politicizing Capital: Giving the Present a Name," reference to pp. 162–3.
37. Wole Soyinka stated, for instance: "They are the blocks in a suspended bridge begun from one end of a chasm which, whether the builders will it or not, must obey the law of matter and crash down beyond a certain point, settling definitively into the widening chasm of suspicion, frustration, and redoubled hate. On that testing ground which, for us, is Southern Africa, that medieval camp of biblical terrors, primitive suspicions, a choice must be made by all lovers of peace: either to bring it into the modern world, into a rational state of being within that spirit of human partnership, a capacity for which has been so amply demonstrated by every liberated black nation on our continent, or – to bring it abjectly to its knees by ejecting it, in every aspect, from humane recognition, so that it caves in internally, through the strategies of its embattled majority." Soyinka, "This Past Must Address Its Present," reprinted in: *Publications of the Modern Language Association of America*, vol. 102, no. 5 (October, 1987): 762–71.
38. Mamdani observed, for instance: The lesson was driven home to me with the forceful impact of a dramatic and personal realization in the early 1990s, when it became possible for an African academic to visit South Africa. At close quarters, apartheid no longer seemed a self-evident exception to the African colonial experience. As the scales came off, I realized that the notion of South African exceptionalism could not be an exclusively South African creation. The argument was also reinforced – regularly – from the northern side of the border, both by those who hold the gun and by those who wield the pen. This is why the creation of a truly African studies, a study of Africa whose starting point is the commonality of the African experience, seems imperative at this historical moment. To do so, however, requires that we proceed from a recognition of our shared legacy which is honest enough not to deny our differences." Mamdani, *Citizen and Subject*, pp. 32–3.
39. These are the countries I have decided to include in this study, but one could use the central concept I am proposing, that of ongoing struggle for meaningful freedom, and flesh out this narrative of uneven results after liberation in Africa by looking at Julius Nyerere in Tanzania, as another example, and discuss his positions on development, nonalignment and against violence.
40. Chantal Zabus, *The African Palimpsest: Indigenization of Language in the West African Europhone Novel* (Amsterdam: Rodopi, 1991).
41. Moradewun Adejunmobi, "Provocations: African Societies and Theories of Creativity," *Rethinking African Cultural Production* (Indiana University Press, 2015), pp. 52–77.
42. Patterson, *Freedom in the Making of Western Culture*, p. xiii.
43. Ibid., p. 3.
44. Amartya Sen, *Development as Freedom* (New York, NY: Anchor Books, 1999). See also: Jeffrey D. Sachs, *The End of Poverty: Economic Possibilities for Our Time* (New York, NY: Penguin, 2005) and for a discussion of the statistics that I provide, see the Appendix. The World Bank, Poverty & Inequality data by country: www.worldbank.org/en/country. Source: UN Human Development Report 2016. http://hdr.undp.org/en/countries/. Source:

United Nations Human Development Report. data.undp.org/dataset/Table-4-Gender-Inequality-Index/pq34-nwq7. This index measures disadvantages facing women and girls in terms of discrimination in such areas as health care, education, and job opportunities.
45. See http://hdr.undp.org/en/content/human-development-index-hdi
46. Sen, *Development as Freedom*, p. 4.
47. This is my adaptation of material that Sen presents in *Development as Freedom*, p. 10.
48. Sen, *Development as Freedom*, p. 10.
49. Ibid., p. 87.
50. Walter D. Mignolo, *The Darker Side of Western Modernity: Global Futures, Decolonial Options*, (Durham, NC: Duke University Press, 2011), pp. 17–19.
51. Mignolo, *The Darker Side of Western Modernity*, pp. 296–7.
52. Ibid., p. 298. Mignolo cites Kishore Mahbubani's four postulates of human freedom that were formulated from working on the concept of freedom in China: (1) freedom from want; (2) freedom of security; (3) freedom to choose; and (4) freedom of expression.
53. Explicit references to the rhetoric and ideals of freedom are established early on when Juana sees a public monument to "freedom and justice" in the opening pages of the novel. Her contemplation of these words sets up the ethical frame of the novel: "Now there was peace in her mind and body and it stayed all along the road past the FREEDOM AND JUSTICE monument so that this time she did not think how troubling these words were to a mind that had sought to know what they should mean, how troubling they were in this place" (Armah, Fragments, p. 23).
54. In *Morning Yet on Creation Day* (1975), Chinua Achebe was among the first to dismiss Armah's "anguished gloom," eliciting a wide-ranging debate that included Wole Soyinka's defense of Armah in *Myth, Literature and the African World* (Cambridge: Cambridge University Press, 1976).
55. Cooper, *Africa since 1940.*

Lustra

Christopher Okigbo

So would I to the hills again
so would I
to where springs the fountain
there to draw from
and to hilltop clamber
body and soul
whitewashed in the moondew
there to see from

So would I from my eye the mist
so would I
through moonmist to hilltop
there for cleansing

Here is a new-laid egg
here a white hen at midterm.

1 The Self

Unfettering Identity after Independence

> The density of History determines none of my acts. I am my own foundation.
>
> And it is by going beyond the historical and instrumental given that I initiate the cycle of my freedom.
>
> *Frantz Fanon*

It was a humid afternoon and the sky was overcast on the day I arrived at Sony Labou Tansi's house in Makélékélé, a popular neighborhood in the capital city of Brazzaville, Republic of Congo, with my friend Nicolas Martin-Granel. Tansi's eldest daughter was sitting in the courtyard with her arms folded across her knees. To the right of the entrance, there was a wrought-iron bench with the author's name scrolled on the backrest, and to the left a door led from the leafy courtyard into a small living room. It was dark inside because of a power outage in the area. I remember vividly the silent heaviness I carried within. I'd decided to cut short my stay in Brazzaville, and this was my last stop on the way to the airport. There was a worrisome tension that hung in the air in the city as I'd participated in roundtables, interviews, and conversations. As writers, journalists, and professors had answered my questions about Tansi's political engagement, it seemed inevitable that there would be more violence to come.

Once inside the house, we stood in the living room and then walked to the right, entering the writer's bedroom where he kept his books, writing table, and an altar that he had made himself. Half-used candles were still standing on the altar, Catholic iconography and dozens of photos were affixed to the wall above, and a kneeler for praying lay on the floor below. The intimate connection between creativity and prayer was evident in the private space of his bedroom. During the 1970s and 1980s, Tansi grew disillusioned with the prospect of political progress through the democratic process in the Congo and started praying for the arrival of his ethnic group in power as the only plausible end to the cycles of violence and injustice.

Marcel Ntsoni was a thirteen-year-old boy on August 15, 1960, when Fulbert Youlou came to power in the newly independent Republic of

Figure 1.1 Sony Labou Tansi's altar in his home in Brazzaville, Congo, 1996
Source: Photo by Phyllis Taoua

Congo Brazzaville. Just two months earlier, Patrice Lumumba had been elected Prime Minister in the Democratic Republic of the Congo on the other side of the river, Ntsoni's native country. In 1959, Ntsoni had left his village of Kimwanza, south of Kinshasa, with his maternal uncle who wanted him to learn "proper" French, and relocated to Congo-Brazzaville. It was a tumultuous time in the region – riots were breaking out across the Belgian Congo as the colony embarked on its path to decolonization, and many people were displaced. On the eve of independence, Ntsoni's Kongo identity was taking on a new political significance before the future writer, who took the pen name Sony Labou Tansi, was old enough to understand the long, burdensome history that helped create it. At the age of thirty-two, Tansi published his first novel, *La vie et demie* (1979; *Life and a Half*, 2011), with Editions du Seuil in Paris, catapulting the writer into the international limelight and revealing his remarkable insight into the turmoil that would engulf the region over the course of his lifetime and beyond. Reading *La vie et demie* in 1989 was my introduction to this talented writer and his complicated world.

Initially, I viewed Tansi as a writer's writer – someone who loved playing with words and who expressed his demand for social justice with passion and moral outrage. I went to Brazzaville in August 1996 to ask questions about the author's political engagement, which intrigued me, because it seemed critically important but remained somewhat mysterious. My visit fell between a period of civil unrest (1993–4) and the civil war that erupted in the run-up to the 1997 elections, and I discovered traces he left behind and the impression he made on those around him.[1]

After this trip, my first instinct was to understand the spiritual and epistemological dimensions of his political engagement in the region at the time, which I published as an essay, "Passionate Engagements: A Reading of Sony Labou Tansi's Private Ancestral Shrine."[2] Twenty years later, I am left with an enduring impression of the privacy with which he devoted himself to prayer, in contrast to the inherently public persona he cultivated as a writer. I have contemplated this schism and the meaning of the space where Tansi's most intimate self was at home as a writer, spiritual guide, and political activist. Trying to account for this author's comprehensive sense of dispossession is what put me on the path to writing this book.

In the years since, I have spent countless hours contemplating the longing for meaningful freedom in Tansi's work, particularly in relation to Amartya Sen's idea that freedom should involve the capacity to live a life we have reason to value. The circumstances that defined Tansi's interpretation of life in Congo-Brazzaville during the 1970s and 1980s were, without a doubt, complex and not of his choosing. When writers and activists are caught up in violent struggles, the terms of conflict are never satisfactory – they are dictated by an imperfect situation fraught with interconnected issues. Consider, for example, the discovery of oil in Nigeria and all that eventually led to Wole Soyinka's arrest and political detention in Nigeria in 1967; or the forces of greed, hypocrisy, and the naked assertion of power that contributed to Nelson Mandela's arrest, the Rivonia trial, and his decades-long imprisonment on Robben Island; or the dynamics of political rivalry and Cold War machinations that led to the macabre assassination of Patrice Lumumba. These are the lessons and stories that Tansi lived with every day. He hung photos of Mandela and Lumumba, among many others, on the wall above his altar. Although Tansi escaped assassination and imprisonment himself, his longing for peace, justice, and shared prosperity remained unfulfilled during his lifetime.

Being in conversation, over the past twenty-odd years, with activists and artists in Africa who were engaged in political struggles for freedom and justice has often left me saddened by the permanent toll it took on their lives. One of the most important lessons I learned from my trip to Brazzaville during the summer of 1996, and all the places in the years since, is that political struggle is sometimes dangerous and always embedded in a specific time and place. Upon reflection, I realize that what my unexpected discovery of Tansi's private ancestral shrine revealed to me is that the struggle for meaningful freedom after national liberation involved this writer's intimate self and his existential longing for a lost wholeness.

Recalibration: Individual Identities Nested within the Collective

While it may not be difficult to accept the notion that the struggle for meaningful freedom in Africa was an ongoing process after decolonization, the reasons for this are far less obvious. Even though new African nations had celebrated freedom from European domination, so much had been irretrievably lost or remained to be seen, as Tansi's life and work eloquently illustrate. This chapter explores the first area of narrative interest and considers how African writers and filmmakers adopted an introspective gaze in order to reveal an intimate self in new ways. This process of self-exploration represented a recalibration away from the overtly collective concerns of anticolonial nationalism that had prevailed in the struggle against European colonial rule since the 1930s. There is a substantial difference between the lyrical poetic voices of writers involved with the Negritude movement, who were deeply committed to evoking a shared sense of community, and the narratives I look at in this chapter, which evolved out of a new awareness of subjectivity initiated by Frantz Fanon's work and his critique of the movement.[3] Once the colonizer/colonized opposition that structured realist novels of the 1950s gave way, a different kind of struggle for meaningful freedom at home emerged with innovative terms and more nuances. From our vantage point today, once individuals were faced with coming to terms with the aftermath of colonization in their private sense of self, turning inward to contemplate the self may make sense as a logical next step in the process of liberation. However, introspection and an ethical interest in the intimate lives of individuals proved, initially, to be more controversial with literary critics than many readers may realize.[4]

If we are to appreciate the innovative significance of this emerging area of narrative interest, we must remember that national liberation movements in Africa were the products of collective efforts and were sustained by a cultural narrative of shared experience. The group-centered politics that gave rise to anticolonial protest after World War I stemmed, in large part, from workers' initiatives and the formation of trade unions based on European leftist models.[5] Once it became clear that the racist ideology that served as a rationale for the colonial exploitation of subjugated peoples would never be adequately challenged with European political organizations' international class-based platform remaining in place, Third World nationalisms responded to this inadequacy during the 1950s.[6] The specificities of colonial dispossession, especially race and ethnicity in addition to class issues, were made explicit as part of the narrative of national liberation that shaped the process of decolonization. Largely as a result of Fanon's interventions in his groundbreaking work *Peau noire, masques blancs* (1952; *Black Skin, White Masks,* 2008), followed by *Les Damnés de la terre* (1961; *The Wretched of the Earth,* 1963), a growing political awareness that had started in the post-war era gained a more finely tuned psychological dimension. As a French-trained psychiatrist of West Indian origin, Fanon provided an urgently needed language for talking about how the human hunger for political self-determination was also emotionally charged with the subject's desire to restore a sense of dignity as an *individual.*[7]

In his first book *Black Skin, White Masks,* Fanon takes his lived experience as the point of departure for analyzing the black subject's psychological alienation. He weaves autobiographical anecdotes about his life in the Caribbean and in France together with his clinical analysis of the colonized subject's existential disorientation and embattled sense of self. The striking way this French-trained black psychiatrist disclosed his private life in intimate terms represented a pivotal shift in the discourse of colonial liberation. The space of the autobiographical self that Fanon carved out for himself as a biracial man was analytically indispensable to his therapeutic project, because the alienation that existed *within him* as a result of his awareness of the tension between his "skin" and his "masks" was the source of a new beginning. At a key moment in his essay "The Lived Experience of the Black Man," Fanon talks about his body, locating his perception of self in time and space in corporal terms:

> And then we were given the occasion to confront the white gaze. An unusual weight descended on us. The real world robbed us of our share. In the white world, the man of color encounters difficulties in elaborating his body schema. The image of one's body is solely negating. It's an image in the third person. All around the body reigns an atmosphere of certain uncertainty. I know that if I want to smoke, I shall have to stretch out my right arm and grab the pack of cigarettes lying at the other end of the table. As for the matches, they are in the

left drawer, and I shall have to move back a little. And I make all these moves, not out of habit, but by implicit knowledge. A slow construction of my self as a body in a spatial and temporal world – such seems to be the schema. It is not imposed on me; it is rather a definitive structuring of my self and the world – definitive because it creates a genuine dialectic between my body and the world.[8]

Fanon chooses to describe a banal act from his daily life as a writer – reaching for a pack of cigarettes and matches, while seated at his desk – to evoke how profoundly alienating it is to be split between an awareness of his black skin, with the mental image of his black arm reaching across the table, and his idealized white identity that he wears as a mask, which triggers Fanon's need to negotiate the dialectic between his body and the world. Anjali Prabhu offers a perceptive interpretation of the split that exists in the narrator as being between the universal-historical black narrator and the particular, individual subject.[9] Building on this distinction, I would like to add that by affirming an autobiographical awareness of himself as a particular individual, Fanon was able to begin to unravel the alienation in his psyche when negotiating the dialectic between his experience of his black body and the white world. Fanon's affective ability to narrate the subject's experience both in terms of his emotional self (in moments of weeping) and his analytical self (explosion from the outside and reconstruction from within) was an inspiration to others.

In *Black Skin, White Masks*, Fanon describes how his discovery of metropolitan racism shattered his sense of self and forced him to take off the white mask that he had grown accustomed to wearing. He skillfully dramatizes the painful process of working out a new identity for himself at the same time as national liberation movements were being organized in Africa. From the outset, Fanon perceived a relationship between economic dispossession and the emergence of an inferiority complex, and he explored how the black man's alienation was embedded within a colonial situation defined by culture, history, and social habits as well as economic factors. As a medical professional, he was interested in the health of individual psyches; however, the revolutionary emerging within him already knew that the question of black people's liberation could not be resolved solely in terms of individual experience and psychiatric treatment.[10]

A theoretical awareness of the colonial subject's emotional life continues in Fanon's second book, *The Wretched of the Earth,* in which he idealizes insurrectional violence as a source of psychological liberation in terms of the colonized "slave" killing the colonial "master."[11] There can be no doubt that armed struggle was necessary to achieve freedom from French rule in Fanon's adopted Algeria. However, eight years of war left victims *and* perpetrators psychologically scarred, as I discuss in more detail later. Fanon's predictions about the liberating effects of insurrectional violence did not prove to be true, and he never engaged in a sustained discussion of freedom as an idea, including in his posthumous work *Ecrits sur l'aliénation et la liberté* (2015). Thus, it is important to recognize that his interest in the therapeutic process of liberation contributed concepts and narrative strategies that would be incorporated into an emerging language of freedom without a specific analytical engagement with the idea itself. I will revisit the issues of violence and collective action in Chapter 3 so, for now, let me sum up by saying that Fanon believed the process of decolonization would create New Men, in the same way Georg W. Hegel proposed that the slave could be transformed by work, and through this process, be awakened to the possibilities of freedom.[12]

Ashis Nandy builds on the work of Fanon and other intellectuals who wrote about European colonial domination in Africa, from Aimé Césaire to Albert Memmi, which Nandy adapts to his situation as a prominent political psychologist and social theorist in India.[13] Nandy expands the cultural scope of Fanon's project to include British colonization in India and offers additional concepts that are useful for thinking about selfhood in the aftermath of colonialism in *The Intimate Enemy: Loss and Recovery of Self under Colonialism* (1983). In this study of postcolonial consciousness, Nandy sees the colonized subject's need to forge a self-image free from the baggage of colonial imposition as an endeavor that involves their "inner lives" and "cultural selves" (xvi). Unlike Fanon, Nandy makes scant reference to his own life experience and undertakes, instead, a careful examination of Rudyard Kipling and Mahatma K. Gandhi, which allows him to formulate analytical terms for rethinking self-image and identity within the cultural context of Western imperialism. The "intimate enemy" is a powerful concept that he uses to represent the colonial subject's alienation within the private sphere of the self that may persist for years after colonialism has officially ended. Nandy argues that the specific way European colonials imposed their ideology of domination in terms of rationality, progress, and gendered notions of masculinity and femininity set up a false choice between being Western *or* Indian, but never both at the same time.[14] He interprets the underlying ambivalence in Kipling's voice as a writer to be an expression of his two cultural selves torn in opposite directions – figuratively, between the sound of the saxophone (imperial masculine hardness) and the oboe (feminine softness, cross-cultural empathy).[15] Nandy sees a connection between how Kipling wrestled with this cultural dichotomy and his self-destructiveness, because, although he chose the saxophone, Kipling was haunted by the sound of the oboe as long as his private Indian self-remained nostalgic for his childhood in Bombay. As a counterpoint to Kipling's culturally divided self, Nandy discusses the life of Sri Aurobindo, who was torn between his European childhood and an exaggerated embrace of Indian spirituality as an adult.[16] With these cross-cultural comparisons, Nandy articulates how the inner life of a victim of colonial culture can be split between two opposing cultural selves. The psychological distress that results from living with an "intimate enemy" can lead to pathologies as in Kipling's self-destruction and Aurobindo's interpersonal withdrawal.

Unlike Fanon, who believed that anticolonial insurrection would create New Men and restore their dignity as individuals, Nandy embraces nonviolent resistance inspired by Gandhi's position of noncompliance. Nandy rejects a defeatist view of the colonial subject as a helpless victim caught in the hinges of history and criticizes a posture of defiance that combats the West on Western terms with weapons, virility, and violence. In a move to de-Westernize his own critical discourse, Nandy looks to Gandhi's position of peaceful noncompliance with respect to Western domination *and* cultural hierarchies as an alternative strategy. In order to formulate a new language of dissent, one must undertake a "minimal redefinition of the self" in relation to Western cultural hierarchies:

> But the meek inherit the earth not by meekness alone. They have to have categories, concepts and, even, defences of mind with which to turn the West into a reasonably manageable vector within the traditional world views still outside the span of modern ideas of universalism. The first concept in such a set has to be the victims' construction of the West, a West which would make sense to the non-West in terms of the non-West's experience of suffering. However, jejune such a concept may seem to the sophisticated scholar, it is a reality for the millions who have learnt the hard way to live with the West during the last two centuries. *(Intimate Enemy, xiii)*

Reconceptualizing the West, or trying to come up with a perspective of the Western world that makes sense from the point of view of a non-Western victim, is vastly more important than it may seem to some readers. That this new construction of the West should make sense from the cultural perspective of the non-West is indispensable to understanding representations of freedom in African narratives that use an introspective gaze to reveal an intimate self in an emerging area of narrative interest that was antihegemonic and formally innovative.

African writers and filmmakers represent characters that wrestle with the specter of the imperial West in their *inner lives* and *cultural selves* in ways that expressed what many ordinary people in Africa were going through after liberation from European colonial rule. As Nandy suggests *alternatives* for dissent that do not reproduce Western norms of masculinity, he also proposes *rejecting* Western models and dichotomies altogether:

> If beating the West at its own game is the preferred means of handling the feelings of self-hatred in the modernized non-West, there is also the West constructed by the savage outsider who is neither willing to be a player nor a counterplayer ... Fidelity to one's inner self, as one translates, and to one's inner voice, when one comments, may not mean adherence to reality in some cultures but in some others they do ... The essays in this book are a paean to the non-players who construct a West which allows them to live with the alternative West, while resisting the loving embrace of the West's dominant self. *(Intimate Enemy, xiii–xiv)*

This celebration of the "savage outsider" who opts out of Western modernity was published in the mid-1980s before Twitter and Facebook transformed this kind of choice.[17] Nonetheless, delinking from the colonial matrix of power as a means of charting alternatives to Western modernity's narrative of "progress" is an idea that continues to inspire social theorists in Asia and Latin America in the twenty-first century, as Walter Mignolo argues. In the early postindependence era, African writers and filmmakers wrestled with a construction of the West that was Janus-faced: oppressive because of the hegemony of capitalist culture and alluring as a source of escape, opportunity, and enlightenment. Artists were searching for a restored identity that would offer a creative synthesis forged as a manageable alternative to these colonial dichotomies and for innovative narrative points of view that would call into question the status quo with daring originality. We will see that gendered notions of "masculine" and "feminine" also intervene in African contexts, although in different ways from those Nandy explores.[18]

Ayi Kwei Armah's *Fragments*

Ayi Kwei Armah's second novel, *Fragments* (1969), is set in Kwame Nkrumah's Ghana and undertakes a bold revision of the cultural narrative of triumphant nationalism from the innovative point of view of an individual's radical noncompliance. A review of the archive of criticism on Armah's early novels reveals how an over-reliance on the collective dimension of decolonization significantly delayed the acceptance of the intimate self and the private lives of individuals as a relevant part of the language of meaningful freedom that was emerging after national liberation. Navigating the relationship between self and community in the immediate postindependence era proved to be a surprisingly thorny issue. The way critics have written about Armah's early novels makes it apparent that there have been opposing interpretations of the introspective gaze as a symptom of sick narcissism or therapeutic restoration.

As late as 1975, Chinua Achebe claimed that Armah's first novel *The Beautyful Ones Are Not Yet Born* (1968) was a "sick" failure. Achebe wrote: "It is a well-written book. Armah's command of language and imagery is of a very high order indeed. But it is a sick book. Sick, not with the sickness of Ghana, but with the sickness of the *human condition*."[19] Achebe finds fault with Armah's "pale and passive" protagonist whose "anguished gloom" was ultimately unconvincing because it did not represent Ghanaian experience in the terms – nationalist, constructive – that Achebe expected at that time, so soon after independence. A lively debate about what constituted a legitimate African literary aesthetic ensued, with interventions by Kofi Awoonor, who joined Achebe, and Wole Soyinka, who offered a qualified, but nonetheless convincing, defense of Armah's writing.[20] If the originality of *The Beautyful Ones Are Not Yet Born* was distressingly iconoclastic in 1968, it has since become a classic. As we come to terms with the central importance of the language of meaningful freedom in the canon of African letters, it is important to remember just how much criticism Armah received for his path-breaking use of an introspective gaze to reveal an intimate self in crisis, because it shows just how innovative this new area of narrative interest actually was.

Professional literary critics had a very hard time making sense of Armah's explicit critique of national liberation in formally provocative terms. Even as late as 1990, influential literary critics still stigmatized the introspection in Armah's early novels as a "perverse obsession" that was a "narcissistic" lamentation of the marginalization of intellectuals after independence.[21] In *Resistance in Postcolonial African Fiction*, Neil Lazarus claimed that the more isolated intellectuals like Armah became in the new African nations, the more their novels exhibited self-centered recriminations instead of productively contributing to the project of nation-building.[22] What these interpretations missed was the very real sense in which Armah's introspective narratives sought to resist Western hegemony and, thereby, contribute to meaningful freedom in a collective sense by recovering a basic existential freedom through a renewed sense of self. It was not until 2000 that Ode Ogede effectively countered the various condemnations of Armah's writing, which he attributes to the novelist's unorthodox views and lacerating criticism of postindependence Africa. In *Ayi Kwei Armah: Radical Iconoclast*, Ogede sees Armah's vision not as sick and narcissistic, but as therapeutic in nature, providing a renewed reflection on the complexities of the African situation in order "to heal the wounds of colonialism, not inflame them."[23] As one reads through the criticism of Armah's novels, one discovers how major critics of African literature wrestled for more than twenty years with how to reconcile Armah's introspective narrative style with the goals of national liberation and the literary conventions associated with them.[24]

Armah was one of a handful of African artists in the immediate postindependence era whose innovative narratives recalibrated the discourse of national liberation to include individual experience and the challenges of navigating other kinds of attachments to one's family, significant others, and ethnic group, in addition to national affiliation. These questions about how to represent individual identity in relation to national experience extended well beyond Armah's representations of Nkrumah's Ghana and whether Achebe could make sense of them. Richard Bjornson, for instance, revisits similar issues in the concluding chapters of *The African Quest for Freedom and Identity: Cameroonian Writing and the National Experience* (1991).[25] He observes how, in Ahmadou Ahidjo's Cameroon, it was inherently subversive for a writer to assert that identity was a dynamic process *open to negotiation* and not fixed within a totalitarian scheme steeped in authenticity Mobutu-style.[26] As African dictators, who Mahmood Mamdani calls the bearers of mainstream nationalism – sought to impose a monolithic "authenticity" on the masses in order to control them, a growing number of writers protested in the name of liberty. By exploring self-identity and social justice as part of a dynamic process over which individuals had some measure of control, Cameroonian writers were writing very much against the grain. Both for men and women, belonging to a community was genuinely important – it substantially informed how writers represented a relational self in dialogue with society. Bjornson observed that, "Because individual identity concepts are always nested in an image of one's place in the group to which one belongs, the individual quest for identity in works by Cameroonian writers implies a parallel attempt to define a sense of collective identity."[27] He astutely pinpointed how writers saw freedom and identity as involving "a series of nested identity concepts that include ethnic affiliation and a commitment to pan-African ideals."[28] Bjornson understood that an individual's relationship to national identity was multifaceted and adjusted the scope of his criticism to allow for various spheres of experience, including the existential self-definition that comes with falling in love. His perceptive idea of "nested identity concepts" provides a way out of the impasse previously discussed in relation to Armah's troubling innovation and is analytically useful when thinking more generally about the language of freedom in Africa, because it allows for multiple spheres of interconnected experience that can be expanded and adapted as needed.

I shall return to Armah's first novel in Chapter 3, but for now I would like to discuss *Fragments* which is less well-known, but presents us with an introspective narrative that is representative of the redirection in African fiction at issue here, as well as an explicit engagement with meaningful freedom. The lack of narrative unity in voice and perspective reflects, in formal terms, the theme of cultural and psychological fragmentation that is of central importance to the story that unfolds.[29] To understand the cultural meaning of the alienation that Baako, the protagonist, feels as an aspiring artist who returns to Ghana after independence, we will need to consider aspects of Armah's life story. Baako is a young man who struggles to comprehend the pieces of his fragmented world at home in Nkrumah's Ghana even as his own sense of self is unraveling. In the same way Fanon needed to articulate his experience as a black man in metropolitan France in terms of his autobiographical self, Armah's protagonist Baako is a narrative construction of the author's lived experience as a Ghanaian in the postindependence era. Like the protagonist in his novel, Armah was a student in the United States. At first, he attended a preparatory school in Massachusetts and then went on to study sociology at Harvard College and creative writing at Columbia University. He went home to Ghana from 1964 to 1966, where he worked as a scriptwriter for television and taught English. After 1966 he chose to live abroad in various places, including the United States, Algeria, Tanzania, and Senegal.[30] Armah was born into a family with financial means and of noble lineage among the Akan people, and as a result, he belonged to Ghana's educated elite in terms of social standing and education, although not in terms of his antihegemonic, anticapitalist sensibility. As we will see, an Akan cultural and linguistic context significantly informs Armah's writing in this work. In an interview in 1987, the novelist told Dimgba Igwe that the nervous breakdown Baako endures in *Fragments* resembles what he went through in Boston during the 1960s.[31] However, living with American racism during the civil rights era, in addition to the moral and existential dilemmas that caused Armah duress while in New England, are different from the problems Baako faces in Accra shortly after independence.[32] Thus *Fragments* is not a straightforward autobiography but, rather, a work of fiction that creatively transposes aspects of Armah's life experience in order to offer a critique of a different situation by analogy.[33] The way Armah appropriates Fanon's therapeutic narrative techniques in an inverted scenario of alienation with the black man returning to Africa is different from other forms of historical autobiography, which is another valuable form of African writing with historical urgency as we see in Mandela's *Long Walk to Freedom*.[34]

Armah stages Baako's dilemma of self-definition with a dramatic use of narrative technique in a manner reminiscent of the best modernist novels. One might think, for example, of how Albert Camus portrays

Meursault in *L'Étranger* (1942; *The Stranger*, 1946) with a first-person narrator and a relentless focus on the way his mind works. Meursault's viewpoint provides the subjective filter through which the moral dilemma takes shape as he finds himself unable to adapt to what society expects of him. Fyodor Dostoevsky uses a close third-person narrator to similar effect in *Crime and Punishment* (1866), where he predominantly focuses on Rashkolnikov's obsessive ruminations while alternating focalization from different characters' perspectives. Like Dostoevsky, Armah adopts a close third-person narrator in *Fragments* and alternates viewpoints with Baako as the dominant subjective anchor. The novel's focalization includes the perspectives of three primary characters: Baako, the artist; Juana, the psychiatrist; and Naana, the grandmother. Armah uses a close third-person narrator to convey these multiple viewpoints, except in the opening and closing chapters where the grandmother speaks in the first person.[35] All of these characters experience some form of social estrangement, which is expressed as a struggle for freedom through their distinct, but overlapping, viewpoints.[36]

My reading of *Fragments* shows how Armah explicitly employs a language of freedom and sets up a Fanonian intertext, which invites readers to reflect on the ideal of meaningful freedom in Ghana in the immediate aftermath of national liberation. However, Armah innovates on Fanon's scenario of the black man's struggle to recover from a shattered self when coming up against white metropolitan racism. In *Fragments*, a black man returns home to Ghana with ideals of meaningful freedom after national liberation, only to find that they have not come to fruition. We witness how the protagonist's sense of self becomes unhinged when he is unable to reintegrate himself in the "new" Ghana. Baako's nervous breakdown is less a reflection of a unique individual's existential failure to achieve self-definition than it is a way of putting a human face on his unfulfilled longing to enjoy meaningful freedom in a society that shares his values. As the novel unfolds and Armah connects the dilemma of the fragmented self to the repressed history of slavery in Ghana, we are able to appreciate how he sees the sphere of individual experience and the national narrative of liberation as necessarily entangled in the language of freedom he employs in the novel.

Baako's identity is doubly fragmented. He suffers a nervous breakdown in New York when he imagines returning to Ghana and making a life for himself as an artist. The crux of this issue relates to the artist's dilemma – how to say something relevant that will be of interest to an audience at home. The second nervous breakdown is more complicated. It mirrors what Fanon went through when he arrived in France in the 1950s, only in reverse. Whereas Fanon experienced a shattering of the self from the outside as a result of the white gaze, Baako's sense of self is shattered when he returns home to Ghana from the West and does not fit in. The way his fellow Ghanaians and, most intensely, his own family look at him undoes Baako's fragile sense of self. Armah uses Naana and Juana – names that rhyme with Ghana – as complementary characters whose perspectives help flesh out the madman's dilemma. In the same way metropolitan racism destroyed Fanon's colonial self in a real autobiographical sense, the novelist represents postindependence Ghana in fictional terms to show how disillusionment destroys Baako's optimistic self as he must contend with the absence of meaningful freedom after national liberation from British rule.[37]

Naana's point of view is the first of three in the novel. The grandmother's perspective is characterized by an introspection that mediates between the modern realm of the living and the world of the ancestors. She examines herself and her values in relation to her family and Ghanaian society with the wisdom of an old woman about to cross the threshold into the ancestral realm. The novel opens with Baako's grandmother speaking in the first person as she remembers her grandson's departure some five years before. This retrospective gaze lets the reader know that Naana still had her eyesight – she says, "I watched everything that night" – when she witnessed the farewell ritual for him (*Fragments*, 4). Naana comments on the ritual and intends to reassure Baako that he is not alone in the world and to remind him that he is part of an Akan community wherever his travels may take him. The purpose of the grandmother's narration in the opening chapter is to explain and interpret tradition, and to nurture her grandson by ensuring that ritual is respected so that the ancestral spirits will protect him. This framing device, with the grandmother speaking in the first person, establishes both the importance of an Akan cultural reference point and Naana as one of Baako's most significant others in the story.[38]

Naana's vision reveals how the ability to perceive things accurately and truthfully is an expression of wisdom in contrast to the moral blindness that modernity brings to members of her family. She attains the level of a visionary because she can see what others cannot or will not see: "If I should see a thing which all around me think they do not see, why will I in my foolishness shout against all the strength of their unseeing eyes?" (*Fragments*, 2). Naana reaches the conclusion that it is futile to try to enlighten her family because her struggle against the influence of capitalist modernity appears to be a battle lost in advance. It is difficult for the grandmother to live with this sense of alienation at home and in society given how interdependent her identity is with Akan cultural traditions and a communal spirit. Although the grandmother loses her eyesight after Baako leaves, she welcomes this limitation as a source of comfort: "Sometimes I know my blindness was sent to me to save me from the madness that would surely have come with seeing so much that was not to be understood" (*Fragments*, 14). She is able to "see," or her visionary consciousness is able to perceive, more than anyone else in the novel. She expresses her incomprehension of African modernity with a strident tone that conveys an inflexible disapproval of those who are governed by the appetite of their flesh. Naana's concept of the West and her critical assessment of Western influence on her family are categorically negative, and this moral condemnation defines her cultural self in terms that resonate with a well-established tradition of African criticism of imperial hegemony expressed in the cultural review *Présence Africaine* and continued by others including Ashis Nandy and Walter Mignolo.

Although the ritual of protection that opens the novel seems to have worked, since Baako returned safely, the homeland he comes back to is clearly headed in the wrong direction. When the grandmother's voice concludes the novel with a farewell, the tone is sad and lonely. The wholeness of her vision crushes her soul and makes her long to leave the world of the living. This other-worldliness is reflected in her name, Naana, which is the singular form of the Akan word, "nananom," which means ancestors.[39] She is a "remnant of something that passed by" (*Fragments*, 278), or a living fragment of the way things used to be. References to sensual perception – hearing, smelling, seeing – as well as to moral perception and comprehension help us to understand how witnessing modernity leads to a folding in of her perceptive self: "From the world and the life around me, nothing comes to me. My eyes are no longer windows through the wall of my flesh but a part of this blinding skin itself. Soon my ears too will be shut, and my soul within my body will be closed up, completely alone" (*Fragments*, 278). Paradoxically the wholeness of her vision allows the old woman to place ancestral values in relation to corrupt modernity, and the overwhelming sense of loss kills off her perceiving self. From her antihegemonic viewpoint, the willingness of ordinary Ghanaians to so passively embrace modern values and aspirations is beyond comprehension. The incompatibility between this African modernity and her world creates an impasse that forecloses the possibility of creative synthesis.

As the old woman contemplates the fragmentation of traditional Akan culture, both her intimate self and her social self in relation to her community appear fractured. Armah places an emphasis on the pain an individual psyche endures when faced with the whole-scale dispossession of a previous way of life. The grandmother imagines how madness would follow her blindness if she had not given up, and, as a result, her state of mind clearly anticipates Baako's madness and validates his inability to adapt, since he never gives up trying to comprehend the new Ghana. When the grandmother grasped the magnitude of what was lost, she felt like "a captured beast," her spirit like "an antelope at the end of its hunting," running this way and that, searching for a "refuge it could not reach" (*Fragments*, 281). As an embodiment of the debilitating effects of Western modernity in Ghana, the grandmother, like Baako, is never able to establish a workable identity that would allow her to adapt to the new dispensation.

Once Armah has established Naana as a pillar of the novel's moral edifice and a voice that provides the most meaningful reference point for comprehending Baako's madness in cultural terms, he introduces explicit references to the history of slavery as a relevant context for thinking about the expansion of capitalism. Naana offers interpretations of significant events including why her family sacrifices her great-grandson during the outdooring ceremony. She sees this as a sign that capitalism, or "the great haste to consume things," is an unfettered force of destruction that has been ravaging Ghana since the beginning of the slave trade:

> The baby was a sacrifice they killed, to satisfy perhaps a new god they have found much like the one that began the same long destruction of our people when the elders first – may their souls never find forgiveness on this head – split their own seed and raised half against half, part selling part to hard-eyed buyers from beyond the horizon, breaking, buying, selling, gaining, spending till the last of our men sells the last woman to any passing white buyer and himself waits to be destroyed by this great haste to consume things we have taken no care nor trouble to produce. *(Fragments, 284)*

The family sacrificed a baby in exchange for banknotes, which the grandmother views as a new version of the commodification of human life that started with African participation in the slave trade and continues in the materialistic values of the new political elite. Naana's interpretation of how her great-grandson's life was exchanged for cash explains the roots of Akan cultural dispossession in terms of values – when people put the accumulation of personal wealth before their own human dignity, their culture was doomed to extinction. She reviews the signs of destruction and laments the toll this decline in moral values has taken on her community just before she crosses over at the end of the novel. The grandmother's promise to protect Baako when she dies – "When I go I will seek out stronger spirits and speak to their souls of his need of them" (*Fragments*, 283) – appears tragically insufficient as a remedy for her grandson's state of alienation.

Armah adds another layer of complexity to his narrative and its engagement with the people's struggle for freedom and justice when he introduces Juana, who provides the second perspective through which he focalizes the story, before introducing Baako, who is the primary narrative voice in *Fragments*. Although Juana does not speak in the first person as Naana does, her perspective is just as emotional and introspective as the grandmother's. Their contrasting viewpoints complement one another and jointly create the fictional world into which the main protagonist enters in chapter three. Juana plays an important role as Baako's most significant other because they develop an intimate friendship and become lovers. Readers get a very clear sense of Juana's emotional life and her intimate self through a narration that closely follows her self-examination and political commentary about Nkrumah's Ghana. Like the grandmother, Juana is remarkably perceptive, and, as a middle-aged divorcée from Puerto Rico, she also finds herself navigating in between two worlds – her homeland and Ghana. This sensitive expatriate often feels like an outsider: "Juana sensed the unavoidable estrangement, the politeness of distances created for strangers like herself" (Fragments, 18). Juana is a psychiatrist who turns this cultural distance as an expat to her advantage. As an observer, she is able to analyze what she sees in the capital city of Accra from the point of view of an outsider trying to understand the new dispensation in Ghana. Her interpretations of what life was like in Accra at the time of narration are intermixed with reflections about herself, her profession, and social justice as she grapples with existential questions.

Juana's perspective overlaps with Naana's in one significant way – they both try to assess the underlying reasons for an absence of meaningful freedom after national liberation in Ghana and the toll it is taking on individuals. Their different vantage points open two spheres of reference: Naana laments a sense of irretrievable loss with respect to Akan values and communal customs, whereas Juana models how a sensitive, healthy psyche can remain reasonable, even when faced with political injustice and personal disappointment. Juana's resilience and tenacity seem to allow for a narrow hopefulness in contrast to the grandmother's sadness and moral solitude as she passes away. These female characters also offer contrasting versions of gendered identity by virtue of their different origins (Akan, Puerto Rican) and generations. The layered complexity of the narrative's form anticipates the crisis that will come into focus once Baako's consciousness takes center stage, which allows the reader to understand how the protagonist's identity is more than nested within multiple spheres of experience.

The novelist not only expands the terrain geographically when Juana takes a drive outside the city, but also surveys the social and cultural landscape from a new clinical point of view as the doctor comments on what she observes along the way. In contrast to Baako's grandmother, Juana thinks about the injustice she perceives in Ghana from a contemporary standpoint – that of a Caribbean expat – and as a psychiatrist, which serves as a rather explicit reference to Fanon's life story. We encounter further evidence of this Fanonian intertext in the way Juana attributes her patients' illnesses to social and political factors in urban Africa. She remarks on "the city itself behind her, made as if by some clever mind to produce exactly these wrecks that were her job" to repair (*Fragments*, 21). The psychiatrist sees plenty of people whose spirits have been broken and wonders what results her efforts at clinical treatment can yield when the capital city seems set up to drive people insane: "She got angry whenever she tried to find what use there was in saving people who had found the mess she needed so often to flee from insupportable and had somehow flipped out of it after too much pain too long endured, only to give them the outer toughening they would need so they could be flipped back to get messed up some more in this town that could break any spirit" (*Fragments*, 21). The fact that she asks herself this question – what's the point of curing an individual when the "mess" is so widespread? – is laden with implicit meaning because it was this very same question that led Fanon to leave his position as a psychiatrist in Blida-Joinville and join the Algerian movement for national liberation.[40] Although Juana does not become a political activist in Ghana, Armah uses her Fanon-inspired questions to reveal the interconnectedness of different types of freedom in a conceptual language that connects existential freedom – especially the absence of alienation – with other forms of freedom, such as an individual's capacity to pursue life as it should be and instrumental freedoms in a participatory democracy. Being a foreign observer allows her to retain a measure of serenity and keep her sense of self intact as these problems are filtered through an outsider's professional attitude: "Now there was peace in her mind and body and it stayed all along the road past the FREEDOM AND JUSTICE arch monument so that this time she did not think how troubling these words were to a mind that had sought to know what they should mean, how troubling they were in this place" (*Fragments*, 23; no emphasis added). Juana is able to preserve her inner peace as she contemplates the tragic gap between what the road sign announces and the society she has discovered, whereas a self-aware citizen who reflects deeply on the status of "freedom and justice" in Ghana during the 1960s might feel more troubled, as Baako discovers. The ironic difference between slogans of freedom and the hard work of bringing social justice to fruition in this passage appears an implicit criticism of Nkrumah who played a leading role in the articulation and deployment of a language of freedom to advance the cause of national liberation. We will see that an even more well-developed critique of the discourse of national liberation is advanced in Armah's first novel, *The Beautyful Ones Are Not Yet Born*. The second novel was published well after a general sense of disillusionment had set in: thirteen years after independence and four years after Nkrumah was deposed by a coup in 1966.[41] Whereas this novel does not reflect on the imperial forces arrayed against the leaders of African national liberation, it does seek to portray what life was like for ordinary people when political power was not effectively used to foster social justice and shared prosperity. Concentration of wealth and power in the hands of Nkrumah's centralized government reproduced the economy and structure of the colonial state, which essentially functioned like a gatekeeper state, as we will see in Armah's first novel, to be discussed in Chapter 3.[42]

The specific political problems that make Ghanaian society dysfunctional are not made explicit in *Fragments*, yet the novelist takes care to foreground Juana's personal sense of distress and frustration in an introspective manner. This creates an intimacy of perspective because Juana's feelings and perceptions motivate the way the story unfolds, rather than theories about why national liberation failed to produce meaningful freedom. When one day Juana takes a trip to the beach, fleeing chaos in the city and futility in the clinic, the reader discovers the depth of her perception. Juana watches a crowd gather in the street and notices a man with a "great personal peculiarity" – the close third-person narrator observes this man's wounded virility with a focalization from Juana's perspective. As "the eye" searches for the "twisting cause" of the man's deformity, the tone becomes hyperbolic, indicating that his unnatural state is symbolic of something larger than the man himself. Juana keeps looking and catches the man's expression: "Juana saw in his eyes a manic shine with far more burn in it than that possessing any of the others, and she knew at once that this was a man who needed something like the first killing of the dog for reasons that lay within and were far more powerful than the mere outside glory open to the hunter with his kill" (*Fragments*, 27). The narrator signals how Juana can see into this man's suffering and the nature of his distress, suggesting that the man's violent impulse – killing a dog in the street – is motivated by a deeper, unacknowledged need to compensate for his compromised masculinity. After the man kills the dog, his swollen scrotum begins to drip like the ejaculation of his soul's misery: "Something that had stayed locked up and poisoned the masculinity of his days was now coming down, and in spite of all his shame he seemed seized by an uncontrollable happiness that made him walk with the high, proud, exaggerated steps of a puppet" (*Fragments*, 29–30). The man – an anonymous passerby – tastes a brief moment of joy after he asserts a small measure of virility by killing a mangy dog on the street in front of other people. Given the way Armah explicitly frames the issue of injured masculinity in terms of the unfinished business of achieving freedom and justice in Ghana, we are left wondering: What would it take for wounded men to attain political awareness so that they feel sufficiently compelled to take meaningful action together?

Although Juana looks at Ghana through the filters of national liberation and the psychiatric health of individuals, she reaches conclusions that reinforce what Naana previously described. After the crowd disperses, Juana contemplates the situation in search of a deeper, hidden meaning as she often does. Juana examines herself and the purpose of her work in the face of ongoing dispossession: "Again, the question rose to force the direction of her thoughts: whether all this was worth anything. What meaning could hope have in an environment so completely seized with danger and so many different kinds of loss? It was too widely spread, the damage" (*Fragments*, 34). These moments of introspection have various purposes: they disclose Juana's intimate self by revealing what she cares about; they remind us that thinking about liberation after national independence requires expanding political ideology to address the needs of an individual human psyche in order to understand "so many different kinds of loss"; and they set up an important context for understanding why Baako drifts into madness. But Armah also gives Juana wounds of her own to heal. She describes herself as a "fugitive" from a never-ending pain that just "burrows inward" and accompanies her wherever she may go (*Fragments*, 42). Juana's divorce left her traumatized, and the fact that she has suffered, in addition to the fact that she is an unattached woman, contributes to the definition of her persona as Baako's future soul mate.

Armah returns to the theme of slavery but, this time, he presents an awareness of the history of slavery as a necessary point of reference in the ongoing struggle for meaningful freedom. While Juana is at the beach, she notices a white slave castle in the distance, not far from where she is walking. She observes: "No one seemed to need forgiveness, and it was no use feeling sorry for oneself, for crimes borne by people with whom one identified. The real crime was ignorance of past crime, and that, it seemed, would be a permanent sort of ignorance in places like this and places like home" (*Fragments*, 44). Although Juana has not yet met Baako, this comment about Ghanaians not coming to terms with the legacy of the slave trade mirrors one of the screenplays he pitches later on. She cannot understand why people in Ghana are not engaged in a struggle for meaningful freedom, and learning to live with this absence of collective awareness is a serious challenge:

> The first months here had been terrible for a mind that had come prepared to find its own part in a struggle assumed to be going on [...] None of the struggle, none of the fire of defiance; just the living defeat of whole peoples – the familiar fabric of her life. After such an understanding, peace should perhaps have come, but that was also impossible, with so many reminders around of the impotence of victims and the blindness of those who had risen to guide them. She had learned ways of making the necessary peace for herself. Adjustment. Something necessary and true, though she had gotten into the habit of laughing at the bald word itself. A matter of knowing what visions people lead their lives by, or by what visions life leads them. And survival. A matter of adopting a narrower vision every time the full vision threatens danger to the visionary self. *(Fragments, 45–46)*

The fact that she must try to make adjustments in order to survive "the living defeat of whole peoples" resembles Baako's consciousness. However, unlike Baako, Juana is relatively successful in scaling back the scope of her perception by "adopting a narrower vision" whenever the fuller "vision threatens danger to the visionary self."

It is remarkable how much of the novel is focused through perspectives other than Baako's, even though his character dominates the story. This stylistic feat even led the literary critic D. S. Izevbaye to remember the novel as a first-person narrative from Baako's perspective.[43] Armah achieves this effect by having everything that is told and revealed contribute to understanding Baako's central dilemma – how to find his place in the new Ghana. When Juana and Baako meet, they fall in love, and their intimate friendship becomes the most compelling and successful aspect of the novel. At the beginning of chapter five, Juana remembers Baako's first visit to her office with a retrospective gaze as she considers how to respond to his invitation: "Will you be my friend?" (*Fragments*, 149). The interest they have in each other is immediately obvious, and Armah tells the story of their love affair in an appropriately unconventional manner – he focalizes the narration primarily from Juana's point of view, which means the psychiatrist reveals how Baako has become the object of her attraction.

During the heyday of nationalist fervor, one can imagine how the fact that Armah reinforces the intimate self and sexuality as part of an individual's well-being in this novel might be seen as anti-conformist. Juana has a gentle, assertive presence, and she takes him by the hand when they are at the beach together for the first time. The narrator describes their first sexual encounter with striking detail and, as is often the case, when the introspective gaze reveals the intimate lives of individuals, sexual intimacy and love relations come into play. Armah rapidly develops the intensity of their intimate connection as they have sex three times within a short time, and the description of their second copulation in the ocean is even longer and more involved than the first. Their sexual intimacy is interwoven with stories of creativity and discovery – they attend a literary event, talk about myths and poetry, go for long drives together, and make love in the ocean. Baako tells one story about how artistic expression can be inspired by a desire to overcome the absence of a love object and that feeling of separateness, which implicitly evokes what is emerging between them.[44] And yet, what seems most vital in this relationship is how they help one another escape the realm of the intellect – "He stopped her thinking with his searching fingers" (*Fragments*, 177) – and explore one another physically in the present.

When Baako's perspective focalizes the narrative, the drama centers on his quest to have a meaningful role as an artist in the new Ghana. This leads inevitably to a sharp critique of the cultural narrative of triumphant nationalism. His desire to be relevant is not a narcissistic endeavor because finding a form of expression that is useful to his community is the ultimate measure of his success. The third-person narrator maintains a consistently close focus on the inner workings of Baako's feverish mind and observes the sequence of events that leads to his descent into madness. When Baako pays a visit to his former art teacher, he tells Ocran that deciding to pursue a life as a writer sent him "all the way around the bend" the first time. Yet Baako returned to Ghana with a carefully considered plan – he wanted to write screenplays rather than novels, because "it's a much clearer way of saying things to people here," given the barriers of language and literacy (*Fragments*, 114). After he lands a job at Ghanavision, Baako comes sharply up against a culture of corruption and hypocrisy that eventually destroys his hopeful vision. The film treatments he pitches to the managers at the television station deal with overtly political topics: leaders coming to power on the backs of the people and Africans selling their brothers and sisters into slavery for financial gain. For Baako, understanding the history of slavery was indispensable to deconstructing the hegemony of Western capitalism in Africa after independence. During a production meeting, Asante-Smith quickly dismisses Baako's ideas as "very peculiar concerns" (*Fragments*, 214) that do not appear to have any relation to their "gigantic task of nation building," since Ghanaians "inherited a glorious culture" and are an "independent people" (*Fragments*, 209). The educated elite who run the country are only interested in stories that perpetuate a false narrative of triumphant nationalism.[45] Rather than help peddle these illusions, Baako resigns from his position at Ghanavision and burns every film treatment one page at a time.[46] Baako's isolation and the rejection of his ideas are reflected in the Akan meaning of his name, the "lonely one." The feeling of being a misfit was stronger than his ability to resist with an alternative vision, and this failure to find his voice as an artist triggers his second downward spiral.

The fact that Baako's existential alienation seems most acute at home with his family foregrounds the vital importance of kinship attachments for his personal equilibrium. When Baako visits Juana in her office, he compares his family to a "concave mirror" that reflects a more intimate image of how the dominant society sees him. The narrator describes Baako's take on his situation from the point of view of the psychiatrist who is listening:

> He talked, very precisely, of the things worrying him, like a doctor probing into a diseased body, locating the node of sickened nerves; all his talk was of a loneliness from which he was finding it impossible to break, of the society he had come back to and the many ways in which it made him feel his aloneness. She asked him about his family, thinking of some possible shelter, but when he spoke of it, his family became only a closer, more intense, more intimate reflection of the society itself, a concave mirror, as he called it, and before long she was left in no doubt at all that in many ways he saw more small possibilities of hope in the larger society than in the family around him. *(Fragments, 145–46)*

Baako appears lucid enough to diagnose the cause of his suffering and see how the "node of sickened nerves" starts with a hyper-awareness of his self in relation to others. He knows that his problems cannot be solved by a narcissistic retreat into himself as he is so conscious of how his self-concept is nested within familial and social spheres in addition to his national affiliation. Baako's loneliness at home stems from the difference in his values and those of his mother, Efua, and his sister, Araba. His family mirrors the dominant perception of Baako as a "been-to" or someone who has been to Europe or America and returned to Africa. The status of a been-to in 1970s Accra was legendary and inspired cultish behavior in materialistic people who indulged fantasies of financial rescue from abroad.[47] Efua, in particular, projects her hopes for social advancement and dreams of financial gain onto her son after he leaves for New York. Thus, when Baako returns from America without cash, a new car, or shiny trinkets, his family is hideously disappointed. Of course, the sense in which the rampant materialism of "larger society" offered so little hope for Baako's aspirations for meaningful freedom and social justice conveys a much deeper disillusionment with Nkrumah's leadership and the promise that national liberation would transform society.

In *Fragments*, things start to fall apart when capitalist hegemony becomes so pervasive that the social fabric begins to unravel. After Baako left his family by flying away in a mysterious machine to an unknown land, he became a ghost or intermediary figure, operating in between the realms of the living and the gods. While he was in America, his mother participated in cult rituals where she gave money to a self-proclaimed prophet as an expression of her faith in his promise that her ghost-son would bring back wealth for her from the other world. In order for Efua to cleanse her soul, she takes her son to the abandoned construction site where she had put down the foundation for a house. During their visit to this bereft place, the narrator gives us Baako's perception of the "jagged edges that gave the eye a feeling of being grated against a thousand snapped fractions of things" where a pile of blocks had "fallen apart" and were "waiting for the ruin of a final fall" (*Fragments*, 254). While the son's eyes are wounded by his painful perception of fragmentation and ruin, a jet plane passes overhead, "silver white itself and trailing a white mist," which provokes a revealing comment from Efua: "If our souls are dirty it's because of the desire to fly too" (*Fragments*, 255). His mother's soul is tainted by her slavish admiration of whiteness, of an idealized West that figures in her mind as a source of redemption in material terms. Baako sees things as having fallen apart – an apostrophe to Chinua Achebe's path-breaking novel of the 1950s – because the materialistic values that were introduced during slavery and colonialism are continuing to spread like a cancer after independence; they have dehumanized his mother to the point where she would curse him for not helping her realize her fanatical materialistic dreams.

This episode about the tragic rupture of his familial attachment is narrated from Baako's point of view as a memory after his family took him to an insane asylum. He sees himself as a disappointment and a failure through their eyes, and he gets stuck in the tragic loneliness of that vision: "One repeated thought took his mind and sped through his head like frames carrying an unchanging accusation: right, right, they're right, right, right" (*Fragments*, 250). When he refused to go along with their plan to celebrate his return with a party, he imagined they saw the "horrifying inner shrinking" of his soul (*Fragments*, 250–1). While in the asylum, he also remembers making a fool of himself during the outdooring ceremony that Efua and Araba organized for his sister's baby. The family disregarded custom and elected to have the ritual early, on the Sunday after payday, hoping to collect as much gift money as possible, even though this meant prematurely exposing the infant at only five days old.[48] The narrator suggests Baako's moral isolation when, "Watching, he felt himself receding physically from the scene, a clown looking at a show turned inside out" (*Fragments*, 266). Baako made a scene when he yanked away the fan that was blowing on the newborn and the "clown let the heavy thing drop into the brass pan, still turning, scattering the gathered notes" (*Fragments*, 266). Baby Baako died and his mother's money was strewn across the yard. As he remembers this painful scene, he sees himself as "a solitary fool walking into the midst of things wearing only reasonable clothes, a shirt and a northern *batakari* over a pair of shorts" (*Fragments*, 259). The narrator presents Baako's intense feeling of disconnection from his family and, as a result, from an authentic sense of himself through the retrospective gaze of a psychiatric patient who remembers what sent him over the edge the second time.

The narrator describes in grotesque detail the physical pain Baako feels in his body and psyche by observing his fever and headaches as he slips into madness. When Juana returns from her vacation leave in Puerto Rico, she finds Baako sitting on the ground in the courtyard outside the acute ward in the asylum. She asks him what really happened, and he replies that it was the cargo mentality that did it: "Who needs what's in a head?" (*Fragments*, 271).[49] As Juana listens to Baako, her closeness as a soul mate is reestablished through physical contact: "She took his hand and held it, caressing it; a fullness of affection she had been unable to let out in words broke through and took complete possession of her. He seemed to have felt it too, and moved closer against her. The resistance that had been so strong in his words was gone, and his body next to hers felt totally willing. He was crying again" (*Fragments*, 272). Baako's vulnerability in the intimate sphere expressed, here again, in physical terms humanizes his existential longing for healthy connections and provides a parallel to his yearning for substantive freedoms as an artist in this carefully layered narrative. Armah uses Eros and intimate friendship to deepen his characters and to evoke how their human longing for connection and community grounds the political ideals they share. Armah's ability to represent the private, intimate sphere of an individual's longing for existential freedom as nested within political ideas and moral values is arguably the most compelling aspect of the novel.

The artist's quest to lead a meaningful life displays in dramatic fashion a process all formerly colonized subjects would have to go through in order to arrive at a sense of self free from an intimate enemy. However, if we reverse the concave mirror metaphor and take Baako as the measure of sanity by which Ghanaian society should be judged, we see his madness in a whole new light. After Nkrumah took office, the wealthy elite who had internalized British class-consciousness carried on imitating white colonials after decolonization had occurred. The power of the ruling elite was never effectively challenged because the dispossessed took out their frustrations on one another or simply imitated their new black masters, rather than confront the injustice of their situation. In

Fragments, Armah represents this class as unaware of their alienation and resistant to attempts by others that might cultivate the necessary self-awareness that could contribute to progressive social change. Those rare individuals who can see what is going on, such as Naana, are maligned and marginalized. The grandmother's social isolation is a sign of the moral disorientation that follows from the fragmentation of traditional social arrangements that started with slavery and continued under colonialism. Efua and Araba have become estranged from the ethical values that might help put the things that have fallen apart back together. They have surrendered to Western hegemony and capitalist values, and they use the extended family network to persuade others to conform to the dominant culture of greed in Ghana, even if it means calling guests by name and holding out a collection basket. As Baako's crisis illustrates, an individual's ability to resist these forces is measured in terms of his willingness to disappoint the expectations of loved ones at home.

In more positive terms, Baako's vision as an artist reflects his ability to make cross-cultural comparisons that are informed by a realistic understanding of the West, which is critical of unfettered capitalism, but open to the acquisition of other kinds of knowledge. What Baako brings back from New York is a guitar, a typewriter, and a cultivated intellect – these are significant elements that defined how he reconceived the West in terms that make sense to his non-Western self. Although his experience studying abroad turned him into an intellectual outsider, at odds with his culture of origin, it is intriguing that *what was learned* is never presented as a source of alienation for Baako. It is implied that he can pick and choose what seems useful. Instead, what troubles him is *how to translate* what he has to say in a purposeful way back home.[50] This quest for relevance is formulated as essentially a social dilemma, and as Baako tries to work this out, we witness the fragmentation of his self-image unfold. His struggle to remain faithful to an authentic self in defiance of his family's expectations takes place within the realm of culture – his values have turned him against Ghanaian society in its modern capitalist drift. Like André Gide's protagonist Michel in *L'Immoraliste* (1901; *The Immoralist*, 1996), Baako is left paralyzed in the end. His unheroic inaction appears an act of moral dissidence inciting readers to find fault with the society, not the individual. Baako's conflict requires that he makes choices as a moral actor, which reveals his values and through them his cultural self. As a protagonist, he lacks the confidence to establish his own priorities in any broad sense. However, his radical position of noncompliance suggests a moral resolve not to adapt to a culture of greed and not to pursue his self-interest at others' expense. The way Baako navigates this terrain – and his need for healthy attachments – seems, above all, a plea for others to resist the cancerous spread of modernity's capitalist values by working together for cultural renewal.

In order to appreciate the central importance of the struggle for meaningful freedom after national liberation in this canonical novel, readers may find it useful to see freedom as multifaceted and involving more than the attainment of political sovereignty. It was not until Ode Ogede published *Ayi Kwei Armah: Radical Iconoclast* that new insight into how Armah's experimental narratives sought "to heal the wounds of colonialism, not inflame them" was finally offered. Yet, it was Richard Bjornson who provided the most useful analytical tools for understanding how an individual's "identity concept is always nested in an image of one's place in the group to which one belongs" in *The African Quest for Freedom and Identity*. My reading of the novel shows how Baako's nervous breakdown, which is refracted in the formal fragmentation of the narrative, is less a reflection of a unique individual's existential failure to achieve self-definition than a way of putting a human face on his unfulfilled longing to achieve meaningful freedom in a society that shares his values.

Djibril Diop Mambety's *Touki Bouki*

Djibril Diop Mambety's *Touki Bouki* (1973) is a formally innovative film that revises the cultural narrative of triumphant nationalism from a boldly original point of view. Whereas Armah's *Fragments* presents a coherent narrative that shows us the painful process of a man's fragmenting sense of self, Mambety gives us a film that experiments with narrative discontinuity in formal terms, but presents the story of a man who makes the sensible decision to stay home and not expose himself to the dislocations inherent in migration. Whereas Armah's novel explicitly evokes the language of freedom that was deployed in the service of national liberation and presents an awareness of the history of slavery as a necessary point of reference, Mambety's film places a primary emphasis on Mory's existential freedom and represents the absence of instrumental and substantive freedoms as contributing factors to the lack of good options in postindependence Senegal. I argue that Mambety gives us another anti-hegemonic narrative that uses an introspective gaze to narrate Mory's journey to reclaim a sense of self that is free from the alluring embrace of an idealized West. I read the signs of disaffection in the film as social and political elements that frame our understanding of the protagonist's existential struggle to lead a meaningful life at home. Indeed, Mory and Anta's fantasy of going to Paris sprouts from the soil of young people's disillusionment with opportunities to live the kind of life they have reason to value in Dakar during the 1970s. *Touki Bouki* resists the double impasse of disaffection at home and a fascination with an idealized West by taking the self as a point of departure.

Mambety's statements about the film as well as his representation of Mory's inner life invite us to interpret the young man as a double for the filmmaker's cultural self. Although *Touki Bouki* is not about a filmmaker in Dakar, it is an intensely personal story about a young man's aspirations in which Mambety sees himself. "The characters of *Touki Bouki* are interesting to me," states Mambety, "because their dreams are not those of ordinary people. Anta and Mory do not dream of building castles in Africa; they dream of finding some sort of Atlantis overseas. Following their dream permitted me to follow my own dreams, and my way of escaping those dreams was to laugh at them."[51] He presents us with anticonformist characters who operate on the margins of society because their difference, with which he identified, allows for criticism of social conventions and mainstream values. The struggle Mory goes through to locate himself within the urban landscape in Dakar of the 1970s can be seen as analogous to the artist's process, which involved introspection and self-examination. Here, again, we notice a parallel with Armah's character Baako, who searches in vain for a way to fit the pieces of African modernity together for himself. Mory frees himself, in the end, and decides to stay home, but his journey was traumatic and seems an indirect reflection of the director's life experience. Mambety said, "*Touki Bouki* was conceived at the time of a very violent crisis in my life. I wanted to make a lot of things explode."[52] With this admission in mind, we can interpret the film's abstraction as a distancing mechanism that allowed the filmmaker to project aspects of his intimate self onto the screen with symbolism, humor, and some violence. African film critics tend to agree that the film is a deeply personal statement on the difficult journey of self-definition in individual and artistic terms. To the extent that Mambety took his temptation to join the flow of postindependence migration to Europe as the subject of his laughter, it helped him move on to different creative endeavors in Colobane. Today, both Armah and Mambety, two deeply introspective artists, are considered classics. Their early works now stand as iconic representations of African identity in the postindependence era.

All of Mambety's films are set in Colobane – the district of Dakar where he was born and raised – in a neighborhood settled by rural migrants to the city.[53] The language most often spoken in his films is Wolof, a language that the majority of the population in Senegal speaks. Dakar, the capital city of Senegal and previously the colonial capital of French West Africa, was more like Paris than a village in the Sahel when *Touki Bouki* was filmed. Mambety was raised in a Muslim household because his father was an imam at a mosque in Colobane, and we see evidence of a complex spirituality in his films, which is more mystical and ironic than patriarchal.[54] The first words uttered in *Touki Bouki* are those of a muezzin calling the faithful to prayer and his message – "those who are not patient will die of hunger" – is not terribly edifying. The inner peace that comes from surrender to one's faith could not be farther from the turbulent, violent quest for self-definition on which Mory embarks in the film. The filmmaker's resolute anticonformism shielded him from too much censorship at school and at home, allowing Mambety to develop arguably the most original film aesthetic in West Africa. There is a consistent focus on self-representation in his oeuvre, and his friends have said that all of Mambety's films have characters that resemble him or are a double of the filmmaker himself.[55] Although choosing to film close to home was no doubt a financial and logistical consideration, it also seems that being rooted in a familiar place – from which he was never estranged – enhanced his confidence as an artist.

In aesthetic terms, Mambety engages in a deconstruction of realist film language and infuses a non-Western narrative style into his storytelling. This allows him to begin to formulate an alternative film language, which is a means of finding an indigenous voice for the expression of dissent.[56] The critical reception of introspection in African cinema was a very different story from what Achebe said about Armah's early novels. In fact, film critics refer to an introspective trend as a means of framing their arguments without feeling compelled to follow up with a justification. In *Black African Cinema* (1994), Nwachukwu Frank Ukadike states, "In the 1970s and 1980s, cinema became more introspective, directed toward addressing contemporary African issues – colonialism and neocolonialism, social and cultural conflicts."[57] Ukadike develops this observation about the increasing introspection in cinema by attributing this orientation to modes of storytelling that were enriched by the oral tradition and claims they attained greater aesthetic "maturity."[58] Ukadike opens his chapter "The Cultural Context of Black African Cinema" with statements like these, which underscore the importance of this trend as a frame of reference for African film criticism.

Olivier Barlet and Françoise Pfaff also cite introspection as an interesting development with specific reference to Mambety.[59] In *African Cinemas* (2001), for instance, Barlet celebrates the "very personal" nature of *Touki Bouki*, which other filmmakers accord "a prophetic status both for its form and for its content."[60] Barlet also uses an introspective gaze to set up his argument in "Closing Your Eyes," a chapter he sums up as follows: "The contradictory relationship with the West, a relationship experienced both as dream and nightmare, haunts African screenplays. It resolves itself today in an opening-up to splintered modern realities, to inwardness."[61] Thus, it is through turning inward – *closing their eyes* – that African filmmakers forge a creative synthesis of the tensions implicit in African modernity and begin to resolve their fraught relationship with the West. Barlet returns to *Touki Bouki* in the final paragraph: "By playing on ambivalence, by drawing deep on the imaginative resources of his cultural reality and employing parodic and ruptural techniques, Mambety reconstructs a battered psyche [...] This is indeed an introspective gaze, an inward gaze."[62] Barlet's interpretation echoes Nandy's proposition that the best way to resolve opposing views of the West and related cultural dichotomies (i.e., nightmare/dream) is through self-examination and non-Western syntheses. *Touki Bouki* is a passionate film that stages the drama of a young man's quest for self-definition while resisting the temptation to leave Africa with exceptional innovation in camera work and editing.[63] Both the story and the way it is told have made the film an enduring statement on the alienation of urban youth after independence.[64]

Touki Bouki adopts an introspective gaze to explore Mory's existential quest for self-definition in the capital city of Dakar during the 1970s. Whereas Armah presents a lucid account of what it is like to drift into insanity when an artist cannot piece together the fragments of African modernity in a way that makes sense to him, *Touki Bouki* gives viewers a fragmented and explosive story about a young man's decision to stay home and not become an African immigrant in Paris. The turbulence in Mambety's storytelling suggests psychological distress similar to what Armah conveys with sane, accessible prose in *Fragments*.

Touki Bouki is Mory's story, and the introspective gaze that Mambety uses to define his character is interesting because of the inner process that it reveals. The film shows Mory's journey of self-discovery that begins with his initiation into African modernity. Mory's transition from a rural setting to a capital city is represented symbolically with images that convey disorientation and loss in psychological terms. Within this context of alienation, Mory pursues a fantasy with his girlfriend Anta to strike it rich in the West and to come back to Dakar and show off. Mambety gives viewers a humorous projection of the been-to fantasy according to which the West is seen as the ultimate source for the acquisition of financial wealth and personal prestige for those who get to show it off. However, in the end, Mory fights against this alluring fantasy and frees himself from its powerful embrace. The way he arrives at his decision to stay home is filmed with a sequence of turbulent images that present an existential struggle of epic proportions. Ultimately Mory is left with no means of transportation – no boat to Paris, no motorcycle in the city, just a fragment of the longhorns he had on his motorcycle as décor. As he contemplates this fragment, which is an eloquent symbol of his new identity, scenes from his been-to fantasy rewind, all the way back to a freeze frame of the opening image. Mory gets over his juvenile dream and gains the necessary self-awareness to try something else at home, rather than "pick the leftovers from the white man's teeth," to borrow a phrase from Armah.[65] *Touki Bouki* became a classic because Mory's existential dilemma resonated with the experience of millions of disaffected youth on the streets of African cities in the 1970s – youth who wondered why they enjoyed so few substantive freedoms a decade after national liberation.

Although existential freedom is in the foreground of *Touki Bouki*, we will see how Mambety sets up the main drama with very explicit references to instrumental and substantive freedoms. Three signature moments in the film will illustrate how Mambety reveals Mory's inner life and quest to live life as it should be with an introspective gaze. The opening sequence represents psychological turmoil symbolically with violent images of animals being killed, which becomes a central motif in the film and is woven into all three of the signature moments of interest here.

Touki Bouki opens with a mid-range shot of cattle being led toward the camera by a boy shepherd with traditional flute music on the soundtrack, which locates the action in a rural setting in the Sahel region of West Africa. A second mid-range shot shows the herd approaching the camera from a different angle, at which point we hear animals and the low sound of cows groaning. Next the camera cuts in for a close-up of a cow's head, then neck and body as the animal is forced into a slaughterhouse. What follows is a scene of graphic violence in which cows like the ones we've just seen are dragged by their horns toward butchers who are waiting with knives in hand and meat hooks overhead. A mid-range shot lingers on the slitting of the cow's neck and also shows its legs jerking around as the animal writhes in pain. The soundtrack captures the ambient noise, amplifying the grotesque realism. Before leaving the meat plant, where the floor is flooded with blood, the camera pans around and stops at a group of familiar-looking cows waiting their turn. Then the sequence jumps back to the Sahel with a shot of the shepherd approaching the camera again, this time by himself – implying that his cattle have been slaughtered – and now the pastoral flute music seems sinister after what just happened. An important transition is announced when the sound of a motorcycle enters the soundtrack and overtakes the flute music. Once the approaching shepherd occupies most of the screen, the image dissolves into one of Mory on his motorcycle filmed with an over-the-shoulder shot of him riding away from the camera into the city. Mambety's use of a steady-cam mounted over Mory's shoulder personalizes the young man's experience and draws attention to his subjective perspective, which will be the film's central focus. In this establishing shot the image is framed from Mory's point of view and shows a set of longhorns fixed to the front of his handlebars like those of the slaughtered cows.

As a trophy on Mory's motorcycle, the longhorns stand out as a symbol of traditional Africa and refer specifically to a pastoral setting where shepherds raise cattle, which viewers familiar with the Sahel will associate with a way of life governed by ancestral beliefs. At the same time, the longhorns are all that is left of the slaughtered cow and are thus a continual reminder of what has been lost. This polyvalent symbol is used to great effect throughout the film to represent Mory's alienation in multiple settings. The camera work and editing explicitly establish the shepherd boy as what precedes Mory, the young man on his motorcycle in the city. However, in another definitive moment when Mory decides not to board the ship headed for Paris, the camera work and soundtrack associate him with a cow being slaughtered. On one level, the opening sequence is a figurative representation of Mory's initiation into African modernity, and this introduces the film's most important psychological content. As it relates to the development of Mory's identity, the slaughterhouse is the first conceptual construction of Western influence in Africa, which I interpret as a symbol for capitalism. Just as cows are turned into meat products for consumers to buy, capitalism is the legacy of colonial exploitation that continues to disrupt the inner lives of men like Mory. As he rides away from the camera into the city of Dakar we have in mind a sense of his disconnection from village life and imagine, given the negative connotations of the symbolic violence, that Mory must carry within him a profound existential alienation.

The second important moment in the representation of Mory's inner life relates to the pleasure of the ego and is revealed during a magnificent seaside scene. But Mambety inserts an important sequence along the way with the first direct reference to national liberation and constraints on instrumental freedoms. When Mory arrives at the university to pick up his girlfriend, he runs into a group of political activists who deride him for not attending their meetings and for distracting Anta from the revolution. In a bizarre parodic scene, the activists capture Mory with a lasso, which mimics how the cows were pulled toward the butchers in the opening sequence. The students tie Mory on the back of their red jeep and display the longhorns from his bike beside him, reinforcing the slaughter motif with visual symbolism. This montage of Mory arrested resembles the archival footage of Patrice Lumumba's capture in the Congo during the 1960s, which suggests that political leaders who intend to defend the people's interests are destined for martyrdom.[66] This symbolic apostrophe to the martyrs of national liberation carries two messages related to the idea of freedom: first, the process of decolonization was compromised by the assassination of patriotic nationalists like Lumumba; and, second, what Georges Nzongola-Ntalaja presents as the people's struggle for unfettered sovereignty in the postindependence era is hampered by a fear of violent repression. It is interesting that the viewer never sees how Mory escapes from his detention, but we imagine that he has learned a lesson about the dangers of activism and is skeptical of the possibility of using instrumental freedoms as a means to social justice when he appears next with Anta at the beach. This tableau that makes use of images familiar to viewers who only recently had watched African decolonization on television contributes to Mory's sense of entrapment and cynicism since national liberation left him in the slums with so few options.

We see Mory and Anta together for the first time at the seaside in a pivotal scene where they have sex and then hatch a plan to strike it rich in Paris. The way Mambety builds up to their off-screen copulation and the fantasy that follows is even more complex and layered in its meaning than the opening sequence. In order to understand what happens between them, we must consider what each of them brings to the encounter and the details of Mambety's intricate mise-en-scène. By the time Anta gets to the beach, the viewer sees her as an unconventional female character with short hair and tight pants, who curses when babies cry and talks back to her mother. Mory's companion has little time for such things as charity, patience, or self-effacement – qualities that are considered feminine virtues within many West African societies. Anta is a politically aware university student who feels trapped in postindependence Senegal and shares Mory's sense of disaffection. Mambety explicitly engages with the absence of substantive freedoms when he represents the human deprivation that results from poverty as clearly and literally as possible in an otherwise densely symbolic film. It is obvious that Mory eats meals on credit (which he cannot repay) and that he and Anta try to avoid his debtor, Tante Oumy, who is a bizarre and strangely materialistic woman. Thus the fact that poverty hinders substantive freedoms and the capacity to live the kind of life Mory and Anta have reason to value, as well as the absence of instrumental freedoms to effect progressive political change, prepares the soil in which the young couple's escapist fantasy plants its roots. As a filmmaker, Mambety continued to explore these ethical issues relating to how the deprivations of poverty inspire fantasies of financial rescue throughout his career, such as in *Le Franc* (1994) and *Hyènes* (1992).

For a moment Mory and Anta enjoy sexual pleasure but afterward, as they lay together overlooking the sea, they long for something more. The aspirations of young people looking for a good time do play a role here, yet other aspects of the mise-en-scène are somber and spiritual in nature. The slaughterhouse motif and anticapitalist imagery reappear in this scene with the recurrent symbol of the longhorns. The seaside sequence begins with Anta running toward the ocean and down to a ledge on a cliff. We see her going down stairs from multiple vantage points with the camera at the bottom and top of the steps. There are eerie noises including the whoosh and squawk of vultures overhead, mixed with the laughter of Tante Oumy, who wields a knife and wishes Mory were dead because he owes her money for a bowl of rice. The strange repetition of shots showing Anta's arrival creates a nightmarish atmosphere when combined with the sounds of vultures intercut with Oumy's menacing gestures. Anta seems in danger of being devoured by the evil forces of greed, and when she extends her arms to mimic the shape of the longhorns, the voracious effects of capitalism are evoked once again.

The camera insists on this symbolism by cutting in for a mid-range shot of her arms extended against the cliffs, followed by a cut-away shot with an extreme close-up of the longhorns on the handlebars. Then the camera moves back to Anta's arms, then to another cut-away, with a lingering close-up of the Dogon fertility symbol on the back of Mory's motorcycle, followed by another reverse shot of the horns on the front of Mory's bike. The filmmaker's playful cross-cutting between close-ups of the horns and the Dogon fertility symbol underscores their contrasting inverted shapes and poses an existential question about Mory and Anta's options: death or fertility? The use of jump cuts and conceptual editing creates a montage effect in which these concepts – death (loss, alienation) and fertility (pleasure, reproduction) – seem to be competing for interpretation in a realm where meanings are relative. The way Mambety lays bare the devices of filmmaking in *Touki Bouki* involves many techniques: disjunctive editing; jump cuts; calculated disparities between sound and image; a violation of continuity with non-diegetic inserts; use of cut-aways (metaphoric or symbolic shots that do not belong to the space and time of the narrative) and cut-ins (a shot, usually a close up, to emphasize visual specificity); suggestive montage; and a cyclical compositional style, among others. Mambety's keen interest in pushing the limits of film language from within his own African context explores a paradoxical form of enunciation where symbols are often placed in ambiguous relation to their contexts, such as the Dogon fertility cross and the zebus longhorns.

Mambety expands the symbolism of violence to include ritual in this scene as he develops Mory's inner life with images that build on the anti-capitalist slaughterhouse motif. A layer of meaning is added when images of a ram's neck being slit according to Islamic custom are intercut during the beginning of the seaside sequence. As with Armah, we observe an opposition between the material realm of greed and capitalism and the spiritual realm of transcendence and connection to the ancestors. But, ritual takes on an allegorical meaning here because of the way the director's insistent repetition of a non-diegetic event – the ram's neck being bled – presents this practice with an abstract image that requires interpretation. Even the ritual act of sacrificing an animal to communicate with the gods would repeat to no avail and so, it would seem, that if Mory and Anta are in danger of being devoured in the slaughterhouses of capitalist modernity, there is little the ancestors can do to protect them. Mambety's evocation of ancestral impotence in the modern era resonates with other scenes in African film and fiction; Naana's pessimism at the end of *Fragments*, the missionaries' survival in the evil forest in Chinua Achebe's *Things Fall Apart* (1958), and the absence of protection for dictators after the Cold War in Ahmadou Kourouma's *En Attendant le vote des bêtes sauvages* (1998; *Waiting for the Vote of the Wild Animals*, 2004) all represent pivotal moments in these narratives.[67]

In *Touki Bouki*, Mambety offers sexual pleasure and fantasy as a response to their grim postcolonial inheritance, since they have little hope for social justice and feel they have lost the protection of the ancestors in the spiritual realm. Mory and Anta's sexual encounter is an exceptional moment in African cinema and is represented with transgressive humor, although not actually shown.[68] When Anta undresses we have a mid-range shot of her naked torso before she kneels down, disappearing from the frame. The camera remains fixed on the horizon and we have a gorgeous shot of the fertility symbol and the ocean meeting the sky in the distance, evoking multiple associations with female sexuality. Then Anta reaches up and begins caressing the Dogon fertility cross as sounds of her moaning mingle with waves breaking on the soundtrack. A powerful wave sends a rush of foamy seawater into the air and Anta releases her grip, as her hand slides down leaving the screen. The way Mambety suggests Anta's orgasm is humorous because girls are raised to view motherhood as the defining purpose of a woman's life, and yet the director lets us know that Anta engages in the sexual act for pleasure rather than reproduction.[69] After their off-screen copulation, we have a panoramic shot of a boat heading out to sea followed by another beautiful long shot of the couple lying together on a ledge overlooking the ocean, which shimmers in the sunlight. Expansive feelings of freedom and the limitlessness of dreams are represented in direct contrast with previous panoramic shots of crowded slums in which Dakar's urban poor find themselves trapped. This is the pivotal moment when Anta and Mory make plans to go to Paris as soon as possible and their been-to fantasy takes hold. Their dialogue in the last part of this scene could be straight out of *Fragments*, mimicking the materialistic mindset of an opportunist like Brempong who plays by the rules that Baako refuses. Josephine Baker singing "Paris, Paris, Paris" blares on the soundtrack as they leave on Mory's motorcycle. This signature moment, when they give into the pleasure of the ego, yields the second conceptual construction of the West as an idealized source of wealth and personal prestige for those who are lucky enough to come back and show off. As Barlet observed, African screenplays are haunted by contradictory images of the West, which we have here in the powerful opposition between the nightmare of the slaughterhouse and the dream of spectacular wealth.

Mory and Anta's various efforts to find enough cash to buy boat tickets for Paris present the funniest moments in the film and unfold with the most narrative coherence. Finally, at Charlie's villa, Mory and Anta steal clothes and a wallet full of cash and then make off in one of Charlie's cars – a convertible painted red, white, and blue to resemble the American flag. This vehicle is a derisive symbol of American values, as their chase is all about greedy consumerism. As they leave, Mory imagines a spectacular victory parade in celebration of their return as rich and powerful people. He strips and stands naked in the back of the car where he makes a speech to himself and to the throngs of people he imagines watching in a rare moment of voiceover narration. In the second direct reference to the failed process of decolonization, Mory talks about the pleasures of power – both political and economic – and how the hyenas (those who are greedy and in power) must all flee, and leave the palace to the children of the victorious lion (i.e., himself). Traveling shots from Mory's point of view show spectators who have come out to celebrate their success, and Mambety mixes in cut-away shots of Mory and Anta who are decked out in fancy suits as they wave to the masses like British royalty. This fantasy parade in which Mory dreams of usurping power ends when they come across people dancing in traditional clothes led by Tante Oumy, who now sings their praises. Mory and Anta puff on cigars from the backseat of the convertible, blowing smoke in the direction of the dancing people who grovel at the sight of crisp bank notes. This deeply ironic scene parallels the anticapitalist ethic in Armah's novels and shows how greed is a powerful and destructive force in postcolonial Africa. In *Touki Bouki*, this fantastically rapid rise from victims of capitalism in the slums of Dakar to the super wealthy elite is a dream that is treated with parodic, derisive humor.

The third, and last, signature moment in Mambety's representation of Mory's inner life starts when passengers are boarding a ship headed for Paris. The sound of the boat's horn inviting passengers to board triggers a memory in Mory of cows being slaughtered, and images of the opening sequence are intercut in the scene. Metonymically the sound of the horn resembles the cow's groan as it was pulled toward the butchers. This final episode is dominated almost exclusively by Mory's subjective viewpoint as he reaches the conclusion that leaving for Paris would entail another form of violence. So, it is his visions of cows being slaughtered, re-presented here as a flashback, that prevent him from boarding the ship with Anta, who does decide to leave. Mory flees the harbor on foot, running through the streets of Dakar, and his desperate effort to extricate himself from such an enthralling fantasy is conveyed in a dramatic manner as the camera spirals around imitating the thrashing movements of a cow's head as it is being pulled by the horns into the slaughterhouse. Mory continues running into the city in an extended segment with jazz on the soundtrack, and then we hear an ambulance siren at the scene of an accident involving Mory's motorcycle. People in the crowd comment on how jumping from a Baobab tree (symbol of tradition) to a motorcycle (symbol of modernity) is a leap that can kill you in reference to the man who crashed the motorcycle, which also echoes the opening sequence. Mory walks off with a piece of the cow's longhorns that were broken during the accident.

As Mory sits on the steps holding the fragment of the horns in his hands, he contemplates his own sense of loss and revisits past experiences that brought him to this point. As Juana in *Fragments* observed, the incomplete process of decolonization left people with so many different kinds of loss. The sequence of images that rewind to the beginning show how Mory's mind wanders to Anta on the boat, then to the seaside cliff where they had sex and dreamed of escaping, then back to the rural setting in the Sahel with a herd of cattle headed toward the slaughterhouse of urban modernity. The very last image is a freeze frame of the lone shepherd riding into the city with his cattle. The fragment Mory is holding in his hands poses another existential question: What does he have left? A logic of fragmentation that was at play in Armah's novel again raises the issue of identity formation in the shadow of imperial domination. The way Mory's gaze lingers on the fragment of the longhorns transforms the symbol into a mirror of his consciousness that has been torn between opposing cultural forces.

Barlet comments on the choice Mory makes to stay home:

> There isn't a good choice and a bad one, there is the inner dynamics of a tension. The director does not explore the difference, or even the clash between tradition

and modernity, but the space which separates and connects the two, the riven nature of a society, all of whose members are split between their roots and a fascination with elsewhere.[70]

It is very clear that staying home does not restore a sense of wholeness; rather Mory's quest to leave Dakar produces the self-knowledge that allows him to escape the fate of a postcolonial migrant. Barlet describes this journey:

> Although the film focuses on a particular social space, it does so through a journey of initiation, a quest, not by fixing its gaze on a referential tradition. The montage of *Touki-Bouki* is like a spiral located within the great circle of origins, which is symbolized from the beginning by the long-horned zebus, linking the cosmos to the land of the ancestors. They are ridden by a shepherd boy representing the young Mory, who will later attach one of these horns as a trophy to the handlebars of his motorcycle.[71]

Mory's future struggle to find a place for himself at home in the city is foreshadowed by a subjective understanding of a lost wholeness, of the need to work with the incomplete options at hand. A first step might be reconceiving the West outside of the nightmare/dream antinomy and then reformulating cultural priorities that make sense to a non-Western sense of self.

Touki Bouki affirms the benefit of remaining rooted in one's culture of origin and, in this sense, presents an interesting parallel to the central theme in Armah's *Fragments*. Mambety's decision to have Mory stay home is not proposed on terms that would be over-determined by religion or tradition. Rather *Touki Bouki* asserts the importance of individual creativity and freedom to define a sense of self against the grain of social conformity. Mambety's defense of individual liberty and the possibilities for achieving a creative synthesis challenges the submission to tradition briefly suggested in the first part of the film. The film's innovative aesthetic, which explores Mory's innermost desires and conflicts via an introspective gaze, conveys a socially progressive message wherein individual self-definition could be the fertilizer that would revitalize society. As with Armah, Mambety's modernity comes with a caveat: although Mambety embraces an avant-garde film aesthetic that is thoroughly modern and the personal freedom implied by self-definition to the point of anticonformism, he shares Armah's critical view of capitalist modernity and presents the losses that come from materialism and greed with a gory slaughterhouse motif. In *Touki Bouki*, the most important way of resisting the destructive forces that deprive young people of the opportunities to live a life they have reason to value – because of injustice at home and the gleam of Western materialism abroad – is to take the self as a new point of departure. Yet Mory's future struggle to find a place for himself at home in the city is foreshadowed by a subjective understanding of a lost wholeness, of the need to work with the incomplete options at hand.

Mariama Bâ's *So Long a Letter*

Finally, let us consider Mariama Bâ's equally canonical *Une si longue lettre* (1979; *So Long a Letter*, 1981), which offers another strikingly innovative narrative, this time for its path-breaking feminist standpoint. In this novel, we have another version of an autobiographical subject as historical witness, insofar as the writer draws inspiration from her lived experience, and from this she fashions an introspective narrative that involves both critical self-examination and the articulation of a position of radical and provocative noncompliance. We will see how the pioneer of Senegalese feminism expanded and refined the language of freedom in relation to the unfinished business of national liberation to include women's viewpoints. The indisputable contribution that women's writing has made on African letters since its inception, including the transformative effect it had on male writing subsequently, has been well established by such critics as Irène d'Almeida and Florence Stratton. However, feminist engagements with the central importance of the idea of freedom in the African canon has only been partially explored.[72]

We know that when women writers find their voice and express a different kind of subjectivity outside of patriarchal expectations, new kinds of discourse can emerge. As Sidonie Smith has argued,

> She seeks instead to pursue her own desires, to shatter the portrait of herself she sees hanging in the textual frames of patriarchy, and to create the conscious and unconscious of her sex by claiming the legitimacy and authority of another subjectivity. With that new subjectivity may come a new system of values, a new kind of language and narrative form, perhaps even a new discourse, an alternative to the prevailing ideology of gender.[73]

This process of exploring a new subjectivity outside the parameters of patriarchal culture is very much at issue in Bâ's first novel, in which she uses introspection to reveal a wife's intimate experience as a widow and abandoned co-wife in order to restore her sense of self as a woman. In so doing, she expands the parameters of what could be said about freedom to include women's perspectives. I argue that the protagonist Ramatoulaye sees the reasons for her existential unfreedom in the intimate sphere of her marriage as interconnected with instrumental and substantive freedoms at issue in the laws, values, and institutions that define women's lives outside the walls of her compound. Bâ's narrative does not disentangle the private, intimate self from the public sphere of national politics – instead we have mutually reinforcing kinds of freedom.

The novelist revises the narrative of triumphant nationalism from a feminist point of view that criticizes the conduct of men in positions of responsibility. Bâ draws our attention to the gender dynamics of power and agency within new African nations in terms that resonate with Anne McClintock's work on the gendered nature of nationalism as a discourse and political practice.[74] In this novel, we see a starkly different relationship to Western hegemony from what we observed in Armah's novel and Mambety's film thus far – this narrative is filtered through a feminist perspective and simultaneously offers criticism of patriarchal values in Senegal at the time of independence. Bâ selectively appropriates some aspects of Western modernity, such as girls' access to higher education and a driver's license, while rejecting some traditional Senegalese practices, such as forced marriage and polygamy. As Susan Andrade has argued, we will see that Bâ's writing, like that of African feminism more generally, has been articulated in diacritical relation to the version of African cultural nationalism that was popular in the years following independence. However, my argument departs from Andrade's reading of the novel insofar as she claims that the narrative of "failed romance in which the betrayal of a woman by her husband *stands in for* the betrayal of the nation by its middle class (emphasis added)."[75] Rather than seeing the private domestic sphere as an allegory that stands in for, or comments on, the public national discourse, I read Bâ's novel as representing different types of freedom that are interdependent and mutually reinforcing – thus, more in line with Amartya Sen's definition of freedom.[76]

Like Armah and Mambety, Bâ was a path-breaking artist with her first radically innovative novel, which has since also become a classic. Stratton demonstrated how *So Long a Letter* was sharply criticized by male critics at first, but has since been translated into seventeen languages and is widely read in Africa and around the world.[77] Here again, much of the author's life experience went into writing the novel, although Bâ insists that Ramatoulaye's "I" does not reflect the author's autobiographical self.[78] She wrote this first novel at the age of fifty after her divorce from Obèye Diop, who, like male protagonists in the story, was an activist and member of parliament.[79] Bâ grew up around politics – her father served as mayor of Dakar and then as the first minister of health under the Loi-Cadre.[80] She was born into a wealthy family and raised as an observant Muslim, attending Koranic school in addition to French colonial school. While she spoke Wolof at home, the novelist gained access to europhone cultures through learning to read and write French. Her father was a progressive man, who decided to have his daughter educated against the wishes of her more conservative and traditional maternal grandparents who were raising the young Mariama after her mother died.[81]

For this novelist, breaking out of the traditional mindset and ethnocentric priorities happened as a result of her education in a cosmopolitan milieu.[82] Educating girls became a life-long career for Bâ; she was among the first women to be trained as teachers at the École Normale in Rufisque, which opened its doors in 1938. During an interview with Alioune Touré Dia in 1979, Bâ remembered her French teachers fondly as women who supported her education and even advocated on her behalf – without Madame LeGoff's and Madame Maubert's interventions, Bâ would not have attained the level of education she did.[83] Even though these French mentors played a decisive role in her life, Bâ wrote with freedom against the politics of colonial assimilation and integrated aspects of Western culture only insofar as it served her interests in social mobility and emancipation as a woman. Bâ's fiercely pragmatic vision was enriched by studying in Rufisque, an intellectual hub where students from West Africa exchanged ideas from different perspectives on a range of social issues.

Mariama Bâ's novel foregrounds the intimate self in the domestic sphere where a woman's existential freedom is central, and then the narrative progressively opens onto the social terrain of marriage and political issues of women running for office. *So Long a Letter* is narrated in the first person from Ramatoulaye's intimate perspective in the form of a personal letter, written to a childhood friend over several days, that she never sends. As with many novels in the epistolary genre, the narrative is hybrid and incorporates passages that resemble a personal journal as well as stylistic influences from African orature (repetition, direct address) and novelistic digressions that provide background.[84] The novel opens in conventional letter style: "Dear Aïssatou, I have received your letter. By way of reply, I am beginning this diary, my prop in my distress. Our long association has taught me that confiding in others allays pain" (Letter, 1). In this first letter, the narrator also tells Aïssatou that she "closes her eyes" – the phrase Mambety used to describe the source of his inspiration as a filmmaker – but, for Ramatoulaye, introspection brings back memories, not dreams (Letter, 1). In contrast to *Touki Bouki*'s surreal imagery, the retrospective narration of Ramatoulaye's intimate life creates an impression of sincerity and the appearance of being a "true story." The way Ramatoulaye reveals her intimate self to a childhood friend, her ostensible interlocutor, makes the reader feel privy to a private conversation between good friends. The narrative's aura of authenticity enhanced the novel's persuasiveness and contributed to its broad appeal as a revision of the portraits African women had seen of themselves "hanging in the textual frames of patriarchy."[85]

Ramatoulaye establishes a comparison between her husband's treatment of her at home and his work in the public sphere. This sets up a parallel between his personal betrayal in the domestic sphere and his behavior as a leader who turned his back on workers whose interests he had previously defended in the name of national liberation. She writes to Aïssatou about this during a moment of crisis and reflects on how her self-image was shattered as a result of the choices Modou made while he was alive. The introspective gaze allows Ramatoulaye to recollect the past, to mourn in the present, and then to project into the future with a growing sense of self-awareness. The story begins when she is in mourning. As a widow, she is sequestered according to Islamic custom during which time she tries to understand why her husband behaved the way he did. Her grieving process is defined, in part, by ritual: "The *mirasse* commanded by the Koran requires that a dead person be stripped of his most intimate secrets; thus is exposed to others what was carefully concealed" (Letter, 9). The narrator explains these revelations as a disturbing discovery: "These exposures crudely explain a man's life. With consternation, I measure the extent of Modou's betrayal. His abandonment ... He rejected us" (Letter, 9). There was a formal meeting with Ramatoulaye, her co-wife and close family members to disclose the deceased's financial situation and handle matters of inheritance at which time Ramatoulaye learns that Modou had mortgaged her home to pay for his second wife's lavish lifestyle. When it is revealed that he pilfered their life-savings, the narrator places his spending alongside unethical professional decisions and explains how Modou used his promotion in the Ministry of Public Works as a means of stopping a trade union revolt. Thus, in this narrative, the husband's identity is clearly represented as nested within multiple spheres of experience so that his ethics as a husband and as a professional are seen as interconnected.

The novelist introduces the convention of *mirasse* to expand the frame of reference beyond a widow's personal reflections to include a ritual that reveals a man's private affairs to the extended family. As Ramatoulaye strives to disentangle herself from the past thirty years of marriage, five of them with a co-wife, she examines Modou's motivations and measures the damage to his reputation:

> Madness or weakness? Heartlessness or irresistible love? What inner torment led Modou Fall to marry Binetou?
>
> And to think that I loved this man passionately, to think that I gave him thirty years of my life, to think that twelve times over I carried his child. The addition of a rival to my life was not enough for him. In loving someone else, he burned his past, both morally and materially. He dared to commit such an act of disavowal ... and yet.
>
> And yet, what didn't he do to make me his wife? *(Letter, 12)*

The first paragraph, with its series of rhetorical questions, is repeated elsewhere in the chapter, and this reiteration conveys the intensity of Ramatoulaye's emotion. Part of what makes *So Long a Letter* so rhetorically powerful is the emotional quality of the narrative voice, which vividly captures what it feels like to love and not be loved back. The extravagance of Modou's debts with grocers, traders, butchers, and car dealerships deals a fatal blow to Ramatoulaye's admiration for her husband and taints his memory in the views of others as well. This is a sensitive matter because the young Modou symbolized success – he had been a trade union leader and was a lawyer with French diplomas who came of age with the first generation of professionals at the time of national liberation. Thus when Ramatoulaye describes in intimate detail Modou's romantic and familial betrayals, she is revealing the private hypocrisy of a man whose public persona had been socially successful and politically progressive. The abstraction of this issue – how men treat women within the intimate sphere *and* what it feels like to women – perpetuates the patriarchal status quo, so when Bâ makes these connections, she extends the parameters of debate about justice and meaningful freedom in Africa.

The widow's reflection on her own sense of unfreedom during the period of sequestration gives rise to an extended meditation on the possibilities for women's liberation outside the walls of her house – her feelings of imprisonment and the bitterness of her memories stimulates this process. A significant aspect of Ramatoulaye's self-restoration involves comparing her life with the lives other women within the context of patriarchal culture as it was defined in Dakar and the West African region during the 1970s. The way she surveys the choices other women make explains both their options as well as the various constraints they faced. Tradition dictates that she must open her home to a "buzzing crowd" of people who come to express their condolences and that she endure this with her co-wife by her side. Once she is finally alone, Ramatoulaye contemplates the confinement she will have to observe as a widow: "The walls that limit my horizon for four months and ten days do not bother me. I have enough memories in me to ruminate upon. And these are what I am afraid of, for they smack of bitterness" (Letter, 8). It is this extended period of rumination that inspires Ramatoulaye to write such a long letter, and the psychological effects of solitude and self-examination are evident in the therapeutic arc of the narrative. Of course, she considers what motivated her co-wife to marry Modou. We know that Binetou's mother agreed to the marriage in exchange for the material comfort Modou promised and that deals were made in writing, including a monthly allowance of 50,000 francs so that Binetou could discontinue her high school education. This transaction is another manifestation of the greedy mother's dream of financial rescue that we encountered in a different form in *Fragments*. Here, the mother-in-law is a patriarchal woman whose willingness to participate in consumer culture on male-stipulated terms only helps to cement social arrangements as defined by the men in charge. Ramatoulaye interprets this deal making as a mother sacrificing her daughter's life on the altar of materialism in terms that echo the anticapitalist values previously discussed. In contrast, Ramatoulaye's own daughter becomes a progressive voice of dissidence and advocates for divorce in line with Aïssatou's more radical values.

The way Ramatoulaye surveys the terrain invites the reader to consider the male behavior represented in the novel as part of a pattern that repeats itself with variations on a common theme. She takes a sober look at her options and continues to examine specific examples in a way that instructs the reader. She looks at her body in the mirror, after thirty years of marriage and twelve pregnancies, and imagines how men like Modou look over their wife's shoulder at what they used to have. Over time, she realizes that her own fate as a woman is part of a broader cultural pattern that concerns many other women. We observe a striking parallel between her situation and Aïssatou's for a number of reasons: their husbands' names, Modou and Mawdo, are similar; their co-wives' names, Binetou and Nabou, are similar; the first marriages are unconventional and based on the free choice of individuals in love; and, both husbands are in advanced middle-age when they take much younger, second wives. It is Mawdo, not Modou, who becomes the voice of the unfaithful husband when he explains what motivates men like him – he justifies his second marriage in crude terms as an expression of "the bestiality of male instincts" and says that wives should accept these biological facts and forgive the "betrayals of the flesh" (Letter, 34). In addition to this biological hypothesis about "male instincts," Ramatoulaye makes a significant cross-cultural comparison that reveals the life-story of a Christian woman from the Ivory Coast. The narrator indulges in a long digression to tell us about Jacqueline, a woman who married a Muslim from Senegal and ended up in a mental hospital recovering from a nervous breakdown. This story-within-a-story further instructs the reader about the differences between Christianity and Islam with regards to women's expectations about love and marriage. As a result, Ramatoulaye draws more conclusions about human nature: men betray women who love them whether they are Christian or Muslim; and women long for mutual love whether they are Senegalese or Ivorian. Ironically the one constraint that used to check the "bestiality of male instincts" was traditional culture, according to Bâ, who believed that the new generation of men showed women less respect than their forefathers did.[86]

This digression sets up Ramatoulaye's revelation of her decision to stay in her marriage, which she presents as a life-defining choice that is an expression of her substantive freedom:

> Why did I recall this friend's ordeal? Was it because of its happy ending? Or merely to delay the formulation of the *choice* I had made, a *choice* that my reason rejected but that accorded with the immense tenderness I felt toward Modou Fall?
>
> Yes, I was well aware of where the right solution lay, the dignified solution. And, to my family's great surprise, unanimously disapproved of by my children, who were under Daba's influence, I *chose* to remain. Modou and Mawdo were surprised, could not understand ...
>
> Forewarned, you, my friend, did not try to dissuade me, respectful of my new *choice* of life.
>
> I cried every day. *(Letter, 45; emphasis added)*

Ramatoulaye defies expectations by choosing love over reason. That she cries every day is a cleverly placed detail that signals the impossibility of a woman's happiness within a polygamous union like this one. She wants to see herself as rising above disappointment with dignity and presents her decision as being faithful to the ideal of mutual love on which she based her original choice to marry Modou. By having Ramatoulaye explain to Aïssatou why she did not follow her example, the novelist opens a second set of questions about why a woman would make *this* choice. From a pragmatic feminist standpoint, it is significant that Bâ structures the plot in this way because it underscores the fact that women do have *choices*. Ramatoulaye's introspection as a co-wife is reform-minded because it reveals what it feels like for a wife who loves her husband to live with polygamy, which is relevant for every African woman who does not imagine happiness outside of marriage. While her idealism reinforces mutual love as the only basis for marriage, living with a co-wife reflects the reality that the majority of women do stay in marriages like Ramatoulaye's wishing their husbands loved them exclusively.[87]

To develop this important contrast with Aïssatou, and how these two women exercise their substantive freedoms differently, the narrator allows the reader to hear her friend's voice directly when Ramatoulaye cites a letter that Aïssatou sent to Mawdo informing him of her decision to divorce and the reasons for her action. She challenges the values Mawdo used to justify polygamy and the social forces at work in the justification he provided when he took a second wife. Aïssatou's letter reads like a fragment of a manifesto that is more revolutionary than reformist, and it offers a second point of reference, a second illustration of the possibilities for female agency and subjectivity in the novel. Aïssatou shares Ramatoulaye's sense that the educated elite did not live up to their ideals and elevates the preservation of a woman's dignity in marriage to the level of a cultural value that is worthy of consideration by the community. Daba, for one, prefers Aïssatou's course of action to her mother's and looks up to Aïssatou as a feminist pioneer who offers an example for other West African women to follow. After divorcing Mawdo, Aïssatou joins the flow of African immigrants – like Baako in *Fragments* and Anta in *Touki Bouki*. Her departure raises the question of what options were available to unmarried professional women like her in Senegal at the time. We learn, for instance, that Ramatoulaye could not go out to the movies by herself without contending with social disapproval from people who thought that a woman unaccompanied by a man should not be out alone. In comparison, Aïssatou works at an embassy in New York City and enjoys a level of social emancipation and financial independence that contrasts sharply with the women in the novel who remain in West Africa. In a gesture of feminist solidarity and, more specifically, African sisterhood, Aïssatou buys Ramatoulaye a new car and has the pleasure of seeing her childhood friend learn to drive it. By helping Ramatoulaye survive outside of marriage and by providing an example of self-sufficiency, Aïssatou subverts a principle of Islamic patriarchy in West Africa, according to which unmarried women had unequal legal rights compared with men and were frequently compelled to (re)marry.[88] With this cross-cultural comparison, Bâ introduces the contingency of gender identity and asks whether Senegalese women should have the same rights as women elsewhere. The narrative does not present the patriarchal status quo in Senegal as immutable and beyond question, but rather open to negotiation. The fact that Ramatoulaye writes to her friend in New York City projects the possibility of new forms of international feminist solidarity. Very clearly, Aïssatou challenges "the internal ordering" of Senegalese society and the immutability of cultural traditions from the pragmatic, ethical standpoint of an emancipated woman. In this feminist narrative, the West is not exclusively constructed as a negative hegemonic force that spreads capitalist values, but as a cultural realm of potential solidarity for women across national borders.

As her mourning comes to an end, Ramatoulaye finds the voice of defiance within her and surprisingly defines her own position of radical noncompliance. A confrontation occurs when Modou's elder brother visits Ramatoulaye at home to announce his intention to marry her at the conclusion of her mourning period. Tamsir's declaration provokes a vigorous refusal when Ramatoulaye breaks thirty years of silence and forcefully defends her ideal of marriage as a mutual choice made by both spouses. These circumstances of a brother-in-law seeking to marry his brother's widow introduce a marital custom known as the levirate, sanctioned by patriarchal Islam in West Africa. If the community upholds the brother-in-law's desire to marry the widow, she often has little choice in the matter and becomes "an object passed from hand to hand." This issue of forced marriage was subsequently taken up in other novels and films, as we will see in Cheik Oumar Sissoko's film *Finzan* (1992). Unlike Ramatoulaye, Nanyuma incurred the wrath of the village patriarch and her family when she refused to marry her brother-in-law. In *So Long a Letter*, the imam and Mawdo who witness Ramatoulaye's stinging rejection of Tamsir's statement of interest help bring the meeting to an amicable end. Even though Tamsir arrogantly asserts his intention to marry Ramatoulaye, as if it were his male prerogative, they are forced to respect Ramatoulaye's position. This noncompliance represented a radical challenge to the treatment of women as objects, to a view of marriage that discounts love as a legitimate motivation and that denies women the freedom to choose their spouse. Ramatoulaye's moral resolve is tested again when the infinitely more compelling Daouda Dieng asks her to consider becoming his second wife. She declines again, this time because mutual love and monogamy, the only solid bases for a healthy marriage, would not have been possible in such a union.

As Ramatoulaye closes her eyes and turns inward during the months of her mourning process, she embarks on an existential journey of self-redefinition as a widow. It becomes clear that the reasons for her existential unfreedom in the intimate sphere of her marriage are unavoidably connected to the laws and political values that define women's lives outside the walls of her compound. How free will she be when this is all over? Her introspection reveals how the restoration of her emotional balance after her experience of polygamy and abandonment is related to the fate of Senegalese women in general. Bâ carefully exposes Ramatoulaye's political views during a discussion with Dieng about the small percentage of women elected to the National Assembly and the lack of legislation protecting women's rights (Letter, 88–90). Their lively exchange shows how the effort of achieving gender equality in Africa can be served by feminist men like Dieng and thwarted by patriarchal women like Binetou's mother, but unless women are willing to get involved in national politics and make use of their instrumental freedoms, the gender asymmetry in elected representatives will never be rectified and the law of the land will reflect the values of the men in charge.

Ramatoulaye's various ruminations about why male cupidity and egoism destroy families sketch a panorama of Senegalese society from the point of view of a moderate Muslim woman. The argument she makes about values is socially progressive, practical and culturally inclusive. She does criticize the influence of Western culture on African societies in terms of consumerism and materialism as moral problems that can disrupt marriages when middle-aged men compete with one another by buying younger wives and treating them lavishly. Ramatoulaye also worries about Western influences on her children who smoke and have premarital sex, behaviors she attributes to the negative effects of modernity on African youth. But her ethical objections to certain aspects of Western cultural influence are practical in nature and not symptomatic of an epistemological disorientation of the kind we see in *Fragments* and *Touki Bouki*. In contrast to Baako and Mory, Ramatoulaye is not confused about the relationship between Africa and the West because she does not perceive the two cultural spheres as opposing forces. Her faith as a Muslim is tempered by her reason as a woman, and this combination is the guiding force that allows her to navigate life's challenges with confidence. She sees African cultural traditions as open to negotiation and in need of reform in some cases. At the same time, she considers a modern education in French as a means to social mobility and enhanced capabilities for girls and women. Ramatoulaye does not lament a sense of spiritual ruin or cultural dispossession – instead she looks to the future with enduring idealism.

At the beginning of the long letter, Ramatoulaye tells Aïssatou, "We were true sisters, destined for the same mission of emancipation" (Letter, 15), merging the fact that they grew up together as girls and shared a sense of mature sisterhood as African women. Access to education in French for women was part of what would shape the "New Africa." As students, they enjoyed more freedom from tradition and direct parental control, and so they chose their husbands in defiance of social expectations. Ramatoulaye describes the effect of her marriage to Modou: "Our marriage was celebrated without dowry, without pomp, under the disapproving looks of my father, before the painful indignation of my frustrated mother, under the sarcasm of my surprised sisters, in our town struck dumb with astonishment" (Letter, 16). Yet Ramatoulaye and her cohort were not marginal anticonformists like Anta and Mory – they were doctors, lawyers, activists and school teachers who embraced social innovation with the "resolutely progressive" values of a cultural vanguard (Letter, 18–19). Thus when Aïssatou's and Ramatoulaye's unconventional marriages end in divorce, this failure signals how the limits of women's substantive freedom constrain their ability to live a life they have reason to value. Their experiment with progressive marriages based on mutual love and respect were thwarted by their husbands and the patriarchal values that protect male prerogatives at the expense of women's freedom.

When the process of personal purification comes to an end, Ramatoulaye takes pleasure in a clean body and a clean house, and she contemplates how she will live in the space she has cleared for herself as a modern Muslim woman in Dakar. The fact that she is ready to love again leaves open the question of whether there is a man prepared to love a woman like her. She explains this "new turn of mind" as she concludes her long letter and anticipates Aïssatou's imminent arrival:

> Till tomorrow, my friend.
>
> We will then have time to ourselves, especially as I have obtained an extension of my widow's leave.
>
> I reflect. My new turn of mind is hardly surprising to you. I cannot help unburdening myself to you. I might as well sum up now.
>
> I am not indifferent to the irreversible currents of women's liberation that are lashing the world. This commotion that is shaking up every aspect of our lives reveals and illustrates our abilities.
>
> My heart rejoices each time a woman emerges from the shadows. I know that the field of our gains is unstable, the retention of conquests difficult: social constraints are ever-present, a male egoism resists.
>
> Instruments for some, baits for others, respected or despised, often muzzled, all women have almost the same fate, which religions or unjust legislation have sealed.
>
> My reflections determine my attitude to the problems of life. I analyse the decisions that decide our future. I widen my scope by taking an interest in current world affairs.
>
> I remain persuaded of the inevitable and necessary complementarity of man and woman.
>
> Love, imperfect as it may be in its content and expression, remains the natural link between these two beings.
>
> To love one another! If only each partner could move sincerely towards the other! If each could only melt into the other! If each would only accept the other's successes and failures! If each would only praise the other's qualities instead of listing his faults! If each could only correct bad habits without harping on about them! If each could only penetrate the other's most secret haunts to forestall failure and be a support while tending to the evils that are repressed!
>
> The success of a family is born of a couple's harmony, as the harmony of multiple instruments creates a pleasant symphony.
>
> The nation is made up of all the families, rich or poor, united or separated, aware or unaware. The success of a nation therefore depends inevitably on the family [...]
>
> I warn you already, I have not given up wanting to refashion my life. Despite everything – disappointments and humiliations – hope still lives on within me. It is from the dirty and nauseating humus that the green plant sprouts into life, and I can feel new buds springing up in me. *(Letter, 88–9)*.

In these farewell remarks, the narrator repeatedly makes statements beginning with "I" that reveal her reflections and feelings. This subjective, emotional language is used alongside theoretical formulations such as "the irreversible currents of women's liberation" and "all women have almost the same fate," which serve to articulate a feminist vision that is personal in tone. The fact that the novelist took the brave step of appealing to women worldwide opened her to criticism as a woman "ruined" by the West.[89] In the end, Ramatoulaye has prepared herself for a new life: her soul will be free to love again and, once the four months and ten days are over, her body will be free to move about the city. In the intimate sphere, the novel celebrates a woman's ability to overcome suffering and to embrace renewal as the image of new buds sprouting in fertile soil suggests. However, because love between a man and a woman is the pivot of her feminist vision, marriage must be redefined as a social institution that does not degrade a woman's dignity. Thus renegotiating the rights of women within the institution of marriage is critical to African women's experience of meaningful freedom. The use of Ramatoulaye's lyrical voice to talk about her own intimate, existential journey – as well as to make social commentary about substantive (access to education, choice of spouse) and instrumental freedoms (legal protections, political rights and representation) – exemplifies Bâ's particularly feminist use of introspection in this novel. The narrator goes as far as presenting her own growing awareness as a model for readers to emulate. This pedagogical intent is developed when the narrator offers a lesson to couples on how to achieve lasting harmony. It is particularly significant that she makes a connection between stable families and the national interest, because this invites men to consider their roles as fathers and husbands through the prism of national liberation, which was an effective rhetorical strategy at the time. Bâ shrewdly formulated her feminist criticism of corrupt male behavior explicitly in relation to the project of nation building.[90]

African women put the introspective gaze to different uses from male writers. The contrast between Bâ's perspective and those of Mambety and Armah allows us to expand and refine our understanding of identity and freedom in Africa. The notion of an intimate enemy takes on new meaning in this novel because Ramatoulaye does not experience alienation from a part of herself that is still overwhelmed by Western influence, as we have seen in *Fragments* and *Touki Bouki*. Instead, her intimate enemy is the specter of a husband who died and left her with a devastated sense of self and without a single franc in savings. But, women were harmed because the men in charge still suffered in the shadow of imperial domination, and we see this most explicitly in how they experience their masculinity and express their virility. Ramatoulaye's husband, Modou, exemplifies the kind of middle-aged African man who gives in to a culture of greed and arriviste competition when he marries his daughter's teenage girlfriend and lavishes her with an Alfa Romeo, an air-conditioned villa, and trips to Mecca for her parents.

Even though Ramatoulaye is injured indirectly from the influence of capitalist culture because of the effects of her husband's cupidity, she does not see Western modernity as an inherently destructive force. For her, certain elements of Western modernity can be used to practical ends. Providing young girls access to an education in French is, for instance, a means for them to gain upward social mobility and personal emancipation, as well as to potentially increase their participation in national politics. In contrast to many male writers, Bâ does not present this scenario as also bringing with it ethical disorientation. There is an asymmetry in how African men and women reconceptualize the West after independence, as rigid repudiations of Western influence tend to carry masculine overtones. As Ramatoulaye seeks to free herself from a different intimate enemy, her introspection uncovers new junctures between patriarchy and capitalism, feminism and nationalism, and the private lives of men at home and in public.

To enjoy meaningful freedom is to benefit from different interconnected kinds of freedoms that operate together within this narrative as an explicit critique of what national liberation failed to deliver. One way the novelist foregrounds the role of instrumental freedoms pertains to participation in the political life of a new African nation and, in particular, to the necessity of women's involvement. Substantive freedoms play a critical role in this novel (and in feminist narratives more generally) in terms of women's capacity to enjoy a life they have reason to value, from getting an education to choosing their spouse (and whether to divorce or not). We see this when the central characters make different choices – whereas Aïssatou and Ramatoulaye get married to similar men for similar reasons, Ramatoulaye remains in her marriage after Modou takes a second wife, while Aïssatou divorces Mawdo after he marries Nabou. The novelist shows how these contrasting characters make different life-defining choices as they come up against oppressive patriarchal customs and become disillusioned with the "new" Africa. Ramatoulaye's existential freedom is of constant importance as the focus of her soul-searching and prayer in this introspective narrative. As a widow engaged in the rituals of mourning, Ramatoulaye cultivates a new sense of existential freedom within the private, spiritual sphere into which she retreats at home.

In *So Long a Letter,* the narrative of national liberation is reconsidered in terms of whether men *and* women enjoy the freedom to live the kind of lives they have reason to value. The question of women's freedom is layered and explicitly inclusive. It involves existential issues and self-definition; instrumental freedoms in a democratic society, as we see in the need for women to run for elected office in Senegal; and substantive freedoms for women, as in getting an education, becoming financially independent, and choosing their own spouses. The kind of stories that men and women told reflected gender asymmetries in social and political power in Senegal and other African societies at the time. Consider, for instance, the number of times African women writers have told stories like this one about the injustices female protagonists endured in their private lives. There is simply no equivalent form of expression by African men. How many novels can you think of with a first-person narrator from the point of view of a Modou or a Mawdo where the husband engages in soul-searching, ultimately confessing his true motivations for taking a second wife, and acknowledging all the consequences of betraying his wife and their children?

Conclusion

Finding a figurative language for talking about the intimate self and existential freedom beginning, here, in West Africa of the 1970s, opens a window onto the broader issue of reconsidering meaningful freedom after national liberation. Looking at the language of individual freedom in these stories allows us to understand the other inter-related aspects of freedom, from gender inequality to the asymmetries created by the expansion of global capital – as we will see later. It is in some ways befitting that these creative statements about unfettering the self after national liberation, which have since become iconic statements about the postindependence era, were formulated in Dakar and Accra. From the 1950s onward, these cities were the epicenters of debates about political freedom that were pan-African in scope. Yet the language of individual freedom as it evolves over time can be seen in every aspect of freedom that will be discussed in the chapters that follow.

There is something distinctive about the creativity in introspective fiction that was inspired by a subjective sense of the unfreedoms that persisted after national liberation. The novels by Armah and Bâ, as well as Mambety's film, reveal the intimate self from within: with Baako's pain conveyed by the fragmentation of narrative voices; with the camera mimicking a cow being slaughtered from Mory's point of view; and with the searing honesty of Ramatoulaye saying what had never been said before in her own voice. The protagonist's subjectivity leads, in each case, to innovation in the way the story is told with an original expression of the underlying quest to liberate the self and renegotiate important filial and social attachments. Representing the private lives of individuals after national liberation became a means of exploring the interconnected spheres of freedom. It also expanded the parameters of what could be said to include the instrumental freedoms of democracy as well as the substantive freedoms for men and women to have the capacity to live the kind of life they had reason to value. Over time, various modes of narration would be used, as the process of representing the self and refining the language of freedom continued to evolve.

The three works discussed in this chapter engaged in a revision of the cultural narrative of triumphant nationalism from innovative points of view. They are multi-layered narratives that represent the self and individual identity as being nested within other identity concepts including gender, ethnicity, class, and national affiliation. The artists represent individual experience at the intersection of competing and conflicting pressures to conform. In this way, the cultural work of creativity presents readers and viewers with provocative anticonformists who challenge the status quo and invite us to bring up for reconsideration some of the social, cultural, and political issues facing new African nations. These narratives thus allow us to reflect on the process of redefining notions of the self in relation to communities, which involves thinking about freedom through the lens of an individual's attachment to groups, a distinction that Tejumola Olaniyan has characterized as attached and unattached freedoms.[91]

The cultural criticism of Western hegemony and capitalism that we see in each of these narratives in different forms had been well established since the 1940s with the founding of *Présence Africaine* and the international congresses the Société de Culture Africaine organized in Paris and Rome during the 1950s. What we have in these innovative narratives of the postindependence era is a new form of antihegemonic criticism that seeks to reconceive the West in terms that are acceptable to those formerly living under Western imperial rule and – to borrow from Ashish Nandy's conceptual vocabulary – to explore the ongoing process of liberating the intimate self from colonial cultural impositions after political independence. We have seen that reconceiving the West intersects with criticism of other forms of domination such as capitalism, patriarchy, and the spread of corruption among the new elites. This intersection is vital because the perpetuation of a kind of alienation that began under colonial rule stemmed from male African leaders who subsequently became the custodians of a neo-colonial dispensation, as Ousmane Sembène's film *Xala* (1979) brilliantly stages. The peaceful transfer of power from European colonial representatives to Kwame Nkrumah in Ghana in 1957, and to Léopold Sédar Senghor in Senegal in 1960, marked a significant transition to political self-determination that was followed by a complex process of soul-searching. Whereas Nkrumah and Senghor had been active in the organization of anticolonial protest in West African and beyond, they had also been groomed as leaders who were willing to step into the role defined by the gatekeeper states they inherited. Read together, these three classics demonstrate the central importance of freedom and an evolution of a complex, multi-faceted language to evoke this emerging ideal in the canon of African cultural expression in the postindependence era.

In this chapter, I articulated how different kinds of freedom are at work in these narratives: instrumental, substantive, and existential.

Instrumental. In *Fragments*, when Baako decides, in a fit of rage, to burn his treatments for films about slavery because the manager of Ghanavision rejected them, this is an act of protest against the constraint on his freedom of expression as an artist. Baako interprets the television station's rejection of his project as political censorship from within a cultural institution that does not value the historiography of slavery because it does not advance the dominant narrative of triumphant nationalism. In *Touki Bouki*, the sequence in which political activists lasso Mory at the university and tie him up on the back of their jeep is an allegorical mise-en-scène of the absence of instrumental freedom in new African nations that implicitly references Lumumba's arrest and assassination. Mambety makes use of this iconography of political dispossession in order to suggest the brutal repression of civic engagement and to set up the absence of opportunities at home as the source of Mory and Anta's escapist fantasy. In *So Long a Letter*, Mariama Bâ evokes the vital importance of women running for elected office during a conversation between Ramatoulaye and Daouda Dieng about gender equity and the National Assembly. It is suggested that without women joining the political conversation as elected representatives, the nation will be governed by men and will consequently reflect men's interests.

Substantive. The meaning of Baako's name in Akan, the "lonely one," conveys the essence of his moral solitude, which stems from his unfulfilled longing for healthy emotional attachments and for social relevance as an artist. Armah represents Baako's madness as a symptom of the absence of substantive freedoms. With each failed attempt to define a life for himself that he has reason to value, with choices that make sense to him, his feelings of loneliness and alienation grow deeper and more intense. Mory and Anta also encounter the absence of opportunities at home, and their escapist fantasy to strike it rich in Paris is an expression of their longing for better choices and more substantive freedom in Senegal. Wealth is an idealized source of pleasure in the dream of financial rescue, but the film implicitly laments with ironic humor the actual lack of opportunities through education, employment, and civic engagement that would afford young people the possibility of meaningful self-definition at home. Ramatoulaye's choices in the marital sphere are the best expression of her substantive freedom – her unconventional choice of spouse, her decision to stay married after Modou takes a second wife, and her refusal to remarry after he dies exhibit best this aspect. Her choices are contrasted with Aïssatou's, as Bâ elaborates a feminist ideal of reciprocal, exclusive love as part of a "New Africa," nourished by cosmopolitan education and a narrative of social progress.

Existential. Armah represents Baako's existential longing for health and wholeness at home in Ghana through his relationship with Naana, who gives voice to his cultural identity as his ancestral soul mate, and with Juana, who is his modern soul mate with whom he explores his capacity for happiness in love and psychological resilience in the present. The scene that most vividly portrays Mory's existential longing for wholeness at home in Dakar is when he holds and contemplates a fragment of the zebus horns that had been on his motorbike at the end of film. This symbol, charged with meaning through an accumulation of references to the effects of capitalist modernity, becomes a mirror of his complex, riven consciousness. Ramatoulaye's existential longing for wholeness permeates the entire narrative, from her earliest soul-searching through to her extended period of mourning as a widow. The novelist's use of Ramatoulaye's introspective self, as she retreats within herself and into the domestic space behind the walls of her family compound, takes on a therapeutic quality in this path-breaking feminist narrative.

Meaningful freedom is achieved when these different kinds of freedoms work in concert, enabling individuals to live the life they have reason to value.

Notes

1. See, for instance, Phyllis Clark, "Sony Labou Tansi and Congolese Politics: An Interview with Jean-Clotaire Hymboud," *Research in African Literatures*, vol. 29, no. 2 (Summer 1998): 183–92.
2. Phyllis Clark, "Passionate Engagements: A Reading of Sony Labou Tansi's Private Ancestral Shrine," *Research in African Literatures*, vol. 31, no. 3 (Fall 2000): 39–68.
3. There has been quite a lot written about the influences, intertexts, and differences between the Negritude movement, both its corpus of poetry and ideas, and postcolonial African fiction. Ayi Kwei Armah and others have been very critical of the Negritude writers, especially Léopold Sédar Senghor, because they see this approach to Africa as inauthentic and ensnared in Western myths about "blackness." On the other hand, literary critics have attempted to point out similarities between the values of the Negritude movement, such as restoring "a lost African dignity" and the ideals of social renewal

and self-restoration in the postcolonial novel. See, for example, Ode Ogede, *Ayi Kwei Armah: Radical Iconoclast* (Athens, OH: Ohio University Press, 2000). In order to sort out these similarities and differences, it is helpful to look at early interventions that framed the evolution of the debate, such as Chinua Achebe's essay "Africa and her Writers" in *Morning Yet on Creation Day* (Garden City, NY: Anchor Books, 1975), pp. 29–45. Wole Soyinka's "Ideology and the Social Vision (2): The Secular Ideal" in *Myth, Literature and the African World* (Cambridge: Cambridge University Press, 1976), pp. 97–140. For a collection of essays on the francophone and anglophone positions with respect to Negritude, see, Francis Abiola Irele's *Négritude et condition africaine* (Paris: Karthala, 2008). For my purposes here, the point I wish to make is that the use of introspection in Negritude poetry of the 1930s and 1940s served purposes that are different from the ones we find in postcolonial novels after the nationalist movements. Whereas the poetry of Negritude offered subjective perspectives that were lyrical and expressive of a pan-African cultural imagination, the narrators in postcolonial fiction tend to be specifically situated in national contexts where the self is explored in relation to the community's ongoing struggle for meaningful freedom after the disillusionment of national independence.

4. For a time, the early fiction of writers such as Ayi Kwei Armah was considered "sick" and "narcissistic." These ideas are developed subsequently in this chapter. For this characterization of Armah's fiction, see: Achebe, *Morning Yet on Creation Day*, pp. 29–45; and, Neil Lazarus, *Resistance in Postcolonial African Fiction* (New Haven, CT: Yale University Press, 1990).
5. The research on the role labor issues played in the development of nationalist movements is extensive. For two places to start, see Frederick Cooper, *Africa Since 1940: The Past of the Present* (Cambridge: Cambridge University Press, 2002) and Basil Davidson, *Let Freedom Come: Africa in Modern History* (Boston, MA: Little Brown, 1978).
6. I use the term "Third World" to refer to the international appeal of Frantz Fanon's writing beyond the specific context of African nationalism that interested him in Algeria's war for independence. See, for example, Kwame Anthony Appiah's foreword to the English translation by Richard Philcox of *Black Skin, White Masks* (New York, NY: Grove Press, 2008).
7. My use of the words "individual" and "subject" requires some comment. In Fanon's writing, there is an awareness of how subjects are constructed through language, ideas, and cultural systems. At the same time, there is the notion of an individual in the sense of a political actor and potential citizen within the context of liberation movements. Fanon was, of course, well aware of the ethnocentrism at work in European humanism and had revealed, as Aimé Césaire did, the false pretense of a European perspective parading as a universal perspective. See Aimé Césaire's *Discourse on Colonialism* (New York, NY: Monthly Review Press, 2000), translation of *Discours sur le colonialisme (1950)* (Présence Africaine, 1989). With that said, questions of method linger *today* about subjectivity and agency for Africanists who are sensitive to the theoretical issues raised by post-structuralism. I use the word "individual" to refer to the concept of a social actor and "subject" to refer to the symbolic, linguistic, or cultural construction of a subject within the realm of

discourse. For a useful discussion of these questions of method, concepts, and vocabulary, consult a volume of essays edited by Richard Werbner, *Postcolonial Subjectivities in Africa* (London: Zed Books, 2002).

8. Frantz Fanon, *Black Skin, White Masks* (New York, NY: Grove Press, 2008), pp. 90–1.
9. Anjali Prabhu, "Narration in Frantz Fanon's *Peau noire, masques blancs*: Some Reconsiderations," *Research in African Literatures*, vol. 37, no. 4 (Winter 2006), pp. 189–210.
10. Fanon makes clear in the introduction to *Black Skin, White Masks* that the black man's problem is not an individual problem, but one that must be seen in terms of cultures, economics, and collective values. See the introduction to *Black Skin, White Masks*, pp. xi–xviii; *Peau noire, masques blancs*, pp. 5–11.
11. See Frantz Fanon, *The Wretched of the Earth* (New York, NY: Grove Press, 2005), pp. 35–106; translation of *Damnés de la terre* (Seuil, 1952), pp. 65–141.
12. Ashis Nandy, *The Intimate Enemy: Loss and Recovery of Self under Colonialism* (Delhi: Oxford University Press, 1983), p. 67.
13. Nandy provides in a postface, written twenty-five years after the original publication, references to his "African connection." He mentions, in particular, Frantz Fanon, Octave Mannoni, Aimé Césaire, Albert Memmi, Amìlcar Cabral, and Léopold Sédar Senghor. He says that except for Fanon, who was introduced via Jean-Paul Sartre, the other writers were not taken seriously in India. He describes how these "francophone intellectuals recognized that colonialism was produced and driven by persons and states of mind in addition to institutions," *The Intimate Enemy*, p. 116.
14. Nandy, *The Intimate Enemy*, pp. 70–1.
15. Ibid., p. 70.
16. Ibid., pp. 85–96.
17. This option of choosing to be a nonplayer and opting out of capitalist modernity was not a ridiculous or trivial proposition in the 1970s and even into the 1980s. However, things have changed substantially since 1990 – even in Africa. Both Ashis Nandy and Fareed Zakaria make comments about how the "natives" are getting good at capitalism. In 2009, Nandy acknowledged in his postface that "good" Indians and Chinese were prepared to "enter the rat race of progress." But, he remains wary of the promises of prosperity after imperialism and questions the virtues of capitalist hegemony: "If victimhood and resistance are indivisible, so are the impoverishment of life and abridgement of the freedom of the dominant" (*The Intimate Enemy*, p. 123). In 2008, Fareed Zakaria presented a very different view of the world in the *Post-American World* (New York, NY: Norton, 2008). Zakaria presents an argument in this book that is less about the decline of America than it is about the "rise of the rest." He predicts a decline in American hegemony as the economies of other nations grow around the world. Zakaria states: "At the politico-military level, we remain in a single-superpower world. But in every other dimension – industrial, financial, educational, social, cultural – the distribution of power is shifting, moving away from American dominance. That does not mean we are entering an anti-American world. But we are moving into a post-American world, one defined and directed from

many different places and by many people" (*The Post-American World*, pp. 4–5). I discuss issues and these shifts as related to Africa and globalization in Chapter 4.

18. See: Ashis Nandy, "The Psychology of Colonialism: Sex, Age and Ideology in British India," *The Intimate Enemy*, pp. 1–63 (Delhi: Oxford University Press, 1983). Nandy analyzes notions of child/adult, masculine/feminine and other concepts such as progress in Western, and particularly British, civilization.
19. Achebe, *Morning Yet on Creation Day*, p. 39.
20. There are at least two discussions of this debate. See Derek Wright's introduction to *Ayi Kwei Armah's Africa* (London and New York, NY: Hans Zell, 1989), pp. 1–16. For a more incisive overview of this issue, see Ogede's introduction to *Ayi Kwei Armah: Radical Iconoclast*, pp. 1–9.
21. See Lazarus, *Resistance in Postcolonial African Fiction*, pp. 1–25. Lazarus has a hard time with Armah's disappointment and misunderstands his disillusionment as a "perversely attractive obsession." Lazarus argued: "Throughout the 1960s, as the marginalization of radical intellectuals advanced, so too did the intensity and the introspection of their work." He goes on to add: "Above all, they remained possessed of the illusion that the era of independence marked a revolutionary conjuncture in African societies. It was this illusion that motivated the intellectual obsession with loss and failure and betrayal in the works of the 1960s" (Lazarus, *Resistance*, pp. 22–3). According to him, the fact that writers like Armah were under the illusion that decolonization was a "revolutionary conjuncture" explains why they then became so depressed and introspective in the late 1960s.
22. It would seem to me that introspective representations of an intimate self were part of a general process of coming to terms with how *that* postcolonial future became *this* postcolonial present, as Lazarus has put it (Lazarus, *Resistance*, p. 191). The obsession with postcolonial dispossession that emerged during the late 1960s, of which Armah's fiction is an example, could not be adequately addressed by political protest at the national level. I find the relationship between theory and criticism in the argument that Lazarus makes simply too formulaic.
23. Ogede, *Ayi Kwei Armah*, p. 56. Ode Ogede also observes that "Armah is a radical iconoclast, and the main reason his works have provoked extremes of praise and censure is because of the lethal originality of his vision" (Ogede, *Ayi Kwei Armah* p. 2). The most controversial aspect of the early novels relates to Armah's lacerating criticism of a postcolonial African mindset in narratives that use an introspective gaze to great effect. Ogede takes issue with those who cast the Ghanaian writer in a negative light and seeks to establish how "the distinctive contours of his voice" are expressive of a commitment to social renewal in Africa rather than of pessimistic disillusionment (Ogede, *Ayi Kwei Armah* p. 5). He describes *Fragments* as a "frank and fearless exposé of the problems of neocolonial Africa" and says that "Armah conceived of his novel in therapeutic terms, as an attempt to heal the wounds of colonialism, not inflame them" (Ogede, *Ayi Kwei Armah* p. 56).
24. Ogede claims that *Fragments* "represents a major literary accomplishment in the sense that – like the work of other great artists of the world, Yeats, Joyce,

Soyinka, Faulkner – its vision of regeneration entails the use of form, images of delight, a lyrical language, and design to combat the novelist's own terror, his fear of the reality of chaos captured in the novel's disordered narrative sequence." Armah's narratives are distinctive because they capture the fresh sense of disorientation that followed decolonization in new African nations – Ghana, Senegal, Algeria, the Congo – where coming to terms with national liberation brought a harrowing sense of disappointment.

25. Much of the literature Richard Bjornson writes about in Cameroon was directly or indirectly influenced by a Christian notion of the individual self. The publishing house Éditions CLE (Centre de Littératture Évangélique/ Center for Evanglical Literature) printed a number of important novels after it was founded in 1963. In this regard, it is noteworthy that Bjornson claims: "This concern with individual self-definition was the center of focus in most of the Cameroonian novels published by CLE during the 1960s and 1970s, but it also characterized the works of Cameroonian poets and novelists living in exile" *The African Quest for Freedom and Identity: Cameroonian Writing and the National Experience* (Bloomington, IN: Indiana University Press, 1994), p. 458. The trend toward introspection in postcolonial film and fiction was by no means limited to, or even dominated by, a Christian concept of the self as multiple examples from Muslim West Africa will show. For now, it should be noted that the concepts Bjornson sometimes uses – such as when he links romantic love and individual self-definition – although appropriate to his context, they reflect a Western Christian influence that is most relevant in other similar contexts.
26. Bjornson, The African Quest for Freedom and Identity, p. 377.
27. Ibid., p. 458.
28. Ibid., p. 459.
29. Ogede writes, "[i]n this sense, *Fragments* provides an opportunity for renewed reflection on the African situation. In it, Armah advocates communal solidarity among the visionaries, while simultaneously also viewing the problem in its global context, as Juana's role illustrates. A more rewarding approach to decolonization, one likely to achieve even more lasting results, would be for the underprivileged people of the Third World in general to unite in a common onslaught on the postcolonial forces of disorder. The multiple point of view Armah employs to dramatize the problems of colonialism broadens our perspective of the problem" (Ogede, *Ayi Kwei Armah*, p. 73).
30. For biographical information on Armah, consult Ogede's *Ayi Kwei Armah* and Robert Fraser, *The Novels of Ayi Kwei Armah* (London: Heinemann, 1980).
31. "Armah's Celebration of Silence: Interview with Dimgba Igwe," *Concord* (Lagos, April 2, 1987): 11–12.
32. Ayi Kwei Armah, "One Writer's Education," *West Africa* (August 26, 1985): 1752–3.
33. In 2008, Ayi Kwei Armah gave a lecture entitled "Awakening" that was posted on YouTube in eight parts at: www.youtube.com/watch?v=Lv7Jzce-MCag. This lecture confirms how much of himself and his ethical vision for Africa's future went into his second novel *Fragments*. Nearly four decades later, Armah still encouraged progressive young people – activists and artists

– to consider the importance of being grounded in a rational moral framework that is nourished by traditional cultural values that put community before individual profit.

34. I am also thinking, for instance, of Wole Soyinka's autobiographical writing – not fictional autobiography, but straightforward memoirs about his life – that has such important historical meaning and a magisterial sense of personal significance as a witness to the people's struggle for democracy in Nigeria. See, for example: Wole Soyinka, *You Must Set Forth at Dawn* (New York, NY: Random House, 2006).
35. D. S. Izevbaye argued, "Although [Armah's] first two novels deal with suffering as the experience of individuals, his heroes are individuals only because they are set against their community. Even as individuals they stand for something larger than themselves in the sense that not only does the author vest some of his themes and values in them, he also makes them the representatives of other suffering individuals in society. Moreover, the centrality of the first-person narrator in the first two novels is mainly an instrument for sounding the depths of social discord, even though the nature of the seeing by either the hero is done in a very personal manner," p. 247 in "Ayi Kwei Armah and the 'I' of the beholder," *Ghanaian Literatures*, ed. Richard Priebe, (New York, NY: Greenwood, 1988), pp. 241–52.
36. Derek Wright describes how Juana's and Baako's "parallel third person narratives have a tonal uniformity and imaginative rapport" in a way that is similar to how the cyclical pattern of Naana's thoughts "infiltrate the mainstream of the narrative so that the intermittently interlocking viewpoints effectively form a single diffused consciousness" (Wright, *Ayi Kwei Armah's Africa*, p. 154). Later, he adds: "The visionary consciousness at the heart of the book is never wholly possessed by any of them and, in the last analysis, has its unity only in the mind of the author, yet each of the narrators participates in and contributes some important mythological fragment to it" (Wright, *Ayi Kwei Armah's Africa*, p. 158).
37. I will discuss the particular poignancy of the situation in Ghana after national liberation in Chapter 3. For now, let me acknowledge that there was a struggle between Kwame Nkrumah and his followers in the Convention People's Party who came up against British colonial policies and efforts to direct the course of Ghana's future independence. Nkrumah took advantage of the centralization of power afforded to him by the colonial state he inherited and consolidated his control of the lucrative cocoa industry to ensure economic power and then banned all political parties with a regional platform, including the Asante's National Liberation Movement. As Cooper points out, Nkrumah's initiatives to preclude opposition to his power went beyond these first two steps as the new president also curtailed the power of chiefs, farmers, and organized labor. So, the sense of disillusionment was real, not merely a figment of the imagination. For more, see Cooper, *Africa Since 1940*, pp. 68–9.
38. Let me provide two references on the Akan cultural and linguistic dimension of the novel *Fragments*. The first, Chantal Zabus's brief discussion of Armah's use of an Akan lexicon with character's names and chapter titles that are Akan words that remain untranslated in "The Ethno-Text Fragmented: Ayi

Kwei Armah's *Fragments*," *The African Palimpsest: Indigenization of Language in the West African Europhone Novel* (Amsterdam: Rodopi, 1991), pp. 148–55. The second, Derek Wright takes up the question of an Akan worldview in the novel in his chapter, "*Fragments* and the Akan World Order," *Ayi Kwei Armah's Africa: The Sources of his Fiction* (London: Hans Zell, 1989), pp. 138–86.

39. See, Derek Wright, Wright, *Ayi Kwei Armah's Africa*, pp. 162–3; and, Chantal Zabus, *The African Palimpsest*, pp. 148–9.
40. See Issac Julien's documentary *Frantz Fanon: Black Skin, White Masks* (San Francisco, CA: California Newsreel, 1996).
41. Cooper summarizes the disillusionment: "There is a particular poignancy to the history of Ghana because it was the pioneer. Kwame Nkrumah was more than a political leader; he was a prophet of independence, of anti-imperialism, of pan-Africanism. His oft-quoted phrase – 'Seek ye first the political kingdom' – was not just a call for Ghanaians to demand a voice in the affairs of the state, but a plea for leaders and ordinary citizens to use power for a purpose – to transform a colonized society into a dynamic and prosperous land of opportunity" (Cooper, *Africa since 1940*, p. 161). After Nkrumah was ousted by a coup while traveling abroad, Ghana was ruled by military regimes from 1966–9, 1972–9 and 1981–92. I return to these issues in Chapter 3.
42. Cooper reminds us: "And one of Nkrumah's first acts as the head of an independent state was to ban all political parties organized on a regional basis – including the NLM" (Cooper, *Africa since 1940*, pp. 68–9). He goes on to discuss how Nkrumah and others took over colonial projects such as building dams and retained their control over revenue streams that had been concentrated in the hands of power within the centralized colonial state, which set up the conditions for the gatekeeper state (Cooper, *Africa since 1940*, pp. 96–7). After defining the concept of the gatekeeper state, Ghana is his first example. He describes how the "pioneer who guarded the gate" put the economy in the hands of multinational aluminum companies and international financial institutions (Cooper, *Africa since 1940*, pp. 161–3). All of this brings to mind Ayi Kwei Armah's first novel *The Beautyful Ones Are Not Yet Born* (Boston, MA: Houghton Mifflin, 1968) where the anonymous man is a clerk at the Railway & Harbour Administrative Block and observes, "[y]et the stories that were sometimes heard about it [an old shop with new name] were not stories of something young and vigorous, but the same old stories of money changing hands and throats getting moistened and palms getting greased. Only this time if the old stories aroused any anger, there was nowhere for it to go. The sons of the nation were now in charge, after all. How completely the new thing took after the old" (Armah, *The Beautyful Ones Are Not Yet Born*, pp. 9–10).
43. See: Izevbaye, "Ayi Kwei Armah and the 'I' of the Beholder," pp. 241–52.
44. Wright observed: "In the fictive space occupied by the dual consciousness of Baako and Juana, the combined artist-psychiatrist, converge the common traits of the carrier and the lover of Mammy Water: a visionary estrangement, a power of healing, and the assumption by an "expanded consciousness" of a

maddening burden of knowledge or, in Baako's words, "all there is to know about loneliness, about love, about power" (pp. 171–2) in *Ayi Kwei Armah's Africa*, p. 139.

45. For more, see Robert Fraser, "The Context: Liberation and Resistance," *The Novels of Ayi Kwei Armah* (London: Heinemann, 1980), pp. 1–14.
46. Ogede sees Baako's resignation as an "honorable act of individual protest" and as a means of distancing himself from the corrupt establishment (Ogede, *Ayi Kwei Armah*, p. 72). He develops his interpretation of Baako's disillusionment at Ghanavision and disagrees with other critics, including Simon Gikandi, who have argued that the social setting in the novel is not realistically depicted.
47. The theme of an African person who has been to France or another Western country and returned home is prevalent in modern film and fiction, as we will see in *Touki Bouki* and *So Long a Letter*. One novel, in particular, that comes to mind is Daniel Biyaoula's *L'Impasse* (Paris: Présence Africaine, 1996), which opens with a scene at the Roissy Charles de Gaulle airport in Paris and explores the difficulties of African migrants returning to their native countries only to discover how much they have changed when faced with their cultures of origin. In Armah's novel *Fragments*, we also have a scene at the airport in Accra when Brempong's sister behaves in an exaggerated manner when he arrives, dancing and singing his praises.
48. Several critics discuss this outdooring ceremony and its implications. Robert Fraser interprets the episode in terms of the timing of Araba's pregnancy that coincides with Baako's arrival and how the perpetrators of the infanticide seem deliberately to destroy their own creative potential. For more, see Fraser, *The Novels of Ayi Kwei Armah*, pp. 39–41. Derek Wright reads this aspect of the novel in relation to Akan ritual and the blood-bond between maternal uncle and child. For more, see Wright, *Ayi Kwei Armah's Africa*, pp. 138–86.
49. Even as he was drifting into madness, Baako described in his writer's notebook the cargo cult (*Fragments*, 223–5) and the cargo mentality (*Fragments*, 228–9). This was an emotional response to the sudden and inexplicable appearance of manufactured goods from capitalist economies in a pre-industrial socio-cultural setting. Believers interpret the incomprehensible phenomenon of boats arriving and airplanes landing loaded with all manner of goods from within their non-Western cultural system. They think the gods must have sent all this wealth, and must have also had a hand in the technological advancement that made it possible. So, cult followers devise rituals inspired by their traditional myths to persuade the gods to drop more wealth into their mortal hands, which includes destroying the little they have in the hope of reaping much more in return. The way the novelist provides direct excerpts from Baako's notebooks with what appears to be pseudo-scientific references to studies of Melanesian cults is curious. It is possible that Armah, as a student in sociology at Harvard, could have been exposed to the writings of early theorists such as Marvin Harris who wrote about cultural materialism with influences from Marxism. In his book *Cows, Pigs, Wars, and Witches: The Riddles of Culture* (New York, NY: Random, 1974), Harris argues that the solution to riddles in culture are best explained by understanding practical circumstances and not by spiritual phenomena. Even today, social scientists

continue to study this controversial topic of cults and cargo mentalities. See, for example Holger Jebens, ed., *Cargo, Cult and Cultural Critique* (Honolulu: University of Hawai'i Press, 2004). In 1983, the Nigerian novelist Chinua Achebe used the phrase "cargo cult mentality" to describe the failure of political leaders in under-developed regions to find a better solution to their nation's problems than waiting for a fairy ship to dock in the harbor. See: Chinua Achebe's *The Trouble with Nigeria* (Portsmouth: Heinemann, 1983).

50. One scene in the novel actually takes place in the West. This is when Baako has a layover in Paris while *en route* from New York to Accra, which he planned to extend long enough to explore the beautiful city. As he walks around observing people and the city an uneasiness overtakes him. At one point, Baako comes across a man who is either praying as he faced a quay wall along the Seine or crazy as he is "in a frozen attitude of prayer" while tourists watch him in his "shut-off world." This symbol of moral solitude foreshadows Baako's inner struggle, but nothing he sees *outside* himself in Paris can be directly attributed to the cause of his *inner* malaise. The narrator comments: "There was nothing outside that he had seen to raise in him such a feeling. And within himself what he was aware of was vague: an unpleasant but not at all sharp sensation that everything he had done in about the last half year had been intended as a postponement, a pushing away of things to which he felt necessarily called" (Armah, *Fragments*, p. 74; emphasis added). The need to continue on his journey home was so intense that Baako arranges to catch a flight to Accra the same day.
51. Ukadike, "Djibril Diop Mambety," *Questioning African Cinema: Conversations with Filmmakers*, Nwachukwu Frank Ukadike, (Minneapolis, MN: University of Minnesota Press, 2002), pp. 121–31.
52. Interview with Djibril Diop Mambety, *Adhoua*, January–March 1981, p. 3.
53. Nar Sène, *Djibril Diop Mambety* (Paris: Harmattan, 2001), p. 11.
54. There are a couple of different attempts to discuss the spiritual dimension of Mambety's filmmaking. I find Sada Niang's *Djibril Diop Mambety, un cinéaste à contre-courant* (Paris: Harmattan, 2002) one of the most valuable contributions because of the author's understanding of Wolof culture in the Senegalese context. Further, David Murphy published an article that considers the role of Islam in his films, "Between Socialism and Sufism: Islam in the Films of Ousmane Sembène and Djibril Diop Mambety," *Third Text* 24:1 (2010), 53–67.
55. Sène, *Djibril Diop Mambety*, p. 19.
56. Ukadike argues that Mambety broke an "aesthetic gridlock" and initiated a whole new way of thinking about film language with *Touki Bouki*. For his discussion, see *Black African Cinema* (Berkeley, CA: University of California Press, 1994), pp. 172–7. For Barlet's discussion of the path-breaking filmmakers who refused to mimic the West, see his chapter "Closing Your Eyes," inspired in large part by Mambety, in *African Cinemas: Decolonizing the Gaze* (London: Zed Books, 2001), pp. 72–81.
57. Ukadike, *Black African Cinema*, p. 166.
58. Ibid.

59. Barlet, *African Cinemas*; translation of *Cinémas d'Afrique Noire* (L'Harmattan, 1996). For Françoise Pfaff, see: "Five West African Filmmakers on their Films." *Issue: A Journal of Opinion* 20.2 (Summer 1992): 31–7.
60. Barlet, *African Cinemas*, p. 79.
61. Ibid., p. 72.
62. Ibid., p. 80.
63. So much has been written about *Touki Bouki* and the film's influence. Françoise Pfaff, has remarked that it captured the alienation of the youth: "The film is, in both content and form, an autobiographical statement intended to disrupt the rules of conventional narrative African cinema and denounce the sociocultural alienation suffered by young Africans" (Pfaff 220). To explore this question of the youth and the generation of the 1970, I recommend Frank Ukadike's chapter "Post-1970s and the Introspective Phase," *Black African Cinema*, pp. 166–200; and, Donal B. Cruise O'Brien's "A Lost Generation? Youth identity and state decay in West Africa," *Postcolonial Identities in Africa*, eds. Richard Werbner and Terrence Ranger (London: Zed Books, 1996), pp. 55–74.
64. Although *Touki Bouki* did not earn immediate international acclaim, today the film is widely recognized by film critics and filmmakers as an African classic. Ukadike claimed: "[*Touki Bouki*] was unlike anything in the history of African cinema; today, film scholars around the world agree that *Touki Bouki* is a classic" (Djibril Diop Mambéty, "The Hyena's Last Laugh," *Transition* 78, p. 138).
65. A phrase from Ayi Kwei Armah's novel *The Beautyful Ones Are Not Yet Born*.
66. For viewers during the early 1970s for whom scenes from Africa's decolonization would have been fresh in mind, the arrest of the rebel activist was no doubt an iconic image. This image in archival footage has been integrated into countless films including Jean-Marie Teno's *Afrique, je te plumerai* (San Francisco, CA: California Newsreel, 1992) and Raoul Peck's *Lumumba: Death of a Prophet* (San Francisco, CA: California Newsreel, 1992).
67. I will deal with the critical discussion of this kind of perceived impotence of the gods and the sense of an absence of spiritual protection from the ancestors that goes with it later in relation to the writing of Sony Labou Tansi. For now, it should be noted that there is a certain ambiguity in *Touki Bouki* on this issue, since there is a recurring longing for transcendence and an apparent pessimism about the potential for healing and restoration through ritual or prayer.
68. This is a brilliant scene in the film that has gone practically unnoticed in the critical discussions. As regards sexuality in general, Ukadike shows a conservative temperament when it comes to African representations of sexuality on the big screen. He discusses Désiré Ecaré's film *Visages de Femmes* (1987) as not "genuinely" African because of a ten minute sequence with explicit physical contact (Ukadike, *Black African Cinemas*, pp. 220–2). For his brief characterization of this scene in *Touki Bouki*, see: pp. 174–5. Mambety is a master of indirection and makes ironic use of the proviso that sexual relations may be referred to, but not portrayed explicitly, in keeping with many traditional African cultures, especially within Muslim West Africa. Although Mambety decides to leave the visuals out, he amplifies the meaning with a dramatic display of sexual satisfaction in symbolic terms.

69. Barlet sees this scene as an affirmation of female desire and relates it to postcolonial identity politics. "African filmmakers' concern with this exemplary affirmation of the desire of woman – unfaithful as she is to cultural norms (without, for all that, rejecting them), but faithful, in her refusal of immobility, to her original life force – may, through the self-examinations it provokes, create fertile ground for social change. And is it not, indeed, a Dogon cross Anta grips in her hand as she copulates with Mory, her moans clothing the violence of their thrashing bodies, in the magnificent *Touki-Bouki*?" (Barlet, *African Cinemas*, p. 106).
70. Barlet, *African Cinemas*, p. 80.
71. Ibid.
72. Irène Assiba d'Almeida, *Francophone African Women Writers: Destroying the Emptiness of Silence* (Gainesville, FL: University Press of Florida, 1994) and Florence Stratton, *Contemporary African Literature and the Politics of Gender* (London: Routledge, 1994).
73. Sidonie Smith, *A Poetics of Women's Autobiography* (Bloomington, IN: Indiana University Press, 1987), p. 59.
74. Anne McClintock, Aamir Mufti et al., *Dangerous Liaisons: Gender, Nation & Postcolonial Perspectives* (Minneapolis, MN: University of Minnesota Press, 1997).
75. Susan Andrade, *The Nation Writ Small* (Durham, NC: Duke University Press, 2011), p. 76.
76. Amartya Sen, *Development as Freedom* (New York, NY: Anchor Books, 2000).
77. Florence Stratton discusses both the international acclaim and readership of the novel, including English-speaking universities in Africa, as well as the critical backlash against the novel in *Contemporary African Literature and the Politics of Gender*, pp. 133–55.
78. For the full interview in French in which Mariama Bâ makes this statement, see: Alioune Touré Dia, "Succès littéraire de Mariama Bâ pour son livre "Une si longue lettre," *Amina* 84 (Nov. 1979), pp. 12–14.
79. Dia, "Succès littéraire de Mariama Bâ pour son livre "Une si longue lettre," pp. 12–14.
80. Ibid.
81. Ibid.
82. She charted her own path, adopting egalitarian views about caste and ethnicity, joining women's associations such as Soroptimist, Club de Dakar and Cercle Femina. See: Dia, "Succès littéraire de Mariama Bâ pour son livre: Une si longue lettre," pp. 12–14.
83. She cites the example of when her father was away on assignment in Niamey and her grandparents were left to decide whether the young Mariama should be able to continue her studies. See: Dia, "Succès littéraire de Mariama Bâ pour son livre: Une si longue lettre," pp. 12–14.
84. There are various discussions of Mariama Bâ's choice and use of the epistolary genre. In 1990, Christopher Miller devoted an entire chapter to Senegalese women writers with an emphasis on Bâ and her novel *So Long a Letter*. Miller remarks how few novels in this genre by African men were in print at the time, whereas the genre had been well established among writers in French since the early modern period. For his discussion, see *Theories of*

Africans: Francophone Literature and Anthropology in Africa (Chicago, IL: The University of Chicago Press, 1990), pp. 246–93.

85. Smith, A Poetics of Women's Autobiography, p. 59.
86. Dia, "Succès littéraire de Mariama Bâ pour son livre 'Une si longue lettre'," pp. 12–14.
87. During her interview with Dia in 1979, Mariama Bâ cites from memory a passage from Aminata Sow Fall's novel *La grève des battus* (Dakar: Nouvelles Editions Africaines, 1979) which she puts like this: "Toutes les femmes ont au moins une fois dans leur vie rêvé d'un mari pour elles toutes seules" (Dia, "Succès littéraire de Mariama Bâ pour son livre: Une si longue lettre," pp. 12–14). When one considers how Bâ talks about her experience and the writing of *So Long a Letter*, it is difficult to imagine why Stratton attributes the source of Ramatoulaye disequilibrium to a "Western model of womanhood" in *Contemporary African Literature and the Politics of Gender*, p. 145. Even if one reads the novel critically looking for symptoms to support this interpretation, how does this reading fit with Aïssatou's emancipation while working in the United States and the international feminist perspective at the conclusion of the novel?
88. In 1972, Senegal enacted the Family Code, which is a set of laws that govern relations between spouses and within families as regards inheritance, polygamy, and other matters. The Family Code remains in effect today, although rights and protections that are accorded to women under the law are often not enforced by the judicial system. According to a 2006 report by the Bureau of Democracy, Human Rights, and Labor with the US State Department, women in Senegal continued to suffer inequalities: "Women faced pervasive discrimination, especially in rural areas where traditional customs including polygyny and rules of inheritance were strongest. Under national law, women have the right to choose when and whom they marry, but traditional practices restricted a woman's choice. The Family Code prohibits marriage for girls younger than 16 years and men younger than 20 years. This law was not enforced in some communities where marriages were arranged. Under certain conditions, a judge may grant a special dispensation for marriage to a person below the age requirement. Women typically married young, usually by the age of 16 in rural areas" (see section 5, Children). URL source consulted October 26, 2011 www.state.gov/g/drl/rls/hrrpt/2006/78754.htm. Various nongovernmental organizations and associations within civil society in Senegal are actively working to promote women's rights and gender equality, such as the Association des Juristes Sénégalaises and Tostan, whose mission is to empower African communities based on respect for human rights, with a program in Senegal that seeks to eradicate the practice of Female Genital Cutting. For a recent feature article, see: Celia Dugger, "Senegal Curbs a Bloody Rite for Girls and Women" *New York Times*, October 18, 2011.
89. The question of African women's relationship to feminism and the West has been fraught with cultural issues from the beginning and critical interpretations of Mariama Bâ's novel *So Long a Letter* is no exception. Christopher Miller observed: "Francophone literacy is a lever that Mariama Bâ uses to advance the cause of the dispossessed, even if it is only one group of relatively

privileged women for whom she speaks. It did not take long for anti-feminist critics to accuse Mariama Bâ of Eurocentrism" (Miller, *Theories of Africans*, p. 276). Here, he identifies a very common tendency among male critics from Africa to discredit critical stances that women take in writing and in action by tagging them as Western or Eurocentric. Miller cites Femi Ojo-Ade's article, "Still A Victim? Mariama Bâ's *Une si longue lettre*," *African Literature Today* 12 (1982): 71–87, as his example, which is also one of the sources Stratton uses to advance a similar argument. While Stratton, like Miller, acknowledge the trap African women writers faced in the early years of being labeled "Western" if they directly challenged patriarchal values, she winds up arguing that Ramatoulaye is not able to free herself because of a "western model of womanhood" (Stratton, *Contemporary African Literature and the Politics of Gender*, p. 145). For Stratton, Ramatoulaye became psychologically trapped during the course of her colonial education in a Western model of femininity and this has made her susceptible to becoming a victim of Islamic patriarchy. This argument seems difficult to reconcile with Bâ's representation of Aïssatou who enjoys a wider margin of freedom in the West after she chooses divorce. By contrast, Mildred Mortimer argues: "The reader learns that Aïssatou faced the issue of polygamy in her own marriage, refusing it before the crisis occurred in Ramatoulaye's home. Aïssatou's revolt and subsequent "escape" to America makes her Ramatoulaye's ideal reader. Her success in the "new world" is convincing testimony; the journey outward is possible," *Journeys Through the African Novel* (Portsmouth, NH: Heinemann, 1990), p. 136. The novel provides ample evidence of a strong sense of complicity and sorority between Aïssatou and Ramatoulaye, which suggests a wide-angle view of the problems facing African women during the 1970s that favors international solidarity. As things progressed, African women did face the question of how to position themselves with respect to feminism in its First World and Third World forms and cultural class biases. For a thoughtful discussion of these issues during the 1980s and 90s, see: Juliana Makuchi Nfah-Abbenyi, *Gender in African Women's Writing* (Bloomington, IN: Indiana, 1997).

90. In the interview with Dia, the author explained that if men had used literature as a weapon to achieve colonial independence, women could use writing as a weapon too. See: Dia, "Succès littéraire de Mariama Bâ pour son livre: Une si longue lettre," pp. 12–14.
91. Tejumola Olaniyan, in presentation entitled "Thinking Afro-Futures II" at Modern Language Association, Philadelphia, PA, January 2017.

The Black Unicorn

Audre Lorde

The black unicorn is greedy.
The black unicorn is impatient.
The black unicorn was mistaken
for a shadow
or symbol
and taken
through a cold country
where mist painted mockeries
of my fury.
It is not on her lap where the horn rests
but deep in her moonpit
growing.

The black unicorn is restless
the black unicorn is unrelenting
the black unicorn is not
free.

2 Gender

Women's Engagement with Freedom

> Now I was making my daughter, who had been ready to settle into her father's country, into the latest fugitive.
>
> Smugglers together from that point on, she and I: bearing what furtive message, what silent desire?
>
> "The desire for freedom," you'd say of course.
>
> "Oh no," I would reply. "Freedom is far too vast a word! Let us be more modest, desiring only to breathe in air that is free."
>
> *Assia Djebar, So Vast the Prison*

> Jaja's defiance seemed to me now like Aunty Ifeoma's experimental purple hibiscus: rare, fragrant with the undertones of freedom, a different kind of freedom from the one the crowds waving green leaves chanted at Government Square after the coup. A freedom to be, to do.
>
> *Chimamanda Ngozi Adichie, Purple Hibiscus*

After I got married, my husband and I were sharing a house with two other couples, also newlyweds, in Niamey, Niger. We lived in a popular neighborhood in the capital city known as Quartier Baghdad. On a summer morning after breakfast, one of the women, and my cousin by marriage, came into my bedroom. I was writing in the cool, quiet room by myself. A standing fan was running.

My new cousin by marriage was in a fit of despair. For a time, she could not stop crying to tell me what was wrong. Eventually, she pulled herself together and told me the story. Her husband, whom she had married in a mining town about 1,000 kilometers to the north two weeks before, had started sleeping away at night after they arrived in Niamey. It was her second marriage. She discovered that he had lied to her. Before they were married, he admitted he had been married to a Hausa woman whom he had allegedly divorced in Niamey. This was not true. This kind soul, who lived in the room across the hallway from me, had been tricked into a polygamous marriage and found herself to be a co-wife against her will. As a Tuareg woman she had not been raised to expect polygamy, and certainly not with a Tuareg husband under false pretences. It was hard to tell what hurt her the most: being deceived, being betrayed by a man she loved, feeling ashamed in front of her family and friends, or having a legal status she never agreed to. As she kept talking, I could tell she wanted out, so I advised her to talk to Sidi-Amar, my husband. She explained to me that Sidi-Amar was related to her husband of two weeks on his father's side of the family, and that because he was older, Sidi would likely feel awkward confronting him on such an intimate issue. I insisted.

We both waited anxiously for Sidi-Amar to get home from work. Finally, they had a chat, and he advised her to leave the marriage as soon as possible. He said that the longer she accommodated the situation the harder it would be to break it off. He told her unequivocally that the community would support her decision, that she was not raised to be a co-wife, and that her husband would find little support among the male elders.

This was, indeed, what happened. Fortunately, this woman gathered the courage to walk away and face divorce a second time with the support of her extended family. Helping her navigate this situation came at the beginning of my socialization as a young woman married to a Tuareg man myself. Marriage in Tuareg society is more complex when families migrate to the city and women lose the traditional safeguard against polygamy. Tuareg men interact with other ethnic communities, such as the Hausa, where women are raised in polygamous households with the very real prospect of being a co-wife as an adult. This can put pressure on the extended family network to uphold traditional objections to polygamy in a multiethnic urban context. Over the past two decades, I have been frequently reminded how important and socially contingent women's substantive freedoms are when it comes to choosing a spouse, especially under new and challenging circumstances. It comes as no surprise to me that the area of narrative interest that has figured most prominently in feminist writing by African women has involved socially embedded marriage plots as the point of entry.

As African women entered onto the scene and found their own voices as writers and filmmakers, they transformed modern African cultural expression with writers leading the way. The first wave of decolonization in Africa, from Ghana's independence in 1957 to the conclusion of the Algerian War in the summer of 1962, coincides with the emergence of a recognized body of writing by African women in European languages. In the midst of this historical change, women writers took themselves and their private lives as new starting points for reflecting on broader social issues of justice, freedom, and equality. We can consider the acts of writing fiction and making films as manifestations of women's instrumental freedoms insofar as they transformed society and women's standing within it. As we observed in Chapter 1, individuals respond to the process of national liberation and relate to the discourse of a collective struggle for freedom from within a set of "nested identity concepts," as Richard Bjornson put it in *The Quest for Freedom and Identity* (1992). We also noted that gender is an important differentiating factor in terms of how artists – in this context, writers and filmmakers – represent their own private, intimate sense of broad questions such as social justice and existential freedom. When women have taken up the question of freedom, particularly from a feminist standpoint, they tend to represent the personal, social, and political spheres of experience as interrelated.[1]

In the first two decades of African women's writing, narratives often concerned courtship and marriage, and they frequently took up the relationship between African and Western cultures. As this new area of narrative interest began to emerge, we notice a cluster of themes that were important to the daily lives of women: the challenges and rewards that come with cross-cultural love relationships; the effects of migration and girls gaining access to education; and the enduring questions of monogamy, reciprocity, and the freedom to choose one's spouse in the intimate sphere. Assia Djebar's first novel, *La soif* (1957; The Mischief), written quickly and with a sense of urgency, tells the story of a Franco-Algerian woman who attempts to make her boyfriend jealous by seducing another man. The following year, Claire Matip published a brief narrative entitled *Ngonda* (1958) that recounts the life of a Cameroonian girl whose father sends her to a French school and how she navigates the changes her education brings, especially her expectations about choosing a spouse she loves. Matip also describes the grandmother's storytelling and the daily activities of women in a rural setting, such as a mother's food preparation, in an effort to flesh out this area of narrative interest with accounts of women's lived experience. In terms of theater, Ama Ata Aidoo's first play, *The Dilemma of a Ghost* (1965), tells the story of a cross-cultural relationship between an African groom and his American bride who finds it difficult to adapt when they arrive in her husband's country. Grace Ogot's *The Promised Land* (1966) presents the experiences of a young Kenyan farmer who migrates to Tanzania with his wife, where they face many challenges in their new community. In 1966, Heinemann's African Writers Series published Flora Nwapa's *Efuru*, its first title by a woman, about a beautiful Nigerian woman who elopes and then suffers disappointment in love as her first and second husbands abandon her. Three years later, Thérèse Kuoh-Moukouri published a novella, *Rencontres Essentielles* (1969; Essential Encounters), that relates an unhappy marriage between two young Cameroonians who meet as students in France and return to Cameroon; the story is told from the perspective of a woman whose husband does not love her. Of course, the earliest publications in this field occupy a unique place in the literary history of women's writing by virtue of setting a precedent, but if we look for trends in this corpus of pioneering works over time, we are able to discern the emergence of a feminist topology in African women's writing in which women's substantive freedoms – choice of spouse, and access to both education and new cultural spheres of reference – were clearly in the foreground. In time, fully fledged female characters who were not willing to conform to patriarchal expectations shifted the terrain for male and female writers alike, expanding, as I will show, the parameters of what could be said about freedom.

While much has been written about how the idea of the nation and discourses of nationalism are marked by gender as well as by normative masculinities and femininities, much less has been said about women's engagement with the ideal of freedom. In *Stories of Women* (2005), Elleke Boehmer notes that during the early 1990s in gender-and-nation studies, critics such as Anne McClintock and Florence Stratton repeatedly cite national concepts and signifiers of femininity as interlocking.[2] Boehmer, along with Sangeeta Ray and others, believe, as I do, that "*no* theory engaging fully with either (national) resistance or sociality at both micropolitical and macropolitical levels can adopt 'a gender-neutral method of inquiry' (her emphasis)."[3] Whereas feminist critics have examined how women writers and filmmakers explore their own subjectivities in relation to different spheres of experience from the private to the public, little attention has been paid to the central idea of meaningful freedom, even though it is – and has been – of central importance in canonical works from Mariama Bâ's *So Long a Letter* to Chimamanda Adichie's *Purple Hibiscus*.

More recently, Susan Andrade, in *The Nation Writ Small: African Fictions and Feminisms, 1958-88* (2011), proposed to investigate how novelists of the first generation, from 1958 to 1988, represented these links between the private and the public spheres: "By focusing on the interconnected nature – indeed, the interpenetration – of the private and public spheres of life (in this case, the domestic and national spheres), [she] redefine[s] the terms of conversation about politics and gender in Africa."[4] Her work draws primarily on critical modes of reading narratives allegorically and pays close attention to texts, discourse, and signification in literary historical perspective. Andrade's study grew out of her sense that novels published by men were widely perceived as engaging directly with the project of national liberation, whereas women's writing, focused on marital and familial issues in the domestic sphere, was wrongly considered to be largely apolitical. As a result of what Andrade calls the "deeply gendered iconography of decolonizing nationalism," women's writing carried specific representational burdens. Part of their challenge involved navigating their complex relationship as feminists to African cultural nationalism – which is a central feature of the masculine narrative of triumphant nationalism.

The conversation Andrade seeks to establish in *The Nation Writ Small* between decolonizing nationalism dominated by men and gender politics advanced by women, strives to make the political content of women's fiction legible to a broad readership and to recuperate women's contributions as politically relevant. As she examines the representation of women's experience in narratives by women, reading allegorically in dialogue with Fredric Jameson's work on allegory and his Marxist definition of the political unconscious, she argues that through allegory the family in women's writing becomes the "nation writ small." From my critical standpoint, I share some common ground with Andrade's project insofar as it suggests, as Anne McClintock did in the 1990s with *Imperial Leather: Race, Gender and Sexuality in the Colonial Contest* (1995), that nationalism is a gendered discourse in which men's and women's agency and subjectivity are viewed differently and have been subject to asymmetrical patriarchal bias. However, the extent to which Andrade's argument aims to cultivate political literacy by making the political content in women's writing legible via allegorical interpretation, wherein the domestic sphere is seen as "standing in for" the national political sphere, gives up more terrain than I am willing to concede. I, too, will offer interpretations of stories by women (novels and films) in which metaphor, symbolism, and allegory are employed in carefully layered narratives that represent the private and public spheres as deeply interconnected. However, I do not interpret this interconnection in terms of domestic life "standing in for" the national political sphere through allegorical allusion or substitution, but rather as portraying interdependent spheres of experience – intimate, gendered, national, global, spiritual – in which different types of freedoms operate together in concert within a single work.

I will be cutting against the grain of criticism that tends to see women's writing about issues of social justice, national liberation, and freedom in the public sphere as essentially allegorical because this mode of interpretation, driven by textual and discursive considerations, tends to occlude the extent to which women represent different kinds of freedoms not only as interconnected, but also as *mutually reinforcing*. In each of the novels that I discuss, the representation of couples is of central interest but always in connection with larger social and political questions of freedom. I see the private lives of men and women in love as being depicted in relation to a complex set of forces – cultural, social, political – that may constrain, define, or facilitate their rights and liberties. The women whose works I consider in this book, and in this chapter as a central focus, represent a woman's personal struggle for meaningful freedom in her private life as embedded within broader questions of social justice and the political legacy of national liberation. Over time, women's narratives evolved away from the early feminist interest in the marriage plot as they began to engage with the idea of freedom in relation to a broader set of circumstances ranging from motherhood to migration.

I will consider works by five women novelists from the 1960s through to the early twenty-first century to give a sense of the range of their engagement with the idea of freedom over time and across the continent. I begin with Nadine Gordimer's response to laws forbidding interracial marriage under apartheid in South Africa – the Prohibition of Mixed Marriages Act of 1949 and the Immorality Act of 1950 – in her third novel, *Occasion for Loving* (1963), in which a black man is deprived of the basic moral right to live with the white woman he loves. With sober realism, Gordimer's narrative represents the private sphere of love as intertwined with the public world of national politics against the backdrop of the repressive political climate that followed the Sharpeville massacre of 1960. Next, I turn to Bessie Head, who fled from South Africa in 1964 when she was twenty-seven, and consider her novel *When Rain Clouds Gather* (1969) in which a mixed community of exiles, both black and white, work together to form a new, utopic social order. The plot in this novel about marriage and community derives its power of denunciation from the dialectic between the "howling inferno" of South Africa that is left behind and the idyllic farming community of Golema Mmidi, where the protagonist Makhaya settles in Botswana. Then I consider Buchi Emecheta's classic novel *The Joys of Motherhood* (1980), which delineates gender relations in West Africa during the mid-twentieth century, which will shift our focus in this area of narrative interest from marriage and communities to the experience of motherhood. Although meticulous in its social observation and painstakingly realistic in its character formation, this narrative introduces strong, new symbolic elements in women's engagement with the idea of freedom, most notably in Emecheta's equation of motherhood with slavery.[5] I build on Emecheta's symbolic use of slavery in relation to the idea of freedom and consider the trope of the prison in Assia Djebar's novel *Vaste est la prison* (1995; *So Vast the Prison: A Novel*, 2001) that offers her most sustained and compelling reflection on gender identity and freedom in the context of her native Algeria. In this text, Djebar also discusses her creative process as a filmmaker, providing us with a window onto the world of cinema for African women. Finally, I look at Adichie's *Purple Hibiscus* (2007) and examine her explicit and multifaceted engagement with the language of freedom from "Aunty Ifeoma's experimental purple hibiscus: rare, fragrant with the undertones of freedom" (*Purple Hibiscus*, 16) to Nigeria's historical struggle for democracy on the streets and in a free press.

Gordimer's refusal to exile herself from South Africa during the apartheid era and her persistent and increasingly radical criticism of that regime, including her willingness to address the complicity of white liberals in the minority like herself, makes her a historically important and morally compelling voice in the opposition to apartheid. Like André P. Brink and others, Gordimer has dealt with these political issues both in her narrative fiction as well as in essays about African literature and culture, such as *The Black Interpreters* (1973). Gordimer has reflected, for instance, on the history of the novel in South Africa and the importance of the emergence of black novelists such as Thomas Mofolo and Sol Plaatje, as well as how she might contribute to cross-cultural fertilization in narrative strategies and to a hybrid cultural model, rather than to contribute unwittingly to an imperial imposition of form and language unilaterally via English. Dominic Head discusses Gordimer's ambiguous relation to the tradition of the modern African novel, noting that, according to Abiola Irele, the works of white South African writers such as Brink, J. M. Coetzee, and Gordimer do not display an "African Imagination" in the way black Africans have in their works.[6] At the same time, Head aptly describes how Gordimer's novels and short stories openly challenge and transgress attempts to separate blacks from whites in multiple ways: by exploring the possibilities for a fusion between cultures, by representing the micropolitics of the body and sexuality in transracial relationships that subvert the fundamental principle of apartheid, and by exploring macropolitical questions of space, territory, and landscape that expose the racial injustice of apartheid's geopolitics and policies.[7]

Although a black man's substantive freedom to love a white woman is in the foreground of Gordimer's *Occasion for Loving*, the plot takes shape against the backdrop of the increasingly violent struggle for black liberation. Gordimer began writing *Occasion for Loving* before the events in Sharpeville in 1960, although she did not publish the novel until three years after the massacre in which sixty-seven demonstrators were killed and one hundred and eighty-six were wounded. She does not specifically refer to this violence, but a growing sense of pessimism hangs over the events in the narrative, reflecting the shrinking possibilities for social interaction and political cooperation between whites and blacks in the aftermath of Sharpeville.[8]

During the 1950s and 1960s when new leaders were negotiating the transition to African rule across the continent from Ghana to Kenya, the situation in southern Africa worsened. "Meanwhile," writes Fredrick Cooper, "white settler politics swung in an increasingly racist direction. The region seethed with tension."[9] Of course, the history of racist exploitation began with the discovery of diamonds in 1867 and gold in 1886, which led to the Anglo-Boer War (1899–1902) – a classic conflict in competition for control of African labor and the exploitation of natural resources.[10] In southern Africa, white settler populations had pursued another version of development, in the style of apartheid, which was a variation on the colonial theme with a political ideology of separate development of territories that were racially designated. This required extensive laws and a legal codification of race that regulated the unequal coexistence of the European population with the "non-whites," including former Indian slaves and African people who were native to the region. In 1948, the Afrikaner-dominated National Party took over, allowing the expansion and further codification of white supremacy, which had been evolving over decades. As a result, still more laws were imposed, defining land ownership and political citizenship in terms of voting rights, banning interracial marriage, limiting access to universities, codifying racial identification, and imposing pass books. Passbooks in South Africa under apartheid stipulated where a black person was allowed to work and travel; they controlled and restricted freedom and movement. In South Africa, the white minority made up 22 percent of the population in 1911, 16 percent in 1980, and 8.9 percent in 2011 – but held 87 percent of all the land at the time of transition from 1990 to 1994, which was the result of the black population having been dispossessed of their property, rights, and previous way of life.[11] White settlers have stayed in South Africa, and the concentration of wealth in the hands of this minority is a long story that has made achieving socioeconomic equality for all South Africans a yet-to-be surmounted challenge.[12]

In the aftermath of Sharpeville, with the whole world watching, the apartheid regime declared a state of emergency following international appeals for the total liberation of the continent once decolonization was underway in the British and French territories. In South Africa, there were widespread arrests in the early 1960s, and many of Gordimer's friends were either fleeing or in jail.[13] It was in this political context that Gordimer brought to life, in her novel *Occasion for Loving*, the people around Jessie and Tom Stilwell in their big old house, with a density of descriptive detail that evokes a strong sense of place. A white liberal living in Johannesburg, Tom Stilwell is a professor of history who is writing about colonialism from the point of view of black Africans (*Occasion*, 15). His political views are made manifest in the novel though his opposition to the Extension of Universities Bill of 1959 which would exclude blacks from white universities. While this law negatively impacted the black population's academic freedom, it also violated their substantive freedoms by denying them access to social, educational, and cultural resources to improve their lives.[14] Stilwell's friend Boaz Davis, also a white South African academic, is conducting research as an ethno-musicologist and has come with his new wife to stay at the Stilwell's house. Ann Davis, his wife, a free spirit in her twenties, has just joined her husband in Johannesburg. As a British expatriate, she approaches the racial dynamics in her new environment with some naïveté because she had not internalized the racist interdictions that apartheid culture worked so hard to instill. The narrative development of this community of white liberals is thick with description, not only of the house as an open tolerant meeting place, but also of their habits as they spend time together, eating and drinking, and of their values regarding politics, love, and life in general. Through the study of history, music, and painting they are all engaged in various creative and intellectual ways with black African cultural expression and welcome social interaction with black South Africans.

In *Occasion for Loving*, Gordimer explores, for the first time, a theme that had dominated South African writing: the politics of interracial relationships. As Stephen Clingman has observed, Peter Abrahams had already done this in *The Path of Thunder* (1952), as did Dan Jacobson in *The Evidence of Love* (1960), and Richard Rive in *Emergency* (1964).[15] What is unique in Gordimer's treatment of this theme is the way she represents personal lives, intimate experiences, and internalized attitudes to effectively reveal underlying political attitudes that originate in the national culture of apartheid. It is worth noting that she conveys these revelations over the course of her career with the kind of narrative mastery and insight that earned her the Nobel Prize in Literature in 1991. The drama starts when Ann Davis falls in love with a talented black painter called Gideon Shibalo; the adults living in the Stilwell's house in Johannesburg eventually learn about the extramarital affair and are uniformly tolerant of what was, at the time, an illegal relationship – including her own husband, who never initiates a confrontation with his wife's black lover. The passionate love that Ann and Gideon come to share seems as authentic as possible; it appears to be the result of pure human chemistry and is free from the sin and abnormality that often characterize such relationships in literature from the apartheid era and beyond as we see, for instance, in Zakes Mda's exquisite novel *The Madonna of Excelsior* (2002). Gordimer rather subversively characterized the love between them as creative, unique, and inspiring – like the paintings Gideon creates while he is in love with Ann – suggesting an analogy between cross-cultural creativity and interracial sexuality as two pathways for challenging the ethos of division under apartheid. The reasons for the group's tolerance of the black man who enters their world are portrayed as a blend of liberal white guilt and genuine admiration for Gideon as an individual. The safety Ann and Gideon enjoy in this haven of racial tolerance and moral flexibility is thoroughly established, with a realism that is free from allegorical abstractions, before they set out on a road trip on their own in search of a space to love one another freely.

The forces that destroy this relationship are both external – as a result of the public interdiction of such a union – and internal, due to the values that individuals, especially Gideon, have internalized in terms of what Clingman calls "the pre-structuring effects of apartheid."[16] Ann and Gideon's flight is an attempt to find a way of actually being together as a couple, but everywhere they go they are faced with the pervasive realities of racism across the country. This interracial couple is not welcome anywhere: not at Gideon's teacher friend's house, not in a field having a picnic, certainly not sharing a hotel room, and not even at Jessie's beach house, where they show up unannounced. Ann and Gideon experience awkward moments of having to impose on friends – moments of danger, such as when they stumble across a white farmer in a field; and moments of raw fear, as when Gideon goes for a walk on the beach and is gone for an agonizingly long period of time, much longer than an ordinary walk should take. Once they run out of ideas and money, the lovers reluctantly return to their liberal cocoon in Johannesburg. Yet Dominic Head has proposed that it is also possible to see a city like Johannesburg as a heterotopia or an urban place "created for individual bodies to resist the organized spaces of incarceration or surveillance and to establish their own spaces of consciousness and freedom."[17] Thus we can add urbanization, specifically urban heterotopias, to sexuality and creativity as one more pathway that offers transgressive potential for resisting apartheid's policies of separation and division. Unfortunately, when Ann and Gideon return to the Stilwell's house, it signals external defeat and is evidence of the absolutely inhospitable landscape that has been created by apartheid's effort to control cultural territories and geographical space at the macropolitical level.

It becomes apparent that as a black man, Gideon has internalized a sense of doom and dread over the years that brutally surfaces once his relationship with Ann fails. In the end, Ann decides to leave South Africa with her husband, fleeing with him to another African country and abandoning her plans with Gideon.[18] The contrast Gordimer sets up between the utopic haven of tolerance at the Stilwell's house and the open hostility toward mixed-race relations in the society at large finds an explicit denunciation in the narrator's comment: "So long as the law remained unchanged, nothing could bring integrity to personal relationships" (*Occasion*, 236). This is one of many statements in the novel that clearly indicts apartheid laws as the source of the deprivation of black people's freedoms. While it is true that Ann and Jessie discover the limits of their options as women, they enjoy a far greater sense of freedom and privilege as white women than Gideon does as a black man in South Africa. Racial discrimination limits his horizons at every turn – he was denied a visa to study art in Italy, although he was the recipient of a scholarship – and he becomes a drunken, bitter man when he is unable to have the woman he loves. In this respect, we encounter what Dominic Head has called a "hierarchy of oppression," such that racism is seen as more destructive of human freedom than the sexism that negatively affected the lives of white women under apartheid.[19]

Yet, the way this novel seeks to uncover the potential for liberation in South Africa is articulated from a woman's point of view in a narrative that explicitly links the private lives of lovers with national politics. Gordimer's narration in *Occasion for Loving* significantly contributes to the emergence of women's writing in Africa because of the way she fleshes out interesting and complex female characters. Jessie Stilwell, the subjective anchor in the novel, is developed with a vividly realistic psychology and far surpasses the strongest female characters in works by men. Clingman notes that Gordimer has rarely dealt with subjectivity as deeply as she did with Jessie.[20] *Occasion for Loving* offers a slice of life from a woman's perspective without a specific focus on gender inequality, yet with a keen interest in the intimate sphere of women's lives at home, at work, and in love. The reader witnesses Jessie's struggle for self-awareness and independence in her relationships with men, her children, and friends with a raw sense of psychological realism. Jessie was married right after completing her education and soon found herself widowed with a young child. Then she married a second time, to Tom, with little opportunity to experiment with personal freedom. When Ann and Gideon visit her beach house, the unexpected event jolts her into a new state of awareness of herself and of the racist society in which they live under apartheid. The way Jessie realizes the limits of her ability to take progressive actions, because of the external system of racial discrimination, exposes the constraints on interracial political cooperation after Sharpeville, while also suggesting "a prescription for the basis of a liberated political consciousness" in the future.[21]

Before writing this novel, Gordimer had travelled to other African countries, including Egypt and the Democratic Republic of Congo, and had an informed understanding of the direction in which the continent was headed.[22] In *Occasion for Loving*, Gordimer chose to deal with life outside the belly of the whale with all the ethical rigor that is required of such a realistic literary imagination. The novel reveals how liberal whites felt frustrated, irrelevant, and trapped in their alienation – without any of the equivocation that dogged Albert Camus's analogous position on French Algeria in the late 1950s.[23] Camus was of European descent and born in Algeria during French rule. When he won the Nobel Prize in Literature in 1957 journalists pressed him to take a side on the Algerian War of independence. Camus opposed the armed struggle and sided with his French mother. Gordimer is very clear: as long as a black man and white woman did not enjoy the private freedom to love and live with each other, there could be no hope for social justice. *Occasion for Loving* would have disabused white liberals in South Africa of any illusion that their tolerant values were the same, or similar, to those of other whites in the country at the time. Gordimer took a radical and uncompromising view of South African society in which an ethical interest in the possibility for meaningful freedom for blacks and whites originated in the intimate sphere of men and women in love.

Over the next two decades, this optimistic vision was severely tested as the apartheid state resolutely held onto power. In Gordimer's later fiction, such as *July's People* (1981), we see her attempting to come to grips with the terms of revolutionary change to come. The novel opens with an epigraph from Antonio Gramsci's *Prison Notebooks*: "The old is dying and the new cannot be born; in this interregnum, there arises a great diversity of morbid symptoms." For Gordimer, in this case, the interregnum pertains to what would be apartheid's twilight years over the next decade – a period of intense political struggle that would lead her to undertake a careful reexamination of identity politics between blacks and whites, masters and servants, and how they get exposed during revolutionary moments of upheaval. The narrative in *July's People* explicitly signals the political context of the violent uprisings that erupted in the area around Johannesburg after Sharpeville in 1960, Soweto in 1976, and Elsie's River in 1980, which reached a chronic state of instability all over the country after so many strikes (*July's People*, 8). As a result, a white, middle-class couple resorted to fleeing from their home and hiding in their (former) servant's village, where they were all forced to constantly renegotiate the meaning of ownership, the use of private and public space, their social status, and their roles as masters and servants. The erosion of white control and possession of property starts with Maureen noticing a wide variety of small objects strewn about that July had pilfered from their home over the years – a knife grinder and a pair of scissors among others – that went unnoticed. In time, the fundamentals of their master/servant relationship completely unravel. July finds the idea of calling the police completely absurd, which prefigures the state's eventual loss of political control and territorial authority. And the white middle-class couple who had previously employed July, now find themselves entirely dependent on their "servant" for food, shelter, access to news, and safety.

One result of this process is that Maureen is forced to contemplate what it means to recognize her servant's dignity, because it moves her to examine her own place in the structure of his oppression. Symbolically, Bam and Maureen Smales finally lose the tools of white bourgeois power in the imperial setting of late apartheid when their "servant" appropriates the keys to their bakkie and a freedom fighter named Daniel takes off with Bam's hunting rifle. Gordimer observes the interconnections between intimacy and power in key moments in the narrative, such as when Bam has a hallucinatory vision as he awakes and mistakes his wife's menstrual blood on his penis, after making love for the first time since they fled home, for the blood of a warthog he had killed the day before while hunting (*July's People*, 80). The killing of the warthog with a rifle is unconsciously associated with the white man's sexuality and his status in the hegemony of the apartheid state, as Dominic Head observes: "The connection is revealing and suggests a latent violence in the bourgeois channeling of male sexuality, an aspect of appropriation and ownership which is merely one aspect of the male's socially encoded power."[24] As in *Occasion for Loving*, external forces – in this instance an escalation in armed conflict – propel individuals to renegotiate their social relationships and re-examine their intimate selves. Once again, Gordimer weaves together external and internal forces in her descriptions of freedom fighters blowing up government buildings, exploding social roles, and setting fire to the master bedroom (*July's People*, 117). The transfer of property from white hands to black hands in the interpersonal narrative mirrors the dynamics of the collective struggle led by the black population. By the 1980s, Gordimer was able to imagine how the false consciousness of white liberals would completely unravel. As Dominic Head sums up, "This is an apocalyptic moment for the bankrupt white identity: the white woman finally accepts that she has no inner resource and no residual power or control to deal with her situation. She runs to accept the inevitability that her fate lies in the hands of others."[25]

Bessie Head makes a very different contribution with *When Rain Clouds Gather*, in which she recreates an African experience that appears uninterrupted by imperial domination. The pastoral setting the novelist imagines in Golema Mmidi is a place where self-renewal is possible and social change is projected in utopic terms from the standpoint of a radical cultural feminist. In this narrative, Head brings to life a village of exiles who are working together to build a new foundation for social justice, rather than a return to a mythical past (one she never knew) in accordance with a masculine version of cultural nationalism. The village of 400 people is located in eastern Botswana – a haven where refugees and various folks have settled to form a community that survives on subsistence agriculture and is about one day's walk from the border with South Africa. The central protagonist is a black man named Makhaya whose life parallels the author's in some significant ways: he immigrates from South Africa to Botswana, he is a political refugee, and he leaves the city for the countryside. It seems to me that this novel allowed Bessie Head, as a "colored woman" from South Africa, to integrate aspects of her fragmented self in a new environment with more distance than straightforward autobiography would allow. The possibility of social renewal through creativity re-emerges here in the context of exile, utopic spaces, and communities that also call to mind Werewere Liking's writing, similarly inspired by cultural feminism, and the Ki-Yi M'Bock village that she established as a Cameroonian expatriate in the Ivory Coast.

The narrative in *When Rain Clouds Gather* displays what Huma Ibrahim calls the author's "exilic consciousness," or her Janus-faced desire to remember her lost home and to find a way of belonging in her new adopted home. The moral fiber of Makhaya's character is developed through this lens, and his evolution as a man within the community of Golema Mmidi are elements of the author's feminist imagination. Bessie Head never knew her black father – and this was, at least in part, *because of his race* – so the way she imagines an ideal man appears as a principled expression of hope. Considering that she was taken from her white mother at birth and raised as a "colored orphan" by missionaries after her white mother was sent to a mental institution, the importance the novelist attributes to marriage within a sane and healthy community strikes an especially poignant chord.[26] The circumstances of Bessie Head's life story help define the moral vision of the novel written at an important moment of historical transition on the continent: *When Rain Clouds Gather* was published five years after Head arrived in Botswana in 1964, fleeing the turmoil in South Africa after the events of 1960, and just two years before Botswana, then a territory in the British Protectorate, gained its independence and the people elected Seretse Khama as their first president in 1966.

When Rain Clouds Gather derives its ideological edge from the dialectical relationship between the "howling inferno" Makhaya left behind in South Africa and the idyllic farming community he finds in Botswana. In this novel written in English – as was the case for much of the antiapartheid literature in South Africa – the possibilities for meaningful freedom in Africa are caught between the dystopia in South Africa and the promise of progress in newly independent nations in a story that connects the intimate sphere of love to the integrity of the political community. While Makhaya was engaged in antiapartheid activities in South Africa, he was arrested for planning to blow up a white-run power plant and was sentenced to two years in prison. As a result of his experience in the slums of South African cities, Makhaya brings a complex legacy with him: he has political awareness of the necessity to resist oppression, a hatred for whites who derive pleasure from treating blacks like dogs, and a personal solitude from a hollow life of using prostitutes, drinking, and urban squalor. He witnessed how thousands of black men had died senselessly to "boost up the manhood of a manless" white man so that "at one stage Makhaya had acquired enough hatred to become a mass murderer" (*Rain Clouds*, 121). The only way out of the "howling inferno" in which his instrumental freedoms were constantly and severely constrained was to leave the country. So, although South Africa remains a dead-end dystopia, immigration represents the first step on the path to self-renewal, and Makhaya is able to save himself as an individual. After settling in Golema Mmidi, he finds this community an "enchanting world" where he is able to fit the "scattered fragments of his life into a coherent and disciplined whole" (*Rain Clouds*, 118). Many things contribute to Makhaya's process, not the least of which is the "completely new experience" of meeting a white man, Gilbert Balfour, who is a kind and generous soul. The friendship and mutual respect that grows between the two men through conversations about life and collaboration on a tobacco growing project allow Makhaya to treat a white man like a normal human being for the first time in his life. Through this liberating experience, he discovers that values, not skin color, are what define our worth as people.

According to Huma Ibrahim's interpretation, Head's imagining Makhaya's desire for integration in Golema Mmidi mirrors the author's longing to be "born again in a different nation," yet it is also an attempt to reconcile both sides of herself in order to achieve a workable identity in a way that does not "erase" the effects of apartheid, as Ibrahim suggests, but rather seeks to transcend them.[27] Makhaya's introspection about human nature in this new world is helped along by a maternal figure named Mma-Millipede, who with a Tswana translation of the Bible preaches a gospel of generosity, solidarity, and faith. During a tête-à-tête over tea one evening at her house, Makhaya catches "an invisible thread of her life and attached it to his own," and this new capacity to trust and to connect allowed the walls he had erected inside himself to begin to dissolve (*Rain Clouds*, 128). Makhaya's willingness to respond to the old black woman's invitation to visit her is a pivotal moment in the novel that is followed by his growing intimacy with Paulina Sebeso, his future wife. The novelist portrayed him, to this point, as an exemplary man: he turns down the opportunity for sex with a young prostitute, he treats women as equals on the tobacco farm, he shows interest in Paulina's children in a country of "fatherless children," and he avoids casual sex with local women while quietly admiring the single-minded love between Gilbert and his black wife Maria. Paulina is also an idealized woman who stands out from the group in Golema Mmidi – although she is curious and adventurous, she is saving herself for a soul mate, and she has an intuitive sense of how society has produced a "whole race of degenerate men" that are untrustworthy and suffer unwittingly from the weakness of their own moral values (*Rain Clouds*, 89). Makhaya and Paulina are exceptional individuals who seem destined to enjoy a harmonious union in which they will both benefit from the wisdom of devoted monogamy in love. Near the novel's conclusion, Mma-Millipede observes that "it was seldom that the Lord ever gave a woman a man like Makhaya" because "he differed from all African men," since he did not like another woman up the hill, or another one in the valley, or another one in the next village in the indiscriminate ways of men (*Rain Clouds*, 169). It is equally important, in the context of this novel, that Paulina and Makhaya join together to help their community progress by expanding from subsistence farming to small-scale tobacco crops for profit. Makhaya supervises the construction of sheds for drying and curing leaves as well as setting up irrigation, while Paulina recruits women as workers and oversees serving tea and preparing meals. Thus, this exemplary relationship is not merely a private affair between two individuals, but also a partnership that benefits the entire village. Certainly, the effort to recreate a community built by shared, collective labor, rather than on the capitalist model of imperial exploitation, is seen to entail a redefinition of the intimate self, especially in terms of gender identity, and interpersonal relationships dominated by the discussion of what makes a healthy marriage.

The multiple collective forces that enable social progress – such as reason, science, knowledge about the land and nature, industriousness, independence, open-mindedness, and a willingness to cooperate with people who are outside one's kinship circle – are rendered with the central metaphor of "rain clouds gathering." During Chief Matenge's absence, much progress was made in practical terms of tilling the fields and establishing a new industry, and in the people's capacity to work hard and to think for themselves. This growing tide of shared initiative against the custodians of an old patriarchal order began to gather momentum quietly but certainly like rain clouds in September (*Rain Clouds*, 142). When the chief realizes that the villagers have emancipated themselves from his tyrannical control, he summons Paulina Sebeso to his court because he says he has a "case against her." Although the chief's messenger does not give a specific reason, it appears that she is guilty of organizing the community against Matenge, and all the villagers who hear about her summons accompany her to the chief's house. In the dramatic conclusion of this scene, the chief cries like a child when confronted with evidence of his demise and then chooses to hang himself from the rafters like a coward. The narrator describes the chief's death as the result of "a strange gathering-together of all their wills," which again evokes the central metaphor of rain clouds and the possibility of rain restoring the earth after a drought (*Rain Clouds*, 179). It is when Makhaya asks Paulina to marry him, after the chief commits suicide, that their hopes for the future take shape. This new couple is poised to play a significant role going forward, as their shared ideals will help cement an emerging egalitarian society that is anticapitalist and antiimperial, made possible by the community's liberation from the grip of dictators driving golden Chevrolets. But, the improbability that an entrenched tyrant would simply choose to hang himself rather than face the shame of having been defeated by grassroots community organizers takes something away from the novel's utopic conclusion. While imagining progressive ideals can be useful for the formulation of innovative strategies and for inspiring people to action, in this instance, the author's idealization of the tyrant's voluntary exit and an egalitarian society made up of happily married couples seems an emotionally satisfying scenario, more than a rigorous response to the harsh realities that prevailed in South Africa under apartheid.[28] It has already been well established that Bessie Head's feminist engagement with a politics of liberation that rejected violence, the armed struggle, and their toxic consequences for masculinity, did not earn her praise from male critics like Lewis Nkosi.[29]

Let us turn now to Buchi Emecheta's best-known novel, *The Joys of Motherhood* (1980), which tells a story about the daily lives of Igbo women in Nigeria under British colonial rule from 1909 to 1960 – a story that Elleke Boehmer characterizes as "compelling for its boldness and honesty."[30] The author of more than ten novels, Emecheta is one of the most prolific and widely read African women writing in English. The fact that she studied sociology at the University of London is clearly evident in this work that reads like a narrative essay on gender identity and the socialization of girls in a traditional family setting.[31] The events represented in this historical novel span some fifty years and establish, retrospectively, an instructive contrast between rural and urban contexts during colonial rule. The female protagonist, Nnu Ego, was born in a village called Ibuza (as was the author), but after fleeing her abusive first husband, she settles in Lagos with her second husband chosen by her father. In our consideration of this novel, we will shift our focus from plots centered on marriage in sociopolitical settings to a narrative that explores the theme of motherhood and more overtly employs political symbolism to engage with ideas of freedom. While the beleaguered Nnu Ego's actions are largely predictable and, therefore, unsurprising, there is a striking polemical edge to this narrative in that Emecheta rather boldly equates a mother's joyless absence of freedom with slavery.

As one might imagine, the way Emecheta took on the charged cultural symbolism of motherhood, which had been prominent in the male canon of African literature, often as a symbolic idealization of "Mother Africa," generated considerable critical debate. Many critics of African women's writing have addressed the central theme of motherhood and very often in relation to Emecheta's seminal text, *The Joys of Motherhood.*[32] Although the time period depicted is later than in Chinua Achebe's *Things Fall Apart*, Emecheta revisits issues of masculinity and femininity in Igboland from a feminist perspective that presents readers with a sharp rebuttal to established patriarchal views. Florence Stratton has documented the responses of male critics who have largely claimed that Emecheta's characterization of Igbo men is unduly harsh, stereotypical, and lacking nuance.[33] Yet, the narrative follows a deliberately chronological sequence of events, depicting one thing after the next with such attention to detail that the story appears as a true-to-life account. In literary debates about the novel's realism, Emecheta has been both praised and criticized for her views.[34]

In her introduction to the novel, Elleke Boehmer observes that women inhabit a hierarchical social structure marked by different levels of oppression, in which they find themselves at the very bottom.[35] What is of particular interest, in terms of the idea of freedom in this narrative, is to consider the extent to which women have been taught to see themselves as the property of men and to tolerate being treated like chattel. This would be a violation of their most basic freedoms, constraining a range of choices to speak and to act, and impeding the possibility of their self-definition. In Emecheta's narrative, it is revealed that the central female protagonist is primarily a victim of her traditional Igbo socialization. The novel begins with her family background, which establishes how the seeds for her subservience were planted during childhood. Her father, Nwokocha Agbadi, was a wealthy local chief whose physical prowess and charismatic image meant that he had many wives and mistresses in addition to being "naturally accepted" as a leader among his people (*Joys*, 10). Agbadi embodies a version of virility that is imposing and idealized to the extreme – he derived pleasure, for instance, from dominating strong-willed women and loved the mistress who refused to marry him the most of all his women. This beautiful mistress who eludes his possession is called Ona, and she later gives birth to their daughter Nnu Ego. In a dramatic scene that follows Ona nursing Agbadi back to health after a hunting accident, the powerful chief who thirsts for ownership engages in aggressive sex play to punish the independent Ona while others are listening: "Having hurt her on purpose for the benefit of his people sleeping in the courtyard, he had had his satisfaction" (*Joys*, 21). The chief's display of sexual potency and physical prowess is matched by Ona's conventional femininity which is idealized as suggested by her attractive bare breasts adorned with coral beads, her proud character, and noble family. Ona accepts the fact that she belongs to her father and submits graciously to his will, even when it is difficult. She is also described as "stubborn" and "arrogant," but only insofar as she excites the forceful chief's domineering appetite (*Joys*, 11). When she must justify being away from her father's house while nursing Agbadi, the narrator comments on Ona's self-perception as fortunate to be the property of men – "she supposed she should regard herself as lucky for two men to want to own her" (*Joys*, 25). Like her mother Ona, Nnu Ego submits to her father's will and ultimately to her second husband's authority, although not without moments of struggle and discord. Though it is true that Ona, and to a lesser extent Nnu Ego, have episodes of defiance, in the end they always relent to male domination. The multiple ways in which Ona and her daughter Nnu Ego conform to social expectations (often conveyed by women) and submit to male authority illustrates how gender identity within patriarchal societies requires a dynamic of female submission to enable the preservation of masculine domination.

The fact that Emecheta published *The Joys of Motherhood* two decades after Nigerian independence afforded her the possibility of reflecting historically, as a sociologist, on gender dynamics before and after decolonization. "Against the exacerbated gender hierarchies that the colonial system produced," notes Boehmer,

> anticolonial nationalist movements by contrast promoted inverted gender attitudes and structures, in particular a vehement masculinity, in order to help dismantle the oppressions of the past. As men sought to regain control over the women who had found limited outlets for their desire for freedom and self-expression under colonialism, masculine authority in the independence period became the more deeply entrenched.[36]

It is useful to bear in mind these historical dynamics when considering the novelist's representation of hardened masculinity. Indeed, even when far from home, Emecheta portrays the Igbo community as profoundly patriarchal and close-knit. After Agbadi's senior wife dies, she must be buried with her cooking utensils and her slave according to Igbo custom, but, when the eldest son fears that his mother's burial will not be completed according to ritual because others feel pity for the slave-woman, he takes it upon himself to kill the slave by striking her on the head with his cutlass (*Joys*, 23). Virility is enacted in this scene with the son's display of inflexible adherence to tradition at the expense of a slave-woman's life, which resonates forcefully with all the quieter moments in the novel when men pursue their own interests at women's expense.

Emecheta offers an instructive opposition between Nnu Ego and Adaku, which resembles the contrast Mariama Bâ setup between Ramatoulaye and Aïssatou in *So Long a Letter*, insofar as Adaku, like Aïssatou, gains financial independence and with this, a capacity to define her life with a measure of substantive freedom. In the context of this novel, there are only relative degrees of freedom for women. Conforming to traditional expectations is a burden that most women are often compelled to accept, in large part because they fear that gossip will tarnish their reputations. However, there are times when senior wives have recourse to obtain a certain standard of treatment and adequate living conditions, even within patriarchal culture – especially if they are the mother of one or more sons. Nnu Ego, for instance, is able to convince Nnaife to rent a larger house when he brings a co-wife into the household by requesting the intervention of older men from Ibuza during a family meeting. On the other hand, when Adaku calls on the same men to hear her complaint about Nnu Ego disrespecting her guest, the male elders treat her as a woman of inferior status, because she has not given birth to sons. Adaku refuses to submit to this subordination of her interests as the mother of daughters, so she chooses to become a prostitute and leaves the household altogether. Although the ambitious and rebellious Adaku is later described as more joyful and financially independent than Nnu Ego, the fact that her escape from Igbo tradition depends on her selling her body to men for their sexual pleasure in Lagos, suggests the narrow options women had.

Underlying this often-dismal tale about women's subjugation is the effort by the central protagonist, who keeps trying with little reward, to forge a new sense of selfhood. "In a narrative that straddles the Nigerian mid-century leading up to independence (1960)," writes Boehmer, "Nnu Ego's name, pronounced 'new ego' and meaning *priceless*, bears the anglophone associations, too, of renewed cultural self-confidence and new selfhood." However, the challenges she constantly faces break down her attempt to assert this new sense of self and contribute, in the end, to an intangible sense of incompleteness, which clearly compromises her existential freedom. The privileged status accorded to women who give birth to boys explicitly serves to perpetuate patriarchal hierarchies. We have another version of this story of male privilege at the expense of girl's substantive freedoms eight years later in Tstitsi Dangarembga's novel *Nervous Conditions* (1988), set in Zimbabwe, in which Tambudzai is only able to go to school after her older brother passes away.[37] The women who comply with these values, whether in Nigeria, Zimbabwe, or elsewhere, become the custodians of a male-dominated system that stigmatizes the female gender. The absence of male offspring in Nnu Ego's family left a legacy that contributed to her entrapment: her mother Ona was not permitted to marry because her father did not have a son to carry on his family line; when Ona did give birth to a child, she was able to keep her daughter since her father was exclusively interested in her son as his male successor; and when Nnu Ego is ready for motherhood, she will feel "complete" as a woman only if she has a son. Nnu Ego's first marriage to Amatokwu does not produce any children and ends badly when he severely beats her and she returns to her father's compound. Desperate to taste the joys of motherhood, Nnu Ego agrees to marry a second husband who lives in Lagos, without ever having seen him. Nnu Ego is appalled by Nnaife from the moment she meets him: his physical appearance disgusts her, as he is short with a fat belly; and his employment in the capital city robs him of his manhood, as he must wash clothes for a white family, including the lady's dirty underwear. In time, Nnu Ego discovers that her second husband lacks sound judgment, which we see in his reckless drinking and spending. Like the other men in the novel, he pursues his own interests at his wife's expense, from bringing a co-wife into their one-room home, to fathering children whose school fees and meals he cannot afford to provide. Nnu Ego's inferior status as a female is a relentless burden that she carries until the end of her life when she dies at the side of the road, a joyless mother, with no one to hold her hand.

The various ways in which Nnu Ego has been deprived of basic freedoms hamper her ability to speak in her own defense in the courtroom, an opportunity to exercise her instrumental freedom, and ultimately leaves her with an existential sense of dispossession. The truth about how Nnaife is a complete failure and Nnu Ego a naïve wife blinded by tradition is revealed with dramatic irony in the courtroom scene near to the end of the novel. The reader has already seen so much evidence of Nnaife's inadequacies and irresponsibility that his conviction seems unavoidable. During cross-examination, Nnu Ego is forced to answer the prosecutor's questions about her husband's behavior while those listening to her testimony laugh at how she makes excuses for him. The judge finds Nnaife guilty and sentences him to five years in prison for nearly killing a Yoruba man his daughter intended to marry. During the hearing, the shallowness of Nnaife's outburst to protect his daughter's honor for ethnic reasons is measured against his life of irresponsibility and the depredation he inflicted on his wives and children. In a clever twist, Emecheta has Adaku, the rebellious wife who fled the household, explain to Nnu Ego that the reason people were laughing at her was because of how absurd her blind submission to tradition sounded. Until women begin to see things differently – to value girls as much as boys, for instance – it will be a man's world, "which women will always help to build" (*Joys*, 187). What Nnu Ego does see, in the end, is how "[h]er love and duty for her children were like her chain of slavery" (*Joys*, 186), and that even after she dies she will remain a "prisoner of [her] own flesh and blood" (*Joys*, 187). Emecheta's novel vividly conveys just how important it is for strong women to find the courage to contest social injustice, to say "no" to their fathers and husbands, and to raise their children with progressive egalitarian values.[38] Nnu Ego's desire to preserve her reputation as an "honorable woman" prevented her from stepping outside the conventions of her role as the daughter of a respected chief from Ibuza. Unless women are willing to resist, in the private space of the home and in the public court of law, the kind of gender equity that ensures meaningful freedom for men and women will never be achieved.

Let us now return to Assia Djebar, a pioneer among African women writers who published two novels in French before independence, including *La Soif*, and two more shortly thereafter. As her country, Algeria, devolved into civil war during the 1990s, she entered a period of intense creativity. I have chosen to write about a novel from this period, *Vaste est la prison* (1995; *So Vast the Prison*), because it provides what is, in my view, the most compelling example of Djebar's engagement with gender and the question of freedom. She also wrote an impressive, introspective narrative about the causes and effects of the civil war in Algeria in *Le Blanc de l'Algérie* (1995; *Algerian White*). I include Djebar in this discussion, following Anne McClintock, who writes about Algeria and South Africa in *Imperial Leather*; and Susan Andrade, who cites Simon Njami in her introduction for his take on the virtues of pan-African perspectives and approaches to thinking about African cultural production. I do so, not because I want to claim that Djebar's writing is representative of Maghrebi women during the author's lifetime, but because her works made a significant feminist contribution to the evolving language of freedom after national liberation in Africa far beyond Algeria, as we also see in her important novel *L'Amour, la fantasia* (1985; *Algerian Cavalcade*). Although she grew up speaking the Algerian Arabic of her mother's people from Cherchell, she heard her father speak Berber and gained access to the Europhone world by learning to read and write French. She also went on to make two films in Arabic, *La Nouba des femmes de mont Chenoua* (1978) and *La Zerda et les chants de l'oubli* (1982), which we will consider in the context of the emerging practice of filmmaking by African women.[39]

So Vast the Prison gives us Djebar's most explicit, complex, and sustained engagement with freedom in all its dimensions. In this novel, prison is not only a real place where people are detained, but also a feminist trope. The title is a phrase taken from a Berber folk song, and the apparent paradox of a "vast prison" announces from the outset a logic of inversion at work in this narrative. *So Vast the Prison* opens with a scene among women in a hammam. The autobiographical narrator describes how she overheard her mother-in-law conversing with an attractive, middle-aged friend who referred to her husband as *l'e'dou* in Arabic, which means "the enemy." The friend said that she cannot stay and chat because her *enemy* is waiting at home. The narrator is shocked to discover that rosy-cheeked women who enjoy all manner of material comfort routinely use this colloquialism to refer to their husbands. What was merely an off-handed comment for this woman has the effect of letting a chilly gust of wind into the warm bathhouse for the narrator. Hearing *l'e'dou* in her mother tongue, which is, for her, the language of love, strikes at the narrator's heart. The other women's cool indifference amplifies the narrator's distress as she realizes how they have all resigned themselves to a degree of hostility between men and women. From this introductory episode, the hammam can be seen as an inverted symbol of unfreedom: within the intimate sphere of the bathhouse women are free, whereas the society outside is a vast prison where patriarchy turns husbands into enemies. The gendered space of the hammam – and by extension the harem, with which the novel opens – forms the moral epicenter from which all other variations on the theme of imprisonment evolve.

In the first of four parts, the narrator tells the story of her divorce as *her* irrevocable repudiation of *him*. This is a dramatic reversal of conventional gender roles and is also accompanied by the daring revelation of her husband's violent temper. Things spiral out of control between them when she confesses that she has been attracted to another man. In a rage, the husband physically lashes out, wounding his wife's face and hands. Once these physical wounds heal, the narrator-wife acquiesces, agreeing to return to a marriage she experiences as a form of imprisonment. However, in spite of strong familial ties, the implacable sense of unfreedom she feels in her marriage ultimately pushes her to take "the first shaky step of [her] freedom" (*Vast*, 119). This means ultimately choosing to divorce her husband, which is presented as a bold act of self-definition in defiance of a whole host of social expectations that keep women silent, sequestered, and subservient.[40]

The novel's second part appears unrelated to the central theme of freedom until we consider the logic of inversion already established and add to it the related effects of *effacement* and *fragmentation*. The narrator is contemplating, once again, all that has been lost for herself and for Algeria, and in this section, she visits Dougga, an ancient Berber village in present-day Tunisia. The passage of time over many centuries has partially effaced inscriptions on a monument at this site, while European explorers added to this natural loss by sawing off pieces of the ancient stele and carting them away to a museum in London. Taken together, the erasure of inscriptions over time and the stele's violent fragmentation create an impasse for visitors who are no longer able to make sense of the ruins that remain in Dougga today. In addition to what the state of these unreadable fragments tells us about imperial history, the narrator also perceives a sense of cultural dispossession especially in terms of her inheritance as a woman. This is because the language that eroded on the stele at Dougga was Tamashek – a precolonial African language spoken by Berbers and Tuaregs in the Sahara – and so the narrator proposes that people in the region also stand to lose the cultural values transmitted by speakers of Tamashek.[41] The narrator laments the disappearance of one Tuareg ancestor in particular: Tin Hinan, who displayed her beauty and strength as a woman in a way that represents the absolute antithesis of Islamic patriarchy's modern invention of a sequestered and silenced Muslim woman. If creativity requires personal freedom and cultural roots, then women writers like Assia Djebar stand to lose the most when faced with the ruins at Dougga. Restoring Tin Hinan to her proper place in the cultural heritage of the Maghreb is of vital importance for all who see patriarchy under modern Islamist rule as a vast prison that continues to unfurl in the wake of Western imperial domination.[42]

In the third part of the novel, the autobiographical narrator weaves together memories of filming *La nouba des femmes de mont Chenoua* (1977; *The Nouba of the Women of Mount Chenoua*) with fragments from her life that span several decades, from early childhood to the present. The narrator, at times referred to as Isma, or "the name," provides a retrospective commentary on the first cinematographic images Djebar captured near the mountains of Chenoua in 1977.[43] She remembers searching for the images in her first film as taking ground-breaking action with implications that would affect the community of women to which she belonged. The image of a woman completely concealed by a white veil was the symbol that became the driving force of her creative endeavor as a filmmaker in the late 1970s. She had to rework her perception of this image-symbol not as something "normal," but as a cultural construction that was "scandalous," and the filmmaker's excitement of rediscovering the veiled woman more than twenty years ago was still emotionally charged in 1995 at the time of writing *So Vast the Prison*.[44] Telling the story of how she struggled personally with the experience of being both inside and outside her culture of origin laces the narration of all of her novels and constitutes her own version of a feminist genealogy. As a pioneer, she challenges the impression that Algerian women are free in theory, while in practice she sees them as being culturally incarcerated. Recasting this image-symbol happened for Djebar when she imagined looking through the lens of her movie camera from the opening in a woman's veil:

> Community of women shut away yesterday and today, an image-symbol that is the true action, the drive behind this hunt for images that is beginning. A female body completely veiled in white cloth, her face completely concealed, only a hole left free for her eyes. Ghost who, reversing appearances, is rendered even more sexual by prohibition; shadowy shape that has strolled along for centuries, never screaming that we were enshrouded, never tearing off the veil and even our skin with it if required. This image is the reality of my childhood, and the childhood of my mother and my aunts, and my girl cousins who were sometimes the same age as me. Suddenly this scandal that I experienced as normal looms at the beginning of this quest: a single silhouette of a woman gathering in the folds of this shroud, her linen veil, the five hundred million or so segregated women in the Muslim world. Suddenly she is the one looking, but from behind the camera, she is the one devouring the world through a hole left in the concealment of a face. *(Vast, 179–80)*

In keeping with a feminist agenda, the narrator clearly connects Djebar's creative insights as an artist with a community of women beyond Algeria to include 500 million women across the Muslim world. By inverting the dynamic of the patriarchal gaze, the small opening that is left in a woman's veil becomes the filmmaker's new pathway for a liberated woman's gaze that is capable of devouring the world.

In *La Nouba*, the object of the woman's gaze is a wounded husband who watches his wife from a wheelchair. Alternating between the viewpoint of the paralyzed man and his wife allows Djebar to explore the dance of the man's impotent desire. Freedom of movement adds another dimension to the dynamic of the gaze in this film – the handicapped husband stays home, never speaks, and is immobilized in stark contrast to his wife who moves about freely and travels outside the home. The wife is seen coming and going, driving down the road, talking about her feelings, and listening to female relatives tell their stories in Algerian Arabic about the war for independence. In many ways, the woman in the film is a double for Djebar the novelist; they both take action, they both desire freedom in addition to the various parallels in their life stories. The point of recreating the steps that went into making *The Nouba of the Women of Mount Chenoua* was to underscore the importance of collective women's action and learning to see the world differently. Describing how she imagined inverting the patriarchal gaze and staging inverted gender roles between husband and wife are presented as potential sites of freedom that may inspire other women to liberate themselves in similar ways.

I will conclude with a discussion of Chimamanda Ngozi Adichie's *Purple Hibiscus*. The way in which Adichie engages with the language of freedom is explicit, symbolic, and of central importance to the novel, which rapidly attained canonical status among the new generation of twenty-first-century writers. The first evocation of freedom occurs early on when Kambili looks out of her bedroom window and sees a purple hibiscus growing in the garden. In her interior monologue, she describes her house as a prison, the windowsill as a threshold, and the flower outside as beautiful and rare, which becomes a symbol for meaningful freedom in the novel (*Hibiscus*, 8–9). The second instance in which the word "freedom" is used occurs again during an interior monologue, just a few pages later, when Kambili is lying in bed and sifting through her family's past in her mind. She reflects on the painful silence that reigned at home before their visits to Nsukka:

> Jaja's defiance seemed to me now like Aunty Ifeoma's experimental purple hibiscus: rare, fragrant with the undertones of freedom, a different kind of freedom from the one the crowds waving green leaves chanted at Government Square after the coup. A freedom to be, to do. *(Hibiscus, 14–15)*

Adichie sets up this distinction between different types of freedoms from the very beginning, as Kambili longs for the "freedom to be and to do," which she differentiates from political activism in the streets. The "freedom to be" relates to what I am calling existential freedom, and the "freedom to do" can involve both instrumental and substantive freedoms. Adichie's engagement with the language of freedom – we may even say with the ideal of meaningful freedom – is explicit, although it is also symbolic and remains to some extent aspirational as Kambili is still a work in progress at the end of the novel.

The story focuses on the protagonist's family with a triangulation involving the father (Eugene), mother (Beatrice), and daughter (Kambili). The story is narrated in the first person by Kambili from an adolescent female point of view. Outside the inner circle of her parents, Kambili has important relationships with her brother Jaja, her aunt Ifeoma, and a Catholic priest named Father Amadi. What is distinctive in this novel is how individuals are represented as making self-defining choices in ways that contrast with other characters. The novel presents opposite types of masculinity with Eugene and Father Amadi, as well as two different kinds of women with Beatrice and Ifeoma. For Adichie, gender identity is not overdetermined by religion or tradition, but is rather the result of a complex set of choices that individuals make in reaction to the circumstances in which they find themselves.

In some important ways, Kambili's father, Eugene, is a modern-day version of the classic Igbo character, Okonkwo, in Chinua Achebe's *Things Fall Apart* (1958). Eugene and Okonkwo both suffer from excessive rigidity, distorted priorities, and limited wisdom in an exaggerated personification of Igbo masculinity.[45] Things start to fall apart for Okonkwo when British colonials forcefully take over his community in Umuofia, resulting in a tragic disruption of their spiritual and cultural order. Adichie recalibrates the scale of what gets lost as a result of colonial imposition and presents Eugene as an example of the depersonalization that can happen when a black man agrees to wear a white mask.[46] This is what Ashish Nandy has called the "intimate enemy" in his analysis of identity formation in the shadow of imperial domination, which we previously considered in Chapter 1. Yet Eugene is completely different from Father Amadi, because the young clergyman refuses to wear a white mask and does not suffer from the same kind of intimate alienation, showing that there are, in fact, alternatives to the grim postcolonial legacy that we see in Eugene's self-loathing and systematic rejection of all things African.

Working with Harry Garuba's essay on animism and magical realism in African fiction, Brenda Cooper offers a reading of *Purple Hibiscus* that pinpoints how African spirits pervade the novel. Cooper cites examples of the enchantment of objects (furniture that seems to move, flowers that exude happiness), which involves blurring the distinctions between animate and inanimate objects. The point of this aspect of the narration, for Cooper, is to convey to the reader the extent to which traditional African beliefs and practices continue to permeate daily life in Nigeria.[47] Having this frame of reference allows us to understand the spiritual dimension of Papa's destructive acts, when he tears up Amaka's painting of Papa-Nnukwu and smashes his wife's figurines.[48] Part of what contributes to this extra dimension in the narrative, is the wealth of description given to material culture, such that thick description infuses furniture, fans, flowers, and figurines with something more than inanimate objecthood. When Papa breaks the figurines on the étagère, in the opening scene, what he has destroyed is the mother's shrine and her gods. This act of spiritual destruction, Cooper argues, provides a staging of the drama to unfold that is echoed in the curious choice of the French word "étagère" that is related to the English word "stage."[49] Unfortunately, Cooper reads this as a "radical" feminist move in which Adichie brings politics into the domestic sphere allegorically and symbolically and thus does not see the two realms as interconnected in the narrative.[50] "The daily life rituals and possessions," Cooper claims, "the special places in the home, in this view, are the basis and framework for political action."[51] In order to make this reading of the domestic sphere as allegorical for political action work, Cooper sees the thread of domestic abuse as what ties everything together. However, this overemphasis on family dynamics, instead of seeing multiple spheres of experience as interconnected and involving mutually reinforcing types of freedoms, leads her astray in the end, as we will see.

Adichie continues a common thread in feminist fiction and reveals the contradiction between Eugene's courage in his public life as an activist for democracy and recipient of an award from Amnesty World (*Hibiscus*, 5) while abusing his wife and children at home. There are scenes in which Eugene brutalizes his family that surpass any episodes of wife beating in *The Joys of Motherhood* or *Things Fall Apart*. One morning, he goes off in a rage, swings his belt in the air, strikes his daughter, and yells that the devil will not win (*Hibiscus*, 102–3); in another, he pours boiling water on the soles of Jaja's and Kambili's feet to punish them for walking into sin because they spent time with their "pagan" grandfather (*Hibiscus*, 193–5). The worst is when Eugene nearly beats Kambili to death in reaction to a dramatic sequence of events that trigger his wrath: first, Ade Coker, the editor of Eugene's opposition newspaper, is assassinated when a letter bomb explodes during breakfast at the kitchen table; next, in the familial realm, Kambili defies his orders not to entertain relations with her paternal grandfather because he is an animist and not a Catholic. Kambili disobeys her father when she brings home Amaka's unfinished painting of their grandfather, which has become a fetish object and Kambili's connection to her ancestor's chi.[52] Eugene takes out these multiple frustrations on his daughter, who ends up so seriously injured that she must be hospitalized. Eugene's sense of political impotence in the national arena and his self-hatred from internalizing racist attitudes about his culture of origin deform his role as father beyond any conventional scheme of patriarchal domination.

Adichie presents Kambili's private life as a teenage girl and introspective thoughts as interconnected with the Nigerian people's struggle for political freedoms and democracy in which men, including her father and Ade Coker, are active participants at the national level, as well as with the spiritual realm. Yet Cooper struggles to makes sense of how these spheres are interwoven: "There is no doubt that, at the deepest level, the novel is locating the stage centrally within the home, where men are judged politically in terms of their domestic relationships."[53] However, there are multiple, interconnected sources that shape Eugene's character and motivate his actions. The first source of his wrath is his willingness to take on the white man's image of himself as a black sinner, which leads Eugene to hate his skin color, reject his native language, and distance himself from kin who disagree with his wicked interpretation of Catholicism. The second source of his rage and abusive behavior comes from the deprivations of his instrumental freedoms as the editor of an independent newspaper engaged in the Nigerian people's struggle for democracy. It is evident from these interwoven layers of experience and the narrative sequence of events that Ade Coker's assassination is what triggers Eugene's downward spiral into rage and that self-hatred has prepared the terrain of his alienation. However, Cooper argues that it is Adichie who has a hard time harmonizing all these different threads: "But Adichie is also aware that at times this harmony is difficult to achieve and elsewhere in the novel she shows an understanding that the 'big' politics of the public, national level are concerned with *different* freedoms" (emphasis added).[54] Rather than see these "different" types of freedom as mutually interdependent, she claims: "If you are fighting for freedom from domestic abuse, if you are searching for an individual identity and voice without a stutter, liberated from terror at home, then a coup, or a rally in Government Square becomes less important, miniaturised by these bigger albeit purportedly smaller concerns."[55] Cooper sees this false distinction as setting up a polarization, rather than perceiving the hybrid nature of Adichie's figure of freedom as a carefully articulated interweaving of the "public" and "private" spheres, and thus she misses the point of Adichie's innovative feminism. *Purple Hibiscus* explicitly undertakes a revision of the unidimensional conception of freedom that had been dominated by men in the name of national liberation and the struggle for democracy.

Eugene's character, whose private alienated sense of self is revealed by the teenage narrator, contrasts sharply with Father Amadi. Although Amadi is a Catholic priest, he incarnates the opposite of Eugene's values: Amadi is warm, kind, and nurturing; he is proud of his African heritage and sings Igbo songs at home, in the car, and even during mass. Cooper interprets these Igbo songs, and all the Igbo words and names in the narrative, as metonymical referents to the invisible sphere of spiritual reference previously discussed. In psychological terms, Father Amadi is a healing presence in Kambili's life, which we see when he visits her in the hospital and when he takes her to get her hair braided, making her feel good about herself. At first Kambili is disoriented by Amadi's gentle, appealing masculinity that seems so unfamiliar to her, but he helps her come out of her shell and she smiles and laughs for the first time with him. The root of Father Amadi's strength is his ability to forge a synthesis of himself as an African man and as a Catholic who respects his culture of origin and his individual sense of self. Amadi becomes a missionary in Germany in a surprising reversal of the European colonial relationship that affirms the solidity of his personal faith and suggests that it is possible to acknowledge the fact that Europeans may have failed in how they practiced their faith in Africa without essentially discrediting the religion itself.

Kambili's mother appears to be the prototype of the passive woman who is disciplined into submission by a domineering husband until she decides to silently and slowly kill Eugene by adding poison to his tea. It is a desperate act of self-definition in which she exercises her substantive freedom by choosing to rid her family of the scourge of domestic abuse using the limited options available to her. While she does not have the force of character to defend her children or herself from being beaten, it would appear that the intensity of her despair ultimately pushes her over the edge. On two occasions, Beatrice is beaten so badly when she is pregnant that she loses her babies, and this theme draws our attention to the feminist symbolism attached to motherhood as we have seen in Emecheta's novel. When Beatrice is beaten the first time, Kambili hears the sickening sound of blows in her parents' bedroom and starts to count out numbers in an effort to focus her mind on something else. Eugene takes his wife to the clinic where it is confirmed that she has suffered a miscarriage, and what Kambili's notices when they return is how vacant her mother's eyes are, suggesting a deeper sense of lost vitality. The fact that the narrator describes how Kambili and Jaja clean up their mother's blood underscores how both children are intimately aware of the extent of the physical abuse (*Hibiscus*, 32–3). It is possible to read her behavior as a mother in keeping with conventional gender roles insofar as the two events that trigger Beatrice's decision to poison her husband relate to her compromised status as a mother unable to have more children. In addition, her devotion to the children she already has suggests that her maternal role as protector was also involved. It is painful, for instance, when Kambili rejects her mother's attempt to comfort her in the hospital; she turns her head and looks the other way when Beatrice starts making excuses for Eugene, saying that he had been by her side for the past three nights. Thus, Beatrice suffers a double sense of failure as a mother: she was not able to protect her children from abuse by their father while he was alive; and she loses two babies from miscarriages after being beaten herself. When the second miscarriage happens, after Ade Coker's assassination and Kambili's hospitalization, the narrator observes how her mother "looked possessed by a different demon," in a phrase that foreshadows the resolve building within her to kill Eugene and free them all from his tyranny (*Hibiscus*, 250).

Aunt Ifeoma, Eugene's sister, represents an entirely different kind of woman, continuing the feminist tradition of contrasting characters, as we saw in Mariama Bâ's novel, and reveals another way in which women have *options* and *choices*. Ifeoma's house is modest with low ceilings and used furniture, but the home she provides for her children is enchanted with warmth, laughter, and the aromas of curry and nutmeg. This contrasts with Beatrice's luxurious residence that seems like a cold fortress entirely governed by Eugene's temper and discipline, which is characterized, as we will see, by the traditional authority associated with red hibiscus bushes. Ifeoma is a university professor and widow who is raising her children alone, showing them wisdom, affection, and a sense of balance between defiance and obedience. What Kambili notices most about Ifeoma is her laughter; she describes how the aunt asks for peace and laughter during her morning prayers and laughs while showing off the purple hibiscus in her garden. The way Kambili associates the rare beauty of the flower with her aunt's laughter suggests that she sees inner peace and happiness as gifts to be cherished. Ifeoma lives free from fear; she is affectionate and even takes a flippant tone with her brother Eugene (*Hibiscus*, 77). As a mother, Ifeoma cultivates independence, cooperation, and mutual respect in her children. Like Father Amadi, her close personal friend, she is proud of her African heritage, which we see in several ways from the Igbo songs she sings with her children to her research position at an African Studies Institute. The values that guide Ifeoma's life embody the ethics of meaningful freedom and once Jaja and Kambili get a taste of this life, the experience has a profoundly liberating effect on them. It is precisely when his wife and children discover their capacity for resistance and begin to defy the father's tyrannical ways that things begin to fall apart for Eugene. Ifeoma is a strong woman who refuses to submit to her brother's abusive authority, and her actions inspire others to follow her example. The narrator explicitly foregrounds the roots of her family's liberation in the opening pages of the novel, "Nsukka started it all; Aunty Ifeoma's little garden next to the verandah of her flat in Nsukka began to lift the silence" (*Hibiscus*, 16). She concludes by saying that her familial memories started when all the hibiscuses in her front yard were a startling red.

Let us now consider Adichie's treatment of the symbolism of red and purple, as colors, and the intertextuality associated with flowers and freedom in African literature. Cooper identifies a compelling intertext in *Purple Hibiscus* with Ngũgĩ Wa Thiong'o's novel *Petals of Blood* and argues that it is possible to see the red associated with blood and revolutionary action in Ngũgĩ's novel as also related to the red hibiscus plants in Papa's garden. Papa frequently stands by these red hibiscus plants as he is giving orders; the red plant symbolizes the strict regime of papa's absolute authority under which the children have grown up that is defined by rigid masculinity and political engagement at the national level.[56] Cooper identifies another intertext in *Purple Hibiscus* with Alice Walker's novel *The Color Purple* (1982) which she associates with the "purple liberation" of Nsukka, feminism, and Ifeoma's experimental hibiscus flowers. It is Jaja who brings home the stalks of purple hibiscuses and thus he is associated, through this symbolism, with an alternative model of masculinity that is measured and balanced.[57] The color distinction Cooper proposes offers an important symbolic contrast, which helps us appreciate, in my view, Adichie's feminist revision of male definitions of freedom that had been dominated by armed conflict, blood, and violence. Building on Cooper's evidence of intertextuality with Ngũgĩ's novel where flowers are described as blooming, we may consider another significant intertextual reference to freedom and flowers in the canon of African literature in Ayi Kwei Armah's novel *The Beautyful Ones Are Not Yet Born*. As we will see in the next chapter, Armah's narrator similarly laments the limited achievements of the kind of freedom that crowds called for in the street, "It may be terrible to think that this was what all the speeches, all the hope, all the love of the first days was for. It is terrible, but it is not a lie" (*Beautyful Ones*, 90). All that remains for real progress to be made is for the people to wake up and to want to be whole again. Armah's novel also concludes with the promise of freedom – like the "single flower, solitary, unexplainable, and very beautiful" that was painted at the center of the inscription, "THE BEAUTYFUL ONES/ARE NOT YET BORN," on the back of the bus – that must be kept alive (*Beautyful Ones*, 183). This promise of meaningful freedom in the future symbolized with a flower is what the man contemplates as he walks home at the end of Armah's novel.

If Ifeoma were the narrator, it would be possible for a greater sense of achievement to be conveyed at the end of *Purple Hibiscus*. However, Adichie chose to have Kambili tell the story, and so freedom, in the end, seems to be a promise that should be realized in the not-so-distant future. The teenager's life is still a work in progress at the end of the novel. Unlike Ifeoma and Amadi, Kambili does not have a rooted sense of her African cultural heritage, so more effort will be necessary in this regard. The importance of establishing this connection for Kambili is revealed when she shows her persistent attachment to the unfinished portrait that her cousin Amaka had given her of their grandfather, and is beaten nearly to death by her father as a result. Pride in one's origins is of critical importance for every character in the novel, and those who fail to work out this aspect of their self-image suffer deeply. The fact that Kambili had always sought her father's approval leaves her with a shattered sense of self after he dies: "there were painfully scattered bits inside me that I could never put back because the places they fit into were gone" (*Hibiscus*, 290). The metaphor used here to suggest that the daughter's identity will have to be reconstructed in a new way brings together images from Achebe's phrase for dispossession as "things falling apart" and an element in Frantz Fanon's theory about the colonial self being shattered from the outside. The daughter will have to forge a new sense of her self free from the father and his destructive values in the shadow of colonial domination – or what Nandy called the postcolonial subject's "intimate enemy."[58] Father Amadi remains a healing influence in this regard, and Kambili says that she carries his letters around with her "because they are long and detailed, because they remind me of my worthiness, because they tug at my feelings" (*Hibiscus*, 303). He urges her not to seek the reasons for her suffering in the past and to move on with grace and self-acceptance.

The final scene in *Purple Hibiscus* looks to the future when Kambili makes plans with her mother as they leave the prison – this second evocation of prison in the novel is quite literal, whereas the first reference to prison was a trope for existential unfreedom within the home – where Jaja is doing time for his father's death because he claimed responsibility to protect his mother. Kambili wants to plant beautiful flowers and visit her aunt in America; these two desires project into the future the possibility of experimenting with the inclusive idea of multiple freedoms – previously evoked as the freedom "to be and to do" – and were compared to the rare beauty of the purple hibiscus. Although Kambili stays in love with Amadi after he leaves and seems willing to share him with God for the time being, she makes progress with her mother whose smile inspires her daughter's laughter as they imagine Jaja's future freedom.

Conclusion

The way women have written about gender from feminist viewpoints expanded the parameters of what could be said about freedom in Africa after the first phase of decolonization. We have seen that early feminist fiction focused on the marriage plot in *So Long a Letter*, *Occasion for Loving*, and *When Rain Clouds Gather*. These narratives tend to foreground the private self, intimate relations, and the domestic sphere. Although an individual's choice of spouse is at the center of the story, these narratives represent this substantive freedom as embedded in a broader network of social, cultural, and political contexts, where different types of freedom are interdependent and mutually reinforcing. Feminist engagements with gender and freedom have dealt with interrogating options for women in a range of different political contexts, including criticism of racism in southern Africa, criticism of patriarchy and modern Islam in Algeria, and a sense of national dispossession in Nigeria under dictatorship. Our theoretical challenge is to articulate the nature of these connections; our critical challenge is in explicating how they are creatively represented in women's narratives. I have argued against the grain of feminist theory by claiming that the politics of love in African women's writing is not an allegorical transposition for national politics and that the intimate sphere and gender identity are embedded within multiple spheres of experience. I do not read representations of domestic life as "standing in" for male-centered politics at the national level, as Susan Andrade and Brenda Cooper have argued. I propose that women, in particular, were more aware of the multifaceted aspects of freedom precisely because of their subjugation within patriarchal societies.

We considered how explicit and sustained engagement with freedom has been of central importance to canonical writing and filmmaking by African women.

Instrumental. Instrumental freedoms in feminist discourse tends to focus on the deprivation of individual rights – with some nuance regarding civil society and instrumental actions in terms of institutions and spaces of confinement that deprive men and women of rights. In Gordimer's *Occasion for Loving*, we see how legal interdictions under apartheid prevented Gideon from studying abroad and marrying Ann Davis. In more abstract terms, the legacy of Sharpeville hangs over the narrative and reminds us of the increasing constraints on black freedoms at universities, in the court room, and in every space subject to apartheid's control. In Head's *When Rain Clouds Gather*, Makhaya immigrates to Botswana to escape the "howling inferno" in South Africa under apartheid. We know that he was arrested for blowing up a white-owned power plant and spent two years in prison before going into exile. Thus, he is involved in exercising his instrumental freedom through political engagement and was subsequently jailed by the state. In Emecheta's *The Joys of Motherhood,* the theme of slavery finally emerges and women are depicted as chattel owned by men. This kind of tyrannical rule by men is further developed with other references to slavery and to scenes, such as when Agbadi hurts Ona in his courtyard in an abusive and public display of his masculinity. This deprives women of their voices and their rights, as we see when Nnu Ego is unable to make a case for herself in the court room. In Djebar's *So Vast a Prison,* the metaphor of the prison is most evident as a symbol of the deprivation of instrumental freedoms. But this trope is also used to represent transgression in spatial terms as women seek to enter new spaces, uncharted territory and to open new possibilities. In Adichie's *Purple Hibiscus*, Ade Coker's assassination is an excellent example of the state's violent repression of a journalist's free speech, which is an obvious deprivation of his instrumental freedom. More generally, the "freedom to do" also refers to other instrumental freedoms such as the right to express dissent, to organize, and to take action.

Substantive. The kinds of substantive freedoms that we have encountered in this chapter pertain largely to an individual's capacity to make choices (i.e., spouse, education) to improve lives with an emphasis on subjective longing for self-definition. In Gordimer's *Occasion for Loving*, not until the law forbidding interracial marriage was struck down could men and women enjoy the freedom to marry irrespective of race. The narrative, more generally, was marked by emotions of fear and unfulfilled longing that were expressions of the persistent human aspiration to have choices, the desire to live a life worth living in accordance with an individual's values. In Head's *When Rain Clouds Gather*, when Makhaya asks Paulina to marry him at the end of the novel, the new couple is presented as the future embodiment of an egalitarian society. This was setup with Head's idealization of them as the "perfect man/husband" and the "perfect woman/wife" within the utopic community she imagines in this narrative inspired by grassroots, cultural feminism. The narrative thrust of Head's novel involves recreating a community where individuals are free to choose. In Emecheta's *The Joys of Motherhood*, the author sets up a contrast between Adaku, who is more joyful and financially independent, and Nnu Ego, who tried to live a virtuous life, but dies at the side of the road with no one to hold her hand. These contrasting characters, like Ramatoulaye and Aïssatou in *So Long a Letter*, invite us to reflect critically on the limited options and substantive freedoms available to women. In Djebar's *So Vast a Prison*, we see a contrast between T in Hinan, the beautiful, strong Tuareg princess, and Djebar's description of the veiled woman against the backdrop of Algeria's civil war during the 1990s. Her excavation of this ancient cultural history was done in order to propose a wider array of references and therefore choices for Algerian women to define their lives as they have reason to value. In Adichie's *Purple Hibiscus*, in addition to the freedom to be and to do, we see Beatrice decide to poison her husband in a radical act of self-definition that liberates herself and her family from his tyrannical abuse. As was the case in Emecheta's novel, the dramatic dénouement in *Purple Hibiscus* calls attention, once again, to the limited options available to Beatrice.

Existential. In terms of existential freedoms, in Gordimer's *Occasion for Loving*, when Gideon goes for a walk on the beach and does not come back for a long time, Ann waits in fear, which takes on an existential dimension after all the running and hiding they have been through since they left the Stilwell's house. In Head's *When Rain Clouds Gather*, Makhaya experiences moments of existential liberation when he meets Gilbert Balfour (a white man who is not racist) and develops a friendship with him, and when he meets with Mma-Millipede who shares the gospel in Tswana and dissolves the walls Makhaya had erected inside himself. In Emecheta's *The Joys of Motherhood*, Nnu Ego cannot feel "complete" without having a son and continues to feel like a prisoner of her own flesh and blood until the day she dies. So, Nnu Ego is unfortunately defined by the persistence of her existential unfreedom. In Djebar's *So Vast a Prison*, we see a woman's desire to exist free from the orthodoxies of puritanical patriarchal Islam. Although the longing is existential and intangible, fulfilling this wish would involve a range of practical things from a woman's desire to move about freely, to not wear a veil, to work outside the home, to speak a foreign language, to be able to divorce her husband, to know about other cultural traditions, and to find inspiration in them. In Adichie's *Purple Hibiscus*, existential freedom is the "freedom to be"; the freedom to forge a creative synthesis between Igbo beliefs and Catholicism, and to develop a workable identity free from the kind of colonial alienation that plagued Eugene, as Aunty Ifeoma has done and as Kambili is in the process of working out for herself. This freedom is the capacity to enjoy a sense of self free from alienation, which is as rare and beautiful as a purple hibiscus.

Notes

1. For an overview of the many theorists and critics who have written about how women sought to expand the parameters of what could be said about social justice and freedom to include the social and domestic spheres was an explicitly feminist move, see Merry Wiesner-Hanks's summary in *Gender in History: Global Perspectives* (West Sussex: Wiley-Blackwell, 2012), pp. 158–66.
2. Elleke Boehmer, *Stories of Women: Gender and Narrative in the Postcolonial Nation* (Manchester: Manchester University Press, 2009), p. 5.
3. Boehmer, *Stories of Women*, p. 5.
4. Susan Andrade, *The Nation Writ Small: African Fictions and Feminisms*, 1958–1988 (Durham, NC: Duke University Press, 2011), p. 1.
5. See Elleke Boehmer's introduction to *The Joys of Motherhood* (Portsmouth: Heinemann, 2008).
6. Dominic Head, *Nadine Gordimer* (Cambridge: Cambridge University Press, 1994), pp. 5–7.
7. Head, *Nadine Gordimer*, p. xii.

8. Stephen Clingman, *The Novels of Nadine Gordimer: History from the Inside* (Boston, MA: University of Massachusetts Press, 1992), pp. 74 et seq.
9. Cooper, *Africa since 1940*, p. 74.
10. For a theoretical discussion of dispossession and resistance in South Africa, see Anne McClintock's *Imperial Leather: Race, Gender and Sexuality in the Colonial Contest* (New York, NY: Routledge, 1995). For a discussion of this history and its repercussions in the present, see Frederick Cooper's *African since 1940*. And for a discussion of the history of dispossession and the ANC's organization of resistance to it, see Anthony Butler's *The Idea of the ANC* (Athens, OH: Ohio University Press, 2012).
11. See Cooper, *Africa since 1940*; the most recent census data from 2011 available online at www.statssa.gov.za/?page_id=3839 (consulted May 13, 2015).
12. See Butler, *The Idea of the ANC*. I should also add that this was a topic of lively debate during my visit to the African Studies Center at the University of Cape Town in South Africa in the fall of 2014.
13. Clingman, *The Novels of Nadine Gordimer*, p. 75.
14. For historical background, see Clingman, *The Novels of Nadine Gordimer: History from the Inside* (Boston, MA/Amherst: University of Massachusetts Press, 1992) second edition.
15. Clingman, *The Novels of Nadine Gordimer*, p. 81
16. Quoted in Head, *Nadine Gordimer*, p. 66.
17. Head, *Nadine Gordimer*, p. 31.
18. Clingman, *The Novels of Nadine Gordimer*, p. 76. Lewis Nkosi describes these mixed love affairs as "nightmares of worry and effort to have some privacy." It has been speculated that the story in this novel may be based on the real-life experience of a friend of Gordimer's Can Themba who was in love with a white Englishwoman, but trapped in South Africa under apartheid.
19. Head, *Nadine Gordimer*, p. 68.
20. Clingman, *The Novels of Nadine Gordimer*, p. 89 et seq.
21. Head, *Nadine Gordimer*, p. 76.
22. Clingman, *The Novels of Nadine Gordimer*, p. 78.
23. The comparison to Albert Camus seems particularly à propos given her interest in existentialism and the ethics of engagement.
24. Head, *Nadine Gordimer*, p. 128.
25. Ibid., p. 134.
26. This novelist's biography is particularly important for understanding her writing. To start with, see "Bessie Emery Head." *Encyclopaedia Britannica*. Encyclopaedia Britannica Online Academic Edition. Encyclopædia Britannica Inc., 2014. Web. 08 February 2014. For more, see Joyce Johnson, *Bessie Head: The Road to Peace of Mind: A Critical Appreciation* (Newark, NJ: University of Delaware Press, 2008).
27. Huma Ibrahim, *Bessie Head: Subversive Identities in Exile* (Charlottesville, VA: University Press of Virginia), p. 63.
28. The way Nadine Gordimer sets up the narrative in *Occasion for Loving* with a thoroughly detailed representation of the white liberal's cocoon, sealed off

from the virulent racism mixed couples were likely to encounter at the end of a white farmer's hunting rifle in the middle of a field or alongside the road, contrasts sharply with Bessie Head's dream of migrating to an integrated community in order to escape from the "howling inferno" that was South Africa in the 1950s and 1960s. James Garrett takes up the politics of representing communities in his article: "Writing Community: Bessie Head and the Politics of Narrative" by James M. Garrett, *Research in African Literatures*, Vol. 30, No. 2 (Summer, 1999), pp. 122–35. See also: Lewis Nkosi, *Tasks and Masks: Themes and Styles of African Literature* (Essex: Longman, 1981).

29. Ibrahim, *Bessie Head*, p. 77.
30. Boehmer, Introduction, *The Joys of Motherhood.*
31. Buchi Emecheta earned a B.Sc. in Sociology at the University of London in 1972. For more on Emecheta's biography, see Brennan, Carol. "Emecheta, Buchi 1944–." *Contemporary Black Biography*. 2002. Encyclopedia.com. (February 8, 2014). For Florence Stratton's discussion of Emecheta's emergence as a writer on the African literary scene, see "'Their New Sister.' Buchi Emecheta and the contemporary African literary tradition," pp. 108–32.
32. For Stratton's discussion of Emecheta and her novel *The Joys of Motherhood* in the context of her awareness of a new "literary sisterhood" within a self-conscious female literary tradition, see "'Their New Sister.' Buchi Emecheta and the contemporary African literary tradition," pp. 108–32. For a more theoretical engagement with Emecheta writing that explores marriage and motherhood in terms of identity and self-definition, see Juliana Makuchi Nfah-Abbenyi, *Gender in African Women's Writing: Identity, Sexuality, and Difference*, chapter 2 "(Re)Constructing Identity and Subjectivity: Buchi Emecheta, Ama Ata Aidoo, Tsitsi Dangarembga," pp. 35–72. For a more recent assessment of Emecheta's contribution to literary debates on the "feminine condition" in African literature, see Nana Wilson-Tagoe, "The African novel and the feminine condition," in *The Cambridge Companion to the African Novel* (Cambridge: Cambridge University Press, 2009), pp. 177–93.
33. Stratton observes male critics' response to Emecheta's novel that have asserted that her male characters appear stereotypical, rather than realistic, and reflect her determination to cast them in a derogatory light in "'Their New Sister.' Buchi Emecheta and the contemporary African literary tradition," p. 117.
34. See Stratton's review of the critical reception of Emecheta and her novel *The Joys of Motherhood*: "'Their New Sister.' Buchi Emecheta and the contemporary African literary tradition," pp. 108–32.
35. Boehmer, Introduction, *The Joys of Motherhood*, p. iii.
36. Ibid., p. iv.
37. Tsitsi Dangarembga, *Nervous Conditions* (Oxfordshire: Ayebia Clarke Publishing, 2004) with a preface by Kwame Anthony Appiah.
38. Some years later we find a very similar situation that tests women's ability and/or willingness to conform to patriarchal expectations in Tsitsi Dangarembga's *Nervous Conditions* (Seattle, WA: Seal Press, 1988). In this novel, a young girl gets to go to school only because her older brother dies and she gets to take

his place. We witness the British colonial influence on both the educational structures and the church in colonial Rhodesia. The gender roles within this colonial scheme involve the school master's wife, who is educated but slow to develop a critical awareness of her subjugation at home. Dangarembga depicts the difficulties of growing up in between two cultures – traditional African culture, associated with cooking and raising children, and modern European culture, where women smoke, wear jeans, and travel. The status of African women under these cross-cultural circumstances is seen as being brought up for renegotiation. Very often, the point of resistance remains: The daughter's willingness and the mother's courage to stand up to the repressive patriarchal father. For more, see Nfah-Abbenyi, *Gender in African Women's Writing*, "(Re)Constructing Identity and Subjectivity: Buchi Emecheta, Ama Ata Aidoo, Tsitsi Dangarembga," pp. 35–72.

39. Her contributions are distinctive in at least three ways: first, her training as an historian gives her stories depth and context; second, the fact that her family was involved in shaping Algerian history through their participation in anticolonial resistance blurs the lines between history and autobiography; and third, her parents withdrew her from koranic school, did not have her wear a veil, and allowed her to attend French colonial school as the only girl in her father's classroom. Although the privileges afforded to her came with various challenges, Djebar assumed the responsibility of being the first Algerian woman to do many things – attend the École Normale Supérieure and be elected to the Académie Française – with grace and wisdom.
40. There is a substantial and growing body of literary and film criticism devoted to the work of Assia Djebar. In terms of literature, an excellent source is John Erickson's *Islam and Postcolonial Narrative*, especially the chapter "Women's Voices and Woman's Space in Assia Djebar's *L'Amour, la fantasia*," where there is some discussion of the themes of freedom and *Vaste est la prison* (Cambridge: Cambridge University Press, 1998), pp. 37–65. Another useful reference is Mildred Mortimer, *Maghrebian Mosaic: A Literature in Transition* (Boulder, CO: Lynne Reiner, 2001), especially Mortimer's essay "Reappropriating the Gaze in Assia Djebar's Fiction and Film," pp. 213–28. For more discussion of the Algerian Quarter of which *Vaste est la prison* is a part, see Mildred Mortimer's "Assia Djebar's *Algerian Quartet:* A Study in Fragmented Autobiography," *Research in African Literature*, vol. 28, no. 2 (Summer 1997), pp. 102–17. For more theoretical discussion of selfhood and Islamic traditions, see Etin Anwar, *Gender and Self in Islam* (New York, NY: Routledge, 2006) and Anouar Majid, *Unveiling Traditions: Postcolonial Islam in a Polycentric World* (Durham, NC: Duke University Press, 2000). For a sustained discussion of freedom in the works of Djebar see Phyllis Taoua, "Of Prisons and Freedom: Liberation in the Work of Assia Djebar," *World Literature Today* (November 2012), pp. 12–18.
41. It should be noted that the Tuareg people, who have lived in the Sahara Desert for thousands of years, observe gender customs that are far more favorable to women than many of the Islamic cultural practices that were imported into North Africa after the sixth century. For instance, women do

not wear veils, whereas Tuareg men wear turbans. Similarly, Tuareg women participate in the Cure Salée festival in the fall where they wear make-up and jewelry and parade on their donkeys in a beauty pageant that bears no resemblance to the puritanical ethic governing the confinement and concealment of the female body. Finally, Tuareg women are considered the owners of the family's tent and cooking tools, so if a man wants a divorce, he takes his sandals and camel saddle and leaves without dispossessing the mother of the household of her property. The Tuareg are related to the Berber people in Algeria – the Berbers became sedentary when they began practicing agriculture, whereas the Tuareg retained their nomadic lifestyle.

42. Regrettably, the Tuareg in northern Mali joined alliances with Islamic extremists in the region during an armed confrontation with the military junta that ousted President Amadou Touré in March 2012. For more, see Chapter 3 on Global Africa.
43. In addition to the article by Mildred Mortimer that deals with the gaze in Djebar' film and fiction, see also: Réda Bensmaïa, *Experimental Nations: Or, the Invention of the Maghreb* (Princeton, NJ: Princeton University Press, 2003), especially Chapter 5, "(Hi)stories of Expatriation," Assia Djebar's *La nouba des femmes de Mont Chenoua*, Introduction to the Cinematic Fragment," pp. 83–97.
44. For an excellent discussion of gender and Islam from a feminist point of view, see Leila Ahmed, *Women and Gender in Islam: Historical Roots of a Modern Debate* (New Haven, CT: Yale University Press, 1992) and Fatima Mernissi *Beyond the Veil: Male-Female Dynamics in Modern Muslim Society* (Bloomington, IN: Indiana University Press, 1987).
45. For background information on Igbo culture and Chinua Achebe's novel *Things Fall Apart*, see Abiola Irele's introduction and notes in the Norton Critical edition, as well as the group of essays in the section "The Igbo-African Background" pp. 221–58 in *Things Fall Apart* Edited by Abiola Irele (New York, NY/London: W. W. Norton & Co, 2009).
46. Frantz Fanon used the metaphor of the black man wearing a white mask to capture the psychological alienation experienced within colonial culture in his seminal set of essays *Black Skin, White Masks*. Some years later, Ashish Nandy added the idea of an "intimate enemy" that persists within the formerly colonized's sense of self, even after official decolonization takes place in a provocative set of essays, *The Intimate Enemy*. For a more thorough discussion, see Chapter 1.
47. Brenda Cooper, "Breaking Gods & Petals of Purple. Chimamanda Ngozi Adichie's *Purple Hibiscus*," *A New Generation of African Writers: Migration, Material Culture & Language* (James Currey/University of KwaZulu-Natal Press, 2008), p. 113.
48. Cooper, *A New Generation of African Writers*, p. 111.
49. Ibid., p. 115.
50. Ibid., p. 117.
51. Ibid., p. 117.
52. Ibid., p. 118.

53. Ibid., p. 128.
54. Ibid., p. 129.
55. Ibid., p. 129
56. Ibid., p. 126.
57. Ibid., pp. 124–5.
58. Nandy, *The Intimate Enemy*.

Country of Grief and Grace
Antjie Krog

(d) because of you
this country no longer lies
between us but within

it breathes becalmed
after being wounded
in its wondrous throat

in the cradle of my skull
it sings, it ignites
my tongue, my inner ear, the cavity of heart
shudders toward the outline
new in soft intimate clicks and gutturals

of my soul the retina learns to expand
daily because by a thousand stories
I was scorched

a new skin.

I am changed forever. I want to say:
forgive me
forgive me
forgive me
You whom I have wronged, please
take me
with you.

3 The Nation

From Liberation to Meaningful Freedom

> In the victorious convergence of the diverse contributions to the building of the road we have walked, lies our hope for a future path together as one nation.
>
> *Nelson Mandela*

I went to Yaoundé, Cameroon, with questions for Mongo Beti about his political engagement during the 1950s and came back with more than I expected. During my visit in 1996, an early draft of *Trop de soleil tue l'amour* (1999; in English, "too much sunshine kills love," not yet translated), was sitting on the author's large, uncluttered desk at the back of his new bookstore Peuples Noirs. Beti had recently returned to Cameroon after living in voluntary exile in France for three decades. I was interested in discussing his political engagement as a young man for my first book, *Forms of Protest,* and with the help of his wife, Odile, we spent three hours reconstructing a fairly detailed account of his post-war positions on engagement, realism, and French intellectual life. That afternoon, while we revisited the polemic around Camara Laye's novel *Enfant noir* and Jean-Paul Sartre's presence in the emerging field of anticolonial thought during the 1950s and 1960s, he also shared his concerns about corruption and violence in Cameroon as well as various projects, since returning, from growing tomatoes in Mbalmayo to starting a radio station. Two aspects of how this retired teacher talked about his novel in progress stood out for me in the summer of 1996: his fascination with, and attempt to capture, the way people spoke French on the street, to which he did not have access while in France, and how he found himself grappling with the reasons for the absence of shared prosperity and social justice in his homeland that seemed far more complex observed firsthand in his day-to-day life. He talked about discovering a new sense of belonging within his community of origin – not without its frustrations – and actively working out a mode of representing what he called the "Francophone African Republics," which are quite similar to Latin American "Banana Republics." I learned as much, if not more, from the unexpected privilege of witnessing such a fertile and creative time in his life as I did from his answers to my pre-formulated research questions as well as from the conversation we initiated that summer which continued until his death in 2001.

A little older than Sony Labou Tansi, Beti came of age under French colonial rule at a time when Ruben Um Nyobé and others in the Union des Populations du Cameroun (UPC) were formulating an ideology of anticolonial nationalism and a popular political discourse within the ranks of Cameroon's most important opposition party. After the French government supplanted the only armed insurrection in French-administered, sub-Saharan Africa and assassinated leaders of the UPC, Beti chose to live in France instead of making a life in Ahmadou Ahidjo's Cameroon. The history of the derailment of decolonization in Cameroon and the accumulation of wealth by gatekeeping dictators became the central preoccupation for Beti while in exile. I had read a lot about this painful history before meeting Beti in Yaoundé, but it was sobering to see for myself the brutal consequences of the deferral of meaningful freedom in Cameroon.[1] One afternoon, I attended a roundtable discussion on freedom of the press with Beti and his wife. Initially I was impressed by the appearance of expanding freedoms because of the frank debate at this event about the critical importance of an independent press with journalists who had, themselves, been detained as political prisoners. However, just two weeks later, men assumed to be Paul Biya's (the president of Cameroon) thugs attacked the editor of La Génération, Vianney Ombe Nzana, (who had hosted the roundtable) with machetes as he was leaving his office – the day before, he had published an article exposing the state's corruption. It was an eye-opening experience to see the journalist again, only days later, under such drastically different circumstances. He had come sharply up against the cold fact that Cameroonians who tested the limits of freedom of expression still lived in fear of violent repression – the harassment of activists continues today.

Even before this happened, Mongo Beti had told me stories about how Biya's regime used repression and violence to intimidate the opposition, including an account of how Biya's secret service physically assaulted him along the road from Mbalmayo to Yaoundé. One evening the president's motorcade was passing along this road into the capital city at dusk, and his security forces had stopped all traffic, including Beti's vehicle. When the nation's most famous writer joined in the popular chorus decrying the annoying interruption, Biya's men (whom Beti called a "parallel police force") struck the side of Beti's head, hitting his temple, and then kicked him in the ribs and stomach after he fell to the ground. Bystanders intervened and saved him from the assailants.

Figure 3.1 Round table in Yaoundé with Mongo Beti. Cameroon, 1996
Source: Photo by Phyllis Taoua

There are many scenes of violence in the street in African literature and films, such as the opening sequence to Jean-Marie Teno's film *Afrique, je te plumerai* (1992; *Africa, I will fleece you*), and allegorical scenes of political dispossession that take place in the street, as in the opening sequence of Ousmane Sembène's film *Xala* (1975). There are also scenes of writers and journalists being beaten, tortured, detained, as in Beti's novel *Trop de soleil tue l'amour* (1999), Ngũgĩ wa Thiong'o's prison memoir *Detained* (1981), Wole Soyinka's *The Man Died* (1972), and in Assia Djebar's *Le blanc de l'Algérie* (1995; *Algerian White* 2003). The prevalence of scenes in which politically engaged writers, filmmakers, journalists, and activists are deprived of their freedom of expression in public places testifies to a popular awareness of both the deferral of meaningful freedom and the dangers of dissidence. Nowhere is the fact that the dynamic relationship between resistance and repression has largely shaped the struggle for freedom in Africa more evident than in the history of national liberation movements.

While a nearly exclusive focus on national liberation during the process of decolonization may have made practical, strategic sense for organizing collective protest, once it became clear that a struggle for meaningful freedom would continue after independence, the language of freedom needed to evolve – and it did. There can be little doubt that national experience remains of crucial importance in the early twenty-first century both in the real world of governments and political policies and in terms of how writers and filmmakers represent their past struggles and future aspirations. Yet while genuine national sovereignty was and continues to be, in my view, indispensable to achieving meaningful freedom, the nation is just *one of several interconnected spheres of experience* linking the intimate self, with gender identity, with global capital, and the spiritual realm. As we have seen, the kinds of freedom I discuss – instrumental, substantive, and existential – are operative in important ways in each of these interconnected spheres, although the realm of national experience has historically received the most critical attention in relation to the idea of freedom because it dominated the discourse of decolonization. Benedict Anderson, for instance, presents national sovereignty as the "ultimate gage" and "emblem of freedom" from dynastic rule in Europe and as an ideal to which those subjugated by colonial rule collectively aspired in *Imagined Communities. Reflections on the Origin and Spread of Nationalism* (1983). While Anderson's bold claims were not untrue, the exclusive focus on the nation would prove problematic for the formerly colonized with time. James Ferguson aptly observes the limitations of this singular focus in *Global Shadows. Africa in the Neoliberal World Order* (2006) when he says that seeing national sovereignty as "synonymous with dignity, freedom and empowerment" had become a trap that was impeding a more complex, nuanced anthropological discussion of wealth, power, and well-being in Africa after independence. Since, in the history of European imperialism in Africa, the idea of the nation and the discourse of national liberation have to a significant extent defined the language of freedom, it is time to consider how this language evolved and is shifting in its importance as new linkages are formed in the Global South.

Let us briefly consider the history of the idea of the nation as it is somewhat paradoxical that the idea of the nation that emerged in the United States and Europe after the Enlightenment informed Western imperial conquest of overseas colonies *and* the anticolonial nationalism that developed in protest against it. From the idea of the nation as an imagined political community in Western culture flowed the inspiration for anticolonial nationalism that became the organizing principle of collective protest in Africa. In order to understand how the idea of the nation was used in the discourse of African liberation, I will consider how two iconic figures – Frantz Fanon and Nelson Mandela – each deployed this discourse in different ways. Understanding the parameters of the performance of the discourse of liberation will allow us to make sense of the specific ways in which leaders, intellectuals, and artists subsequently responded to challenges and disappointments after independence. It has already been well established that national liberation produced uneven results and different forms of political sovereignty from a multiracial democracy in South Africa, to brittle, embattled sovereignty in gatekeeper states such as in Nigeria and Cameroon, as well as failed states, as we have seen in Somalia.

The rest of the chapter discusses how writers and filmmakers have responded to the fact that the promise of freedom has been so unevenly fulfilled and to creating a context for understanding the social and political implications of this history on the present. In anticipation of the next chapter, I will be mindful of the fact that as global capital expands, the nation-state has become the subject of intense critical debate about the possibilities for effective political intervention within, between, or beyond national boundaries.

Of Nations and Nationalisms

Histories of the idea of the nation often start with the French philosopher Ernest Renan's lecture "What is a nation?" given at the Sorbonne in 1882.[2] In his famous address, Renan described nationality as rooted in shared experiences in the past and the desire to live together in the future – a political idea which came to define the French model, in contrast to the German idea of the nation that was, at the time, more focused on birth and blood relations.[3] Renan proposed:

> A nation is a soul, a spiritual principle. Only two things, actually, constitute this soul, this spiritual principle. One is the past, the other is in the present. One is the possession in common of a rich legacy of remembrance; the other is the actual consent, the desire to live together, the will to continue to value the heritage which all hold in common. Man, sirs, does not improvise. The nation, even as the individual, is the end product of a long period of work, sacrifice and devotion. The worship of ancestors is understandably justifiable, since our ancestors have made us what we are.[4]

This definition of the nation is Janus-faced; Renan looks to both the past and present in his description of the people's sense of a common heritage and their consent to continue to work and sacrifice for the community. The comparisons of the nation to a "soul" and a "spiritual principle" convey an intangible feeling of solidarity that is socially persuasive and inspirational in terms of an individual's psychological identification. Renan's late-nineteenth-century defense of the nation was a wide-ranging and comprehensive statement that helped shape a malleable and powerful national discourse at a time when European imperial conquest was on the march. It was just a few years later in 1884–5 that Europe's leaders convened at the Berlin Conference to consult and agree among themselves on how to partition Africa into territories for colonial development and exploitation. A core component of European-style nationalism during the late nineteenth and twentieth centuries – including French, British, and Afrikaner nationalisms with variations on a central theme – was the claim to be advancing through a historical phase of development.[5] The French people's "work, sacrifice, and devotion" was inspired as much by worship of their Gaulois ancestors as by their belief in progress together in the future that was worthy of their investment.

Nationalism as a rationale for imperialism made possible by the expansion of capitalism after the industrialization of Europe can be seen as "Marxism's great historical failure," to borrow Tom Nairn's phrase.[6] We might say that nationalism's success in defining conflicts in terms of exclusion and inclusion within communities during the twentieth century stems from Marxism's failure during the previous century to make socioeconomic class a more compelling factor. During the twentieth century, nationalism inspired people to work and die for their country far more effectively than Marxist philosophies of class-based revolution had mobilized citizens to agitate for economic justice. Yet Karl Marx had anticipated some forty years earlier, in 1848, that: "The need of a constantly expanding market for its products chases the bourgeoisie over the whole surface of the globe. It must nestle everywhere, settle everywhere, establish connections everywhere."[7] So, if the spread of capitalism was destined to go global, why the need to differentiate between different *national* bourgeoisies as European leaders did, for instance, in Berlin when they created the Belgian Congo and French West Africa?

An astute observer of nationalism's origins in Europe and its appeal to others around the world, Anderson addresses these issues in his book *Imagined Communities. Reflections on the Origin and Spread of Nationalism.* Anderson defines the nation as "an imagined political community – and imagined as both inherently limited and sovereign."[8] Anderson goes on to elaborate on the concepts in his definition by saying that: (1) communities are to be distinguished, not by how false or genuine they seem, but by the *style* in which they are imagined; (2) communities are *limited* insofar as no nation imagines itself as coterminous with all of mankind; (3) communities are *sovereign* because the concept of the nation came about in an age in which Enlightenment and Revolution were destroying the legitimacy of the divinely-ordained, hierarchical dynastic realm and the gage and emblem of that *freedom* was the sovereign state; and (4) it is imagined as a community because, regardless of the actual inequality and exploitation that may exist, the nation is always conceived of as a deep, horizontal *comradeship* and preserving this fraternity is a cause worth dying for.[9] It was during the late nineteenth and early twentieth centuries that European nations expanded their sense of community through imperial conquest and developed their markets and infrastructure through the exploitation of colonial labor and resources.

An innovative observation that Anderson contributed was that new modes of communication brought about by increased access to printing presses and the growth of market capitalism helped make the imagination of national communities possible. He proposed that nations are cultural artefacts of a particular kind linking fraternity, power, and time in a way that allowed people to think about themselves and relate to others simultaneously. As it turned out, the print-languages involved in the expansion of European national communities – French, English, and Spanish – were also vehicular languages in the colonial territories, which enabled cultural connections around the world, and across time and space. This was one of many unintended consequences of European imperialism. Historians of the emergence of anticolonial nationalism in the non-Western world have frequently noted, as Anderson does, how the literature and ideology of Negritude in French inspired a new sense of community based on the shared experience of dispossession under colonial rule.[10] Anderson observed, in this regard, how anticolonial nationalism was "a response to the new-style global imperialism made possible by the achievements of industrial capitalism."[11] The early years of anticolonial resistance witnessed the emergence of forms of protest that fostered an antiracist solidarity and that were pan-African in scope, which were eventually overtaken by a discourse of emancipation derived from colonial ideas of the nation, progress, and development during the 1940s and 1950s. It remains to be seen whether these early forms of pan-African protest can be recuperated and adapted in our global era. While the colonial school house and opportunities for employment as translators, teachers or administrators within the European colonial scheme created the possibility for "natives" to imagine themselves as "nationals," Anderson describes the early spokespersons for anticolonial nationalism as "lonely, bilingual intelligentsias unattached to sturdy local bourgeoisies."[12] I would like to set aside, for the moment, the question of "sturdy local bourgeoisies" and take up the issue of nationalism's spokespersons in order to understand how the discourse of nationalism was used to inspire collective action in Africa.

Two Pioneers of African National Liberation

Fanon and Mandela were among the leading spokesmen for national liberation in Africa during the twentieth century. Born in 1925, Fanon grew up with Martinican Creole and French on the West Indian island of Martinique. He went on to earn a medical degree in psychiatry in Lyons, France, and to practice at a clinic in Blida-Joinville, Algeria, before joining the National Liberation Front. Born in 1918, Mandela grew up in the Transkei, a former Bantustan bordering South Africa, with isiXhosa, Afrikaans, and English. He went on to earn a law degree, open a law office in Johannesburg, South Africa, with his friend Oliver Tambo, and joined the African National Congress. Fanon and Mandela both had access, inside and outside the classroom, to what Anderson calls "models of nation, nation-ness, and nationalism distilled from the turbulent, chaotic experiences of more than a century of American and European history."[13] The styles in which Fanon and Mandela defended the cause of national liberation varied in tone and emphasis reflecting their individual and social backgrounds, but, in both cases, their feelings of political solidarity reflected a deep comradeship worth dying for.

National liberation became *the* organizing principle of collective protest in Africa for the generation of leaders and activists who came of age after World War II. In historically important speeches, we can observe how the discourse of nationalism was used to articulate and defend the principles of protest in real time while the struggle for freedom was underway. Both Fanon and Mandela were rhetorically persuasive speakers, politically inspirational, and directly involved in the struggle as members of nationalist organizations. Yet they had unique viewpoints that came, in part, from their different professions and personalities. Fanon often sounded like a psychiatrist and digressed into self-descriptive therapeutic assessment, as Freud also did, whereas Mandela emphasized legal rights, equal opportunities, and inclusive principles of democracy from the standpoint of a lawyer. Both men honed their language as the ideas and values of their nationalist platforms evolved in response to the violence and repression they encountered. On the one hand, the reach of their influence as spokesmen is a testament to their unique gifts as well as to the currency of national liberation as a discourse with relevance beyond the borders of their respective battles in Algeria and South Africa. On the other hand, their fame and influence also demonstrates the powerful conceptual currency that came with speaking the language of nationalism – a language that both colonizer and colonized understood – which, in the end, proved to be a double-edged sword.

It was in Rome in 1959 that Fanon gave his famous address entitled, "On National Culture," at a meeting organized by the Society of African Culture. The speech, delivered when Fanon was 34 years old, is a distillation of his thinking on the challenges and promises of nationalism for African liberation at that time. Founded in 1956, this society consisted of prominent members of the French-speaking intelligentsia from Africa and the diaspora with close ties to the review *Présence Africaine*. Arguing against an amorphous concept of "black culture" that would include the diaspora, Fanon draws a distinction between the specific nature of the African-American struggle for civil rights and national liberation in Africa. He also differentiates between the psychological and historical exigencies that motivated the negritude movement of the previous generation and the literature of combat that should be productively engaged in the people's current struggle for freedom. The lyrical terms with which negritude had affirmed the value of black African culture, initiating a cultural dialectic in response to the injury of European racism was being overtaken in 1959 by the need to contribute directly to African struggles for national sovereignty across the continent. While speaking to writers, intellectuals, and activists, Fanon echoed Renan's Janus-faced vision of the nation, linking the past to the present:

> The colonized man who writes for his people ought to use the past with the intention of opening the future, as an invitation to action and a basis for hope. But to ensure that hope and to give it form, he must take part in action and throw himself body and soul into the national struggle. You may speak about everything under the sun; but when you decide to speak of that unique thing in man's life that is represented by the fact of opening up new horizons, by bringing light to your own country, and by raising yourself and your people to their feet, then you must collaborate on the physical plane. *(Fanon, Wretched of the Earth, 232)*
>
> ...
>
> To fight for national culture means in the first place to fight for the liberation of the nation, that material keystone which makes the building of a culture possible. *(Fanon, Wretched of the Earth, 233)*

Fanon's muscular speech defends the moral legitimacy and historical necessity of nationalist struggles in Africa. Although he was wary of African traditions associated with the past and cautiously advocates their progressive use, he made frequent reference to the people's shared experience of suffering under colonial rule as an impetus for protest in the present. He sees culture as a dynamic field of popular expression in which writers, artists, and intellectuals should be collectively and purposefully engaged in charting a path to political sovereignty, the restoration of the colonized subject's self-esteem, and ultimately a renewal of culture. Fanon's language is steeped in metaphors related to the body, sexuality, and consciousness. In this passage he tells writers that they may write and talk about anything, but when it comes to national struggles for sovereignty, they must collaborate "on the physical plane" or, in his French phase, "with their *muscles*." He also equates the nation with the "material keystone" or, in his French phrase, "the material *matrix* or *womb*," that makes giving birth to national culture possible. As an ideal to be fully realized in the future, the psychiatrist imagines that national culture would restore the colonized intellectual's "psycho-affective equilibrium." Fanon's forward-looking nationalism was defined by the Hegelian dialectical vision that runs throughout his writing according to which anticolonial protest would finally overcome the colonial devalorization of native cultures, history, and experience, not with a rhetorical defense of black African culture, but through political combat for national sovereignty. As a West Indian who adopted the Algerian cause, Fanon does not use "national" as a geographically specific adjective; he used the phrase "national culture" as a flexible pan-African ideal – as it was often used on the pages of *Présence Africaine* during the 1950s – that could apply, in theory, to struggles for freedom anywhere on the continent. While the theoretical flexibility of Fanon's idea of pan-African nationalism contributed to its popularity, it needs to be distinguished from other forms of the discourse that were more specific and constrained by regional dynamics and practical considerations – as we see in the speeches of Kwame Nkrumah in Ghana and Patrice Lumumba in the Democratic Republic of Congo. In one respect, Fanon's prescience in *Wretched of the Earth* echoes Marx's in the *Manifesto*. As Fanon watched the Cold War unfold, he knew that the struggle for freedom was no longer only against the French or British, but against neoliberal imperialism and specifically refers to this threat. In his timely speech, "On National Culture," Fanon exhorted his audience not to settle for protesting with their pens with politically engaged writing à la Sartre, but to actually join the movement "body and soul" as he had.

Let me briefly acknowledge, at this point, that as narratives of nationalist liberation have been brought up for reconsideration, it has often been remarked that nationalism in Fanon's writing during the Algerian War is riven by a paradox. The dynamics of anticolonial protest are both Manichean – defined by the opposing camps of black/white and colonized/colonizer – and they are messy, unpredictable, and, at times, even contradictory.[14] In my view, the split opens along the divide between hope and realism, between theory and direct observation of nationalism tested in the crucible of violent insurrection on the battlefield in Algeria. Violence was Fanon's point of departure in defining national liberation as we see in his essay, "On Violence," which opens *Wretched of the Earth*. "National liberation, national renaissance, the restoration of nationhood to the people, commonwealth: whatever may be the headings used or the new formulas introduced, decolonization is always a violent phenomenon."[15] The core idea is this: in order for a new order to be established, the old one must be destroyed. Decolonization may involve armed insurrection as was the case in Algeria, Cameroon and Kenya, but Fanon went further and described the process as *inherently* violent insofar as it should entail the ordering of colonial society from the bottom up, even in places where not a shot was fired. The historical record shows that this social revolution did not happen often enough, and in Fanon's more self-descriptive moments he reveals his fears that the decolonial process would not deliver the promised revolution. In "Pitfalls of National Consciousness," Fanon recognized that: "National consciousness, instead of being the all-embracing crystallization of the innermost hopes of the whole people, instead of being the immediate and most obvious result of the mobilization of the people, will be in any case only a shell, a crude and fragile travesty of what it might have been."[16] Fanon's personal involvement in Algeria's war of independence made him aware that the ideals of nationalism and facts on the ground were not going to line up as he and many others had hoped. However, at no point does Fanon show an interest in defining what freedom means, neither as an idea with a particular history, nor as collectively shared ideal that was emerging – as we see in the speeches and writing of Nkrumah, Lumumba, and Mandela, among others. If we look carefully at the history of the discourse of national liberation in Africa, Fanon's lack of interest in defining the idea of freedom appears as a revealing omission – in his writing about national liberation and personal alienation – which helps explain, in my view, why so much postcolonial theory that has been built with Fanon's concepts fails to give freedom the attention it deserves.

Anne McClintock, in her critique of Fanon's articulation of African nationalism, has observed that, "Nationalism becomes … constitutive of people's identities through social contests that are frequently violent and always gendered."[17] Her reading of Fanon's idea of violence opened up important new terrain for feminist critics almost twenty years ago. "Not only are the needs of the nation typically identified with the frustrations and aspirations of men," she writes, "but the representation of male *national* power depends on the prior construction of *gender* difference. All too often in male nationalisms gender difference between women and men serves to symbolically define the limits of national difference between *men*."[18] McClintock shows how nationalism, according to Fanon and many other male theorists, is constituted from the beginning as a gendered discourse, replete with familial metaphors of "motherlands" and "fatherlands" and references to birth as we have seen in the language of Renan and Fanon. McClintock was among the first to point out the absence of a theory of gender power in discussions of nationalism and shows how male-centered nationalism depends on the social subordination of women and children to the domestic sphere. She proposes that if Fanon's vision of nationalism is *anticipatory*, women's agency as contributors to the national liberation struggle is *designated* – "an agency by invitation only."[19] McClintock takes issue with Fanon's view that women enter into history through their participation in the nationalist movement and points out the ambiguous status of women's rights *after* the revolution. McClintock's realm of critical engagement overlaps with Terry Eagleton's who writes about Fanon's theories of liberation as being articulated primarily in the "subjunctive tense" with hypothetical statements about future achievements, and with Edward Said's who advanced a contrapuntal critique of the Hegelian metaphysics in Fanon's writing. The essence of these critiques of Fanon's writing about national liberation draws our attention to the problems with his Manichean vocabulary and his vacillation between redemption and dispossession as he contemplated the future, but they do not engage specifically with the idea of freedom. After McClintock demonstrates the male-centered bias in theories of nationalism, she asks: What in practice did national liberation deliver for women, notably in South Africa? This is a rich question that will allow us to return to the question of freedom in South Africa in more detail later in relation to Antjie Krog's *In the Skull of My Country* (1998) and films about the Truth and Reconciliation Commission. In her chapter on gender and nationalism, McClintock leaves this an open question and concludes on a challenging note by citing a famous phrase from Gillo Pontecorvo's classic film, *Battle of Algiers* (1966), "It is difficult to start a revolution, more difficult to sustain it. But it's later, when we've won, that the real difficulties will begin." In the years since McClintock's intervention, feminist historians have worked on fleshing out the archive, paying more attention to the gendered language of national liberation and the actual participation of women in national protest movements – so often not made visible in male scholarship – including the ways women shaped the articulation and performance of discourses of liberation with clothing, dancing, and songs that women composed.[20]

To continue to explore how the discourse of national liberation was deployed by leaders, let us return to the case made by Mandela during the Rivonia Trial that sent him to Robben Island, which I cited in the introduction, and consider his statement in more detail. Mandela's speech is of particular interest here because of the contrast it offers with Fanon's discourse. Not only does Mandela explicitly engage with the idea of freedom in terms of democracy, rights, and institutions, he titled his autobiography, *Long Walk to Freedom* (1995). It was on April 20, 1964 in the Palace of Justice in Pretoria that Nelson Mandela made his statement during the Rivonia Trial in defense of the African National Congress's (ANC) principles and of his life. The state had charged him, and several others, with sabotage and conspiracy and Mandela faced the death penalty at the age of fourty-five. When Mandela and his fellow defendants arrived at the courthouse in Pretoria in October 1963 it was "with a convoy of police trucks," they entered the rear of the building "through great iron gates" as a massive crowd of supporters were singing and chanting. "Once inside," Mandela wrote, "we were held in cells below the courtroom before the opening of what was depicted in the newspapers at home and around the world as the most significant political trial in the history of South Africa."[21] Mandela and his codefendants, including his close friend Walter Sisulu, were allowed to consult one another on strategy and with lawyers in the preparation of their defense. "We were not concerned with getting off or lessening our punishment," Mandela writes, "but with having the trial strengthen the cause for which we were all struggling – at whatever cost to ourselves. We would not defend ourselves in a legal sense so much as in a moral sense. We saw the trial as a continuation of the struggle by other means."[22]

It was decided that Mandela would read a statement from the dock, which could not be subjected to cross-examination. He explains: "We believed it was important to open the defence with a statement of our politics and ideals, which would establish the context for all that followed."[23] Mandela spent two weeks drafting his statement alone in his cell at night and then read it to his fellow accused. Bram Fischer, who represented them before Judge Quartus de Wet, begged Mandela not to read the last paragraph – to no avail. The speech was explicitly intended as a public statement of the ANC's principles and had been polished, read by others and, apparently, edited by Nadine Gordimer and Anthony Sampson at Mandela's request.[24]

In his autobiography *Long Walk to Freedom*, written in English as was the case for most antiapartheid writing, Mandela summarizes the main points of the complete statement, which took him four hours to read in court without pause or interruption.[25] He admitted to helping establish *Umkhonto we Sizwe* (the military wing of the ANC often referred to as MK) in November 1961 with the goal of making limited and deliberate use of sabotage (part of the armed struggle) to try to avoid having the country drift into civil war. Mandela denied allegations that foreign powers influenced the ANC's mission and affirmed that his inspiration to be a leader came from stories that elders told him as a child: "Amongst the tales they related to me were those of wars fought by our ancestors in defence of the fatherland. The names of Dingane and Bambatha, Hintsa and Makanna, Squngthi and Dalasile, Moshoeshoe and Sekhukhuni, were praised as the pride and glory of the entire African nation. I hoped then that life might offer me the opportunity to serve my people and make my own humble contribution to their freedom struggle."[26] Mandela explained that planning sabotage was the result of a "calm and sober assessment of the political situation that had arisen after many years of tyranny, exploitation, and oppression of my people by whites."[27]

He reiterated the ANC's commitment to nonracial democracy and claimed that preparation for guerrilla warfare was part of a contingency plan for the future, only if sabotage did not work. Mandela talked about the military training he received outside South Africa, which he sought so that he could fight alongside his people, and clarified the circumstances of the ANC's strategic alliance with the Communist Party. He professed admiration for British and American democratic institutions – especially the separation of branches of government, defense of formal rights and parliament. Mandela also detailed the "terrible disparities" between blacks and whites in South Africa and blamed the legal system for enforcing white supremacy before reaching his dramatic conclusion. At this point, it is worth observing that his commitment to the ideal of democracy was derived from a precolonial notion of *patrie* according to which land belonged to all South Africans, a devotion to the rule of law in the Western tradition of formal rights and a political conscience that extended well beyond these geographical and conceptual parameters to embrace a shared sense of humanity in the broadest possible terms.[28] He carried within him an ideal that would not be realized for decades and a commitment to the language of law, which his adversaries provided to him insofar as they discriminated and oppressed his people "legally."

On the day of his statement he wore a suit and tie and there was silence in the courthouse while he was reading. But as Mandela and his fellow defendants entered the courtroom on October 9, 1963, to face charges the first time, they greeted the crowd with the clenched-fist ANC salute and their supporters in the visitors' gallery participated in the customary call and response "*Amandla! Ngawethu*!" (The Power! Is Ours!) and "*Mayibuye iAfrika*!" (Bring back Africa!) When Mandela previously appeared in court as a defendant in 1962 he was alone and wore a traditional Xhosa leopard-skin kaross instead of a suit and tie, which he said "electrified the spectators," and made him feel like "the embodiment of African nationalism, the inheritor of Africa's difficult but noble past and her uncertain future."[29] Thus it was with his keen awareness as a lawyer of the drama of the courtroom that Mandela made his statement, a defense that he turned into an indictment of their system in which he explained the principles to which he had devoted his life:

> Africans want a just share in the whole of South Africa; they want security and a stake in society. Above all, we want equal political rights, because without them our disabilities will be permanent. I know this sounds revolutionary to the whites in this country, because the majority of voters will be Africans. This makes the white man fear democracy …
>
> This then is what the ANC is fighting for. Their struggle is a truly national one. It is a struggle of the African people, inspired by their own suffering and their own experience. It is a struggle for the right to live.

> During my lifetime I have dedicated myself to this struggle of the African people. I have fought against black domination. I have cherished the ideal of a democratic and free society in which all persons live together in harmony and with equal opportunities. It is an ideal which I hope to live for and to achieve. But if needs be, it is an ideal for which I am prepared to die. *(Long Walk to Freedom, 178)*

The language he chose to express his dedication to the cause of African freedom comes from the tradition of democratic ideals that ensures rights, justice, and equal opportunity. While his pride in ancestral traditions had already been established and dramatically enacted under different circumstances, he does not use metaphors of "birth," "soul," and "spiritual principles" as Fanon and Renan did. Mandela and the ANC sought to avoid over-emphasizing tribalism and racialism because under apartheid these were traps of divisiveness. While Mandela admitted to being inspired by Marxist ideas, his alliance with the communists did not diminish his commitment to democratic ideals and a multiracial society. The phrase, "a just share in the whole of South Africa," expresses their crucial objection to the injustice of apartheid and asserts the simple, but powerful idea that the people of South Africa had a right to choose their government and to benefit from the resources of their own land.

Mandela captured the world's attention during the Rivonia Trial and then from his jail cell on Robben Island after Judge De Wet sentenced him to life in prison, and not to death by hanging. While Mandela delivered his statement in English, Fanon spoke in French and had an immediate impact on theories of liberation in the French-speaking world and worldwide through translations in English and other languages. Nonetheless, I find that cultural critics and theorists who have knowledge of both the French-speaking and English-speaking traditions have a richer conceptual repertoire to draw from.[30] Fanon did not leave a legacy as the leader of an independent nation or of a movement; he was not destined to become head of state and, unfortunately, he died of leukemia in 1961, before the end of the war in Algeria. Mandela's legacy is very different. Against all odds, he survived prison and became the first democratically elected president of South Africa in 1994 taking 62.65 percent of the popular vote as head of the ANC. Fanon's and Mandela's visions of liberation have fared differently as well. Fanon's theories about national liberation's potential to revalorize the individual's sense of self and contribute to a cultural renaissance for the people were noble goals that inspired artists and intellectuals of his generation, but yielded mixed results in practice.[31] By contrast, Mandela and his comrades in the ANC called for freedom in terms of the people's just share in the whole of South Africa – its land, wealth, resources – and their rights to full citizenship, security and a stake in the nation's future. Mandela's dual emphasis on: (1) the people's right to choose their government and leaders; and, (2) to benefit from their country's resources, are still relevant to the ongoing struggle for meaningful freedom in Africa today as globalization transforms the landscape, as we will see in the next chapter.

Although the National Liberation Front had a hard time pivoting to the new task of building a just society in an independent Algeria after 1962, the ANC still faces persistent challenges in their effort to realize the goals of their party's Freedom Charter and of representing the aspirations of the people, including those of a growing black middle class, in postapartheid South Africa. Unfortunately, some South Africans today regard Mandela not as an icon of African national liberation, but as a sell-out to brand-name capitalism.[32] While neo-Marxists on the left still have a healthy appetite for radical social change and more tangible evidence of progress toward equality and justice for all South Africans, leaders of the opposition in the Democratic Alliance and the Economic Freedom Fighters are faced with a governing party that is corrupt and struggling to maintain its ideological coherence and political legitimacy as the drawn-out recall of President Jacob Zuma in early 2018 demonstrates.[33]

Nations, Narratives, and the Language of Freedom

Written from the standpoint of a Ghanaian in 1968, Ayi Kwei Armah's novel *The Beautyful Ones Are Not Yet Born* (1968) was the first to give voice to the people's postindependence disillusionment. As we saw in Chapter 1, when Nkrumah became Ghana's prime minister in 1957, he gave a speech that not only proclaimed the dawn of a new era and celebrated the people's freedom as the triumph of popular protest, he also promised to transform the country into a prosperous land of opportunity. And yet, within less than ten years this man, who had been the most influential spokesmen for national liberation in West Africa, would be deposed by a coup d'état leaving behind a difficult, bitter legacy of corruption and compromised leadership. The ideals of political self-determination and socioeconomic progress that Nkrumah had championed as a means of remaking colonial societies from the ground up proved difficult to realize in practice and this was due, in part, to obstacles embedded within the structure of the state itself, as we will see in Armah's narrative and in the historiography of African decolonization.

The Beautyful Ones Are Not Yet Born is of particular interest here because of the way the author explicitly employs a language of freedom and reflects on its meaning as part of his critical reconsideration of national liberation. The novel offers a window onto the dysfunction of the state and the corruption of society from the vantage point of a railway clerk who monitors cargo freight trains. This was a strategic choice in terms of the narrator's point of view that gave the narrative deep political resonance in the context of the 1960s. By 1958, one year after taking power, Nkrumah was already ruling by decree and had severely curtailed the autonomy of the powerful trade union movement.[34] In 1961, railway workers led a general strike, which marked a turning point in the short history of Nkrumah's presidency. Thus, it is pertinent that Armah's protagonist (who is nameless) acquires first-hand knowledge of what it is like to be a railway worker and that he also observes, while on the job, the effects of capitalist bosses exploiting railway workers, since these conditions led to the first historically significant protest in Ghana after independence.

While at work, the man spends his time monitoring a network of cargo trains that transport natural resources to the harbor for export. This transit system was a lifeline that allowed the commerce of the emerging gatekeeper state to function in addition to being the site of important labor disputes. When the man examines the huge chart on the wall above his desk he is essentially looking at a map of the flow of timber and manganese from their points of extraction to the harbor in Accra, where they enter the export market. It is because of the man's ability to cut off or speed up the traffic of cargo trains in this network that he becomes subject to bribery and subsequently faced with a moral dilemma. The narrator describes a corpulent timber contractor who enters the man's office, one day, belly first as if defined by how much he "eats," invoking colloquial associations between eating and corruption. The contractor offers a bribe of twenty cedi to ensure that his wood will not rot in the forest before it reaches the market. Amankwa, the contractor, is insistent and asks the man to get his colleague, the booking clerk, to expedite the transportation of his timber, but the man refuses. His moral opposition to this specific bribe, as a low-level agent in the business of regulating infrastructure essential to the gatekeeping state, implicitly condemns the general culture of corruption that has taken over the administration of the railway system. Armah expands the scope of his social criticism by depicting a hierarchy among railway workers from the janitor, at the bottom of the socioeconomic food chain who performs his duties as if he were "sleepwalking," to the biggest bosses, who do not report to work after the coup as they wait to find out who the next gatekeeper will be. Meanwhile, rank and file workers who endure hunger, debt, and despair are described as the "living dead" and personify the alienation that results from callous capitalist exploitation.

As Ato Quayson has observed, when the man enters the city he enters a space of transitions.[35] The phrase, "the beautyful ones are *not yet* born," that the man sees on the back of the bus at the end of the novel refers to the historical transition from colonial rule to independence, and how the promises of freedom and prosperity have not yet been, and may never be, realized. While walking in the city the man reads signs of this deferral and longs for something more, something better, everywhere he goes. While moving through urban space is explicitly connected to the theme of transportation, with important references to taxis, buses, and trains, movement is also symbolically associated with social and historical progress. During his lunch hour, the man leaves his desk and decides to walk along the train tracks, mapping the railway system from a different vantage point than that of a man on the ground alongside workers, while hunger unabated clarifies his "famished vision." The symbolism associated with movement is even evident at a micro-level in Armah's deliberate use of verbs in a particular sequence such as "leap," "jump," and "sail," which draws our attention to the ideal of progress and the yearning for it to take off. Yet these verb phrases convey a *desire* to move, rather than *actual* movement or progress. Similarly, the cargo trains the man watches move along the railway system but they loop along an itinerary of exploitation, running from sites of extraction (the mines, forests) to the harbor (for foreign export) and back, without contributing to social progress or shared prosperity at home.

Armah's symbolism of movement with negative progress continues when the man helps Koomson, his former classmate, who became a corrupt party man, flee Ghana after the coup. The scene begins rather dramatically when the man helps Koomson escape after the regime he supported crumbles and their only way out of the house is through a shit-smeared latrine. What is more, once they enter the city they resort to following sewer lines as they make their way to the waterfront in search of Koomson's get-away boat. The network they use to navigate through the city on the way to the harbor conjures up numerous other references in the narrative to excrement and bodily fluids. Armah's symbolic itinerary for the fleeing party man is evocative of the regressive system of corruption that runs throughout the society because the novel is saturated with detailed observations of the accretion of filth in public spaces, beginning with the wooden banister at the railway office that was dirtied by so many hands, stained with snot, urine, sweat, and fecal matter. The novel represents the deferral of freedom with filth in public that has become so pervasive that trash heaps appear banal and citizens must remember that they should be seen as offensive, just as citizens must make an effort to resist the gleam and realize that unchecked corruption can ruin a culture.

Armah elaborates a sensitive and sharp portrait of the reckless pursuit of material wealth in the decade after independence in this emerging gatekeeper state. The socioeconomic stratification that existed among railway workers mirrors the society at large, as we see when the man takes public transportation and observes interactions among ordinary people in the street from orange vendors to taxi drivers. The poor grab at coins. The driver spits on the man when he gets off the bus. Socialists who have turned their backs on the people grow more corpulent, wear expensive suits, and use fancy perfume. Armah develops the corrosive effects of corruption that pervade every aspect of Ghanaian society through contrasting characters. The nameless protagonist wrestles with his conscience as he fends off the temptation to join his countrymen who are drawn to the bright light of rapidly acquired wealth. Whereas the man seeks a way of living in society without compromising his ethical integrity, his teacher friend withdraws from society vowing never to hope again after enduring such a profound sense of disappointment. Yet both the man and the teacher criticize the hegemony of the new ruling elite which perpetuated the values and commercial relationships that the former colonial authorities left behind. By contrast, the man's wife, Oyo, longs for the comfortable, predictable life material wealth affords and brings considerable guilt to bear on her husband for not putting his family's lifestyle and social status before his ethical integrity. Oyo, like her mother, speaks the language of social conformity and they are both willing to play the get-rich-quick game until Oyo witnesses Koomson's decline after the coup. Koomson loses his property and his dignity when he hears boots in the street as new leaders round up supporters of the deposed president and he is forced to flee through a latrine.

It is particularly striking how Armah portrays the people as waiting for the next gatekeeper, as if everyone in Ghana recognized that competition for control of the gate defined political rivalries – as if everyone was prepared to follow whomever the revolving door favored next. The fact that Oyo discovers renewed respect for her husband's choices only after Koomson's misfortune reveals how the consequences of political dispossession reached into the private lives of ordinary husbands and wives. Armah affirms his hope in humanity when Oyo recognizes her husband's integrity, which helps the man overcome his sense of emasculation in the public sphere and to express sexual desire for his wife again in the private space of the bedroom. The narrator explains the survival of the man's sexual instinct by saying that something human within him refused to die. Yet, when the man shares his moral burden as a husband with his friend, saying that he envies his freedom as a single man without familial pressures, the teacher replies: "If we can't consume ourselves for something we believe in, *freedom* makes no difference at all" (*Beautyful Ones*, 61; emphasis added). The way the teacher uses the word "freedom" in this sentence equates the idea with "national liberation as promised."

For the teacher, whether married or single every citizen suffers from the same absence of opportunities, the same limits on substantive freedoms as long as the people's political freedom does not serve the purpose of building a more just society.

While the man enjoys a privileged vantage point from which to observe the exploitation of resources and labor within an emerging gatekeeper state, his moral solitude conveys the existential disorientation average people felt. Similar to Antonio Gramsci's idea of hegemony in *The Prison Notebooks*, Armah's representation of the gleam – where power resides in its ability to compel the under classes to imitate the elite – shows people who endure the effects of grinding poverty. They feel ashamed of their poverty and status and are frustrated that they too have not yet arrived, rather than feel the anger of the dispossessed.[36] Although it may be tempting to interpret the people's appetite for the gleam as the sole source of Ghana's corruption and stalled progress, the introspective monologues in chapter six of the novel make it clear that Armah thought real opportunities did, in fact, exist but they were foreclosed. When the man "said something earnest about the connectedness of words and the *freedom* of enslaved men," the teacher responded with a discussion of the myth of Plato's cave (*Beautyful Ones*, 79; emphasis added). The moral of the teacher's story is that men accustomed to the darkness of the cave and the familiarity of their chains refuse to believe in the possibility of freedom and light outside, which serves to illustrate Armah's conviction that a failure of imagination limited opportunities during Ghana's transition to self-rule and the decade following independence. In this instance, the fault does not lie with the enlightened ones, like the man and the teacher who speak of freedom, but in the inability of those in the cave to see the light, to perceive the meaning of words spoken, and thus to enter into a new realm of awareness and understanding.

Next in the sequence of Armah's criticism is leadership: "How long will Africa be cursed with its leaders?" (*Beautyful Ones*, 80). While the people, especially the uneducated people to which the teacher refers, may not have been sufficiently well prepared for independence, Armah reserves his strongest condemnation for leaders and their friends in the new bourgeoisie who content themselves with "picking leftovers from the teeth of British colonials." Yet he does allow for the fact that some of the people, at least, refused to wear the white mask of alienation and turned away in disgusted laughter as the new gatekeepers imitated the departing colonials. To explore this question of leadership with obvious references to Nkrumah, the novelist combines introspective monologues, dialogue between characters, and direct citation of the intoxicating rhetoric that the "new men" used when making speeches. The "new men" proclaim,

"We are our own enslavers first. Only we can free ourselves. Today, when we say it, it is a promise, not yet a fact … Freedom!" (*Beautyful Ones*, 86; emphasis added). Here the prophet of freedom evokes the emotional experience of the inner self in terms that echo Fanon as the origin of freedom as he deploys the persuasive discourse of national liberation to rally the people. In the same way Nkrumah explicitly used the language of freedom in his speeches during meetings in Accra with African freedom fighters and on the eve of independence, the "new men" in Armah's novel mimic the historical discourse of national liberation.

The new men got to act like messiahs because enough people were willing to follow, too eager to believe in promises and taken by charisma, as Etse, a woman in the crowd, wryly remarks of another woman, "Maanan is wetting her womanhood over this new man," when she and other young Ghanaians listened to the political speech at a rally for independence (*Beautyful Ones*, 87). The man wonders how such beautiful words could have given birth to a sick and dying baby and asks, "How could this have grown rotten with such obscene haste?" (*Beautyful Ones*, 88). Armah depicts this rotten state of affairs with female characters who are toys in the hands of charismatic men who are defined by their men's club and values, including corruption, callous self-interest, a willingness to exploit workers, and unbridled womanizing. The teacher uses a language of shocking vulgarity as a means to express the extent of his moral condemnation when he observes: "Women, so horribly young, fucked and changed like pants, asking only for blouses and perfume from diplomatic bags and wigs of human hair scraped from which decayed white woman's corpse?" (*Beautyful Ones*, 89). In a narrative style that resembles Alejo Carpentier's in *The Kingdom of this World* (1949), Armah employs the voice of the teacher to reveal the sad and ugly face of how capitalism dehumanizes the victims who would be content wearing wigs made from the hair of European corpses. In ethical terms, the new men's cynical disregard for women, workers, and the citizenry at large is woven into one fabric of political alienation. "It may be terrible to think that this was what all the speeches, all the hope, all the love of the first days was for. It is terrible, but it is not a lie" (*Beautyful Ones*, 90). All that remains is for the people to wake up and to want to be whole again. The promise of freedom like the "single flower, solitary, unexplainable, and very beautiful" that was painted at the center of the inscription "THE BEAUTYFUL ONES/ARE NOT YET BORN" on the back of the bus, must be kept alive and this is what the man contemplates as he walks home at the end of the novel.

Given the importance of freedom as an idea and emerging ideal in Armah's novel, it seems worthwhile to think more carefully about what this narrative is saying in historical context. In terms of the historiography of African decolonization, a good place to start reassessing the fate of "triumphant nationalism" as a discourse in relation to the kind of nations that actually emerged from liberation movements is Basil Davidson's *The Black Man's Burden. Africa and the Curse of the Nation-State* (1992). I say this because Davidson's scholarship before, during, and after decolonization and his interpretation of what went wrong with "triumphant nationalism," in particular, has been influential beyond the field of African history, including literary and cultural studies.[37] In *The Black Man's Burden*, Davidson concludes that it was both the institutions and models inherited from Europe that meant that liberation produced its own denial in Africa.[38] He sees the pioneers of nationalism – such as Nkrumah in Ghana – as overly optimistic about their future triumph without sufficiently scrutinizing the tools they were using, particularly the idea of the nation and its institutions, or the geographical boundaries of the territories they would inherit.[39] For both Davidson and Armah, among others, cultural attitudes were decisive. Those Africans who were influenced by the "European project" had been taught that nothing good could come of their own traditions: "It taught that nothing useful could develop without denying Africa's past, without a ruthless severing from Africa's roots and a slavish acceptance of models drawn from entirely different histories."[40] The problems associated with this kind of cultural rupture are more evident in Armah's second novel *Fragments* (1970), which was discussed in Chapter 1. Davidson does acknowledge the utility of nationalism as a political discourse that allowed African leaders to communicate with European officials as *interlocuteurs valables* in a "respectable" language.[41] Yet, for Davidson, this created an appearance of validity that did not last: "This nation-statism looked like liberation, and really began as one. But it did not continue as one."[42]

Ironically, Davidson uses the failure of European nationalism to deliver social justice in Italy as the model for explaining similarities in African decolonization and concludes: "The breaking of the promise of freedom was the outcome, as is easily understood now, of the victory of the 'national' over the 'social'."[43] There are two main reasons for this victory of the "national" over the "social" in African liberation movements, according to Davidson: (1) allowing the political demands of the state to precede the articulation of the nation as a community; and, (2) new leaders insufficiently tending to socioeconomic class relations such that the dispossessed would be left to fend for themselves. Here, we return to Anderson's observation that the pioneers of African nationalism, spokesmen like Fanon and Mandela, were well-educated and spoke European languages, but were not connected to "sturdy local bourgeoisies." For Davidson, it is primarily a question of the new leaders actually turning their backs on the people once they got into power, as Fanon feared they would. In his conclusion, Davidson revisits the writing of Amìlcar Cabral and recalls how, for Cabral in *Unity and Struggle* (1979), the way the people managed the dynamics of popular protest, including armed insurrection, should lay the ground work for social justice after independence through their cultivation of such practices as democracy, self-governance, and self-criticism in the service of social unity.[44] Of course, these ideals in theory did not always yield results in practice. In the end, Davidson offers a dystopic narrative of African decolonization according to which the nation-state tragically becomes the "black man's burden." But his analysis of the process remains essentially descriptive; he describes a whole host of reasons – institutions, cultural attitudes, disregard for the dispossessed – without articulating how these factors impact one another. In my view, this kind of criticism is largely idealistic, without seriously grappling with the imperfect options that were actually at hand. Davidson's historiography does share a great deal with other fictional narratives after independence whether Ousmane Sembène's novella *Xala* (1973) or Chinua Achebe's novel *Anthills of the Savannah* (1987). Yet the essence of these kinds of critiques that find fault with culture, values, and failures in leadership do little to explain how the gatekeeper state that Armah's protagonist observes with stunning insight in *The Beautyful Ones Are Not Yet Born* emerged historically.

Frederick Cooper's *Africa since 1940: the Past of the Present* (2002) will allow us to push ahead analytically and to reflect more carefully on the options that were at hand and to consider what the archive shows about how the gatekeeper state succeeded the colonial state. For Cooper, the process of African decolonization was like a tug-of-war that was shaped by African and European actors on either side of the struggle. I find this approach compelling because it takes leadership seriously without idealizing the options available. Writing in the era after structural adjustment plans and the implementation of neoliberal financial policies, Cooper chooses to structure his argument around the overlapping issues of economic development and political self-determination. As the path to decolonization was being prepared, development was on everyone's mind, which we see with Fanon's discussion in *Wretched of the Earth* of how colonial administrators made belated promises to improve conditions in the colonies as a means of staving off mounting protest. When new African heads of state were eventually faced with the challenge of building new nations, they used the resources that were at their disposal to consolidate their hold on power,

> The core of the agenda for the new political class owed something to the post-war agenda of British and French colonial rule, but it was given a new twist. The development project, to colonial administrators, implied that the possessors of knowledge and capital would slowly but generously disperse these critical resources to those less well endowed. But to African political parties, development meant resources to build constituencies and opportunities to make the nation-state a meaningful part of people's lives.[45]

To flesh out his argument about development with a "new twist" Cooper considers how Nkrumah built alliances and marginalized his opposition among the Asante and organized labor in Ghana.[46] Through his discussion of different styles of leadership, what Cooper's interpretation of decolonization shows is that the process was shaped in part by the kinds of claims and demands that nationalist leaders made as well as by the fact that: "Amidst one of the great political openings of the twentieth century, the closures of a particular decolonization were becoming visible."[47] So, understanding what was not possible and what the real constraints on freedom would be, proved to be critically important.

When trying to understand the dynamic relationship between resistance and repression in the struggle for national liberation, turning to the historical archive is indispensable. Cooper sheds some light on how European colonial administrators prepared the transition to African independence in deliberate ways that anticipated ongoing influence once the end of the colonial era seemed inevitable. He discusses how the British tried to draw lines, establishing what was acceptable, but with some difficulty, in the Gold Coast and Kenya; and how the French responded with violent repression to demands made in Madagascar and Cameroon. Quoting from the archive of official British correspondence, he states:

> If defending colonial rule would be prohibitively expensive, the key to policy was managing the transition: "during the period when we can still exercise control in any territory, it is most important to take every step open to us to ensure, as far as we can, that British standards and methods of business and administration permeate the whole life of the territory."[48]

This statement of policy reads like a page out of one of Ngũgĩ wa Thiong'o's novels about the transition to self-rule in Kenya. As a matter of historical record the general ambition to exercise control directly for as long as possible and in specific ways that would ensure indirect European influence in the future is evident in the colonial archive in several ways. In terms of leadership, Cooper discusses how certain leaders like Léopold Sédar Senghor in Senegal were encouraged, while others like Sékou Touré in Guinea or Ruben Um Nyobé in Cameroon were thwarted or assassinated, and how European colonial administrators made strategic decisions to devolve power to geographical territories that would be inherently weak politically. With the hindsight that observing the expansion of global capitalism affords us, we can see that once European officials realized that their "administrative units" overseas had made possible the conditions for "natives" to imagine themselves as "nationals," they took consciously planned steps to create enclaves for future capital investment that would be difficult to govern. Yet when leaders such as Jomo Kenyatta in Kenya and Nkrumah in Ghana challenged European authority, they "forced colonial regimes to move the boundaries of the permissible; they, too, helped define a certain kind of decolonization."[49] Cooper does not consider the pioneers of national liberation as pupils or subservient admirers of Western culture or even as simply worthy interlocutors, he sees nationalist leaders such as Kenyatta, Senghor, Sékou Touré, and Nkrumah as actors with their own agendas which have often been misunderstood and mischaracterized in Western accounts of this historical process. Differences in the style and substance of African leadership were consequential and thus we do not have a single set of images for decolonization in Africa.

In this contest for control over territories and resources, Cooper pinpoints how departing colonials also prepared the terrain in Africa to their moral advantage. He concludes his chapter, "Ending empire and imagining the future," with this assessment:

> France and Britain transformed their colonial development apparatus into a foreign aid system, with the crucial difference that it reaffirmed generous superiority while denying responsibility for the social and political consequences of economic change. Other figures on the world scene, including the US and the USSR, began to look at the disintegrating colonial empires as spaces that were being internationalized, still at the bottom of a developmental hierarchy, but now the object of concern of all "advanced" nations. Africa would become the world's project for uplift, and also a magnet for power politics and exploitative interest.[50]

Two things are important to underscore here. First, Cooper establishes a direct connection between the "colonial development apparatus" of the postwar years and the appearance of a humanitarian project during the second half of the twentieth century, which will become more important in the next chapter. But the transformation of colonial development into foreign aid managed by European- and American-led institutions, which made Africa into the world's "project for uplift," also shifted responsibility for any mismanagement in the future to the recipients of international aid, while allowing Western donors the guise of "generous superiority." Cooper's archival documentation and analysis of this sequence of

Western forms of exploitation in Africa invites us to consider just how hard it is to disentangle the conjuncture of decolonization and the rise of neoliberal capitalism.[51]

With this in mind it is not hard to imagine that the expansion of capitalist markets that went hand-in-hand with European imperialism in Africa, would adapt – as Marx, Fanon and Nkrumah foresaw – to the new circumstances that decolonization presented. The discourse of national liberation that presented national sovereignty as the ultimate gage of freedom – to which Nkrumah and others contributed – came sharply up against imperial counter-measures that were taken to ensure that the nation-states African leaders inherited were fragile communities. Cooper's analysis of how the new African nations that emerged were successor states with a gatekeeping function helps explain how this worked in practice:

> The early governments thus aspired both to define their authority over territory which, however arbitrary its borders, was now theirs, and to build something on that territory. But the dual project was born into the limitations of the old one, the colonial version of development. African states, like their predecessors, had great difficulty getting beyond the limitations of a gatekeeper state. Their survival depended precisely on the fact that formal sovereignty was recognized *from outside*, and that resources such as foreign aid and military assistance, came to governments for that reason. Like colonial regimes, they had trouble extending their power and their command of people's respect, if not support, inward. They had trouble collecting taxes, except on imports and exports; they had trouble setting economic priorities and policies, except for the distribution of resources like oil revenues and customs receipts; they had trouble making the nation-state into a symbol that inspired loyalty. What they could do was sit astride the interface between a territory and the rest of the world, collecting and distributing resources that derived from the gate itself: customs revenue and foreign aid; permits to do business in the territory; entry and exit visas; and permission to move currency in and out. *(Africa since 1940, 156–7)*

Once in power new leaders had the "dual project" of imposing their authority and building something meaningful on their new territories. But, their options as political actors building new nations were significantly constrained by the structures and institutions of the colonial states that they inherited at independence, the contours of which had been set up for European strategic, economic, and moral advantage. Instead of Fanon's idea that decolonization would remake society from the ground up, we have the absence of conditions to realize meaningful freedom within gatekeeper states. Instead of being inspired by intangible feelings of solidarity through collective and individual identification with the nation as a "soul" and "spiritual principle" the imagination of a political community came up against new sources of division and fragmentation in these gatekeeper states. If the promise of making progress together in the future was integral to nationalism's persuasive power, the people could no longer give their consent to live, work, and devote their lives to the nation if dictators in charge of the gate trampled their rights and deprived them of opportunities. If we are to evaluate national liberation in terms of whether robust political sovereignty was achieved, which was one of its stated objectives, then the pattern of gatekeeper states with weak, embattled sovereignty reveals perhaps the most significant limitation to what decolonization achieved in Africa. It is within the framework of gatekeeper states embedded within an international web of relations that we should consider the pattern of corruption and dictatorship that defined the first generation of leaders after a devolution of power under these circumstances.

Let us turn now to Sony Labou Tansi's novel set in Congo-Brazzaville in the late 1970s to explore how he represents the people surviving a gatekeeper state. From his point of view in this region during the Cold War, Lumumba's legacy as a martyr for national liberation, the problem of foreign interference, and the defeat of a second independence movement are foremost on the agenda.[52] After nearly two decades of revolving dictatorships in Congo-Brazzaville, Tansi's first novel *La vie et demie* (1979; *Life and a Half*, 2011) offered a satirical critique of foreign-sponsored gatekeepers, repressive political violence, and the seemingly endless deferral of meaningful freedom. Arguably just as innovative and important in the canon of African letters as Armah's *The Beautyful Ones Are Not Yet Born*, this novel gives us a comprehensive interpretation of political dispossession in the last decade of the Cold War and the obstacles to unity, democracy, and engaged citizenship that this put in people's way. Tansi's lamentation of the effects of dictatorship's in *Life and a Half* resonated, more broadly, with political themes in the African novel at the time as we see in Tierno Monénembo's *Les crapauds-brousse* (1972), Alioum Fantouré's *Le cercle des tropiques* (1979) and Ngũgĩ Wa Thiong'o's *Petals of Blood* (1977) to cite just a few. At the time of writing, Tansi was facing a violent political climate in the Congo and this is reflected in the way his narrative connects the nation's history of dispossession, a sense of personal loss after the regime killed his activist friends, and the first signs of spiritual disorientation. Written a decade before the fall of the Berlin Wall and the organization of national conferences in Africa, *Life and a Half* is a dystopic narrative that depicts the deprivation of the people's instrumental freedoms and shows the societal effects of dispossession that erode the people's substantive and existential freedoms. Whereas Armah rather explicitly frames his narrative as a reconsideration of the language of freedom in relation to the promise of national liberation, Tansi approaches the question of freedom conceptually and comprehensively, ten years later, with an emphasis on interconnected spheres of experience, as we saw in Chapter 1.

Lumumba's status as a martyr in the struggle against Western imperialism in Africa certainly still held an appeal for Tansi at this time. In my essay "Passionate Engagements," I document how the novelist was sensitive to the legacy of political martyrdom in the region and discuss his collection of images – some photographs, some printed images – of martyrs on both sides of the Congo River that he included as part of his private ancestral shrine.[53] His personal investment in the history of martyrdom helps us understand why he structured the plot of *Life and a Half* around the political figure of Martial, a martyr who haunts the living through his daughter Chaïdana. Written in a "tropical" French infused with Kongo references, this novel reveals a local conception of political power that grounds the author's representation of the vital relationship between real and symbolic forms of power in a surreal story about the devastating legacy of national liberation in the Congo.

Tansi had to navigate a political terrain that remained riven by divisions and that pitted pan-African ideals of total liberation, national unity, and continental solidarity against the regional dynamics of ethnic separatism that had evolved over two decades from the forces at work that led to Lumumba's demise. In addition to Cooper's work on the gatekeeper state and his discussion of the rise to power of Mobutu Sese Seko in *Africa since 1940*, Georges Nzongola-Ntalaja provides in *The Congo from Leopold to Kabila* (2002) a detailed account of the people's ongoing struggle after the progressive forces aligned with Lumumba were tracked down and defeated, to which I shall return later. It is important to note from the outset that the promise of national liberation does not appear dead on arrival in *Life and a Half* because dissident citizens are represented as still longing for, and believing in, the ideal of a representative government with unfettered sovereignty. Tansi's faith in that promise did eventually die, which is evident in his last novel *Le commencement des douleurs* (1995) where civil discord has become so bitter and irrevocable that the old idea of national unity seems morally offensive. A long-standing tension between national unity and ethnic separatism existed on both sides of the river within the Bakongo community from the turbulent days of Joseph Kasavubu's Abako party that helped unseat Lumumba. Whereas Sese Seko survived competition for control of the gate from 1965 to 1997, and amassed a stunning personal fortune, the first president in Congo-Brazzaville, Fulbert Youlou, was one of many in a succession of dictators beginning in 1963. Given the vertiginous succession of dictators in *Life and a Half* it is useful to recall the sequence of leaders in Congo-Brazzaville as a point of historical reference, which includes: Alphonse

Massamba-Débat (1963–8), Marien Ngouabi (1968–77), Joachim Yhombi-Opango (1977–9), and Sassou Nguesso (1979–92). In 1997 competition for power involving Pascal Lissouba who had been elected president and his rival Nguesso led to years of civil war and political instability. After the war, it is remarkable that Nguesso held onto power for so long; "winning" two controversial elections in 2002 and 2009 and then proposing to revise the constitution to further prolong his rule. For Tansi and others in the Bakongo community in Congo-Brazzaville, especially in the Pool region near the capital, they experienced this era of Cold War dictatorship as a toxic combination of political dispossession and ethnic persecution.

In *Life and A Half* two central themes are interwoven: the embattled existence of opposition leaders who see life on earth as governed by an invisible realm of spiritual forces, and a state that is defined by a revolving door of dictators who are enabled by "the foreign powers that supplied the guides." This is a frequently repeated phrase that evokes the foreign patronage of gatekeepers to the point of becoming a slogan in the novel, insistently reiterating the destructive effects on leadership. The legacy of European interference in the region extends well beyond what Nzongola-Ntalaja has called the most consequential assassination of the twentieth century in reference to Lumumba,[54] to include other popular figures such as Simon Kimbangu and André Matswa. This created a widespread sense that the people were deprived of leaders who were capable of representing their interests.[55] All of this violent repression of political dissidence has a direct bearing on the mindset of the novelist who has said that the assassination of his personal friends for their activism was the impetus for writing *Life and a Half*. Since the author wrote at a time when resistance to dictatorship was a dangerous business in Congo-Brazzaville, a climate of fear and repression hangs over the novel and pushes Tansi to find artful ways of representing this very real political world with an indirect literary style that incorporates elements of magical realism from Latin American fiction. The novelist creates symbolic characters that he calls "flesh passwords" and imagines a surreal country named Katamalanasie where grotesque things happen. All of these narrative elements take us into a bizarre world of political turmoil formulated from a Kongo perspective from outside the walls of power. The writer's predicament as a dissident is figured in the novel with a character named Layisho; a writer whose ideas have not yet found a receptive audience in what Carpentier calls "The Kingdom of This World" and thus Layisho is forced to spend his improbably long life detained inside a cage. This outlandish display makes visible the inhuman deprivation of his instrumental, substantive, and existential freedoms.

The opening scene of the novel takes place in the presidential palace where the Providential Guide attempts to kill the leader of the opposition in front of his family in keeping with Bakongo rituals of violence that involve perpetrator, victim, and witness. The dictator's name conveys a harsh irony given the deadly serious relationship between the spiritual realm and the exercise of political power.[56] Martial and his family represent the political opposition in Katamalanasie and are engaged in a violent conversation with the Providential Guide about power. The symbolic language they use suggests an existential struggle for justice and a political competition for dominance and legitimacy. The dictator tries unsuccessfully to kill Martial; he cuts his belly open with a knife, he fires rounds with automatic rifles and tears him to shreds with cutlery, but the opposition leader's body stubbornly hovers in the air in front of him. The tools of war (knifes, guns) cannot defeat the leader's presence because, in a symbolic sense, his body is a container of power that exceeds the physical realm.[57] Martial's belly – the spiritual seat of his personal power – is opened with a knife and his guts spill onto the floor, but his capacity to resist in the face of such an assault is beyond the reach of the dictator's knife.[58] It is a language of confrontation that involves bodies and objects and explicitly assumes human conflict and a spiritual contest not consensus.[59]

As the title indicates, Tansi envisions the political drama in the narrative as involving this life (objective, real) that is connected to and dependent on another realm of life (occult, imaginary). The contest of power between the Providential Guide and Martial is embedded in the Bakongo practice of *kindoki* (literally, "power or force" also translated as "witchcraft"): this involves the use of invisible forces by *banganga* (those who use "protecting kindoki") to achieve balance within the community or by *bandoki* (those who use "eating kindoki") for destructive purposes.[60] Simon Bockie's essay on *kindoki* helps us understand how, in the realm of the living it is possible to see Martial's body as the physical envelope of his intimate self, whereas in the spiritual realm his belly is the seat of personal power and has a symbolic significance. In the author's Kongo conception of power, drawing a distinction between "real" and "imaginary" power becomes problematic because, as Wyatt MacGaffey points out, in Bakongo culture political leaders are widely assumed to be involved in self-seeking traffic in the occult.[61] Thus the macabre opening scene in *Life and a Half* produces two apparently contradictory meanings. It is a representation of a contest that condemns the Guide's use of repressive political violence and establishes the fact that, if dictators can kill individual dissidents, they will never be able to completely eliminate resistance to injustice. This scene can also be read as a zero-sum game with winners and losers that is not open to negotiation or compromise.

After this dramatic opening, a struggle for political dominance structures the rest of the narrative and begins with a triangulation of power. Part of what makes the conversation about power, legitimacy, and dominance so interesting is that the perpetrator and victim speak the same language as Achille Mbembe has noted.[62] Martial (leader of the resistance) haunts the Providential Guide (dictator) through his daughter, Chaïdana (Martial's survivor). Martial's legacy on earth, in the realm of the living, as a political martyr lives on through his beautiful daughter. When she says she lives "life and a half" in her body, she means that her physical envelope is her own body, but it is also an intermediary link between her ancestor who has become a ghost to haunt the living through her. The Providential Guide is condemned to share his bed with Chaïdana and every time the dictator seeks to assert his virility by initiating sexual relations with her, the father reappears. Martial's ghostlike presence hovers in the air above the bed and the permanence of his censoring presence is symbolized by black ink – the black ink of Martial – that stains the dictator's body (hands, face) and his bed sheets. This triangulation neutralizes the dictator's virility as a man which is intimately linked to his power and authority as a political leader. The gender dynamics at work in this novel are complex and involve women who are both perpetrators and victims of political violence. In other scenes the novelist repurposes stereotypes of women as sexual objects and turns them into political agents who seduce and then kill men with spiked champagne. Tansi's female characters have agency, but this does not lead to liberating alternatives as they are doubly constrained; first, by conventional gender roles (female seduction, heterosexual behavior) and, second, by the same existential struggle for social justice and meaningful freedom.

The way the novelist engages with sexuality and gender is evident during an episode, near the end of the novel, designated as "Virgin Week" in which the production of limitless successors to the Providential Guide becomes possible. During this week fifty beds are made in one of the 3,000 rooms in the Palace of Mirrors, paid for by the national budget that is actually borrowed from "the foreign powers who furnished the guides." Fifty of the most beautiful virgins in the country were selected, bathed, perfumed, massaged, and equipped with linens and robes; they all had bodies made to sexually excite the male imagination. Virgin Week was filmed and televised as, "The Guide and Production," despite the warnings of the Pope, the United Nations and a number of nations friendly with Kawangotara (the nation-state's new name). Each of the virgins was marked with a number on their bellies from 2 to 51 with the Guide marked number 1. It was reported that Jean-Coeur-de-Pierre finished his first round of copulating with the virgins in three hours, twenty-six minutes, and twelve seconds. The combination of hyperbole with specificity in the description throughout the scene creates a critical tension between the real world of political power and the symbolic realm of his imagination. Women's bodies are objectified, once again, as tools in a scheme to satisfy male pleasure and, this time, to prolong indefinitely the scourge of foreign-sponsored dictatorship. The offspring from Virgin Week are so plentiful that they are named in alphabetical series starting with the letters C, S, and V and their comical names signal the depressing array of future leaders willing to collaborate with "foreign powers who supply the guides."

In *Life and a Half* questions of capital, profit and access to resources remain implicit, whereas particular emphasis is given to the revolving door of African dictators funded by external sponsors. On one level, Virgin Week is a humorous scenario that indirectly invokes the expanding hegemony of global capital in the last decade of the Cold War and the obstacles to political citizenship that this created in Africa after independence. Yet Virgin Week is also a pivotal symbolic element in Tansi's fable that increasingly focuses on the obscene absence of progress in Congo-Brazzaville. The endless supply of dictators that can be explained by the structure of the gatekeeper state is depicted here with sexual humor and irony to portray an indecent situation of dispossession that is not at all funny in real life. While a sharp satirical tone gives voice to the author's moral outrage in this scene, it is significant that the symbolic language of the body, at other moments in the novel, integrates spiritual and political experience in terms of the body's memory of repression. As the novel concludes, for instance, the narrator expands his frame of reference in this direction by referring to dissidents who receive "internal slaps" that injure both their intimate and spiritual selves. There are frequent references to malediction and life on earth as hell, to men raping women in order to assert power, and to the existence of communal graves where the bodies of opposition leaders rot covered with flies. Thus, the impossibility of forming a coherent sovereign nation-state and delivering on the promises of national liberation – unity, prosperity, social justice – appears to derive, in this narrative, from political and spiritual factors in equal measure. One of Tansi's unique contributions to literary representations of African decolonization is how the Congolese people interpret objective political factors from their point of view as an experience of dispossession with a spiritual component that makes the struggle for meaningful freedom seem a zero-sum game with an apocalyptic end.

In Cooper's account of African decolonization, the Belgian Congo offers one of the most notorious and egregious illustrations of the tug-of-war that produced gatekeeper states in Africa. Opportunities for an advanced education were not available to the emerging elite in the Belgian Congo in comparison with the education Fanon got in France and Mandela in South Africa. In fact, the paternalism and persistent obstacles to advancement that Lumumba encountered within the Belgian colony, where he was only partially assimilated into European colonial society and yet distanced from the Congolese masses, strengthened his conviction that political independence was absolutely necessary. The "mature nationalism" he developed was inspired by Fanon and Nkrumah (in addition to Gamal Abdul Nasser and Touré whom he met in Accra) and advanced a message of unity that continues to define Lumumbism.[63] But this proved unconvincing to some who were more receptive to Kasavubu's brand of messianic anti-imperialism. Opposition to Belgian rule in the Congo was split between Lumumba's vision of national unity and other regional political figures with a strong ethnic base of support, such as Kasavubu in the south. A competition between these two paths to self-rule led to a fragile power sharing arrangement between Kasavubu, the first president and leader of the Bakongo party Abako, and Lumumba, the first prime minister and leader of the only inclusive nationalist party, Mouvement National Congolais. In practice, Lumumba's adherence to the ideal of national unity backfired. When he attempted to maintain control of the territory with force during the secession of Katanga, his rivals cast him as a Jacobin, while they continued to pursue their own regional and ethnic-based politics in competition for control of the centralized state structure that was emerging. Multiple political rivalries at the regional level spiraled out of control and the absence of one unifying revolutionary sentiment among the people contributed to a situation of fragmentation that devolved into a crisis.

A confluence of internal and external factors complicated the transition to African rule in this colony. Lumumba found himself at odds with his own class, the new African elite who hungered for more privilege, and was seen as an unacceptable partner by leaders of Western nations. The fact that Lumumba did not speak the language of liberation in sufficiently muted tones for the King of Belgium's ears in his speech at the independence ceremony would have grave consequences. Cooper remarks that Lumumba's speech "spelled out a devastating – and accurate – portrayal of the violence and exploitation of Belgian colonialism" and this "encouraged Belgian intrigues against him and helped attach the labels of radical or communist to his name in western capitals."[64] Lumumba's bold frankness combined with his unique potential to organize a movement of national unity was perceived as threatening by European and American governments and incompatible with their strategic interests in the territory's natural resources.[65] While the British planned for continued indirect influence and the French engaged in costly wars in Vietnam and Algeria, the Belgian king appointed a leader whose assassination would pave the way to a gatekeeping dictatorship. "Belgium's abdication of responsibility," writes Cooper, "for its brutal colonization and inept decolonization opened the way to the United States, the Soviet Union, France, and the United Nations to inject their own interests, while allegedly trying to bring order to a land whose people had never been allowed to enjoy the riches their country possessed."[66] Jihan El-Tahri adds to the documentation of this history with her film *Cuba: An African Odyssey* (2008) where she shows the direct involvement of the United States in securing access to resources in the Congo and in preventing the Russians and their allies from gaining influence in the region including Fidel Castro and Che Guevara.[67]

Internal divisions among Congolese leaders allowed Belgium, assisted by the United States, to plan and implement the arrest and assassination of Lumumba, which opened the door for Joseph Mobutu to take power in 1965. Once on his throne Mobutu changed his name to Mobutu Sese Seko and ruled as a shrewd gatekeeper for more than thirty years.[68] Elsewhere in Africa the nature of this competition for influence in the African colonies sometimes involved armed insurrection (i.e., Cameroon, Kenya), violent repression (i.e., Madagascar), or assassination (i.e., Congo-Brazzaville, Niger) – and sometimes the transition was more peaceful (i.e., Ghana, Senegal). With or without violence, deliberate measures to prevent unfettered sovereignty could be taken and were often achieved. While the disastrous path that decolonization took in the Congo does not provide an accurate portrait of the process everywhere else on the continent, the effects of the cold and calculating steps that European colonials and their Western allies took to maintain their influence in this African country helps illustrate the kind of maneuvering that went on a smaller scale and out of view elsewhere whenever possible. At the same time, it is important to acknowledge, in my view, that the Congolese people's political dispossession could not have happened without African actors who made choices and helped shape the outcome including Kasavubu, Moïse Tshombe, and Mobutu.

Nzongola-Ntalaja sums up the Congolese people's attempt to mount a second independence movement as follows, "The first major resistance against the postcolonial state in Africa took place between 1963 and 1968 in the Congo ... The objectives of the movement were basically the same during the two periods [the first taking place from 1956 to 1960], namely, freedom from foreign control and expanded democratic and economic rights."[69] He sees the second movement as consistent with Amìlcar Cabral's notion of the liberation struggle that consists of two phases: the national and the social phases. For Nzongola-Ntalaja, this second movement was a mass movement against the neocolonial regime in the Congo that challenged the uninterrupted exploitation of the country's resources by Western powers and minority white regimes in southern Africa with the cooperation of the new ruling elite.[70] His conclusion about this movement in the Congo in terms of how it defined the people's response to independence helps us also understand Tansi's fiction in its historical context: "Coming on the heels of the political violence and dislocations of the independence struggle, this first war of liberation against the postcolonial state in Africa has taught the Congolese people the value of being sceptical about the would-be saviours who seem to thrive in destroying rather than building the country. At the same time, one of the legacies of the second independence movement is that a culture of resistance against illegitimate state authority has become a major feature of Congolese political life."[71] Tansi's writing and activism suggests that he was split in his allegiance between the ideals of national liberation that Lumumba incarnated and the messianic vision of a struggle for spiritual redemption that Matswa, Kimbangu, and Kasavubu espoused. While Tansi's faith in the promises of national liberation and the Congolese people's efforts to realize them even in the face of violent repression persisted into the late 1970s, his interpretation of the situation of widening conflict and deepening divisions became more rigid and partisan as we will see in Chapter 5.

I would like to turn now to two narratives from the 1990s that are less canonical than the two novels we just looked at. I am interested in them less for the status of their contribution to African cultural expression than for their capacity to elucidate a complex moment of historical transition. The decade of the 1990s represented an extremely important and pivotal moment after the fall of the Berlin Wall and the end of the Cold War. This ideological détente led to a recalibration of Western investment and intervention in Africa and opened the way for African people to participate in multiparty politics, organize national conferences and, in some cases, vote in presidential and legislative elections. At the 2015 African Studies Association meeting, I attended the two roundtables "Post-Cold War, Post-Nation?" chaired by David Pratten and Peter Geschiere with several participants and an active audience. I observed an overwhelming sense among Africanist scholars that the 1990s were as important, if not more so, than the 1960s in terms of the transformational change that happened in many African countries. Beyond the question of national conferences invoked at the beginning of Jean-Marie Teno's film *Afrique, je te plumerai* (1992; *Africa, I Will Fleece You*) and discussed by Eboussi Boulaga in *Les conférences nationales en Afrique: Une affaire à suivre* (1993) the decade is of particular interest here because it was a time when many ideas, including the nation itself, were brought up for reconsideration. Cooper opened the introduction to *Africa since 1940: The Past of the Present* (2002) by juxtaposing two apparently contradictory events of decisive importance – the election of Mandela in South Africa and the genocide in Rwanda – that both took place during the spring of 1994. To explore how the first decade of the post-Cold War era reshaped the conversation about African freedom I will shift my focus slightly with less emphasis on context from historiographies of case studies to patterns and dynamics of general interest.

Cheick Oumar Sissoko's film *Finzan. Dance of the Heroes* (1990) was the first film of the decade to frame the people's struggle for political freedoms in relation to women's rights as human rights. Set in Mali and filmed during a period of civic engagement and political protest in the streets – involving women, students, and workers – that ushered in the country's transition to democracy 1991, Sissoko's film tells the story of women's oppression and resistance in terms that evoke the political ethos in the country. It is evident to me that Sissoko's film narrative, which helped me lay the conceptual foundation for this book, was written by someone with a background in sociology and African history because *Finzan* incorporates all the significant social factors contributing to meaningful freedom and weaves them into a deceptively simple story about two women, Fili and Nanyuma, in a Bambara village in Mali. Alongside Sissoko's *Finzan*, I would like to consider Beti's novel *Trop de soleil tue l'amour* (1999) mentioned in the introduction to this chapter. Beti was an accomplished novelist in his sixties and recently retired from teaching high school in France when he wrote this novel – his first narrative written entirely in Cameroon after he returned from exile. The way *Trop de soleil tue l'amour* seeks to instruct the reader about Francophone African Republics from the hybrid viewpoint of someone who is both an insider (born in Akométan near Mbalmayo) and an outsider (lived abroad for thirty years) goes a long way toward explaining what it was like to still be grappling with the delay of meaningful freedom at the end of the decade.

In a series of interviews with Frank Ukadike conducted between 1993 and 1995 when asked whether *Finzan* was a film about female genital cutting (excision), Sissoko replied emphatically that is was not and quickly offered, instead, that it was a film about freedom.[72] Unfortunately, film critics tend to emphasize the question of women's rights – especially the controversial criticism of female genital cutting – in the film to the detriment of the narrative's complex political implications.[73] In *African Experiences of Cinema* (1996), Mbye Cham and Imruh Bakari cite Sissoko's films *Finzan* and *Guimba, the Tyrant* (1995) as examples of African films by men that specifically raise issues related to women's emancipation. Yet in the Ukadike interview Sissoko further explained why he was drawn to filmmaking: "I chose cinema because of its relation to politics. So each time I make a film, I try to accomplish my objective. With *Finzan* it was clearly the problem of the oppression of women and the necessity for their emancipation. But there is also the essential question of legal rights and liberty for a nation, and for a continent."[74] As we will see, the main female characters each face their own kind of oppression: Nanyuma contends with forced marriage and Fili resists, unsuccessfully, against female genital cutting. But the deprivation of their substantive freedoms as women also serves as an illustration – according to Sissoko's explanations and my understanding of the film – of the people's quest for political freedoms vis-à-vis the state. Sissoko's feminist film explicitly poses women's substantive freedoms (choice of spouse, genital cutting) as being at odds with the patriarchal values in a Bambara village, which allows him to explore how constraints on individual freedoms originate within the community and are exacerbated by a number of interconnected factors. In *Finzan*, Sissoko brings to bear his sociological and historical research on specific issues, his political activism in favor of democracy and women's rights and his interest, as an artist, in provoking civic debate on important and controversial issues.[75]

Finzan opens with a statement about the status of women with data from the United Nations: "[women] receive a double blow both inside and outside of the family because of their sex and social conditions. As fifty percent of the population they do two-thirds of the housework and receive ten percent of the income and own less than one percent of property." This reference to the injustices that actual women faced around the world invites the viewer to consider the story that is about to unfold through a feminist lens and mindful of worldwide conditions in 1990. As we discussed in the preceding chapter, issues such as women's choices to select a spouse and to willingly submit to genital cutting or not are substantive freedoms that feminist writers and filmmakers had been exploring as part of an inclusive discussion of freedom since Mariama Bâ's novels of the 1970s and 80s. In addition, writing by men had previously addressed these specific issues of genital cutting and forced marriage as we see in Ahmadou Kourouma's allegorical novel *Les soleils des indépendances* (1968; *The Suns of Independence*) and in Nuruddin Farah's *From a Crooked Rib* (1970). More generally, male writers and filmmakers had long since been exploring gender asymmetries with humor and political satire as we see in Wole Soyinka's play *The Lion and the Jewel* (1959) and Ousmane Sembène's novella and film *Xala* (1973 and 1975). Sissoko's innovation in *Finzan* is to show that the repercussions of the absence of meaningful freedom at the national level adversely affect women and children disproportionately because they find themselves on the lowest rung of the social hierarchy.

When her husband Sugo dies, Nanyuma does not mourn his passing because she was forced into the marriage as a teenager and endured beatings while he was alive. As soon as her much older husband is buried, his brother Bala – a nickname for the common name Moussa, not incidentally the name of the military dictator, Moussa Traoré, who had ruled Mali since 1968 – seeks to acquire her as his wife according to the levirate custom. This kind of marital request is subject to familial discussion and community approval, which the village chief hears and to which he ultimately consents. When we see Nanyuma bound up – with close-ups that show her wrists and feet tethered – and delivered to Bala against her will, the deprivation of her personal freedom allegorically represents the mistreatment of the Malian people under dictatorship. Although the husband is portrayed as a ridiculous, power-hungry fool by an actor from koteba theater, within the context of this patriarchal village Bala symbolizes male power and, more broadly, in the context of Mali's transition to democracy he symbolizes political oppression and the use of force, which is later reinforced when he handles a gun. Sissoko's negative portrait of Bala and his ally in the village chief, who adheres with such inflexibility to patriarchal customs, stands as an unambiguous critique of patriarchy and dictatorship as well as their implicit interconnection.

In a parallel narrative development, Fili is subjected to female genital cutting against medical advice due to the fact that her mother – who suffered from hemophilia – died during child birth from hemorrhaging as a result of her genital cutting. Fili, who lives in the city, and is engaged to Segi, a young man who has studied abroad, asserts her right to decide not to be cut and says, "My body is mine. I feel good that way. I will not be excised." For Sissoko, the way she takes charge of herself represents "a larger democratic tradition of taking charge of one's person" and the way she uses her voice reflects an increased freedom for women in the city compared to rural areas.[76] At least, this was Sissoko's perspective on women in Mali during the 1990s; in Niger, the opposite seems to be the case for Tuareg women whose rights can be eroded, if they leave their rural kinship networks and migrate to the city. Yet Segi refuses to marry Fili unless she consents to genital cutting. Although a number of the village women support her case to do as she pleases with her body and even threaten to withhold sex with their husbands, some of the elder women are scandalized and finally take Fili by force. They carry her off by her arms and legs and brutally cut her against her will. The way Fili is physically restrained and deprived of her substantive freedom echoes the treatment Nanyuma receives as a wife forced into marriage. In a dramatic turn of events, the details of her medical condition are revealed too late, after she is cut, and as she is rushed to the hospital, we assume she will die.

The film shows discussion and dissent in the exchanges between the villagers of different ages and genders, which reveals the complexity of the culturally embedded practices of marriage and female genital cutting. When it comes to women's emancipation the village chief categorically refuses to go against patriarchal customs – an inflexible position older patriarchal women also support. Sissoko has pointed out that the absence of unity prohibits the villagers from going against the chief's tyrannical authority in defense of women's rights in the same way sociopolitical divisions prevented the Malian people from effectively challenging dictatorship for many years. The filmmaker admits that these implicit political meanings are easier for Malians to perceive at a moment of historical political change in the country.[77] At the end of the film, Fili will likely die and Nanyuma – who refuses to consummate the forced marriage with Bala – desperately defends herself from his sexual advances with knife in hand. To underscore the central theme of freedom, Sissoko includes observational footage – as establishing shots and cut-away shots – of common animals in the village that are tethered to posts or with their limbs bound as visual comments on the scenarios in which humans are deprived of their freedom. As Sissoko has noted: "Being tied up represents the loss of all freedoms. It shows the suppression of individual abilities to function when all fundamental human rights are taken away."[78] In order to fully comprehend why the chief allows Fili to be cut and Nanyuma to be carted off, bound like a goat for sale, we must consider the web of relations that explains why emasculated patriarchs compensate for their diminished authority nationally and internationally by wielding the little power they have over women and children.

The pivotal scene of confrontation in this film happens when the district commissioner (who is a representative of the national government) has come to request that the villagers sell their grain – two tons of millet – at a below-market price to an interested buyer. This unfair and exploitative demand is made during a draught when the price of grain should go up as a result of increased demand and limited supply. The rapport is openly hostile between these men from the state who sit on chairs, speak in French and wear expensive clothes and the villagers who sit on mats on the ground in the shade of trees and speak Bambara. Sissoko represents the villagers' subordination to the nation-state and to the forms of colonial power that preceded it with men who communicate through a translator and seem as convinced of their authority to set the price of grain as a colonial official collecting taxes. The district commissioner resorts to force and takes the Bambara chief hostage as he waits for the villagers to deliver their grain at the imposed below-market price. Of course, the way the patriarch is arrested and physically detained parallels other forms of physical restraint used against women in the film. Yet when the entire village and surrounding area support the chief's refusal to submit to this extortion, the old man is set free as a result of their show of unity. This scene illustrates what a day in the life of villagers is like when their rights to negotiate (the price of grain, which language they speak) and have their interests represented by elected officials have been confiscated. The way the narrative clearly establishes a parallel between the two narrative strands of women who resist patriarchal oppression and the village chief's desire for freedom from coercion by the state advances thinly veiled criticism of another abuse of power in the form of dictatorship. As a matter of fact, women traders started the popular protest in the street against Moussa Traoré (the president of Mali from 1968 to 1991) initiating the transition to democracy in Mali. So, for viewers familiar with these events, the fact that in *Finzan* Sissoko evokes national politics, resistance to dictatorship, and a pro-democracy sentiment in direct relation to the emancipation of women would not have been elusive or surprising.

With an intricately layered plot a confluence of factors can be discerned in this narrative. Mali's economic hardships during the crisis of the 1990s, associated with the implementation of structural adjustment programs, put pressure on prices (i.e., millet) and created difficulties for the rural poor. In this instance, Bambara villagers are subordinated to the state's authority via the district commissioner who sets prices (i.e., millet, rice) and collects taxes, but the same scenario could happen in any number of villages across the region. The Bambara chief's authority is diminished in his village and within the nation-state when he is emasculated during a confrontation with the district commissioner, which as Mamdani argues in *Citizen and Subject* (1996) reproduces power asymmetries set up during the colonial period. The village chief and patriarchs who rely on his authority seem to enjoy the subjugation of women in the domestic sphere, as we witness most dramatically in the lives of Nanyuma and Fili, in order to compensate for their impotence in the public sphere when confronted by agents of the neocolonial nation-state. The narrative suggests that women are so brutally deprived of their substantive freedoms in this village because the patriarch feels emasculated in front of his kinsfolk when national officials disrespect his authority. If gatekeepers compete to improve their strategic and economic advantages at the helm of the nation, men without power in the nation-state take out their frustrations on those who are weaker and more vulnerable than they are. It is important to note that the village chief's insult happens for reasons that reach beyond his Bambara cultural setting to the global politics of economic development. Thus, when Sissoko makes a plea for the liberation of women he effectively challenges a complex network of interconnected forms of subordination. In her succinct summary of *Finzan*, Sharon Russell aptly observed that "Sissoko takes the more radical position that freedom must be total and that all oppression must be abandoned."[79] Since the women he represents in *Finzan* occupy the lowest position in the hierarchy of power at issue in the film, to emancipate them would necessarily call into question all the factors contributing to their subjugation. Sissoko returned, in his next film – *Guimba, the Tyrant* which won best film at FESPACO in 1995 – to the theme of tyrannical male rule that is developed as a gendered critique of dictatorship in an effort to strengthen the emergence of a democratic culture in Mali and on the continent, more broadly. Sissoko's political allegories represent substantive and instrumental freedoms as mutually reinforcing types of freedom. He does this in his films by invoking the historical activism of women who exercised their instrumental freedoms in street and by showing female characters who explicitly seek greater substantive freedoms in the face of patriarchal oppression. For Sissoko, women exemplify the people's struggle and play a leading role in *Finzan* to the extent that Fili and Nanyuma offer an alternative to submitting to tyranny. Their feisty desire for emancipation invites the people to reflect on what it would take for them to work together to expand their instrumental freedoms. At the beginning of an important decade for Africa, both *Finzan* and *Guimba* sought to cultivate an awareness of the importance of women's liberation as well as the value of freedom – especially from political tyranny – as essential components of emerging African democracies.

Let us turn now to Beti's novel *Trop de soleil tue l'amour* (1999) which explores the causes and consequences of the deprivation of men's instrumental freedoms and women's substantive freedoms at the end of the decade. An African nation in the vicinity of Gabon and the former Zaïre is the setting for *Trop de soleil tue l'amour*, though not named, it would seem that Cameroon serves as the author's model for the "Francophone African Republic." In *Africa since Independence* (2004) Nugent presents Mali as an example of a successful transition to democracy, whereas he includes Cameroon among those countries who opted for a "controlled release" from dictatorship. After the military dictator Traoré – who usurped power in Mali in 1968 – faced street protest in 1990 initiated by women traders, a national conference was held in 1991 and elections prepared in 1992. The historian Alpha Konaré won the presidential election in 1992, was reelected in 1997, and stepped aside in 2002, making Mali an example of democracy in the region due, in no small part, to the civic engagement of women.[80] In Cameroon, the opposition was unsuccessful in getting a national conference despite widespread popular protest including *villes mortes* (strikes that shut down cities) and independent election observers say that significant irregularities have marred the presidential elections in 1992, 1997, 2004, and 2011 that Paul Biya claims to have won, since he took over from Ahidjo in 1982.[81] In his film *Africa, I will fleece you* (1992), Jean-Marie Teno made famous the open letter, "La Democratie truquée" (1988), that Célestin Monga wrote in which he roundly criticized President Biya for refusing a national conference and countering his claim that democratic rule had already come to Cameroon.[82] Emboldened by the support of the French government, Biya managed to fend off the opposition by theoretically allowing opposition parties to run candidates against him and claiming to lift restrictions on the media, while thwarting every attempt that was made to establish a true democracy and resorting to brutal, violent repression when needed.[83]

Among African novelists of the twentieth century who wrote in French, Beti stands out as the author with perhaps the most passionate, long-standing obsession with the defeat of national liberation in Africa, especially in his native Cameroon, as we see in his essay *Main basse sur le Cameroun* (1972) and his novels from *Remember Ruben* (1974) to *La Revanche de Guillaume Ismaël Dzewatama* (1984). As Richard Bjornson discusses in *The African Quest for Freedom and Identity. Cameroon Writing and the National Experiment* (1994), Cameroon was the only French-administered colony in sub-Saharan Africa to mount an armed resistance to French rule. Unlike the colonial wars in Vietnam and Algeria, the French colonial administration swiftly defeated the popular uprising led by Ruben Um Nyobe and his party Union des populations du Cameroun (UPC) with troops on the ground and by assassinating the leadership of the opposition including Nyobe. This prepared the way for Ahidjo to take power in 1960 as the first president of Cameroon with the blessing of the French and to the bitter dismay of citizens who had been engaged in the struggle for national liberation. During the three decades Beti spent in France teaching Greek and Latin at a high school in Rouen and raising children with his wife Odile, he remained committed to the cause of democracy and achieving meaningful freedom in Cameroon and to pan-African solidarity with the publication of their review *Peuples noirs, peuples africains* (1978–1991).

In her homage to Beti, his wife entitled her essay "Une singulaire liberté" (a "singular freedom") in which she singles out his most important trait: the visceral defense of his own existential freedom.[84] While it is true that Beti carefully guarded his independence in terms of ideology and political parties, he used his instrumental freedoms as a writer and critic in defense of social justice and political progress and cited Martin Luther King Jr as his model of a transformational leader. As a pro-democracy activist, he published numerous articles in the local media, which we have in an edited volume *Mongo Beti à Yaoundé, 1991–2001* (2005), and was deeply invested in promoting journalism in the form of independent newspapers and radio. In *Mongo Beti parle* (2002), the author identifies the problem of the nation-state as the defining issue in Cameroon and in Africa, more generally:

L'État du Cameroun existe, mais à mon humble avis, c'est une coquille vide. L'État, c'est un ensemble d'institutions ... Mais ce qui compte, c'est l'âme qui donne une vie à ces institutions. Si cette âme n'existe pas, l'État est un cadavre. Or, l'âme, qu'est-ce que c'est? C'est la nation. Estce qu'il y a une nation camerounaise? Voilà la grande question qui se pose. Est-ce qu'il y a un souffle, un dynamisme capable de transcender les ethnies et de constituer, au-dessus des ethnies, une entité moderne, avec une sorte d'unité d'aspirations, une volonté de vivre en commun? Notre grand problème, c'est celui de la nation camerounaise. Cette nation n'a jamais pu se constituer parce qu'on a dressé sur son chemin toutes sortes d'obstacles ... Mais nous sommes là dans une situation qui est celle de presque tous les États africains.

(The State of Cameroon exists, but in my humble opinion, it is an empty shell. The State is made up of various institutions ... But what matters is the soul that gives life to these institutions. If this soul does not exist, the State is a corpse. Yet what is the soul? It's the nation. In this sense, is there a Cameroonian nation? Now there's the big question that must be asked. Is there a kind of breath, a dynamism capable of transcending ethnicity and of constituting, above ethnic groups, a modern entity, with a sort of unity of aspirations, a will to live together? Our big problem is that of the Cameroonian nation. This nation never had the chance of taking shape because all sorts of obstacles were put in the way ... But, in this regard, we are in a situation that is the same for almost all African States. *(Mongo Beti parle, p. 140; my translation)*

After spending a decade in his homeland, Beti arrived at the conclusion that achieving unfettered sovereignty and resuscitating the nation – its spirit, its soul, and a shared sense of purpose – were the most important existential challenges that Cameroonians faced at the end of the 1990s. In addition to the echoes from Renan and Fanon in his articulation of the idea of the nation, we see an increased importance attributed to ethnic attachments, by comparison to Beti's earlier writing, as one of the most significant impediments to national unity.[85]

The way Beti wrestled with the legacy of national liberation after he returned to Cameroon evolved over time. The categorical tone of his first two books before he settled in Yaoundé in 1994, *La France contre l'Afrique, retour au Cameroun* (1993) and *Histoire du fou* (1994), reveal how his criticism of those who stayed behind was formulated from the distanced perspective of someone who had spent three decades in exile.[86] In *Histoire du fou* (History of the madman) Beti creates a world in which anticolonial militants who believed in the 1960s ideal of achieving national sovereignty have gone mad. It was not until *Trop de soleil tue l'amour,* written in French with inflections of urban slang and published in installments in the local newspaper, that we see the author represent the country of his birth and youth in a new way that offers a complex, original synthesis.[87] However, the most obvious contrast with Sissoko's *Finzan* and *Guimba* is the absence of feminism in Beti's novel that maintains a conventionally gendered discourse of national liberation according to which men are the agents of historical change, as feminist critics have long since noted.[88] In *Trop de soleil tue l'amour* men are politically oppressed as journalists and activists because they do not enjoy freedom of expression, and as citizens in a corrupt society without institutions to enforce laws or protect human rights. Once again, we also have a thoroughly patriarchal society in which men oppress women as they take out their frustrations on young urban women who are poor, vulnerable, and in need of love and protection. Whereas Beti does not represent women's liberation as essential to democracy, the way he portrays the difficulties women face in getting their basic needs met and being treated with respect stands as condemnation of a degenerate society. As in previous narratives, the author embeds the Cameroonian people's dispossession in a transnational network of relations in *Trop de soleil tue l'amour* with explicit references to the persistence of a gatekeeper state, most notably with the wealthy Haroun al-Rashid who lives in a palace in the forest and runs a mysterious, illicit business with diplomatic cover. While there are international references to other scenarios of progress in African nations as in Laurent Kabila's overthrow of Mobutu, to African-American civil rights icons like Rosa Park and Martin Luther King Jr. who make change via non-violent protest but, in the final analysis, the nation's destiny will always be "calamitous" in a Banana Republic because the potential for unhappiness is endless.

In *Trop de soleil tue l'amour* the absence of historical progress and social disarray are mirrored in the narrative with a plot that zigzags, but does not develop toward a satisfying conclusion. The novel tells the story of an unhappy couple, Zam and Bébète, that is intercut with various bizarre subplots so that the narrative's dramatic arc is fractured. The characters are confronted with obstacles, such as finding a way to protect political journalists from a violent regime; however, they prove insurmountable and so, at the novel's end, the characters remain essentially unchanged.

The plot is splintered into a sequence of brief episodes that do not follow in logical order, rather they seem to be disjointed elements assembled according to the author's subjective sense of things. Two of the main characters, Eddie and Zam, love classical jazz and, in addition to the rich references to jazz, the principles of improvisation and self-expression in that musical genre also inflect the storytelling style. Within individual chapters coups de théâtre are used at key moments amplifying the plot's unreal and fragmented quality. An example of this is when Zam miraculously falls into Bébète's arms as he is released from police detention; the reader never learns why Bébète decided to return to her abusive boyfriend and her sudden reappearance falls at a dramatic juncture, just moments after Zam was picked up by the police during a raid of the headquarters for the newspaper *Aujourd'hui la démocratie!* where he works as a political journalist for the opposition. Yet if this unconventional, innovative narrative gleefully dispenses with the constraints of verisimilitude and realistic psychological motivation that were characteristic of Beti's earlier fiction, the social commentary is, nevertheless, very carefully considered.

Beti's social criticism is primarily character driven as regards historical progress and the legacy of national liberation. Zam is a historically symbolic character; as a father, he came of age at independence, whereas his son was born after 1960. Their agency as men belongs to the sphere of national politics that is exclusively male in this novel. As a journalist Zam lives under constant duress and fears violent repression, which illustrates the deprivation of the people's instrumental freedoms in this Francophone African Republic and explains his personal anger and alcoholism. When the editor of *Aujourd'hui la démocratie!* calls meetings to discuss freedom of expression, government officials tell him to quit publishing critical articles about deforestation and foreign investment. Zam's frustration in a country ravaged by violent dictatorship and a culture of impunity builds up over time and culminates in a humiliating sense of vulnerability at the hands of police interrogators when he is detained after the police raid the newspaper's offices. The opposition's failure to come up with effective strategies to counter the state's repressive use of violence perpetuates an atmosphere of insecurity to which Zam responds with excessive drinking and sexual compensation.

Near the end of the novel Zam is detained, once again, by a man who claims to be his son. This character that abruptly appears in the final chapter says he was born of an illicit affair in 1963 when Zam was working in the man's village as an informant for the state, denouncing militants in the opposition. Thus, not only had Zam worked in concert with the first French-backed dictator, he also apparently took advantage of an innocent girl at the same time. The consequences of Zam's unethical choices in the past come back to haunt him and are revealed unexpectedly in this confrontation that his ill-begotten son has orchestrated. The vengeful bastard, who insists on a complete confession from his father, dramatically claims responsibility for all that has happened to Zam during the course of the novel beginning with the body of Maurice Mzilikazi that was dumped in his apartment. Yet a sense of mystery lingers given that the reader is unable to verify the son's surprising account against any subsequent statements since the novel simply ends with his unconfirmed avowal. What is clear, however, is that the sins of the sons of independence are visited on the present and this explains the nation's current state of affairs. It should be noted that Beti's representation of how the historical past – notably male elders who betrayed the cause of national liberation – haunts the present generation in *Trop de soleil tue l'amour* intersects with an important motif throughout African literature that we also find, for instance, in Kourouma's *Les Soleils des indépendances* (1968) and Chris Abani's *Graceland* (2004).

Zam's girlfriend, Bébète, is another socially symbolic character who is primarily defined by the deprivation of her substantive freedoms. She is a woman without the means to support herself so she is at the mercy of men like Zam to meet her material and emotional needs. Although she is mostly motivated by necessity in her relationships with men, Bébète is represented as a sexually attractive woman and thus a conventional object of male desire. Women who live in poverty, as Bébète does, have few options to define their lives productively without the help of men and, thus, they often tolerate domestic abuse until something better comes along. The narrator makes bitingly ironic comments about how reciprocal, romantic love seems a bourgeois luxury for women stuck in the slums, while also lamenting how Zam is so profoundly insecure in his masculinity that he cannot develop affective attachments and admit loving feelings for a woman. Formal prostitution, in the form of men paying women for sex, also exists in this society and, once women become sex workers, they are often no longer capable of tenderness, which is seen as having long-term negative consequences for men, women, and children. Beti's social and political criticism comes through when the narrator explicitly relates Zam's emasculation in the public arena to his pathological jealousy and abusive treatment of Bébète in private. It is through a form of compensatory sexuality that this angry, frustrated man seeks the pleasure of control and domination in the intimate sphere.

Trop de soleil tue l'amour does not revise gender stereotypes in any significant way; fathers are criticized for not protecting their families, lovers for not being gallant and respectful. Yet Beti represents Zam's emasculation and Bébète's vulnerability as a means of humanizing the travails of citizens trying to survive the chaos of dictatorship. In the end, the author defends reciprocal love, based on mutual respect, as a universal value and not a bourgeois luxury. Beti's defense of love, combined with his exploration of the toxic psychosexual dynamics of Zam's pathological jealousy and abusive treatment of Bébète, accords an importance to the sphere of intimacy in complex terms that are political, social, and interpersonal. Whereas mutual respect and reciprocity in love would certainly improve women's lives in this Francophone African Republic, the remedy to Bébète's situation is seen as men's responsibility and not in terms of a feminist reorganization of gender hierarchies. Feminist scholars and literary critics have frequently remarked on the fact that gender identity can come under pressure during moments of historical change, as what happened in Africa during the 1990s.[89] There is so much evidence for this in the world of African letters that one hardly knows which examples to cite by way of illustration. In Algeria, for instance, Assia Djebar's *So Vast the Prison* (1995) and *Algerian White* (1995) brilliantly testify to the gendered dynamics of political anxiety and the violent subjugation of women – in addition to political activists, journalists, and writers – during the civil war that erupted in the early 1990s.[90] In Farah's *Blood in the Sun* trilogy set in Somalia, the author masterfully explores gender, identity, and democracy in relation to themes of national affiliation, territory, and family in *Maps* (1986), women's substantive freedoms and foreign aid in *Gifts* (1992), and facing personal and collective trauma in *Secrets* (1998).[91]

In the last section of this chapter we will focus on narratives about the nation during the transition to multiracial democracy and the Truth and Reconciliation Commission (TRC) in South Africa. The TRC is of particular interest here because the debate about what it did and did not accomplish provides a productive case study for understanding the struggle for meaningful freedom after national liberation. In the year following Mandela's election as president the TRC was formed and conducted under the leadership of Archbishop Desmond Tutu. At this time, the majority of South Africans, black, white, and colored, were still searching for a language of reconciliation. The TRC's mandate was to facilitate national reconciliation through a series of hearings that took place from 1995 to 1998. During hearings at cities and villages across the country individual victims of human rights abuses were invited to testify in public and to confront their perpetrators. Those guilty of politically motivated crimes could apply for amnesty on the condition that they fully disclose all of the details in public and possibly in front of victims and their families. The fact that the TRC allowed the voices of victims to be heard in public was a way of ending the silence and bridging the separateness that had officially kept these different communities apart since 1948. One of the TRC's most significant contributions to national unity was the fact that the hearings fleshed out a portrait of what actually happened to the black community, identified white perpetrators, and recorded the scope and nature of Afrikaner violence.

If we consider Cooper's *Africa since 1940*, it is possible to see the struggle for national liberation in South Africa as another tug-of-war, this time between the mostly Afrikaner National Party and the broad coalition that joined forces with the ANC. Cooper argues that the cracks in the edifice of the apartheid state did not come from the effects of extreme polarization, but rather from incremental reforms from within that ultimately unraveled the legitimacy of the system that had been enforcing white supremacy. By 1988, the year Richard Attenborough released his film *Cry Freedom* about the assassination of Black Consciousness Movement leader Steve Biko, the apartheid regime's decision whether to censor the film or not was completely overtaken by popular protest forcing open the door to greater freedoms.[92] Connie Field's documentary *Have You Heard from Johannesburg* (2010) further illustrates this point. The series portrays how the white South African elite suffered international ostracism in a country that had become recognized around the world as a pariah and shows how external pressure, especially in terms of divestment, boycotts, and banning from sports competitions was brought to bear on an increasingly embattled regime. In addition to internal and external pressures, human factors shaped the process such as F. W. de Klerk's willingness to negotiate after he replaced P. W. Botha at the head of the National Party and Mandela's uncompromising commitment to multiracial democracy. Cooper wryly observes that, "Mandela and his colleagues understood the irony: in offering to the [National Party] the rights long denied the ANC, they could complete the long march to freedom."[93]

The first multiracial presidential election on April 27, 1994 was a historic affair. The endless lines of people waiting to vote for the first time in their lives "revealed just how meaningful the act of voting can be."[94] It is my view that the preservation of democracy in the years since, beginning with Mandela ceding power to Thabo Mbeki in 1999, represents the best hope for achieving meaningful freedom for a majority of the population in the future. While Mandela's election in 1994 was the culmination of one of the most intense and long-lasting struggles for national liberation on the continent, it could not *in itself* right the wrongs of the past, "the history of how resources – land, gold mines, factories, urban real estate – got into the hands of particular people and the consequences of such unequal access is a deep one, and that history did not suddenly turn a new page on April 27."[95]

In his essay "Paradoxes of Sovereignty," James Ferguson considered how the root causes of poverty in South Africa in 2006 could be obscured by Botha's old logic of apartheid according to which black areas are supposed to be sealed off as separate areas of development. Ferguson's work as an anthropologist helps us see how the limits of the very concept of *apartheid* must be exposed by radical critiques advanced by Biko and others that reveal hierarchies of power and the extent to which *interconnections* actually enabled exploitation. Ferguson proposes that the ideas of the "nation," "bantustans," and "separate development" can camouflage the interconnected relationships that made it possible for a powerful white minority to exploit black labor and resources under apartheid. Today, our own analytical frame of reference should not present poverty in a single African country as a *national* problem as this risks closing off from view the role transnational corporations such as Elf-Aquitaine, De Beers, or Areva have played, and continue to play, in creating dramatic socioeconomic inequality within nation-states. "For what is," Ferguson asks, "the international order of nations if not just such a 'constellation of states' that segments off the exploited and impoverished regions within discrete national compartments with 'their own problems,' thereby masking the relations that link the rich and poor regions behind the false fronts of a sovereignty and independence that have never existed?"[96] While Ferguson admits that national liberation accomplished some good, he challenges us to keep in mind the "false" sovereignty of bantusans as we examine the politics of powerlessness and poverty within and between nations during the expansion of a neoliberal world order. Whereas the global dynamics of neoliberal capitalism is an issue that will be pursued in more detail in the next chapter, for now, it is analytically useful to acknowledge that the nation and what happens socioeconomically within the nation's boundaries should not be separated from the international networks that fetter its sovereignty as we have seen in representations of the gatekeeper state.

In *Country of My Skull. Guilt, Sorrow and the Limits of Forgiveness in the New South Africa* (1998), Antjie Krog, an Afrikaner poet and journalist, gives us a detailed and perceptive case-by-case account of the TRC hearings. John Boorman loosely adapted her stunning memoir of the process as a gritty Hollywood film *In My Country* (2004), starring Samuel Jackson and Juliet Binoche. As the harrowing narrative of what happened under apartheid unfolds in Krog's *Country of My Skull*, she relates grim stories about black activists being tortured on farms in dungeons and scenes in which their bones are dug up, both in order to return their remains to loved ones, but also to verify the accuracy of testimony. As a poet in a multilingual society, the author who speaks Afrikaans and English was especially attentive to the politics of language choice, affect, and comprehension. While the primary language of the commission was English, witnesses were allowed to testify before the commissioners in their native languages with the provision of translators. However, Krog and others have noted that the speaker's affect often got lost in the process of translation which unfortunately complicated the audience's ability to comprehend the full scope of the stories. Details related to a high-profile case before the TRC that had been in the national news involving the shooting of Richard and Irene Mutase in Temba (a black suburb or so-called township) illustrates the discursive complexity of testimony during hearings. Their six-year-old son Tshidiso survived because a white policeman defied orders and did not shoot the child after killing his parents in front of him. In Boorman's film, Tshidiso forgives the white officer who spared his life but shot his parents in a dramatic courtroom scene that rather idealistically captures the TRC's spirit of forgiveness. By contrast, Krog grapples in her narrative with the subjective nature of testifying given the circumstances required for amnesty, noting that Paul Van Vuuren, Captain Hechter, and Mamasela each provide their own self-interested version of the facts about the Mutase's murder in Temba. Krog suggests that translation in a multilingual context, human subjectivity, and the conditions set for amnesty all played a role in shaping the national narrative the TRC created of the apartheid era.

Krog discusses the politics of gender from her perspective as a woman and the significant sexual violence that was perpetrated against black women and men. In the chapter, "Truth is a Woman," she quotes the chairperson of the special Gender Commission, Thenjiwe Mtintso, who said that behind every black African woman's story lurked the possibility of assault at the hands of white men in the state security forces, that "men use women's bodies as a terrain of struggle – as a battleground."[97] Krog includes, for instance, Ms. Tsobileyo's testimony about still having bullets in the private parts of her body; and Ms. Khutwane's story about escaping rape at the hands of white security forces only to find, after her release, that her house had been burnt down and one child died in the fire; and Ms. Jaffer's story about how her prison experience turned her into a full-time activist. As a white South African who grew up in an Afrikaner family, Krog sums up the chapter by reflecting on how racist myths about black women served the purpose of reconciling a false sense of superiority in the inner world of some white Afrikaners with the outer world of facts that contradicted their assumptions.

Near the end of her memoir, Krog provides powerful verbatim testimony that a shepherd named Lekotse made at the last human rights hearing, which took place amid considerable tension in Ladybrand in the Northern Province. The shepherd's tale comes after so much has already been established and may be one of the most gripping accounts Krog narrates. The shepherd's hearing illustrates the challenge of reconciling perpetrators and victims, black and white communities, as well as the impossibility of ever restoring some victim's lives. Lekotse has come to tell the TRC about how his life was ruined the day the police broke down his door, turned his house upside down, and arrested his son. The leader of testimony (who is responsible for making sure that necessary facts are revealed) presses the shepherd for specific information, which disrupts the man's narration. Lekotse does eventually confirm that the police arrested his son for activism with the Pan African Congress during the raid on his house. More importantly, however, he wants to convey why "his life was affected since that day." Krog summarizes the transcript and adds a discourse analysis that demonstrates her superb attentiveness to language use. The details in his story reveal how Lekotse's "entire life's philosophy, his perception of the world and his own place in it, was destroyed" (*Country of My Skull*, 286). He is thrown off course when asked for dates because those facts seem irrelevant to why his life was destroyed. He describes the police invasion of his house as "worse than cunning jackals among sheep," a reference Krog interprets as meaning they "exceeded his worst expectations of evil" (*Country of My Skull*, 287). When the shepherd asked the police questions – "Are you hungry?" "When are you going to fix my door?" – they provided no answers and thus withheld the possibility for him to make sense of their world and the reasons for their brutal violation of his privacy. The shepherd longs for a stepladder to give to the commissioners so they could *see* his newly mended door and *understand* him and his world. But his longing for comprehension across different worlds – the police's, the commissioner's, his own – will never be satisfied as he ends by saying: "I'd be happy if one of them comes to the stage and kills me immediately" (*Country of My Skull*, 285). He is unable to make sense of why his feeling of home, safety, and privacy have been permanently violated. His worth as a father and as a man have been destroyed because he has been treated like a donkey, like a *kaffir*. In the end, he asks for his bewilderment in spiritual death to be completed by immediate physical death (*Country of My Skull*, 290). Krog acknowledges the limits of the TRC to accomplish its goals in some cases and sees Lekotse's loses as irreparable because of the cold, inhospitable, and impenetrable world of predominantly white Afrikaner violence.

Biko's life and work provide an important point of reference for understanding the limits of the TRC because his family refused to appear before the commission. Krog tells us that the Biko family considered the TRC a "vehicle for political expediency" that robbed them of justice. The core of Biko's ideas as the founder of the Black Consciousness Movement during the late 1960s and 70s are collected in the volume *I Write What I Like* (2002; first published in 1978). The foreword ends with an appeal: "Read his thoughts and participate in their continued cry to the present and the future as they call for a consciousness committed to truth in the continued struggle for freedom, freedom, *freedom!*" (no emphasis added)[98] Biko saw black consciousness as a means of cultivating existential freedom for black men (and women, although this is not often made explicit) from which the power to resist white oppression must come. In his essay, "Fear, an important determinant in South African politics," Biko maintained that "ever since the white man arrived as a settler in Southern Africa he had created and then preserved for himself a special position of privilege. This position was created and preserved by the use of violence and fear, but the use of these methods was in itself a result of the white's fear of the black population."[99] Black consciousness evolved out of Biko's conviction that resisting white Afrikaner violence was an *existential* battle of the first order –as the shepherd's tale that Krog relates so painfully illustrates. In his essay "Fragmentation of the Black Resistance," Biko laments the patterns of black resistance to apartheid over time: first, resistance is open and marked by defiant rejection; then, it becomes sullen acquiescence and reluctant collaboration; and lastly, black resistance is threated by capitulation and corruption.[100] Given Biko's uncompromising commitment to the truth, his refusal to submit to torture without fighting back, and the absence of mystery about his murder, his family understandably refused to appear before the TRC and wanted, instead, their day in court. It is safe to say that the circumstances of Biko's death while in police custody – made famous by Donald Woods's reporting and *Cry Freedom* – were no longer a secret, least of all for South Africans.

Mahmood Mamdani has advanced similar criticism of the TRC's role in the transition to democracy and takes issue with the decision to frame the reconciliation process in terms of hearings about *individual* human rights abuse cases.[101] For Mamdani, the TRC passed up an opportunity to contribute to a greater sense of social justice by not framing the national narrative more broadly in terms of abuses that injured black South Africans as a group, collectively. In the years since the TRC, the persistence of serious socioeconomic inequality – as the United Nation's human development data show – has made the ANC's attempt to advance a narrative of national reconciliation that is compelling for the disadvantaged black majority more difficult (see Appendix). We have seen that Mandela presented national liberation as a struggle for equality, a sense of security, and a just share in the whole of South Africa. If we consider

Amartya Sen's work on freedom and development as it relates to rights and resources, it helps us consider the issue of national reconciliation in postapartheid South Africa as a debate about the role of democracy to develop the capacity for all South Africans to live the kind of lives they have reason to value. While achieving meaningful freedom could not have been the TRC's objective, the decision to frame the debate in terms of individual injury obviously limited the TRC's contribution to national unity and did little to improve the lives of black South Africans as a group.

In *Mother to Mother* (1998), Sindiwe Magona, South African writer and activist, reflects on the roots of violence in black townships during the transition to democracy.[102] Written in English with isiXhosa phrases and references, the novel offers a fictional interpretation of a murder that took place in Gugulethu, a township outside Cape Town, on August 25, 1993. A group of young black men killed Amy Biehl, a white American Fulbright scholar, and the "outpouring of grief, outrage and support for the Biehl family" that followed was "unprecedented in the country" (Preface, *Mother to Mother*, p. v). Four young men were convicted of the crime and then granted amnesty during a TRC hearing in 1998.[103] While much attention was paid to the white American victim, Magona asks, "are there no lessons to be had from knowing something of the other world?" (*Mother to Mother*, p. v). Her fictional narrative tells the story of a single perpetrator named Mxolisi that consists of letters that his black South African mother writes to Biehl's mother. This correspondence describes what Mxolisi's life was like before August 25, 1993 and conveys his mother's guilt and grief in the time since her son was accused of participating in the killing. This narrative situation mirrors a racially inclusive view of motherhood that black feminist activists within the ANC and other antiapartheid organizations had embraced since the 1950s, as we see in the 1958 pamphlet, "Federation of South African Women." Similarly, Albertina Sisulu once said: "A mother is a mother, black or white. Stand up and be counted with other women."[104] Even though stark inequalities define the lives Mandisa and Mrs Biehl are able to live, Magona appeals to all mothers' capacity for compassion and understanding across race, class, and culture from the ethical stand point that every life matters.

Magona's life story informs the way she approaches the narrative in *Mother to Mother*. As a single mother working as a housekeeper and then as a teacher, Magona struggled to feed and care for her children until she managed to leave South Africa. She was able to earn a Master's degree in social work at Columbia University and went on to a career in development at the United Nations until 2003.[105] As Mandisa, the narrator, tells the story of her own upbringing we discover how Mxolisi's mother struggled with the deprivations of her substantive freedoms in everyday life. The degrading treatment of the mother's body and the censorship of her sexuality introduce feminist issues that are critical to women's freedom and contribute to motherhood as a complex political issue in the novel. Mandisa grew up with an agonizing sense of vulnerability from the time the state compelled her parents to leave their home in Blouvlei and relocate to the dusty township of Gugulethu tearing apart their community to the day she realizes that an unplanned pregnancy will lead to the unraveling of her existential freedom as a woman.

If women are not empowered during the struggle for national liberation, they are not likely to be empowered afterwards. As Anne McClintock observes: "If nationalism is not transformed by an analysis of gender power, the nation-state will remain a repository of male hopes, male aspirations and male privilege."[106] For years, black South African men had defined the struggle for national liberation in terms of economic exploitation and racial discrimination, which dominated the discourse on freedom largely to the exclusion of women's issues. Magona's novel productively engages the debate about the status of women in postapartheid South Africa, which involved political rights drafted into the constitution and proclaimed in the ANC's statement on the emancipation of women as well as other literary representations such as Lauretta Ngcobo's novel *And They Didn't Die* (1999) about the resistance of rural women. Magona does not explicitly raise the question of women's political agency in *Mother to Mother*, but rather explores the indirect violence of poverty and the toll it takes on women and children in townships.

The novel vividly portrays how children who are subjected to police brutality at a young age are "scorched" by the experience (*Mother*, 150).[107] Mandisa describes two events when the police caused trouble in her home. The first involved a night-time raid in August 1993 when an army of policemen invade her house and turn it upside down leaving everyone frightened of the police who even kill "important people like Biko" (*Mother*, 84). The mother also shares memories of her son's childhood with Mrs Biehl. She tells another story about the impunity the police have in their indiscriminate use of lethal force. One day, when Mxolisi was a boy, the police were looking to arrest two boys who were his playmates, Zazi and Mzamo, and he innocently gives up their hiding place mistaking the search for a game of hide-and-seek. The police find Zazi and Mzamo and shoot them dead in front of Mxolisi. The traumatizing loss of his friends, an overwhelming sense of guilt, and an inability to comprehend the police's violence leaves Mxolisi mute for two years. He is only able to recover his speech when Lungile, a positive male role model who has fathered a child with Mandisa, leaves the household to join the antiapartheid movement outside South Africa. Mxolisi's first words are, "Where is my own father?" (*Mother*, 158). His father had abandoned them without warning or explanation in search of better opportunities elsewhere. After Lungile joins the movement, Mxolisi grows into a politically aware young man who faces his childhood fear of police and becomes a respected youth activist in Gugulethu. During student-led protests calling for the youth to boycott their schools, activists in the crowd use the slogan, "ONE BULLET, ONE SETTLER! LIBERATION NOW, EDUCATION LATER!" (*Mother*, 161), which reflected the ideals of the Pan African Congress. However, the narrative embraces, in broad terms, the ethics of black consciousness as we see when Mxolisi joins black youth in taking responsibility for their own liberation as an expression of self-esteem and of conquering fear, which explicitly evokes Biko's formidable example.

The son's absence when he goes missing while police are looking for him allows room in the narrative for background information on the history of the Xhosa community's dispossession. Mandisa recounts a story her grandfather told about the time when Xhosa people slaughtered all their cattle on a wide scale. The voluntary destruction of their wealth and property was committed as an act of faith in ancestral protection following the divine inspiration of a young prophetess, Nongqawuse. Yet when the white people do not leave and the amaXhosa do not regain their land and their rights, as Nongqawuse's prophecy predicted, their loss of faith entails a deeper sense of spiritual dispossession (*Mother*, 173–82). This oral narrative – passed on from generation to generation – evokes a broader historical process in South Africa, which is a long story about how substantial wealth became concentrated in the hands of a white minority.

Magona makes a valuable contribution to the national conversation in postapartheid South Africa with this novel. She connects the politics of motherhood with a broader set of issues about what liberation did not achieve for a majority of women and children in townships. *Mother to Mother* raises the issue of what would be involved in emancipating South Africans from sexism as well as from the structures of inequality that were implemented by white settlers and systematically codified under apartheid. Without answers to these questions, the protections of rights and liberties that were put in place for all South Africans with a new constitution and democratic elections left millions of black citizens without assets and skills, and thus effectively in chains.[108] With the timing of her novel and choice of a high-profile case, Magona establishes a context for understanding that Amy Biehl was killed in the midst of widespread political violence. In 1990, in South Africa 1,500 people lost their lives as a result of political violence and 1993 marked the lowest point in the black population's morale after two white extremists assassinated MK leader Chris Hani and nearly brought the negotiation process to the brink of collapse.[109] The novel, as an imaginative expression of a mother's life during the last years of apartheid, invites an interracial, intercultural conversation on the legacy of national liberation in South Africa.

In the two decades since the TRC, dozens of South African narratives about the nation in transition have represented both the conduct of the commission and its complex legacy. In her book *African Film and Literature: Adapting Violence to the Screen* (2009) Lindiwe Dovey remarks: "Films about the TRC, or film adaptations of written accounts of the TRC, are participating in the movement toward a narrative-based form of nation-building by exploring South Africa's violent past through the mode of fiction."[110] I am not sure to what extent films can participate in nation-building but, in my view, South African narratives, audiovisual and written, have contributed to a national conversation about the TRC and what it will take to achieve meaningful freedom. In spirit, these narratives share in the TRC's effort to find a language for expressing black anger and to heal wounds in South Africa. Sechaba Morojele's film *Ubuntu's Wounds* (2002), which represents revenge rather than reconciliation, takes up the persistence of anger and injury after the TRC. Suleman Ramadan's film *Zulu Love Letter* (2004) explores the emotional burden that generations of black women carry in the present as they cope with their traumatizing past under apartheid. Ramadan's film set during the TRC weaves together elements from two narratives – that of national politics and the private lives of women – and ends with a scene in which families gather to participate in a cleansing ritual in memory of the "warriors who died for our freedom." In films representing the TRC, the motif of searching for human remains in the unmarked militant's grave recurs. In *Zulu Love Letter*, Me'Tau asks Thandeka Khumalo to help her find the remains of her daughter Dineo so that she can have a proper burial. In Tom Hooper's film *Red Dust* (2006), based on Slovo's novel, Sarah Barcant is employed to help Alex Mpondo testify before the TRC to hold Dirk Hendricks and Piet Muller responsible for torture. Perhaps, more importantly, she helps locate Steve Sizela's remains in an unmarked grave so that his family may find closure and bury him in accordance with custom. While Dovey points out that the state has been more likely to fund films that promote the ANC's narrative about the "new South Africa," others like Morojele still manage to devote themselves to representing residual black anger that is more closely aligned with neo-Marxist critiques of postapartheid South Africa. The impressive

Figure 3.2 Mural on Robben Island, South Africa, 2014
Source: Photo by Phyllis Taoua

array of voices participating through written and film narratives in a conversation about national reconciliation initiated by the TRC testifies both to the people's collective commitment to achieving meaningful freedom for the majority in the future, and to the fact that so much remains to be done.

In this chapter, we have brought the discourse of national liberation up for reconsideration in relation to other kinds of freedom. We explored Anderson's proposition that national sovereignty was seen as the ultimate gage of freedom and the evident limitations of this viewpoint after independence. To create a context for understanding narratives that engage with national liberation and its imperfect legacy, we looked at the way Fanon and Mandela deployed the discourse of liberation. For the postindependence period of the 1960s and 1970s, we considered two representations of how the people survived the gatekeeper state in Armah's novel *The Beautyful Ones Are Not Yet Born* and in Tansi's *Life and a Half*. During the 1990s and the transition to multi-party rule, we considered two critiques of dictatorship as intersectional engagements with multiple aspects of freedom in Sissoko's film *Finzan* and Beti's novel

Trop de soleil tue l'amour. Finally, we considered the ongoing struggle for national reconciliation and meaningful freedom in postapartheid South Africa in Krog's memoir *Country of My Skull*, Magona's novel *Mother to Mother* and in related South African films. The texts under consideration demonstrate that national liberation did not deliver meaningful freedom to a majority of the people and how ongoing struggles come up against limited opportunities within the nation-state.

While national liberation dominated the discourse of African freedom during the twentieth century, we have seen that the attainment of political self-determination through emancipation from foreign rule is just one aspect of freedom in African narratives that represent national sovereignty in relation to other spheres of experience and different kinds of freedom.

Instrumental. Armah raises the question of instrumental freedoms under dictatorship, when employees at the railway station wait to see who will fill the power vacuum, rather than talk about organizing an election, after the dictator is deposed via a coup. Tansi employs a discourse of hyperbole and satire to evoke the deprivation of the people's instrumental freedoms, such as Layisho's life in a cage as a political dissident, when there is a revolving door of dictators sponsored by foreign powers. Sissoko evokes women's rights and human rights and explicitly engages with the question of instrumental freedom in the contest between the village chief and the district commissioner when the chief is arrested and detained for not agreeing to the price of millet. Beti deals in a very forthright manner with issues of instrumental freedom when journalists working for the newspaper *Aujourd'hui la démocratie!* come up against constraints on their freedom of speech and political rights under dictatorship. In Krog's memoir and other narratives that engage with the TRC, accounts of the violation of human rights under apartheid in South Africa convey in vivid terms the way in which black people were deprived of instrumental freedoms, such as when Lekotse's son was arrested for his resistance to apartheid. While human rights abuses were recognized individually on a case-by-case basis, the TRC did not create institutional structures to address grievances between white and black South Africans as groups, which would have been a powerful instrument for the cause of freedom.

Substantive. Armah raises many issues related to substantive freedoms; an important one being the fact that the railway clerk refuses the timber merchant's bribe, choosing ethical integrity over a comfortable lifestyle. The teacher, in conversation with the man, also questions the point of freedom (understood as national liberation), if he cannot devote himself to causes he believes in. Tansi incorporates all of the aspects of freedom deferred in Layisho who is detained in a cage and displayed. Layisho is deprived of his substantive freedom as a writer with ideas to change the world, but they are censored because the society is not yet ready. Sissoko represents the negative effects of patriarchal constraints on women's choices and thus their substantive freedoms to define their lives: in Fili's case not to undergo genital cutting and in Nanyuma's to choose when and whom to marry. Beti creates the character of Bébète, one of many frustrated individuals who struggle to define their lives with choices that makes sense to them, who is trapped in a cycle of poverty and domestic abuse without any good options to improve her life through education, employment, or a loving relationship. In South African narratives about the TRC, Krog's discussion of the radical deprivation of black women's rights during apartheid when their bodies became a battlefield stands out from the many stories of people losing their physical dignity and sense of safety at home.

Existential. Armah accords enormous importance to the main protagonist's moral solitude that conveys his existential disorientation in postindependence Ghana. All that remains is for the people to wake up and want to be whole again, but, as the novel's title *The Beautyful Ones Are Not Yet Born* indicates, meaningful freedom had been deferred and was projected into the future as a possibility worth striving for. Tansi engages in a systemic and deeply personal way with spiritual forces and existential freedoms, perhaps more than any other African novelist of his generation. The resistance figure Martial refuses to die and when he becomes a martyr he operates in the invisible realm of power haunting the living in a spiritual contest for dominance. Sissoko conveys Bambara women's existential alienation under the rule of a village chief who brutally subjugates them because he feels emasculated within the nation-state and because of economic pressures created by growing inequality as a result of the expansion of global capital. The spiritual damage that this kind of imbalance in power does to the community's existence is suggested in *Finzan* and explicitly developed in *Guimba*. Beti foregrounds the theme of love in his novel that represents reciprocal love based on mutual respect as a universal value, not a bourgeois luxury. In this narrative, the intangibles of happiness serve to humanize the people's unfulfilled longing for social justice and meaningful freedom. In South African narratives about the TRC, Krog's account of Lekotse's testimony at the last hearing in the Northern Province is quite striking. The shepherd who cannot find a language for his existential loss, struggles to adequately convey to the commissioners the extent to which his life was "affected" since the day the police raided his house. Lekotse's intangible dispossession comes from his perception that his place in the world was destroyed. This man's existential battle to resist the violence perpetrated against him relates directly to the cause of Biko's Black Consciousness Movement.

Notes

1. Two books on this topic that I read prior to departure were: Mongo Beti, *La France contre l'Afrique: Retour au Cameroun* (Paris: La Découverte, 1993) and Richard Bjornson, *The African Quest for Freedom and Identity: Cameroonian Writing and the National Experience* (Bloomington, IN: Indiana University Press, 1991).
2. An excerpt from Renan's famous lecture, originally in French, "Qu'est-ce qu'une nation?" translated in English "What is a nation?" is the first entry in the section, "The Question of Definition," that opens Oxford's Reader on *Nationalism* (Oxford: Oxford University Press, 1994), pp. 17–18. Renan's entire lecture is included, also as the first entry after the introduction, in the volume Homi Bhabha edited *Nation and Narration* (London: Routledge, 1990), pp. 8–22.
3. For a theoretical discussion of European ideas of the nation and nationality, see Geoff Eley and Ronald G. Suny's introduction to *Becoming National: A Reader* (Oxford: Oxford University Press, 1996).
4. Renan, "Qu'est-ce qu'une nation?" translated in English "What is a nation?" *Nationalism* (Oxford: Oxford University Press, 1994), p. 17.
5. See, for instance, Tom Nairn, "The Maladies of Development," in *Nationalism,* eds. John Hutchinson and Anthony Smith, (Oxford: Oxford University Press, 1994), pp. 70–6.
6. For Anderson's differentiation of his position from Tom Nairn's on Marxism and nationalism, see *Imagined Communities*, pp. 2–4. For Anderson, whereas Nairn sees nationalism as the sign of Marxism's failure, Anderson proposes that it is an "anomaly" because it has been elided not confronted.
7. Karl Marx, "Manifesto of the Communist Party," in *The Marx-Engels Reader*, ed. Robert C. Tucker, (New York, NY: Norton, 1978 [1848]), p. 476.
8. Benedict Anderson, *Imagined Communities: Reflections on the Origin and Spread of Nationalism* (London; New York, NY: Verso, 1991), pp. 5–6.
9. Ibid., pp. 6–7.
10. As someone who has worked on Negritude, I find it interesting how pervasive reference to this movement is when trying to explain the emergence of anticolonial nationalism, especially in Africa and the diaspora. Frederick Cooper mentions these connections in *African since 1940* and Elizabeth Schmidt does as well in her essay "Top Down or Bottom Up?" both of which I cite later on. For my take on this, see Phyllis Taoua, *Forms of Protest: Anti-Colonialism and Avant-Gardes in Africa, the Caribbean and France* (Portsmouth, NH: Heinemann, 2002).
11. Anderson, *Imagined Communities*, p. 139.
12. Ibid., p. 140. For a critique of Anderson's definition of the nation as imagined community and a discussion of the nation after colonialism, see

Partha Chatterjee, *The Nation and Its Fragments: Colonial and Postcolonial Histories* (Princeton, NJ: Princeton University Press, 1993).

13. Ibid., p. 140.
14. Anne McClintock, "'No Longer in a Future Heaven': Gender, Race and Nationalism," in *Dangerous Liaisons: Gender, Nation, & Postcolonial Perspectives*, eds. Anne McClintock, Aamir Mufti and Ella Shohat. Minneapolis, MN: University of Minnesota Press, 1997, p. 96.
15. Frantz Fanon, *Wretched of the Earth* (New York, NY: Grove Press, 2005), p. 35.
16. Ibid., p. 148.
17. McClintock, "'No Longer in a Future Heaven': Gender, Race and Nationalism," p. 89.
18. Ibid., p. 89.
19. Ibid., p. 98.
20. For a study of women's participation at the grassroots level in Guinea, see Elizabeth Schmidt, "Top Down or Bottom Up? Nationalist Mobilization Reconsidered, with Special Reference to Guinea (French West Africa)," *The American Historical Review*, vol. 110, no. 4 (October 2005): 975–1014. Schmidt engages with the work of John Lonsdale, Susan Geiger, and Partha Chatterjee to broaden the scope of historiographies of national liberation to include the grassroots activities of the nonliterate majority and women. For an essay on women's participation in the war of liberation in Algeria, see Danièle Djamila Amrane-Minne, "Women and Politics in Algeria from the War of Independence to Our Day," *Research in African Literatures*, vol. 30, no. 3 (Fall 1999): 62–77. This essay appears in a special issue on dissident Algeria and shares some overlap with Assia Djebar's film and fiction on women's participation in the war in Algeria. For a discussion of women's activism in South Africa, see Shireen Hassim, *Women's Organizations and Democracy in South Africa: Contesting Authority* (Madison, WI: University of Wisconsin Press, 2006).
21. Nelson Mandela, *Long Walk to Freedom: The Autobiography of Nelson Mandela* (Austin, TX: Holt, Rinehart and Winston, 1995), p. 157.
22. Ibid., p. 168.
23. Ibid., p. 169.
24. Glenn Frankel, "When Mandela's, and the World's Fate Changed at Historic Rivonia Trial," *Washington Post* (December 5, 2013).
25. Nelson Mandela's statement about nationhood that I cited as an epigraph comes from a short preface he wrote in 1996 for André P. Brink's collection of essays *Reinventing a Continent: Writing and Politics in South Africa* (Cambridge, MA: Zoland Books, 1998). But his most comprehensive discussion of the struggle for freedom and nationhood in South Africa, and the involvement of key ANC members such as Walter Sisulu and Oliver Tambo, is Mandela's autobiography *Long Walk to Freedom*.
26. Mandela, *Long Walk to Freedom*, p. 172.
27. Ibid., p. 172.
28. Jacques Derrida contributed an insightful essay to a collected volume on Mandela in 1986; four years before the ANC leader was set free and the same year Wole Soyinka devoted his Nobel Prize acceptance speech, in

part, to the open wound of apartheid in South Africa. See Jacques Derrida, "Admiration de Nelson Mandela ou les lois de la réflexion," *Pour Nelson Mandela* (Paris: Gallimard, 1986), pp. 1–44.

29. Mandela, *Long Walk to Freedom*, p. 124.
30. After watching Jean-Pierre Bekolo's 2017 film *Les Ateliers de la pensée* about the meeting Felwine Sarr and Achille Mbembe organized in Dakar, I was struck by how Mbembe and Françoise Vergès stood out in terms of the range of references they were able to draw upon. It was striking to me that no one ever took up the question of freedom as the subject of explicit theoretical inquiry. At one point, Vergès does make reference to "la liberté" in the quotidian sense of personal liberties in our daily lives.
31. In her essay "No Longer in a Future Heaven," McClintock discusses Fanon's use of the idea of liberation in the subjunctive tense and relates this to anticipatory freedom.
32. I had the privilege of sharing an early draft of this chapter with colleagues at the Center for African Studies at the University of Cape Town in South Africa. During our discussion, I learned that some South Africans have come to regard Nelson Mandela as a sell-out who gave his tacit approval to the ANC's accommodation of brand-name capitalism.
33. For a history of the ANC, see Anthony Butler's *The Idea of the ANC* (Athens, OH: Ohio University Press, 2012). Butler reviews the history of the idea of the ANC from its inception in 1912 and offers insightful analysis of the ideological challenges the party faces now that it is in charge of Africa's second largest capitalist economy with stark socioeconomic disparities that still reflect the legacy of half a century of apartheid.
34. See Frederick Cooper's *Africa since 1940: The Past of the Present* (Cambridge: Cambridge University Press, 2002) and Schmidt's essay "Top Down or Bottom Up? Nationalist Mobilization Reconsidered, with Special Reference to Guinea (French West Africa)."
35. Ato Quayson, *Oxford Street, Accra: City Life and the Itineraries of Transnationalism* (Durham, NC: Duke University Press, 2014).
36. Antonio Gramsci, *Selections from the Prison Notebooks of Antonio Gramsci* (New York, NY: International Publishers, 1971).
37. An example of this is in Edward Said's *Culture and Imperialism* (New York, NY: Knopf, 1993) where Davidson's version of history is engaged with and cited in epigraph.
38. Davidson discusses the precolonial polity that existed in the Asante nation and remarks that for the king of the Asante, "as for others of his kind, this independence could only be a perverse denial of the old independence, and the new nationalists no more than usurpers of the legacy of Africa's own development" (Davidson, *The Black Man's Burden*, p. 73).
39. He, in fact, chides nationalist leaders for their "intellectual poverty"; a phrase that is repeated more than once. Basil Davidson, *The Black Man's Burden: Africa and the Curse of the Nation-State* (New York, NY: Random House, 1992), p. 165
40. Davidson, *The Black Man's Burden*, p. 42.
41. Ibid., p. 172.
42. Ibid., p. 10.

43. Ibid., p. 138.
44. Ibid., pp. 298–301.
45. Cooper, *Africa since 1940*, p. 67.
46. As we will see in the next chapter, Cooper also looks at the complicated contest for power in Nigeria where the structure of federation, "had the perverse effect of encouraging first a winner-takes-all quest for power *within* each of the three regions, and then competition *between* the regions for power at the federal level" (Cooper, *Africa since 1940,* p. 69). He concludes this part with an analysis of how Houphouët-Boigny in the Ivory Coast and Senghor in Senegal managed political alliances with trade union organizations while avoiding challenges from the radical left in contrast to the more apparently militant Sékou Touré in Guinea who "assembled a populist coalition of considerable breadth" (Cooper, *Africa since 1940,* p. 71).
47. Cooper, *Africa since 1940,* p. 71.
48. Ibid., p. 76.
49. Ibid., p. 76.
50. Ibid., p. 84.
51. See, for instance, interventions by Stuart Hall and Geoff Eley.
52. Georges Nzongola-Ntalaja, *The Congo from Leopold to Kabila: A People's History* (London: Zed Books, 1992).
53. Phyllis Clark, "Passionate Engagements: Sony Labou Tansi's Ancestral Shrine," *Research in African Literatures*, vol. 31, no. 3 (Autumn 2000): 39–68.
54. Georges Nzongola-Ntalaja published an article in *The Guardian*'s poverty matters blog commemorating the fiftieth anniversary of Lumumba's assassination entitled, "Patrice Lumumba: the most important assassination of the 20th century" (January 17, 2011). URL: www.theguardian.com/global-development/poverty-matters/2011/jan/17/patrice-lumumba-50th-anniversary-assassination (consulted: August 6, 2014).
55. For discussion of these historical figures, see Clark, "Passionate Engagements: Sony Labou Tansi's Ancestral Shrine," and Wyatt MacGaffey, *Kongo Political Culture: The Conceptual Challenge of the Particular* (Bloomington: Indiana University Press, 2000).
56. For an excellent discussion of the exercise of power in the Bakongo cultural context, see MacGaffey's *Kongo Political Culture.* For a magisterial presentation of the history of the political tradition in Equatorial Africa, see Jan Vansina's *Paths in the Rainforests: Toward a History of Political Tradition in Equatorial Africa* (Madison, WI: University of Wisconsin Press, 1990). For an anthropological study of invisible powers from a Bakongo perspective, see Simon Bockie's *Death and the Invisible Powers: The World of Kongo Belief* (Bloomington, IN: Indiana University Press, 1993).
57. MacGaffey, *Kongo Political Culture.*
58. For a discussion of the belly and its spiritual and political significance in the Bakongo context, see Bockie, *Death and the Invisible Powers* and MacGaffey, *Kongo Political Culture.* For a more general discussion of the politics of the belly in Africa, see Jean-François Bayart, *The State in Africa: The Politics of the Belly* (London: Longman, 1993).

59. MacGaffey, *Kongo Political Culture.*
60. Ibid., pp. 134–59; Bockie, *Death and the Invisible Powers*, pp. 36–82.
61. MacGaffey, *Kongo Political Culture.*
62. See Achille Mbembe's article "The Banality of Power and the Aesthetics of Vulgarity in the Postcolony," *Public Culture*, vol. 4, no. 2 (Spring 1992): 1–30.
63. Nzongola-Ntalaja, *The Congo from Leopold to Kabila: A People's History*, p. 84.
64. Cooper, *Africa since 1940*, p.164.
65. In 1963, Jean-Paul Sartre – a reader of Aimé Césaire, Frantz Fanon, and Richard Wright – and an intellectual tuned into world events as the editor of *Les Temps modernes*, aptly noted that the fight over mineral resources in the Katanga region was a decisive issue that was ultimately sorted out among the Belgians, English, French, Americans, and the minority white regimes in southern Africa. In his perceptive essay on Lumumba's political thought, Sartre made clear that the pattern of governance in the Congo that was based on (a) arriviste leadership, (b) the army defending a corrupt middle class, and (c) international organizations like the United Nations ensuring just enough stability for multi-national corporations to do business resembled the political landscape in Latin America. See Jean-Paul Sartre, "La pensée politique de Patrice Emery Lumumba," *Présence Africaine* (no. 47, juillet-septembre 1963), p. 19.
66. Cooper, *Africa since 1940*, p. 83.
67. Raoul Peck made two films, *Lumumba: Death of a Prophet* (1992) and *Lumumba* (2000), that were, in my view, less effective representations of the Congolese experience.
68. While the bibliography on decolonization in the Congo is extensive, an excellent book that uses ethnography and painting to present this history in the paintings of Tshibumba Kanda Matulu, accompanied by the painter's own personal narrative of this painful and troubling history, is by Johannes Fabian, *Remembering the Present: Painting and Popular History in Zaire* (Berkeley, CA: University of California Press, 1996). Jihan El-Tahri's documentary, *Cuba: An African Odyssey* (2008) gives an international perspective on decolonization in Congo-Kinshasa and delves into the classified archive with informative interviews featuring retired American government officials. See Nzongola-Ntalaja, "Patrice Lumumba."
69. Nzongola-Ntalaja, *The Congo from Leopold to Kabila*, p. 121.
70. Ibid., p. 126.
71. Ibid., p. 139.
72. "Djibril Diop Mambety," *Questioning African Cinema: Conversations with African Filmmakers*, ed. Nwachukwu Frank Ukadike, (Minneapolis, MN: Minnesota University Press, 2002), p. 189.
73. See, for instance, Laura DeLuca and Shadrack Kamenya, "Representation of Female Circumcision in *Finzan, a Dance for the Heroes*," *Research in African Literatures*, vol. 26, no. 3 (Fall 1995): 83–7.
74. Ukadike, *Questioning African Cinema*, p. 187.
75. For a discussion of Sissoko's early political engagement around the time of *Finzan*, see Josef Gugler, *African Film: Re-imagining a Continent*

(Bloomington, IN: Indiana University Press, 2003), p. 161. In 1996, Sissoko participated in founding a national political party in Mali called African Solidarity for Democracy and Independence.

76. Ukadike, *Questioning African Cinema*, p. 188.
77. Ibid., p. 188.
78. Ibid., p. 196.
79. Sharon Russell, *Guide to African Cinema* (Westport, CT: Greendwood, 1998), p. 65.
80. Paul Nugent, *Africa since Independence* (New York, NY: Palgrave, 2004), p. 390.
81. Ibid., pp. 396–8.
82. For the complete text, see http://mongobeti.arts.uwa.edu.au/issues/pnpa63_66/pnpa63_24.html (consulted August 18, 2017).
83. See Nugent, *Africa since Independence*; Ambroise Kom, ed, *Mongo Beti parle: Interview réalisée et éditée par Ambroise Kom* (Bayreuth: Bayreuth African Studies, 2002); Cilas Kemedjio, *Mongo Beti, le combattant fatigué* (Berlin: Littératures et cultures francophones hors d'Europe, 2003).
84. Odile Biyidi-Awala, "Une singulière liberté," *Remember Mongo Beti*, ed. Ambroise Kom, (Bayreuth: Bayreuth African Studies), pp. 243–7.
85. I would like to thank Moradewun Adejunmobi and Tejumola Olaniyan for engaging me in conversation about ethnicity and attachments to kinship groups as factors that define attached freedoms as opposed to unattached freedoms. In addition, please see Cilas Kemedjio, "Mongo Beti: les ultimes défis d'un ancien combattant (1999–2000)," *Etudes littéraires africaines*, no. 42 (2016): 21–36.
86. See my essay, "Aliénation et appartenance dans l'écriture de Mongo Beti après son retour au Cameroun," *Etudes littéraires africaines*, no. 42 (2016): 55–67.
87. See Yvonne-Marie Mokam, "Mongo Beti de retour d'exil: du roman-feuilleton au roman," *Etudes littéraires africaines*, no. 42 (2016): 37–54.
88. See, for example, Anne McClintock, *Imperial Leather: Race, Gender and Sexuality in the Colonial Contest* (New York, NY/London: Routledge, 1995); Elleke Boehmer, *Stories of Women: Gender and Narrative in the Postcolonial Nation* (Manchester, UK: Manchester University Press, 2009); Susan Z. Andrade, *The Nation Writ Small: African Fictions and Feminisims, 1958–1988* (Durham, NC: Duke University Press, 2011).
89. See Merry E. Wiesner-Hanks's summary in *Gender in History: Global Perspectives* (West Sussex: Wiley-Blackwell, 2012).
90. See Phyllis Taoua, "Of Prisons and Freedom: Liberation in the Work of Assia Djebar," *World Literature Today* (November 2012), 12–18. See also the Special Issue of *Research in African Literatures*, vol. 30, no. 3 (1999) on "Dissident Algeria."
91. See Phyllis Taoua, "The Postcolonial Condition," *The Companion to the African Novel* (Cambridge: Cambridge University Press, 2010), pp. 209–26.
92. It is quite instructive to look at the media coverage of the release of Attenborough's film in the summer of 1988 because it illustrates beautifully how the legitimacy of apartheid was unraveling in the years before

Mandela's release from prison. It is a story of failed censorship: first the apartheid censorship committee approved the film for nationwide viewing, then when riots and violence erupted in response to the outrageous facts surrounding Steve Biko's assassination (Steve Biko is masterfully played by Denzel Washington) the censors banned the film in an attempt to quite things down, but this backfired and more violence followed in response to the state's banning of the film. See, for example, "'Cry Freedom' Seized by South African Police," *New York Times* (July 30, 1988); "Woman Killed in S. African Bomb Blast," *The Washington Post* (July 31, 1988); Michael Hornsby, "Police end Biko film's short run; South African Government overturns censors' ruling; Cry Freedom," *The Times* (London) (July 30, 1988); David Niddrie, "'Cry Freedom' film seized at theatres across South Africa," *The Globe and Mail* (Canada) (July 30, 1988).

93. Cooper, *Africa since 1940*, p. 154.
94. Ibid., p. 154.
95. Ibid., p. 11.
96. James Ferguson, "Paradoxes of Sovereignty and Independence," *Global Shadows: Africa in the Neoliberal World Order* (Duke, NC: Duke University Press, 2006), p. 65.
97. Antjie Krog, *Country of My Skull* (New York, NY: Three River Press, 1998), p. 235.
98. "Foreword" to Steve Biko, *I Write What I Like: Selected Writings* (Chicago, IL: The University of Chicago Press, 2002), p. xiii.
99. Ibid., p. 73.
100. Ibid., p. 33.
101. Mahmood Mamdani, "Beyond Nuremberg. The Historical Significance of the Post-Apartheid Transition in South Africa," *Politics and Society*, vol. 43, no. 1 (December 2014): 61–88. DOI: https://doi.org/10.1177/0032329214554387
102. In addition to being a writer, Sindiwe Magona has an extensive record as an activist. She is the founder and Executive Director of South Africa 2033 and was a worker for peaceful change during the struggle against apartheid and a founding member of the Women's Peace Movement in 1976. For a brief online biography, see South African History Online at www.sahistory.org.za/people/sindiwe-magona (consulted January 4, 2015).
103. See Krog, *Country of My Skull*, p. 383.
104. Quoted in McClintock, *Imperial Leather*, p. 381.
105. Magona credits this international experience as the primary reason she became a writer. For a series of informative interviews with Sindiwe Magona, see "I Am Woman: Leap of Faith," (Episode 18 Acts 1–3) a South African Television Series produced by Lauren Groenewald, Miki Redelinghuys and Lisa Chait. www.youtube.com/watch?v=mRzJh82xjiw (consulted June 19, 2014).
106. McClintock, *Imperial Leather*, p. 385.
107. Many stories about white security forces violating blacks were finally exposed to the public during the TRC hearings about which Krog writes in *Country of My Skull*. Krog describes, for instance, people in their homes

who are deprived of the basic human right to security and privacy, pp. 288–90.

108. Butler, *The Idea of the ANC*, p. 96. Butler offers a full discussion of the idea of liberation in the evolving history of the ANC, in his chapter "Liberation," pp. 92–118.
109. Mandela, *Long Walk to Freedom*, p. 427.
110. Lindiwe Dovey, *African Film and Literature: Adapting Violence to the Screen* (New York, NY: Columbia University Press, 2009), p. 54.

Nightsong: City
Dennis Brutus

Sleep well, my love, sleep well:
the harbour lights glaze over restless docks,
police cars cockroach through the tunnel streets

from the shanties creaking iron-sheets
violence like a bug-infested rag is tossed
and fear is immanent as sound in the wind-swung bell;

the long day's anger pants from sand and rocks;
but for this breathing night at least,
my land, my love, sleep well.

4 Global Africa

Pillaging with Less Impunity in the Era of Neoliberal Capital

> One thought alone preoccupies the submerged mind of Empire: how not to end, how not to die, how to prolong its era. By day it pursues its enemies. It is cunning and ruthless, it sends its bloodhounds everywhere. By night it feeds on images of disaster: the sack of cities, the rape of populations, pyramids of bones, acres of desolation.
>
> *J. M. Coetzee, Waiting for the Barbarians*

During the winter of 1998 I traveled to the West African country of Niger and into the Sahara for the first time. As circumstances would have it, I met leaders of the Tuareg rebellion in Niger on the terrace of the Grand Hotel my first evening in Niamey. They were negotiating the implementation of a peace agreement with the government and staying in bungalows at the hotel. The Tuareg uprising of the 1980s and 1990s in Niger, unlike the war in Rwanda, had hardly been reported on in the United States media so there was much for me to learn. About three weeks after arriving in Niamey, I left the capital city for the north, even as Tuareg leaders were working on implementing a peace and reconciliation agreement with the national government. Sidi-Amar Taoua and former rebels in the UFRA movement organized the trip for me.[1] As I headed north of Tahoua on the road to Agadez with Sidi-Amar's men, one of them readied his AK-47 in the back of the Land Cruiser and the sharp sound startled me. The driver attempted to allay my fears by explaining that we had crossed into what had been their previous zone of operations. The sudden precaution of a ready weapon in hand was something of a surprise since they had, until then, kept their guns completely out of sight during the trip with me.

The after effects of combat were so fresh. Years of fighting had only recently ended. Some chain-smoked cigarettes; some stared vaguely at the horizon. Those who were armed held their weapons with a strange intimacy, like an appendage they had grown accustomed to. In Agadez I was introduced to Ismaghil, a former rebel and close friend of

Figure 4.1 On the road to Agadez with armed escort, Niger, 1998
Source: Photo by Phyllis Taoua

Sidi-Amar's, who would be my guide on a short trip out of the city and into the desert. Ismaghil and I set out the next evening heading toward Tiguidit. Once the sun had dropped behind the mountains in front of us, we set up camp and prepared dinner together. He had forgotten a knife, so I had to chase a whole peeled onion around in the pot with a wooden spoon until it softened over the fire till I was finally able to mash it up. He used the sharp edge of a rock to cut up some mutton that we simmered in a spicy tomato sauce with cumin and garlic. Dinner was tastier than you might imagine given our frugal means, and when the stars filled the night sky I marveled at the stunning array and at how useful they must be for navigating by night. Ismaghil and I stayed up until the last embers of our campfire died. He talked about the rebellion, especially surviving the months-long siege in the Aïr Mountains; I mostly listened and drank sweet green tea that he poured in little glasses.

The next morning, we had a dramatic situation to contend with: the old Toyota wouldn't start. I waited inside the vehicle (as I was told), while Ismaghil walked to a Tuareg settlement he could see (but I could not) in the distance. I had written four pages in my journal by the time two men were in view approaching by foot; one of them, mercifully, was Ismaghil. Together they push-started the Toyota and we were off. The three of us spent the day together, driving, talking, and sharing lunch. The helper we recruited, a Tuareg nomad wearing the traditional indigo tunic and white turban, fetched firewood and observed me so keenly that I felt like an extraterrestrial. Finally, I asked Ismaghil to assure him that

Figure 4.2 Tuareg settlement in Sahara near Agadez, Niger, 1998
Source: Photo by Phyllis Taoua

I had no intention of setting up Disneyland in this part of the Sahara. They exchanged words in Tamashek that were translated into French for me. The man Ismaghil had happened upon in his tent in the middle of the desert had absolutely no idea what I was talking about because he'd never heard of Disneyland. He had never met an American before. Today multinational corporations are still making billions of dollars in profit exploiting uranium in Niger while nomadic Tuaregs can dust the sand off their tunics without any hope of ever owning a cellphone or watching satellite television.

It was striking for me to discover that the road that links Niamey and Agadez, which runs from Niger's uranium mines all the way to the port of Cotonou, is paved for thousands of kilometers. But profits from this extractive industry that maintain a paved inter-state road, with bridges, to the Atlantic coast had not improved the well-being of the people who live on the land where the ore was extracted. In my understanding of the region, the fact of this Tuareg nomad not being tuned into global culture sits alongside the communal graves I saw heading north on the road to Agadez, where Tuareg men had been buried together during a rebellion waged over a quintessentially global issue: the exploitation of uranium.[2] When we think historically about globalization in Africa, one thing we notice is how lumpy and uneven the process has been with a patchy integration of markets.[3] James Ferguson has observed how when, "capital *has* come to Africa in recent years, it has been overwhelmingly in the area of mineral-resource extraction," which takes place in "capital-intensive enclaves that are substantially insulated from the local economy."[4] Ferguson discusses many scenarios of mineral-resource extraction from gold mining in Ghana to diamonds in the Democratic Republic of the Congo and off-shore oil in Angola, where capital flows from point to point hopping over vast areas of unusable territory.[5]

Figure 4.3 JFK bridge across the Niger River on road to the Atlantic coast, Niger, 1999
Source: Photo by Phyllis Taoua

Major factors contributing to the Tuareg rebellion of the 1980s and 1990s were the exploitation of natural resources on Tuareg land and of their labor under deplorable conditions while the gatekeeper state excluded them from public discussions about the mining industry and its impact on their community.[6] Unfortunately, Niger's current situation starkly illustrates the persistence of gross inequality between those who profit and those who are exploited: the French nuclear-energy company Areva posted record profits in the first quarter of 2013 at 2.279 billion euros, while Niger, the world's fourth largest producer of uranium, ranks at the bottom of the 2016 Human Development Index (see Appendix).[7] France, the former colonial power in Niger, has exerted direct influence over the exploitation of Niger's uranium since it was discovered in 1957 and this continues to this day. Areva extracts thousands of tons of uranium every year near Arlit and is also the primary shareholder in two Nigerien companies, SOMAIR and COMINAK.[8] Niger supplies roughly one third of the raw materials that power some fifty-eight French nuclear-energy reactors, which produce 75 percent of France's electricity.[9] Also, Niger has the highest-grade uranium in Africa and France's nuclear-weapons arsenal is the world's third largest after the United States and Russia.[10]

A significant player in this history was the gatekeeping dictator Seyni Kountché who ruled Niger from 1974 to 1987. Kountché arrived in power via a military coup while a couple thousand French troops were on the ground in a residual supervisory capacity. The deposed president, Hamani Diori, had requested that France pay a higher price for uranium. During Kountché's reign France enjoyed a reduction in the price of uranium while the nomadic Tuareg who lived in the uranium-rich zone were socially persecuted and politically marginalized.[11] This is one of many instances in which a former European colonial power was able to widen the profit margin from the exploitation of Africa's resources by contributing to an absence of meaningful sovereignty in order to extend the gatekeeping function of the colonial state.[12] Ferguson observes that states with the poorest governance according to IMF and World Bank criteria – Liberia, Sierra Leone, Congo/Zaire, Nigeria – soaked up over half of private capital inflows to sub-Saharan Africa (excluding South Africa) between 1994 and 1995.[13]

The geopolitical importance of Niger's uranium is of particular concern today given that several radical groups – including Ansar Dine, al-Qaeda in the Islamic Maghreb, and the Movement for Oneness and Jihad in West Africa – could gain access, if reports of car-bombings and kidnappings targeting people in the mining industry are any indication.[14] When tensions flared up in neighboring Mali after a military coup in March 2012, France quietly deployed special forces to protect their uranium mines in Niger.[15] The use of special forces and private security firms for the protection of Western business interests is widespread across the continent, as Ferguson describes:

> Today, enclaves of mineral-extracting investment in Africa are usually tightly integrated with the head offices of multinational corporations and metropolitan centers but sharply walled off from their own national societies (often literally walled off with bricks, razor wire, and security guards).[16]

A critical aspect of the asymmetry and inequality that define the political landscape of global Africa is that the First World uses fire power (drones, security forces) to protect enclaves where multinationals make billions in profit, while the people who live on the land are trapped in endemic poverty and often traumatized by armed conflict.[17] After the French military intervened to end the occupation of northern Mali by Islamist militias, the Obama administration approved the construction of a landing strip for drone aircraft near Agadez to patrol the desert where the Islamist radicals retreated.[18] The familiar nexus of fragile nation-states with poor governance and the debilitating effects of extreme poverty over decades will have a decisive impact on how the battle for geopolitical control across the region unfolds from Mauritania to the Sudan.[19]

At the turn of the twenty-first century, Amartya Sen asked us to re-evaluate development. In *Development as Freedom* (1999) Sen advances an elegant proposition: development should be assessed in terms of whether it enhances people's freedom. It is a simple formulation with radical implications. This demand was made a decade after the Cold War ended, forty years after African decolonization in the former French and British colonies, and near the end of Nelson Mandela's first term in office as president of South Africa. For our purposes, Sen's central thesis can be reformulated, more specifically, in relation to Africa after national liberation as a question: Can development schemes set up by European colonial administrations for their financial and moral benefit be transformed to improve the lives of the majority of Africans via civic debate and unfettered democracy?

Thinking historically about how African leaders make choices and take action within the peculiar Euro-African structure of the gatekeeper state explains a great deal about how the past of European domination continues to shape Africa's present. Of central importance to overcoming the obstacles that have been impeding greater freedom and prosperity in Africa is the need to fundamentally reconceptualize what we mean by development after the implementation of neoliberal policies and the globalization of capitalism. Sen has experience working with the United Nations on development policy issues as an economist. The way Sen brings his experiences growing up in India (with family ties to Bangladesh) into play with his studies of economics and moral philosophy at Cambridge University allowed him to bridge significant gaps in cultural understanding that had impeded others from articulating successful theories of, and policies for, development.

Sen's view of development is revolutionary because of his emphasis on enhancing the people's freedom as the legitimate measure of successful development. Quite simply: enjoying a measure of personal wealth is valuable because it gives us choices, provides options, and enhances our freedom to lead the kind of lives we have reason to value.[20] His argument brings sharply into focus how the absence of instrumental freedoms is what makes it possible for autocratic leaders to neglect the people's economic needs and quality of life in a way that erodes their substantive freedoms. This innovative vision challenges two key objectives of Western imperialism: creating modern workers earning wages and living in cities, and the instrumentalization of foreign aid to buy influence in the midst of geopolitical rivalries. More importantly, Sen's moral philosophy represents a fundamental recalibration of priorities so that development policies are no longer governed solely by the rules of the market place – regulated or not – and are evaluated, instead, by the single most relevant criterium: do they enhance people's freedom and thereby improve the lives of those they claim to be helping?

The implications of such an approach are profound and contribute directly to the people's ongoing struggle for meaningful freedom in Africa. Sen observes:

> Seeing development in terms of the substantive freedoms of people has far-reaching implications for our understanding of the process of development and

> also for the ways and means of promoting it. On the evaluative side, this involves the need to assess the requirements of development in terms of removing the unfreedoms from which the members of society may suffer. The process of development, in this view, is not essentially different from the history of overcoming these unfreedoms. While this history is not by any means unrelated to the process of economic growth and accumulation of physical and human capital, its reach and coverage go much beyond these variables.[21]

For Amilcar Cabral and Georges Nzongola-Ntalaja, overcoming the history of colonial domination had a first phase, that of attaining political sovereignty and self-government, and a second phase, that of rebuilding African societies along the same lines that Sen is advocating. For Sen, development is not only about lifting people out of extreme poverty, it is also about building human capabilities and transforming society through open debate and civic participation. Sen recommends including the people in (a) the discussion of issues, and (b) the formulation of priorities. Sen's reasons for asking us to hear the voices and perspectives of local people in conversations about development as freedom are not different from my reasons for wanting to write about writers and filmmakers who have been participating in an evolving conversation about how to achieve meaningful freedom in Africa.

Sen establishes an imperative connection between political freedoms and the economy: "The real issues that have to be addressed lie elsewhere, and they involve taking note of extensive interconnections between political freedoms and the understanding and fulfillment of economic needs."[22] Again, he calls for the active participation of the people in the discussion of ideas and the formation of values in terms that challenge any residual imperial authority or tolerance for autocratic rule: "Our conceptualization of economic needs depends crucially on open public debates and discussions, the guaranteeing of which requires insistence on basic personal liberty and civil rights."[23] These rights and liberties are important for:

> (1) their *direct* importance in human living associated with basic capabilities (including that of political and social participation); (2) their *instrumental* role in enhancing the hearing that people get in expressing and supporting their claims to political attention (including the claims of economic needs); and (3) their *constructive* role in the conceptualization of "needs" (including the understanding of "economic needs" in a social context).[24]

One illustration of the utility of these imperatives is his observation that famine has never occurred in a democratic country. He interprets this fact as evidence for the persuasive effect of the people's right to vote, to voice dissent, and to hold leaders accountable in meeting people's basic needs.[25] As we will see in this chapter, many African writers and filmmakers are sensitive to the political implications of Sen's questions: Who gets to participate in the discussion about globalization? Who gets to set the parameters of the public debate on political and economic issues? Who gets to speak the language of freedom?

Sen explicitly advocates for the people's participation in setting the agenda in broad terms: "Also, informed and unregimented *formation* of our values requires openness of communication and arguments, and political freedoms and civil rights can be central for this process. Furthermore, to express publicly what we value and to demand that attention be paid to it, we need free speech and democratic choice."[26] He affirms dissent and debate as essential civic virtues; the effect of dissident voices is critical because they express countervailing perspectives that challenge political leaders to improve governance by holding them accountable. Sen's defense of the freedom to express dissent also underscores the general benefit of public discussion in the formation of values and the vitality of democracy as a process to which artists and activists contribute in direct and constructive ways.

As we saw in my introduction to this book, the thorny question of whether capitalism can be reformed to work for the good of the many, instead of only making the rich richer, is taken up directly. Sen offers an economist's perspective on this moral issue:

> While capitalism is often seen as an arrangement that works only on the basis of the greed of everyone, the efficient working of the capitalist economy is, in fact, dependent on powerful systems of values and norms. Indeed, to see capitalism as nothing other than a system based on a conglomeration of greedy behavior is to underestimate vastly the ethics of capitalism, which has richly contributed to its redoubtable achievements.[27]

Sen sees capitalism as an economic system that is not inherently unjust, but is dependent on proper rules and regulation to function efficiently. He draws a crucial distinction between the ethics of the market itself and the politics of the environment in which the market operates in the evaluation of capitalism:

> Despite its effectiveness, capitalist ethics is, in fact, deeply limited in some respects, dealing particularly with issues of economic inequality, environmental protection and the need for cooperation of different kinds that operate outside the market. But within its domain, capitalism works effectively through a system of ethics that provides the vision and trust needed for successful use of the market mechanism and related institutions.[28]

For Sen, capitalism is an economic system with its own set of internal ethics and values which are limited in scope to the rules of the market, involving such things as trust and transparency in transactions. The solutions for resolving socioeconomic inequality must be found in social and moral behavior, which fall outside the economic realm of the market, strictly speaking. Although Sen acknowledges the practical need to develop institutions that can regulate codes of behavior to avoid mafia-style relationships that can rig things in favor of the most powerful – and, I might add, gatekeepers in Africa who issue permits and collect rents – his project primarily aims to provide a moral vision for rethinking development as a means of creating shared prosperity and enhancing people's freedom.

To understand, more specifically, African perspectives on capitalism at the turn of the twenty-first century it will be helpful to review the historical conditions for the emergence of neoliberalism in relation to the gatekeeper state. In *Africa since 1940: The Past of the Present* (2002), Fredrick Cooper argues that the formation of gatekeeper states in Africa was a peculiar Euro-African historical phenomenon.[29] Part of this history included colonial policies that set up in deliberate ways a transition from imperial development schemes of the postwar era to foreign aid programs after decolonization as a means of retaining indirect influence and shirking responsibility. Understanding how new African leaders managed their political power as gatekeepers in the neoliberal marketplace will make it clear how the structure of the state itself helped shape the landscape of growing inequality in Africa.

In the chapter "Development and Disappointment, 1945–2000," Cooper acknowledges the declining economic situation in Africa and the interpretive challenge this presents: "The continued poverty, the high indebtedness, the deteriorating infrastructure, and above all the absence of any clear trajectory toward a better future in Africa in the 1980s and 1990s have given rise to a blame game."[30] From his vantage point as an Africanist with historical knowledge of labor and markets on the continent going back to his early work on slavery, the answers do not appear "neat" and make asking "more precise questions" even harder. Cooper invites us to consider the complexity involved in trying to decide who, or what, to blame for the failures of many African economies after independence by reviewing seven propositions. As regards neoliberalism and banks, he writes:

> The blame, some would say, lies in the world economy that turned so decisively against Africa in the 1970s and the policies of the IMF and other international institutions that made it impossible for Africa to "develop" its way out of its limitations. Perhaps development did not go far enough, and an outside world which had long treated Africa as a zone of extraction did not devote sufficient resources to giving the continent a chance to find a different vocation.[31]

These factors are only part of the explanation. Those who blame African governments for not taking better advantage of the market get Cooper's strongest condemnation:

> These are counter-factual propositions, and one must ask what the imagined alternative was. Africans never had the choice of simply entering "the market"; they were up against real markets, some of them controlled by giant foreign firms like the United Africa Company or Union Minière or De Beers, which concentrated capital and power and had no interest in widening the narrow channels of African economies or building the institutions needed to build a diverse and self-sustaining society.[32]

The crux of the matter lies in our ability to understand how managing the economy and wielding political power were inextricably linked as Cooper's concept of the gatekeeper state brings into analytical focus.

He opens the chapter, "The recurrent crises of the gatekeeper state," with a succinct statement, "African states were successors in a double sense."[33] He explains how they, in the first instance, inherited a set of European-style institutions and territorial borders from the colonial era, which we discussed in the previous chapter. "Second," he adds, "African states took up a particular, and more recent, form of the state project of colonialism: development."[34] His analysis helps us see how the gatekeeping function inherited from the structure of the colonial state paved the way for global capitalism to unfold as it did, when formal sovereignty concentrated power in the hands of a leader who sat "astride the interface between a territory and the rest of the world." It is within this context of the nation-state that we should imagine the pressures exerted on African governments whose power was socially thin and structurally precarious. Cooper's discussion of oil money in Nigeria helps us understand the nexus of political power and the market in an economy based on extraction and limited by narrow channels for growth. He presents this nation's economy as an extreme manifestation of gatekeeping:

> Oil can turn a gatekeeper state into a caricature of itself. Unlike agriculture, which involves vast numbers of people in the production and marketing of exports, oil requires little labor, and much of it from foreigners. It also entails relationships between the few global firms capable of extracting it and the state rulers who collect the rents. It defines a spigot economy: whoever controls access to the tap, collects the rent.[35]

The fact that the oil industry dominated Nigeria's economy thwarted diversification and growth in other sectors. While this is not beneficial to the economy as a whole, it also has nefarious political consequences by concentrating enormous wealth in the hands of the powerful few. For obvious structural reasons this heightened competition for control of the gate – that single point of tension, which has been exacerbated in Nigeria by regional political rivalries with ethnic platforms dating back to British territorial policies. It is significant, and Cooper points this out: Nigeria was plunged into civil war soon after oil exports began and, although there have been outbursts of violent ethno-religious conflict in Nigeria, the "most important tensions have been over the control of the gate."[36] What James Ferguson and Geoff Eley will help us understand is that these historical dynamics of exploitation within gatekeeper states continue in the twenty-first century to engender economic inequality, asymmetries in power and weak national sovereignty.

"The remedies proposed," Cooper reminds us, "under the rubric of structural adjustment, do not necessarily address the structural or historical conditions that gave rise to gatekeeper states."[37] Understanding how the past continues to shape the present and coming to terms with the specific ways in which global relations contribute to, rather than alleviate, the existence of extreme poverty are both essential. Solutions that do not productively involve the people's participation in ways that realistically address the sources of exploitation and injustice will never lead to equality and prosperity.[38] He cautions that disappointment after experiments with a transition to democracy during the 1990s should not come as a surprise, "since the historical patterns and global conditions which gave rise to gatekeeper states in the first place have not fundamentally been altered, and the political economy of an African state cannot necessarily be remade by an act of will of even the most enlightened leadership."[39] Even the most dramatic transition to democracy cannot remake the structural relationship between political power and the economy as postapartheid South Africa has shown us. Looking forward, Cooper speculates about factors that could shake up the gatekeeping structure and contribute to pro-democracy movements in Africa, but he presents them as open questions worthy of future debate.[40] His work leaves open the question of whether democracy and civic debate can transform society and improve the lives of the majority.

Let us further explore the ethics of development and its potential to foster greater freedom in Africa from the perspective of an economist whose practice was transformed by working in Africa. In *The End of Poverty: Economic Possibilities for Our Time* (2005), Jeffrey Sachs lays out a detailed proposal for ending extreme poverty worldwide by 2025 with a checklist for a differential diagnosis of what is wrong with a nation's economy in order to most effectively fix the critical problems as rapidly as possible. The bottom line for Sachs is that the poorest of the poor, who are concentrated in Southeast Asia and Africa, must be able to get a foot on the lowest rung of the economic ladder that can lead them to prosperity. This, in his view, is the best hope for lifting one sixth of humanity out of extreme poverty and thereby making the world a safer place. Two aspects of his argument that specifically relate to Africa are relevant here. First, his comprehension of how markets, policy, and finance actually work changed rather dramatically after a decade of working in Africa starting in Malawi in 1995. His book is written from the standpoint of an American economist who discovered the importance of fieldwork when developing policies designed to help others. Second, with his post-Africa perspective as an economist, Sachs claims that with the proper reforms and investments, First World countries have the potential to create a more just world for everyone if they take steps to end extreme poverty. Considering this proposition will allow us to challenge what role the West should play, and whether capitalism can be reformed to benefit the majority of Africans.

Sachs comes to view the International Monetary Fund's philosophy of economic development during the structural adjustment period as akin to eighteenth-century medicine, "when doctors used leeches to draw blood from their patients, often killing them in the process."[41] He proposes that the entire development community "lacks the requisite ethical and professional standards" and "does not take on its work with the sense of responsibility that the tasks require."[42] Sachs assesses the effects of neoliberal policies that First World banks, including the US-led World Bank, implemented in Africa in these terms:

> Western governments enforced draconian budget policies in Africa during the 1980s and 1990s. The IMF and World Bank virtually ran the economic policies of the debt-ridden continent, recommending regimens of budgetary belt tightening known technically as structural adjustment programs. These programs had little scientific merit and produced even fewer results. By the start of the twenty-first century Africa was poorer than during the late 1960s, when the IMF and World Bank had first arrived on the scene, with disease, population growth, and environmental degradation spiraling out of control.[43]

It is helpful to have someone with Sachs' credentials provide such forthright criticism of the development community and its failed policies after grappling with realities on the ground during the course of a decade of work in Africa. At the same time, his discussion of the emergence of the first era of globalization in Europe unfortunately omits Africa's contribution to that phase of European prosperity in terms of human labor and natural resources. Further, his description of the Third World's emergence leaves out how Africa's place in the world after 1960 resulted, directly and indirectly, from European colonial policies.[44] Thus his interpretation of the reasons for First World prosperity and Third World poverty remains invested in a Western perspective of history that simply does not admit, and cannot account for, the complicated way Europe's imperial past in Africa continues to shape the present.

Given Sen's thesis that development should enhance freedom and Cooper's claim that African gatekeeper states are Euro-African in origin, wrestling with the role Western economists see themselves playing is unavoidable at some point. Sachs goes on to ask some probing questions: "How do we negotiate new rules of the game to ensure that the emerging global economy would truly serve the needs of all the countries of the world, not only the richest and most powerful?"[45] The first part of what Sachs is asking for, is for rich and powerful First World nations to promise billions more in financial aid and to forgive some of the Third World's debt as the beginning of a solution to end the inequalities engendered by neoliberal capitalism, in general, and structural adjustment programs, in particular. And secondly, more rigorous professionalism would be needed in implementing an array of programs from public health initiatives to building adequate infrastructure so as to even the economic playing field for the poorest of the poor.

Sachs central question is: "How can the rich and powerful in the First World help Africa end poverty?" Yet this question *in itself* perpetuates the colonial development scheme. His projects do not fundamentally incorporate Sen's advice about civic debate and engagement with the people whose lives are under discussion. It is a call for the rich to help the poor in order to make the world a safer place. For Sachs, the problem is that bankers in international development need more field work; if they listened to women selling tomatoes in the market, they might avoid "killing their patients with leeches" or making unwise loans and implementing unsound policy. In my view, Sachs's argument is best approached in terms of its ends and means. The ends, for him, are for the Western world to set ending extreme poverty by 2025 as its goal. The means to accomplishing this ambitious goal are for wealthy Western nations to deliver aid, forgive debt, and implement loan programs so that poor people can get their foot on the lowest rung of the economic ladder. His is a values-driven argument: Powerful rich nations in the West can, and must, do better. My primary objection to Sachs's argument is that he imagines reforming neoliberalism to do better and wants to help capitalist societies remake the world in their image. The question of whether capitalism, and especially the expansion of a neoliberal world order, in Africa can be reformed to serve the interests of the majority is more complicated than his argument admits and Sachs's being disinterested in the colonial archive does not help resolve the problem. *The End of Poverty* leaves me skeptical about Western bankers coming to Africa to level the playing field and generate shared prosperity in Africa.

James Ferguson in *Global Shadows. Africa in the Neoliberal World Order* (2006) has made a valuable contribution to the debate about development and neoliberalism by depicting what globalization looks like from African perspectives based on his fieldwork as an anthropologist. One of his conclusions, as we saw previously, is that it is important to keep in mind the limits of retaining national liberation as a structuring concept at the beginning of the twenty-first century, which has been useful to our definition of meaningful freedom in Africa after independence. Ferguson's innovative anthropology of power that explores the concepts of sovereignty and governance, the effects of poverty, and of different forms of longing for, what I would call, existential freedom have reshaped the debate of neoliberalism in Africa. Both Cooper and Ferguson have argued persuasively that globalization, as seen from Africa, is lumpy and uneven. Rather than the seamless interconnection that Western narratives of globalization can sometimes suggest, Ferguson describes capital-intensive enclaves for the extraction of uranium, oil, gold, or diamonds sitting right next to empty, vast unusable space where toxic waste is dumped and migrants die on their way to Europe. So, according to Ferguson, the neoliberal world order and globalization have not leveled the playing field, instead they have segmented space and created profit-seeking structures that feed off inequality:

The global, as seen from Africa, is not a seamless, shiny, round, and all-encompassing totality (as the word seems to imply). Nor is it a higher level of planetary unity, interconnection, and communication. Rather, the "global" we see in recent studies of Africa has sharp, jagged edges; rich and dangerous traffic amid zones of generalized abjection; razor-wired enclaves next to abandoned hinterlands. It features entire countries with estimated life expectancies in the mid-thirties and dropping; warfare seemingly without end; and the steepest economic inequalities seen in human history to date. It is a global where capital flows and markets are at once lightning fast and patchy and incomplete; where the globally networked enclave sits right beside the ungovernable humanitarian disaster zone. It is a global not of planetary communion, but of disconnection, segmentation, and segregation – not a seamless world without borders, but a patchwork of discontinuous and hierarchically ranked spaces, whose edges are carefully delimited, guarded, and enforced.[46]

While it is true that Ferguson's assessment of the landscape of inequality in global Africa that features "the steepest economic inequalities seen in human history to date" lines up with human development data (which Sachs also cites in *The End of Poverty*) that shows a majority of the poorest nations with negative growth rates were in sub-Saharan Africa in 2005.[47] However, some of Ferguson's other claims are not, as it turns out, supported by facts. The lowest average life expectancy in any of the countries under consideration in this book was, surprisingly, in Nigeria and it went from forty-six years in 2000 to fifty-three years in 2016 (see Appendix). Further development data shows that all of the countries under discussion (including the DRC, Mali, Niger, and Rwanda) have made progress extending life expectancy since 1990.[48] Nonetheless, Ferguson's analysis of the neoliberal world order as seen from Africa raises many fruitful questions: Can the symptoms of inequality that Ferguson describes be overcome by promoting democracy and civic debate as Sen proposes? Will this allow the people to choose governments that represent their collective interests? Can making African voices part of the global conversation contribute to achieving meaningful freedom on the continent? If capitalism can be humanized in theory does it happen in practice? Or, is the story of globalization in Africa just the naked face of human greed, where the powerful pursue their own profit with open disdain for the powerless?

Although poverty can be exacerbated by natural factors like malaria in tropical climates as Sachs discovered, it is not part of the landscape, as he seems to suggest in *The End of Poverty*. The socioeconomic inequality that increased in Africa after 1960 was a man-made problem that emerged under historical circumstances specific to the region. Eley's essay, "Historicizing the Global, Politicizing Capital: Giving the Present a Name," helps us advance in our analysis of the history of globalization from his perspective as a Marxist scholar of markets and capitalism. Eley begins by observing how the neoliberal worldview, according to which the First World must step up to its responsibility to remake the rest of the world in its image, is comfortably embedded in a political philosophy that imagines free-market capitalism as necessarily wedded to the expansion of democracy.[49] While this may largely be true, Sen does not take the relationship for granted. Nor do I. The historian's first challenge is to find a way to handle the relationship between language and actual facts on the ground:

> The *ideology* or the *discourse of globalization* is arguably a better starting point for analysis than either economics or sociology in the more structural or materialist sense, because it's at this discursive level that the operative purchase of globalization on public understanding has been constituted and secured, including the terms under which particular ideas and policies can be admitted into its frame and the issue of who gets to speak in its languages, who gets to set the dominant tone. By the "ideology or discourse of globalization" I mean both the insistence on globalization as the organizing reality of the emerging international order and the crystallizing of specific practices, policies, and institutions around that insistence. In other words, the history of globalization has become inseparable from the history of the category. Globalization has emerged during the past ten-fifteen years as a set of discursive claims about the international world seeking aggressively to reorder that world in terms of itself.[50]

Asking the questions – what do we mean by globalization? who gets to define the parameters of the debate? who sets the tone and can "speak in its languages"? – is necessary for a recalibration of the First World's discourse, if we want to be able to adequately deal with "facts on the ground" in Africa. The issues Eley raises here dovetail with Sen's project and are frequently taken up by African writers and filmmakers where the questions "who is speaking?" and "in what language?" are of central importance. Divergent perspectives on what is really happening on the ground in Mali or Nigeria is often staged as a competition over who controls the discourse and which language is used. Thus, Eley's point about challenging categories and discursive claims allows us to bring up for reconsideration how globalization is said to be reordering the lives of Africans today.

Historians such as Cooper and Eley have called for a more precise language when talking about globalization in Africa. Part of the problem is finding a way to hear what Africans say about their own experiences and their sense of Africa's place in the world. To flesh out this aspect of his discussion Eley turns to Ferguson's work on African perceptions of inequality in global Africa and quotes the same passage from *Global Shadows* that we considered above. The way Eley sums up the situation builds on Ferguson's anthropology of global capital and goes one step further:

> In other words, globalization as an actual set of processes affecting the world (as against the idealized claims of the globalizing grand narrative) necessarily presumes and produces, in fact specifically feeds off, dynamics of destabilizing and destructive unevenness and inequality.[51]

If we admit, for now, that globalization as it is presently working feeds off inequality, disconnection, and the segregation of the poor and powerless from the rich and powerful, rather than promoting democracy and increasing prosperity for more Africans, we should then ask: Why is this the case?

For Eley, the place to look for an answer is contrasting neoliberal theories of the marketplace with a global history of labor. Eley wryly points out how the neoliberal emphasis on markets ironically echoes classical Marxist ideas: "The well-nigh universal triumph of market principles – not just as a system of ideas for describing an untrammelled capitalist economy, but as a set of precepts for all areas of public policy and social life – have become the fundament for a brutally frank materialist theory of politics based on the movement of the economy."[52] Faith in the power of capitalism and what market principles can, or cannot, do for poor people around the world is everywhere in the First World's discourse of globalization. Yet Eley considers the *New York Times* columnist Thomas Friedman the most "vociferous loudmouth" adding to the "din of globalization."[53] The fact that Friedman and others advocate the use of American military might to police the emergence of a new globalized world order creates a sense of practical urgency for Eley who urges historians to avoid the rabbit-hole of endless conceptual refinement and to figure out what is actually happening on the ground so that we may articulate a language that appropriately captures it.

To this end, Eley offers a provocative and compelling discussion of how we need to rethink the historical antecedents for the kind of exploitation of labor and natural resources that we are witnessing in Africa (i.e., recent reports of child labor in gold mines in Burkina Faso, miners' strikes in South Africa) and elsewhere around the world (i.e., news from the garment industry in Bangladesh where more than one thousand people died inside substandard factories that went up in flames).[54] The extravagant stripping away of workers' rights and the abuse of labor as cheaply as possible in the extraction of natural resources currently underway requires us to adjust our conceptual tools and historical frame of reference. Eley argues that the Industrial Revolution only transformed labor for a "brief slice of historical time" in the First World and cannot help us understand the nature of growing inequalities under global capitalism. Instead, he argues that we should consider *slavery* and *domestic servitude* from a broader, more geographically inclusive, perspective to understand these dynamics at the turn of the twenty-first century:

> If we then put these two social regimes of labour together, that of the enslaved mass worker of the New World and that of the servile labourers of the households, workshops, and farms of the Old, then we have the makings of a radically different account of the dynamics of the rise of capitalism and the modes of social subordination that allowed it to occur.[55]

Looking at these "modes of social subordination" on a scale that extends beyond First World industrialization reveals how the simultaneous forms of New World slavery and Old World servitude helps us pinpoint what has been changing in the era of global capital, which is the radically stripped-down conditions of labor since the late twentieth century. "*This* is what is characteristic for the circulation of labour power in the globalized and post-Fordist economies of the late capitalist world," Eley argues, "and *this* is where we should begin the task of specifying the distinctiveness of the present."[56]

This chapter will allow us to refine the central thesis of this book that national liberation did not deliver meaningful freedom to a majority of the people by looking at the effects of neoliberal capitalism in the twenty-first century. Before we turn to the discussion of films and fiction, I would like to underscore the two most important analytical questions that we should keep in mind going forward:

1. Who gets to participate in the conversation about globalization in the twenty-first century? The question of the people's voice is critical because it relates to voting, to the expression of dissidence, to allowing opposition and resistance, and to the political representation of their collective interests. It implies a culture of democracy and not dictatorship (Sen). The role of the people's voice has direct implications for instrumental freedoms. It also raises the issues of who gets to define the ideology and discourse of globalization (Eley). Including African voices in the conversation about meaningful freedom is indispensable. Their visibility and presence leave the custodians of capitalist exploitation with less impunity.
2. Can capitalism be humanized to serve the majority's interests? The historical roots of neoliberal capitalism are in the postwar schemes of colonial development. We have seen that gatekeeper states emerged after decolonization in Africa and how departing colonials prepared the terrain to their moral and economic advantage. The question of humanizing capitalism cannot therefore be answered without considering how the past continues to shape the present. Let us also keep in mind that the stated goals of African national liberation were to remake society and generate shared prosperity, which dovetails in many respects with Sen's goals. Yet Marxist criticism of neoliberal capitalism in Africa maintains that this economic system is rigged against the poor and in favor of the rich. In the absence of evidence to the contrary, this is what we have to work with for now. Thus, Eley is quite right, in my view, to propose that slavery and servitude are the most helpful antecedents for thinking analytically about the radically stripped-down conditions of labor in Africa during the twenty-first century. Is it impossible to humanize capitalism? Perhaps. Yet if African economies were developed to benefit the majority of people, I believe, as Sen's work helps us see, that this would enhance the people's instrumental, substantive, and existential freedoms.

The remainder of this chapter will explore African films and fiction that engage with issues related to global Africa in the neoliberal world. Let us briefly consider two significant precursors to twenty-first century narratives that illustrate long-standing interests in freedom. Two films, in particular, Ousmane Sembène's *La noire de …* (1966; *Black Girl*) and Jean-Marie Teno's *Afrique, je te plumerai* (1992; *Africa, I Will Fleece You*), suggest new modalities for thinking about the deferral of meaningful freedom after independence in ways that anticipate later perspectives on global capital and the neoliberal world order from African viewpoints.

In *La noire de …* Ousmane Sembène renews themes in the literature of national liberation – to which his own novel *Les bouts de bois de dieu* (1960; *God's Bits of Wood*, 1962) contributed – with a feature film about freedom and the exploitation of migrant labor after independence in Senegal. Eley's proposition, in his essay on historicizing the global, that slavery and servitude are the most appropriate precursors to neoliberal capitalism invite us to think about how filmmakers and writers represent global Africa in terms that seem to evolve directly from Sembène's 1966 film *La noire de …* In this classic film, Diouana is hired by a French family to work as their nanny in France. The theme of slavery is woven throughout the film and visually operative in the scene where *madame* selects Diounna out of a group of black women on the street, evoking the public sale of slaves. Once the Senegalese nanny arrives in France, she discovers that *monsieur* and *madame* misrepresented the conditions of her employment and instead of tending to the children, they ask Diouana to do the cooking and cleaning as well. In French West Africa under colonial rule, these three tasks would be done by three different individuals, so the escalation in their exploitation of her labor is considerable.

Sembène's film dramatizes the conflict that ensues between a white French family and a black Senegalese woman when she refuses to submit to the exploitation of her labor and the subjugation of her person that they seek to impose. We see how her French masters attempt to subjugate her socially when *madame* asks her not to wear high-heel shoes (because a black maid need not dress up) and when a white male dinner guest is allowed to kiss her exotic black woman's cheek (because he has never kissed a négresse before). In dismay, Diouanna relents to begin with, but as soon as she understands her white masters' true intentions, she stops capitulating. As the narrative develops, Sembène employs an unambiguous, demonstrative discourse of refusal. Diouanna refuses the bonds of friendship through gift exchange by taking back the mask she had given her employers and she eventually refuses to perform her duties as a domestic servant. Sembène shows us a woman who refuses to accept dehumanization in exchange for cash; she refuses to accept the exploitation of her labor under false pretences; she refuses to submit to a regime of labor that perpetuates the asymmetries in power that were set up under European colonial rule. Thus, Diouanna instrumentalizes the language of refusal and resistance in the service of her freedom.

In the final scene with Diouana we see her preparing to leave. Yet rather than take a boat back to Senegal, she gets ready for the ultimate journey of departure by committing suicide. Diouana's last words in the film are, "madame m'a mentie, elle m'a toujours mentie, elle ne me mentirai plus, jamais plus elle me mentira, elle voulait me garder ici comme une *esclave.*" ["madame lied to me, she has always lied to me, she will no longer lie to me, she will never lie to me again, she wanted to keep me like her *slave.*"] After saying these words, Diouana goes into the bathroom and commits suicide in the bathtub desperately asserting the one thing that had not been stripped away by the conditions of her servitude: her own sense of the inviolability of her human dignity. With *La noire de ...* Sembène advances a Marxist critique of domestic servitude by establishing an allegorical relationship with slavery. This parallel in the film draws our attention, more broadly, to what Eley referred to as the "social regime of labor." The possibilities for an escalation in white exploitation of black labor are evident in this film from Diouanna being hired in the street to her "radically stripped down conditions of labor." The element of deception, lying, and false pretences that runs through Sembène's filmmaking from *Xala* (1973) and *Camp de Thiaroye* (1989) to *Faat Kiné* (2000) is critically important in *La noire de ...* The way the French couple deceive Diouanna conveys at least two important messages: (1) skepticism about the appearance of independence, and (2) a Marxist critique of the bourgeoisie's hypocrisy in the ongoing exploitation of workers. Whereas we see the deprivation of her substantive freedoms in the cultural realm of Diouanna's social subjugation, her refusal to submit to slavery through suicide expresses an existential struggle for the worker's humanity.

Teno's documentary *Afrique, je te plumerai* is another significant precursor to the stories that writers and filmmakers went on to tell about global Africa. From his editorial point of view, Teno establishes the exploitation of Africa's natural resources (bananas and timber) by European colonial powers – Germany, England, and France, in the case of Cameroon – as part of a more general narrative of dispossession. The title borrows the metaphor of a lark being plucked of its feathers from a French nursery rhyme, "Alouette, je te plumerai," to convey a literal meaning of losing something tangible – feathers, hair, fur – and the figurative meaning of being ripped off or swindled out of some money. As we will see, the theme of pillaging whereby Africa's wealth is extracted and exported to the detriment of people who live on the land continues in twenty-first century narratives.

Teno carefully layers the dual meaning of pillaging in his narrative. He includes archival footage from colonial films showing how industrious European administrators were at exporting products from Africa. He then contrasts their propaganda featuring tons of bananas and wood being loaded onto ships with present-day interviews of Cameroonians, who were subjected to forced labor and what Eley would call "the radically stripped-down conditions" of colonial workers. This colonial-era exploitation reminds us of those modes of social subordination that produced New World slavery and Old World servitude. In 1992, Teno directly connected these images of Europeans pillaging natural resources and using forced labor to the process of decolonization that produced what Cooper calls "successor states," defined by their gatekeeping function and Euro-African history. Teno makes the continuation of European influence visually explicit when we see more archival footage. This time of French military personnel smoking cigarettes and manning their machine guns while they watch over the celebration of Cameroon's independence. As we saw in the previous chapter, Cameroon's status as a "successor state" has been widely discussed elsewhere, most notably by Mongo Beti in his investigative reporting on decolonization and those who profited from it.[57] In *Afrique, je te plumerai* Teno repurposes images from the colonial archive – including Patrice Lumumba's assassination – by juxtaposing them with observational footage of street protests in the 1990s calling for a national conference and eyewitness interviews describing colonial abuses in order to document local perspectives and rectify the historical record from an African point of view.

Teno narrates the film in French and cites statistics on the high percentage of Cameroonians living in poverty and with low literacy rates, and relates what Sen would call the deprivation of human capabilities to the state's repression of political freedoms (see Appendix). We as viewers can easily imagine that if the people enjoyed the liberty to express dissent, then the government would do a better job of satisfying the people's economic needs. As an artist and intellectual Teno is also interested in another factor that hinders progress at home: he considers what role cultural life plays in perpetuating the status quo. In addition to showing how pro-democracy protest is violently repressed and how open public debate is not allowed, Teno also probes issues related to inadequate cultural institutions. The important work of building libraries, radio stations, newspapers, and local publishing houses that are free from censorship and foreign influence would help foster an informed and engaged electorate and promote civic debate. Teno's film came at a pivotal historical moment as pro-democracy activists took to the streets in cities from Bamenda to Bamako demanding national conferences and calling for elections during the 1990s. The themes and images Teno uses in *Afrique, je te plumerai* to represent the absence of a national conference in Cameroon during the transition to democracy reflects the deprivation of the people's instrumental freedoms. He shows scenes of the state's violent suppression of protest and tells us of journalists who have been put in jail. Thus he makes explicit the connection between defeat of national liberation movement led by UPC (Union des populations du Cameroun) in the 1960s – and others elsewhere on the continent – and the deferral of meaningful freedom in Africa during the 1990s. Teno's filmmaking contributes to the conversation about what freedom means in Africa after independence by challenging the dominance of a Western imperial narrative and anticipating two persistent questions raised by the expansion of global capital on the continent: (1) Who gets to participate in the discourse of globalization? (2) To what extent can capitalism improve the lives of Africans?

Let us turn now to two more recent films on the extraction of African resources from the twenty-first century. Idrissou Mora-Kpai's film *Arlit: Deuxième Paris* (2004; *Arlit: Second Paris*) and Robert Nugent's film *End of the Rainbow* (2009) both represent enclaves of intensive foreign capital investment. In *Arlit*, we return to the extraction of uranium in northern Niger discussed earlier, while in *End of the Rainbow* we follow a gold mine that is dismantled in Borneo and reassembled in Guinea-Conakry. These documentaries show us, in vivid detail, the pillaging of Africa's wealth as natural resources are extracted and exported to the detriment of the people who live off the land. Unlike agriculture, these extractive industries are socially thin and lead to the destruction of the environment, by tearing down forests and dumping toxic waste in the desert. We encounter subsistence farmers who have been kicked off their land with little to no compensation and workers who have retired from the uranium mines dying of lung cancer without adequate medical care. Although observational footage of the "radically stripped-down conditions of labor" in what are open-pit uranium and gold mines is stunning and eye-opening, what is more valuable, in my view, is the way the filmmakers allow local people to share their perspectives on what globalization looks like to them.

Arlit: Deuxième Paris looks at the extraction of uranium in Niger from the under-represented point of view of the inhabitants of Arlit who work in the mines. This film introduces us to a panoply of characters. We meet mine workers and their families; the doctors who run the on-site clinics for multinational corporations; destitute women who turn to sex work and bartending; migrants from other African countries on their way to Europe; unemployed men who have resorted to illegal trafficking and the mechanics who repair the Toyotas they use to cross the desert. These people – who are forced to navigate inequalities on the ground in this part of Africa – seem like a portrait gallery illustrating the landscape of global Africa in the way Ferguson describes it in *Global Shadows*. As it turns out, one migrant whose story we get to hear is fleeing Cameroon and on his way to Europe, but the issue of migration stays in the background as another point of reference for people in search of better options. Doctors in the clinics that are financed and run by the mines tell workers who get sick that they have eczema from chemicals used to process uranium or have difficulty breathing because they smoke. Members of the local Tuareg community started a nongovernmental organization that sought to reveal how the pattern of illness and death observed in the mine workers can be directly related to the substandard working conditions to which they had been subjected. In addition to scenes that show the exploitation of the land and people's labor the filmmaker includes interviews with villagers who talk about picking up scrap metal dumped in the desert and using it for household projects only to discover, when it is too late, that these objects are contaminated with radio-active poison.

In *Arlit* we have another layered narrative where pillaging happens in a literal and figurative sense. Viewers learn about multinational corporations – Areva, COMINAK and SOMAIR – reaping billions in profit while extracting thousands of tons of uranium a year. These corporations, dominated by France and the former colonial power's interest in the industry, allow this exploitation to continue in a way that feeds off social inequality and political disenfranchisement. It is obvious that the corporation's cavalier disregard for the workers' health and the natural environment can continue as long as the people find themselves essentially powerless within the gatekeeper state. To substantiate this point, Mora-K'pai includes a sitting interview with Almoustapha Alhacen who leads "Aghir In'Man" ("Human Shield" in Tamashek) a local NGO in Arlit defending workers' rights and the environment. Alhacen counters every claim the corporations make. Corporations say they are providing adequate social and medical services to their workers and we see they are not. They deny subjecting workers to unsafe and unhealthy conditions, which they are obviously doing as an inordinate number of retired workers die of lung or liver cancer every year. With the decline in the price of uranium after Chernobyl in 1989 the town of Arlit hit a serious economic downturn, which is another part of the history recounted in this film. We see mine workers and their families treated like scrap metal, cast aside when no longer useful without any consideration for social security measures to protect them either by the corporations or the national government that negotiates contracts and collects taxes. The absence of other opportunities illustrates both the lack of diversification and how socially thin the uranium industry is in Niger.

Mora-Kpai's film is somewhat limited in its focus in comparison with other narratives that we will look at in this chapter since it does not offer reflections on neoliberal philosophies about capitalism and democracy. Mora-Kpai does not develop the connection between the exploitation of uranium and the politics of a gatekeeper state via voiceover narration.

However, it does allow people on the ground to tell their stories and in their own voices. Indeed, the power of this film derives from its unique focus on under-represented voices that are so often excluded from public discussion about social, political, and economic matters that concern them directly. We know from Sen's work how important it is to include these voices through open debate and civic participation; in this regard, activists and filmmakers have important roles to play. Activists can foster debate within the country and filmmakers can raise international awareness. Since *Arlit* was released in 2004, Alhacen has continued in his efforts to allow the corporations less impunity in their exploitation of Niger's resources: he works with legal advisers who interview workers, physicists who analyse samples, Greenpeace activists who take sand samples, and he lectures widely on these issues. In 2009, Alhacen went to Germany where he had five minutes to tell the CEO of Deutsche Bank what their commerce with Areva was doing to the Tuareg people and their land.[58] Similarly, popular protest erupted on the streets of Niger when Areva's contract expired in December 2013 and was open to renegotiation, which put pressure on the process and encouraged public scrutiny of the Nigerien government and its multinational partner, Areva. The renegotiation amid protest resulted in increasing the taxes Areva pays from 5.5 percent established in the 1960s to 12 percent as of May 2014.[59] If the political elite does not put this new tax revenue to good use, Niger will continue to rank at the bottom of the United Nation's Human Development index, with the Tuareg in the uranium-rich north suffering most directly from the inequality and exploitation (see Appendix).

The unfinished, imperfect process of African decolonization that allowed successor states and gatekeepers to emerge, and the leverage this gives multinational corporations, makes articulating exactly what this means for the people's freedom a challenge in the era of global capital. Extreme poverty in the case of Niger where 45.7 percent of the population still lived on $1.90 a day in 2016 obviously negatively impacts the people's substantive freedom and their capacity to live a life they have reason to value (see Appendix). The possibilities for Nigeriens to express dissent and to participate in civic debate, which are essential instrumental freedoms, do exist in what is a fragile democracy and should be encouraged and supported as they are imperative to improving lives and enhancing freedoms.

Robert Nugent's film *End of the Rainbow* adds new dimension to this story of multinational corporations and extractive industries in Africa.[60] While Nugent is of Australian origin his documentary set in Guinea-Conakry took second place in its category at FESPACO (Panafrican Film and Television Festival of Ouagadougou) in 2009 and vividly captures what the expansion of global capital looks like on the ground and reveals its transnational scope.[61] This striking film shows a gold mine's relocation from beginning to end; starting in Borneo where it was dismantled and then transported around the world to be reassembled in Mandinka country near the border with Mali. Nugent presents the meeting of two fundamentally different worlds: the international team of expatriates running the mine and an agrarian community nestled in the fertile hills of northeastern Guinea. In this film we have ordinary Guineans – mine workers, farmers, families, and village elders – giving their perspectives in their own voices and native language. The local point of view is presented most forcefully by a village chief who in Bambara explains their way of life before and after the central government sold the people's land to the multinational mining company for an undisclosed sum of money. As the gold mine is established, we also meet a familiar cast of characters – the mine's manager, engineers, armed security guards, state police, and army men – who oversee operations and patrol the property to protect the corporation's capital investment. In the end, the two worlds of expatriates and locals remain essentially sealed off from one another even though only one kilometer separates them. The white managers hang out in a whites-only pub, drink Stella Artois, watch soccer on satellite television, and pack solid gold bars in wood boxes that are flown off in the corporation's private jet. The PBS Global Voices press release describes them as "full-fledged citizens of the new global economy" and, on the screen, the foreign managers say they live only for the moment and put nothing into savings.[62] Many of the Mandinka farmers lose their land and homes and with this dislocation come new challenges; they try to imagine what white people do with gold and why it is so valuable on the global market; they resort to stealing and clandestine mining, during the dry season, to make ends meet; they deliberate collectively and try to protect the rights of the poor among them. In the end, when the village chief recognizes how powerless he is when dealing with the corporation backed by the national government, he concludes, "the gods who protected Africa have abandoned us."[63]

Before the gold mine was established villagers lived in a relatively peaceful agrarian community that was sustained by subsistence farming and small-scale gold mining with baskets in rivers. There is a quietly sinister quality to the arrival on flatbed trucks of the machinery used to operate the mine. Nugent gives us extreme close-ups of gargantuan machines dragging tropical green foliage behind as they tear across the landscape and transport the mine in oversized pieces deep into the bush. He also uses clever camera work to comment on the obscenity of the mine's scale by starting a sequence from the bottom of the pit and then progressively panning out, pulling back and then still further back to reveal just how unbelievably huge the open pit really is when seen from the top. Such hyperbolic camera work – lingering extreme close-ups and progressive panning out – evokes our astonishment at the devastation of the natural landscape.

In social terms, the effects of exploitation are perhaps even more disconcerting. We have a scene where armed security guards who have been recruited from the local population apprehend their fellow villagers, including mothers who have resorted to "illegal" mining on the premises of the new gold mine in order to feed their children. They are arrested at gunpoint for this now-unauthorized activity, patted down for any gold they may have collected and aggressively loaded into a minivan with less care than a tired shepherd would take with wayward goats. After being lectured on how the managers have ordered their arrest for their own safety, the women are let go and the men are detained in a commercial shipping container that serves as a makeshift jail. The film's distribution poster features a film still of one man peering out a window cut in the side of this container symbolizing in a single image how these Mandinka men have literally become prisoners of global capital on their own land. Nugent makes clear the circumstances that have led to their dispossession when he opens with this information:

> Conakry Guinea, West Africa, is a one-party state ruled by Lansana Conté since 1984. In 2006 the government granted a 925 square mile concession in the remote northeastern part of the country to a transnational gold mining corporation. Apart from unspecified payments to the central government, the local population, the Mandinka, would receive only 0.4% of the profits from the mine.

End of the Rainbow offers a raw, at times, unscripted portrait of what it is like to work in a capital-intensive enclave sealed off by barbed wire from the people who used to live on the land and patrolled by armed men – some of whom are employed by the state – which has come to define one aspect of the global world order seen from an African perspective. The capacity to resist is entirely absent from this film in terms of productive instrumental freedoms. One young man who is caught stealing is reduced to tears when he has explain to the police that he was hungry and his family is desperate. To put this in perspective, Guinea is ranked at the bottom of the human development scale (183 out of 186) and is ranked among the most corrupt countries (142 out of 177) worldwide (see Appendix). The limited options for survival, in terms of the villagers' substantive freedoms pale in comparison to the chief's admission that his community's spiritual understanding of the world has been unhinged.

Next, we will look at three narratives that represent other key aspects of the global era as seen from Africa at the beginning of the twenty-first century. Abderrahmane Sissako's film *Bamako* (2006) offers a data-rich critique of the effect of international banking policies and structural adjustment plans in Mali. Chris Abani's novel *Graceland* (2004) presents the complex circumstances of social injustice and political repression that lead to Nigerian migration. And, Ngũgĩ wa Thiong'o's novel *Wizard of the Crow* (2006), a wide-ranging epic from Kenya exploring many facets of the neoliberal world order from corporations to existential alienation in the form of "White Ache."

Bamako, like *Arlit* and *End of the Rainbow*, allows ordinary people to tell the story of globalization in their own voice. Yet *Bamako* also offers well-researched criticism of the economic rationale driving neoliberal policies in Africa. The film challenges viewers to think about who has been setting priorities and stages a trial that makes explicit the asymmetries that enabled the unfolding of the neoliberal world order. With this film, Sissako advances an argument that thoughtfully engages the primary aspects of the debate on neoliberalism thus far: (1) it brings up for reconsideration the *discourse* and *ideology* of globalization (Eley); (2) it takes into consideration the perspectives of ordinary people in both the public debate of issues and the formulation of new priorities (Sen); and (3) it recognizes the catastrophic consequences of banking policies during the era of structural adjustment programs (Cooper, Sachs). The trial format provides for the expression of differing opinions and demonstrates that representatives of Western banks and Malian citizens have conflicting viewpoints.

A prosecutor on behalf of Malian civil society brings charges against international banks. The format for this utopic trial of the people versus global capital takes the form of a tribunal that resembles the truth and reconciliation commissions in South Africa (1996–8), Sierra Leone (2002–4), and Liberia (2005–9) which was underway at the time of filming. The camera shows people from the community sitting in the audience in rows facing forward according to Western cultural customs and witnesses who are allowed to approach the microphone to share their grievances when it is their turn. The "official" language of the trial is French, but some villagers speak in African languages in open defiance of the rules. The presiding judge and his jury sit facing the people at a long table piled high with documents and Mr. Rappaport, the attorney who defends the policies of the IMF and the World Bank, stands opposite the prosecuting attorney who brings charges on behalf of goat herders, peasants, civil servants, and students – the people. Given its historical resonance, this trial by public commission suggests an equivalence between apartheid and West African civil wars, on the one hand, and the destruction of Mali's economy and the people's way of life as a result of structural adjustment programs, on the other. Of course the purpose of the truth and reconciliation commissions, and this trial, was not to produce a guilty verdict, but to engage in a thorough, public debate so that all the facts could be fully disclosed. Victims of global capital enter the public square – in this instance, the courtyard of the filmmaker's home in Bamako – to share their impression of the facts on the ground. This narrative situation creates a venue for public discussion of economic policies that challenges the impunity of powerful international banks.

The exchange between those representing the bankers and the villagers reveals fundamentally opposed perspectives. Such a forum should, in theory, level the terrain and allow everyone's voice to be given an equal hearing in the service of a shared ideal of social justice. However, we witness one peasant's consternation when he approaches the microphone and would like to express his views but he is told to be quiet, to take a seat, and wait his turn. In another scene, the pompous Mr. Rappaport, a white lawyer defending the banks' neoliberal policies, talks longer and louder than seems decent when it is his turn to make a closing statement. This stark inequality in the way the bankers and the people have access to the microphone mirrors an asymmetry in the real world where those with the money dictate the terms of the loans and recipients are expected to accept without discussion. Near the end of the film, in a dramatic act of defiance, the farmer who finally grew tired of waiting for his turn interrupts the hearing, approaches the microphone and launches into a monologue in his native language, making a lyrical declaration about how farmers are starving now while they were not hungry before the banks got involved. The man's passionate, irrepressible intervention, not translated with subtitles, stands as an irrefutable statement of his humanity.

Sissako personifies the consequences of neoliberal policies that are denounced in theory by focusing on the private life of a young Malian couple. Melé is a beautiful young woman who works as a singer in a café-bar and supports her husband, Chaka, who is unemployed and their child, Ina, who is sick. Living with unemployment, illness, and poverty bring tears to Melé's eyes and her sadness finds lyrical expression in her singing. Her tenacious humanity is admirable and painful to watch. In the end the family's hardships culminate in Chaka's tragic death – an apparent suicide, which throws the entire community into mourning. After the sudden, unexpected loss of his life, his body is placed in the middle of the courtyard where the tribunal took place as a symbolic manifestation of the human consequences of the neoliberal world order in Mali. The fact that Chaka (who shares his name with a notorious Zulu warrior-king in South Africa) ends his life out of despair by refusing to submit to degrading circumstances distinctly resembles Diouana's choice at the end of Sembène's *La noire de ...* (1966; *Black Girl*). Sissako's film exposes to public debate the ways in which Western policies for economic "development" in Africa actually destroyed the social fabric in this community and, at the same time, paints a portrait of the human consequences of those policies. As in Sissako's other films *Vie sur terre* (1999; *Life on Earth*) and *En attendant le bonheur* (2002; *Waiting for Happiness*), the filmmaker uses elliptical editing to convey simultaneous activities; we see people go about their lives, listening to the radio; pedestrians walking by; women dyeing cloth, and friends talking about the trial. The sequence of these images evokes a village setting and communal way of life that interrupts the rigid rules of the tribunal set up according to Western cultural norms where the audience sits silently in rows facing forward, which adds texture to the ethical and political drama at issue.

The Malian people who get to speak during the tribunal offer testimony about the erosion of the self-sufficient way of life in villages and cities across the country, which is supported with a combination of statistics, analysis, and passionate oratory by the prosecution. Once structural adjustment programs were implemented, the percentage of this nation's economy used to service debt was as much as 40 percent, whereas between 4 percent and 12 percent of the national budget was devoted to education, health, transportation, and communication. Citing consequences for national sovereignty, the prosecution claims that democracy and elections are at best theatrical when so much foreign influence is brought to bear on social and economic decision-making. Nations that hand over control of the lifelines of their economy to private industry and no longer manage their telecommunications companies, their own systems of public transportation, their healthcare facilities, and their public education sector are not really sovereign nation-states in any meaningful sense of the term. But none of this is news to the unemployed youth who pass the time drinking tea and listening to the radio; they stop listening as a sign of protest. The absence of opportunity at home and obstacles to productive intervention at the national level make immigration seem like the best choice for disaffected youth, which remains in the background of this narrative, but is more broadly reflected in twenty-first century African cultural expression.[64]

Sissako appeals to African viewers to reconnect with their faith in utopia in order to keep hoping and ideally working together to build a better future. These ideals stand alongside an ironic judgment given, in the end, to the bankers sentencing them to community service in perpetuity. In the penultimate scene, people who have been milling around the house where the tribunal took place gather to pray over Chaka's coffin. Finally, a procession of men leaves the courtyard carrying the coffin on their shoulders as they enter the street and go into the city giving viewers a sense of how the loss of one man's life serves as a poignant symbol for their collective dispossession.

As Tejumola Olaniyan remarks in his essay on the film: "Their struggles are heroic and heart-touching, though. Those yield mostly empathy, not justice. As Anthony Biten, a reviewer for Channel 4 (UK) perceptively writes, 'the film gives voice to people and ideas rarely allowed to speak, and allows Africa its day in court – even if it is a court whose grim dignity is its only power'."[65] Olaniyan's essay raises a core question at issue in this chapter. Does the simple fact of letting viewers hear under-represented African voices, as poignant as they are, contribute to social justice? The trial in this film is important, I would argue, not because it can deliver justice in a legal or social sense, but because it creates a public forum for the disclosure of facts and opinions. Although the pillaging of Africa's resources that started with the expansion of colonial empires continues through multinational corporations and interference with representative democracies, I submit that this happens today with less impunity. When the Belgians were building railroads in the Republic of Congo and chopping the hands off recalcitrant workers, bystanders could not take a photo with their smartphones and share it with the world on Facebook or Twitter. More importantly, African writers and filmmakers have wider access to production and distribution networks within mainstream cultural institutions these days than they had at independence. During the first two decades of the twenty-first century, we have observed on the streets of African cities innovative challenges to corrupt leadership and the deferral of meaningful freedom. These protests are plural and take on new forms every day from *Y'en-a-marre* in Senegal to *Balai Citoyen* in Burkina Faso, and their efforts to share ideas about how to organize with activists in the Democratic Republic of Congo. Yet we share some skepticism about the potential for a single film like *Bamako* to deliver justice as Olaniyan has observed. During an interview at the Cannes Film Festival in 2014 Teno made a similar point by drawing a distinction between the ease of sharing a photo of injustice on social media and the difficulty of changing the institutional dynamics at issue. Even so, the possibilities for speaking to an international audience from a local point of view are expanding with new technologies in the hands of dissidents in cities and villages across Africa. This ever-widening zone of protest is happening simultaneously with the expansion of a cosmopolitan audience for African films and fiction that engage with these issues in artistically compelling ways.

Abani's novel *Graceland* is a post-national narrative about giving up on the gatekeeper state and choosing migration instead. One of the reasons the protagonist, Elvis, decides to leave Nigeria is because he has reached the conclusion that intervention at the national level is no longer possible. A growing number of literary critics have observed trends in twenty-first-century African fiction that suggest that the project of nation-building never came to fruition in Africa.[66] A familiar cluster of problems such as weak national sovereignty, gatekeepers in charge of oil, competition for control of the gate, the absence of opportunities, and the violation of human rights has caused some contemporary novelists to imagine immigration to the United States as a more reasonable plot device, a better choice for their protagonists than political engagement in national politics at home. "In short," writes Adélékè Adéèkó, "the new Nigerians appear bent on repudiating the defining markers of the celebrated novels of high postcoloniality. Single-minded, self-assured protagonists fail to become centers of progress in these novels not because nationalists embody some inherent epistemological deficiency; they fail because the Nigerian nation state lacks sturdy democratic guarantees for its citizens."[67] It is because of political disaffection that questions of self-definition and personal freedom are accorded more importance in this new writing than ethical obligations to further the cause of freedom in Africa. Adéèkó argues that "the use of permanent emigration to America as a virtuous plot resolution mechanism signals the beginning of something different."[68]

Abani belongs to the generation of novelists born after 1960 and offers his perspective on post-national identity and options for young people in Lagos during the 1970s and 1980s. In *Graceland*, written in English with strong Igbo and pidgin inflections in style and phrasing, Abani opens with an epigraph from Bessie Head, "It seemed almost incidental that he was African. So vast had his inner perceptions grown over the years ..." This lets us know that the humanity of the character we are about to meet transcends the specificity of his local identity. His name is Elvis – after his mother's favorite singer, Elvis Presley – and, in one of the first scenes in the novel, we see the son reach into his bag of tricks to make himself up with sparkle paint to resemble the famous white performer. While it is true that Elvis's playfulness with race and gender comes up against rigid patriarchal censorship, his aspiration to live a life he has reason to value is persistent and defiant and appeals to a basic sense of human freedom.[69]

Abani who is biracial, with a British mother and Igbo father, handles the question of racial identity with humor and irreverence. Oye, Elvis's grandmother, who is Igbo, jokes with him about how he cannot wash off his skin color. In her English with a Scottish accent she picked up while working for missionaries, Oye says, "Dinna cry about tha' things you canna change" (*Graceland*, 11). Race is, in the most immediate sense, simply a visible fact of pigment. Yet Elvis dreams of living elsewhere. And so, like Anta in *Touki Bouki*, Elvis takes an experimental approach to his identity; dressing up as a girl while playing with his aunt, and like Elvis Presley, while dancing for money on the beach. If Anta's fantasy of herself in the West involves strolling the streets of Paris in a pink polyester pantsuit, the myth of the West that Elvis acquires involves gangsters with Afros in America:

> "States is the place where dreams come true, not like dis Lagos dat betray your dreams," Redemption would say. "It is full of blacks like us, you know, American Negroes wearing big Afros, walking with style, talking anyhow to the police; real gangsters," he continued.
>
> "Uhumm."
>
> "Dat's right. Dese gangsters drive 1965 Ford Mustangs, you see. Like cowboys."
>
> "I thought cowboys rode horses?" Elvis would challenge, already knowing the answer.
>
> "De horse is dere, on de hood of de Mustang. Same thing." *(Graceland, 26)*.

The possibility of escaping to the United States is introduced early on and consistently developed in contrast to the shrinking horizon of possibilities for Elvis in Nigeria.[70] Redemption presents a utopic construction of life in the West where black men have swagger and artists can get rich making movies. Yet, for Elvis, the dream that might come true in America is first and foremost one of self-realization as an artist. The allure of America, for him, is a country where he could do what makes him happy and thus fulfill his longing for substantive freedoms.

Given the cosmopolitan sensibility Abani shares with Chimamanda Ngozi Adichie, insofar as characters in their novels are often individuals who define their lives by choices they make, it is significant that in *Graceland* there are factors that limit Elvis's options in ways that are beyond his control. The first of these is the staggering socioeconomic inequality that exists in Nigeria, where "a higher percentage of millionaires – in dollars, not local currency – than nearly any other country in the world" thrive in their sprawling mansions right next to "a higher percentage of poor people than nearly any other country in the world" who survive in abject poverty in ghettos like Maroko. The editorial that Elvis read on this topic "failed to mention that their wealth had been made over the years with the help of crooked politicians, criminal soldiers, bent contractors, and greedy oil-company executives" (*Graceland*, 7–8). The haunting reality of poverty that gnaws at Elvis's sense of himself defines his existence by depriving him of proper nutrition, continuing his education, and fully developing his human capabilities. The second fact of life with which the young Elvis must contend, and that is beyond his control, is the culture of impunity that protects patriarchs and dictators in a country where fathers who are frustrated by their political impotence take out their rage on women and children. This abuse of patriarchal power within the family is used in similar ways by the regime and its security forces within the nation-state as they wield their power with a cavalier disregard for their victims. Finally, in addition to socioeconomic inequality and a patriarchal culture of impunity, there are the effects of global capitalism in this oil-rich country where men who enjoy power as gatekeepers in control of the petroleum spigot get financial support from the World Bank and the IMF. The novelist specifically names these institutions at the moment it becomes clear that a group of "tiefs" (thieves) in charge of the state have rigged the system against a majority of the population who want fairness, opportunity, and progress. These social, economic, and political forces arrayed against him as an individual who longs for freedom prove insurmountable in the end.

Abani portrays the slums of Lagos as a place of confinement, sickness, and filth. The sense of entrapment that this evokes takes on an important historical dimension as the narrative develops and stands in condemnation of the betrayal of national liberation, which paved the way for Nigeria's spigot economy. He provides descriptive detail of excrement floating in the lagoon under plank walkways, rats washing up into bedrooms, and beggars scrounging for grains of rice on dirt floors with an explicitness reminiscent of Ayi Kwei Armah's novel *The Beautyful Ones Are Not Yet Born* (1968).[71] This intertextual engagement with Armah's classic novel conjures up a powerful literary reference to the deferral of meaningful freedom. Abani also enlists imagery of the sun to create an existential sense of oppression that hangs over the nasty, chaotic ghetto with, "A pale watery sun rose over the ghetto of Maroko," that distinctly recalls Kourouma's metaphorical use the sun in his novel *Les Soleils des indépendances* (1968; *The Suns of Independence*, 1997). Abani's aesthetic and thematic references to these canonical postindependence novels adds layers of meaning to the central theme of political disillusionment in *Graceland*. These intertexts add texture, dimension, and definition to the sense we have of an entire generation of men losing hope in the possibility of productive intervention at the national level. National liberation's promise of rebuilding African societies from the ground up on the model of unity and shared prosperity has been overtaken and unraveled by a culture of corruption, violence, and division.

Yet it is Sunday, not his son Elvis, who came of age during the struggle for national liberation. Thus, in *Graceland,* it is the legacy of their loss – what the second generation inherited from their fathers and mothers – that interests Abani. The narrator tells stories about how Sunday started out in life as a well-educated man with income and status as a Board of Education superintendent with an idealistic passion for progress that led him to get involved in politics and eventually to run for office. As it turns out he lost the election to a clever, opportunistic rival and found himself with more debt than he could afford to pay off with his personal finances. After Sunday lost his job, his source of income, his social status, and his hope in the country's democratic process, he decides to start over in Lagos. As bad as things get for Sunday in his downward spiral into alcoholism, prospects are worse still for Nigerian democracy because it does not really matter that the electoral process is rigged against idealistic candidates because the threat of a military coup overturning the will of the people is all too real. Political corruption and the repression of dissent deprive the father's generation of their instrumental freedoms, which generates feelings of impotence and rage, as we also see in the earlier novels by Armah and Kourouma.

Abani approaches the often-discussed question of African masculinity from the perspective of an Igbo man who has grown tired of patriarchy and dictatorship in Nigeria.[72] Depressed and disgruntled, Sunday becomes one of those emasculated patriarchs who takes out the frustrations he suffers in the public sphere on the women and children in his charge. But the bleakness of political life and a diminished social status create vulnerabilities that are exacerbated by the father's undigested intimate loss. This happens when the wife he loved dies of breast cancer and he is forbidden to officially mourn her passing, "The entire family had performed the full rites, with the exception of his father. Igbo men didn't mourn women publicly. It was considered bad taste" (*Graceland,* 60). The burden of life inside the box of Igbo masculinity seems heaviest when Elvis confronts his father about having witnessed Uncle Joseph raping his adolescent daughter Efua. Sunday responds with patriarchal rage, protecting the father who rapes his daughter and insisting on his son's silent complicity. This triggers an unexpected confession from Elvis about how he, too, was raped in a church by a man whose identity is not disclosed. Sunday categorically rejects his son's right to speak openly about the incest he witnessed and the rape he experienced, insisting that these accusations be buried in silence. Another aspect of Igbo masculinity is revealed when the male elders hire Innocent, a former boy soldier during the Biafran War, to secretly kill Godfrey who was tarnishing the family's honor with his shameful behavior as a thief. Thus the novelist develops this theme throughout and represents masculinity as belonging to a cultural pattern that extends from Igboland to the capital. It is impossible not to associate the impunity accorded the Igbo patriarch, for instance, with the colonel's reckless self-importance on the dance floor in Lagos. When Elvis inadvertently bumps into the colonel while dancing in a nightclub he is nearly killed. The way the nightclub owner and Redemption fall into line, obeying the colonel's terrifying authority makes explicit how the regime's security forces can shoot a man in the head for such a trivial offense. The overlap that Abani establishes between patriarchy and dictatorship in the novel resides primarily in his criticism of this culture of male violence, abuse of power, and impunity. This implacable culture is an important factor contributing to Elvis's decision to leave.

Elvis's generation inherited a country some twenty years after independence during which time the IMF and World Bank implemented their policies and the gap between rich and poor worsened. Abani describes the injustice of gross socioeconomic disparity and the deprivation of human capabilities for those trapped in extreme poverty in vivid detail. In particular, the contrast between fancy neighborhoods and the ghetto of Maroko evokes the inequality that defines globalization as seen from Africa:

> Lagos did have its fair share of rich people and fancy neighborhoods, though, and since arriving he had found that one-third of the city seemed transplanted from the rich suburbs of the west. There were beautiful brownstones set in well-landscaped yards, sprawling Spanish-style haciendas in brilliant white and ocher, elegant Frank Lloyd Wright-styled buildings and cars that were new and foreign. *(Graceland, 7–8)*

And, this:

> As he left the buka and walked to the bus stop, Elvis realized that nothing prepared you for Maroko. Half of the town was built of a confused mix of clapboard, wood, cement and zinc sheets, raised above a swamp by means of stilts and wooden walkways. The other half, built on solid ground reclaimed from the sea, seemed to be clawing its way out of the primordial swamp, attempting to become something else. *(Graceland, 48)*

The absence of opportunity is tough for Elvis to accept in the face of such drastic socioeconomic disparity. He is intellectually curious and politically aware enough to understand the historical roots of this injustice, but he is unable to find a workable solution beyond participating in petty criminal activity, trafficking in drugs, and doing temporary gigs as a gigolo. Elvis drops out of school and is left by a depressed, drunken father to fend for himself. One afternoon the narrator observes, "Elvis leaned back and watched life unraveling in the ghetto settlement under the bridge" (*Graceland*, 116). It is not just his own life that is unraveling, but life for everyone in this Lagos slum during the 1980s. The political reasons behind the absence of opportunity to live life as it should be – to have the freedom to pursue the kind of life Elvis has reason to value – creates an existential sense of dispossession.

Before deciding to take the ultimate step of leaving Nigeria and immigrating to America, Elvis considers all his options. The way Abani allows Elvis to survey the social landscape of global Africa before giving up on Nigeria fleshes out his criticism of the society that has emerged. At the conclusion of Book One, Elvis's father finally reaches a dead end in Afikpo after suffering so many different kinds of loss. Book Two opens with an epigraph from Armah's *The Beautyful Ones Are Not Yet Born* and streets scenes of poverty, chaos, crime, and violence in which people accused of stealing are stoned to death and set on fire. As the horizon of opportunity in Lagos shrinks Elvis considers his choices: he feels reluctant to follow King of Beggars who offers a path to old school activism that seems a dead end; he does not look for Efua in the capital as Oye requested; and so, he decides to go with the schemes that Redemption presents, even though he fears his "criminal side." After Elvis discovers that Redemption has them involved in trafficking human body parts and kidnapped children, he is appalled by the fact that money can buy a sick person a new and healthy organ at the expense of another human being's life. It seems that Elvis has finally reached the culmination of his disillusionment when he says, "Shit. A nation of prophets and devotees is a damned place" (*Graceland*, 245).

Finally, it is Elvis's brutal, first-hand experience of political repression that seals his fate as a future immigrant. This happens when the narrative focus shifts to a collective discussion of the state's new initiative ironically called "Operation Clean the Nation." The government has decided to dispatch bulldozers to Maroko in order to raze the dwellings people have erected ostensibly in the name of ridding the nation of crime and poverty. When the people get together to resist and sing Bob Marley's "Get up, Stand up" on the barricades, a bulldozer kills Sunday and Elvis is arrested and tortured. Abani dramatically stages the naked power of the state to violently repress the people's call for freedom and democracy with "Operation Clean the Nation." The colonel who ordered Elvis's torture while detained in prison does not shoot King of Beggars whom he had in the crosshairs of his sniper's rifle only because journalists from the BBC are there and have their cameras rolling. The fact that the presence of international media can limit the impunity with which dictatorial regimes assassinate opposition leaders is one positive effect of global interconnections. However, the narrator quickly points out that the financial support keeping dictators in power are international institutions like the IMF and the World Bank. King of Beggars puts it like this, "De majority of our people are honest, hard-working people. But dey are at de mercy of dese army bastards and dose tiefs in the IMF, de World Bank and de US" (*Graceland*, 280). The idealism of a collective revolt to overthrow the government comes up against the sharp-edged reality of the question: Who wants to die? After he survives torture, Elvis is dumped out of a moving van somewhere in town, like the activist in Teno's film *Clando* (1996). It is at this point that he must finally come to grips with the unfreedom he faces outside of prison and says: "The tears that wouldn't come for his father streamed freely now as he felt worthless in the face of blind, unreasoning power" (*Graceland*, 306).[73] After "Operation Clean the Nation," the poor who have been dispossessed of their homes relocate to Bridge City where Okon has "broken in" a twelve-year-old girl as a sex worker and school children get fondled for a few coins. These circumstances are the last in a series that incite Elvis to use Redemption's passport and to borrow his name in order to immigrate to the United States. The novel concludes with bitter irony leaving the reader to contemplate what grace there is in a land like Nigeria and what kind of redemption Elvis will find in America.

The underlying problem of the deprivation of instrumental freedoms in post-national narratives that give up on the ideal of progressive intervention within the nation-state has sparked a wide-ranging theoretical debate about whether, or to what extent, the nation remains a locus of power.[74] The post-nationalist turn in twenty-first-century African fiction must be seen as a major development, if one remembers how important national liberation, national literatures, and national languages were in establishing African literatures and literary criticism from the outset.[75] In fact, I argue in Chapter 1 that, until the middle of the 1990s, African writers and literary critics were rigidly invested in the idea of the nation as they developed a critical vocabulary for writing about literatures in European languages from Africa. As we have seen writers, activists, and critics who were pioneers in this field relied on ideas of community and collective aspirations that were informed by the language of nationalism as Benedict Anderson and others have defined it.[76] Faith in the possibility to intervene persisted, as we observed in Chapter 3, even if intervention in the nation's affairs was defined and articulated from the standpoint of the political opposition. Thus, to find that this foundation, the bedrock of twentieth-century African cultural expression, appears to be shifting today is hardly a trivial matter.

Thiong'o's *Wizard of the Crow*, written in Gikuyu, a Bantu language spoken by roughly 7 million Kikuyu people in the area around Nairobi, and translated into English by the author, is our third text in this section and an ambitious novel about the neoliberal world order. In this novel Thiong'o attempts a comprehensive treatment of the effects of global capital in Africa as he weaves a Marxist critique of corporations, banks, loans, and the development discourse with elements from magical realism to creatively represent the bizarre affliction known as "White Ache" and depict the last, spectacular gasps of dictatorship. These impressive, innovative narrative techniques are handled with the verve of a traditional African storyteller in what Thiongo has called a "global epic from Africa."[77] *Wizard of the Crow* explores the failure of political leadership in Africa and the people's unsteady commitment to progressive ideals in Aburiria, a fictional African republic.

The author advances a Marxist critique of global capital and the neoliberal world order through the interrelated themes of leadership and illness. Thiongo's epic narrative begins with questions about why the Ruler in the Free Republic of Aburiria is sick. The narrator runs down five different theories about possible sources of the tyrant's illness: (1) he got angry when denied an interview on Global Network News; (2) the Ruler has been disturbed by the cry of a she-goat whose anus has been sewed shut; (3) he has gone mad from staying in power too long, to the point of no longer being able to distinguish himself from the country; (4) his frustrated obsession with wanting to see his wife's tears; and (5) the daemons in his house have turned on him and withdrawn their protective powers. Underlying these improbable causes is the painfully obvious problem of gatekeeping dictators clinging to power. In this fantastical world of daemons and unhealthy desires, Kamiti becomes a wizard who treats a recurring illness that plagues those in power called "White Ache." This illness is a neoliberal version of Frantz Fanon's "black skin, white mask" and comes with a linguistic impediment so that patients afflicted with the disease are limited to saying the word "IF." This is short-hand for saying, "If I were white ..." The black gatekeepers in the Free Republic of Aburiria want to be white like the bankers and messengers at Global Bank and are determined to remake their world according to the model of Western capitalism.

As part of Thiong'o's criticism of the neoliberal world order, he contrasts plans for frivolous global "development" schemes with the persistence of grinding poverty in Aburiria. Since the sources of human competition and conflict in the narrative are primarily driven by access to employment and business opportunities, this keeps development and the politics of gatekeeping at the center of the action. Meanwhile, the intricate and, at times, convoluted plot in this novel about a fantastically corrupt Ruler is spun around his improbable project of building a skyscraper into space called "Marching to Heaven," which is under consideration for funding by the Global Bank. The landscape of neoliberalism that serves as the backdrop for these whimsical "development" projects does not present a flattering image of the Ruler and his people. The narrator describes at length how the unemployed stand in line for jobs, beggars loiter in front of fancy hotels and sex workers walk the streets and die of Aids. Thus we encounter, once again, the fraying social fabric that results from persistent inequality and political corruption, which has come to define globalization as seen from many African perspectives.

In his Marxist representation of neoliberal capitalism that borrows from Latin American magical realism, it is striking how Thiong'o creates a political atmosphere that is especially hard to decipher. He describes a world where identities change and are not to be trusted as with Kamiti's wizardry, where characters symbolize political functions like the clique surrounding the Ruler and where national priorities seem guided by remote control rather than by a legitimate, sovereign leader. The author uses intricately interwoven narrative fragments to convey a surreal world; his focus is mainly on questions of identity (i.e., how to cure "White Ache"), ideals (the birth of democracy), and the various forces – old and new – that define the familiar contest between the Ruler and his opponents (rumor, the media, banks, and foreign diplomats). The obscenity of the Ruler's entrenched dictatorship is represented with grotesque physical detail; he is bloated with rage and exploding with noxious gases and excrement. His ministers are merely the extension of his ears (Sikiokuu, chief spy), his eyes (Machokali, minister of foreign affairs), and his tongue (Big Ben Mambo, minister of information) – all fatally connected by the same sick instinct to preserve their stranglehold on political power. Underlying the aesthetic complexity of magical realism in this narrative are social, political, and economic dynamics that operate in the real world such as debt, dictatorship, and global capitalism and thus readers are compelled to figure out how to make sense of the narrator's obscene exaggeration of how the world works.

The hermeneutical challenge the narrative presents has practical implications for the opposition as they look for ways of resisting tyranny and corruption. Finding a solution to this problem is at the origin of Kamiti's epic quest. Kamiti's journey begins with looking for work where he meets Nyawira, who will become his wife and inspire him to join the movement for democracy. He retreats to the forest where he discovers his ancestral roots in healing; then, he is led by a curious set of circumstances to become the Wizard of the Crow, which allows him to heal sick tyrants and fly around the world on a "global journey in search of the source of black power" (*Wizard*, 731). Along the way, Kamiti struggles with homelessness and alcoholism; ultimately, he reintegrates into society, plans on getting married, and joining the political opposition. His synthetic identity and crisis of faith in the possibility of achieving social justice suggests that old-fashioned militants have reason to be confused and discouraged. Existential freedom and the absence of alienation have taken on new importance. The opposition's struggle to realize the principles of national liberation – shared prosperity, unity, pan-African solidarity – must be fundamentally reconsidered and rearticulated at the turn of the twenty-first century when faced with global banks set on remaking the world in the image of Western capitalism in partnership with African gatekeepers, who are aching to be white. Thiongo had himself contributed to these ideals of national liberation and freedom with his earlier fiction including *A Grain of Wheat* (1967) and *Petals of Blood* (1977).

The Ruler clings to power with a shallow concern for his country's image in the press and in front of international bankers, but with complete disregard for any meaningful sense of justice, prosperity, and freedom for a majority of the people. Women lead the opposition and resort to shaming the Ruler when they lift up their dresses and show their naked buttocks in front of messengers from the Global Bank. Before the Ruler leaves for the United States to discuss his Marching to Heaven project with people at the Global Bank, he orders the arrest of Nyawira, the leading female dissident. Throughout the novel there are repeated attempts to detain dissidents and neutralize those who seek to usurp power, but these appear to be an endless battle doomed to fail as long as there are people willing to oppose tyranny. The Ruler develops a new illness while in America: his body starts puffing up with SIE or "self-induced expansion" after the Global Bank gives him one week to come up with a better rationale for his project to build a tower to heaven. In the end, after the Wizard of the Crow arrives in New York City to cure the Ruler, the Global Bank decides not to move forward with the project in part due to the appearance of public disorder back in the Free Republic of Aburiria where the people have taken to standing in line and women have started beating their husbands. Apparently, some actions have consequences; some instrumental freedoms can serve a purpose. In fact, the Ruler returns from America defeated by these images of chaos and faced with rumors about his new illness that spread when he does not appear on television.

Eley's proposition that the ideology and discourse of globalization should be our starting point for thinking about the "operative purchase of globalization on public understanding" is relevant here. At this point in the narrative the plot begins to unravel and the Ruler's hold on power slips away. Strange things happen. The Ruler discovers corruption in the handling of his pet project and in the process learns of a tree that grows dollars only to discover that it has been eaten by termites. His control over ideas and the language of power may be in trouble. The Ruler's body eventually explodes and we see that the evil tyrant had a forked tongue. Baby Democracy is born and a ceremony planned, but then Tajirika, next in line after the Ruler, stages a coup that is televised. Thus, the struggle for power becomes explicitly about who controls the message. Tajirika declares Baby Democracy dead, declares the Free Republic of Aburiria an empire and names himself Emperor Titus Flavius White Head. When it appears that he has reclaimed the language of power, bearded spirits arrive in the city on motorcycles from the four corners of Aburiria. In all this, Western institutions are still feared to be setting the country's priorities from abroad via remote-control interference. The would-be leader – who appears to be yet another puppet of global capital – finally admits, "The world will become one corporate globe divided into the incorporated and the incorporating" (*Wizard,* 746). The neoliberal enterprise of remaking the "developing" world according to the model of corporate capitalism appears to be the dominant ideology and exclusive discourse of progress.

Yet there is one ray of hope: Nyawira's idealism and willingness to persist in her belief in progressive political change led by the people, which inspires Kamiti to join her underground movement. Their decision to marry, in the end, hints at the potential for a revitalized social order and is an expression of their substantive freedom and capacity for self-definition in an otherwise unpredictable world. Yet this plot resolution seems somewhat old-fashioned at the beginning of the twenty-first century. How the Movement for the Voice of the People will bring change when Abruriria has become an empire and is on the way to becoming a corporate colony, or "corporony," where the state will be wholly managed by private capital, where nongovernmental actors will provide social services, and where the entire country will be the dictator's real estate remains an open question. Yet it is significant that the Ruler and his inner circle have lost their control over what the people are saying – from rumor to storytelling – and thus their operative purchase on the discourse of globalization. They can no longer manage the country's image in the international spotlight because it leaves them open to public scrutiny. Quite a lot of emphasis is given to who controls the message, the spin in the media, and to the mechanism of transmission in the newspapers, on the radio, and television. This is not without consequence since pivotal moments in this narrative hinge on the country's image and who controls the discourse: foreign diplomats issue warnings, Global Bank loans are withheld, and massive popular protest can happen in the streets. Perhaps these will be the new frontlines of twenty-first century protest going forward.

Eley asks whether a "nationally conceived anti-imperialist sovereignty" has been canceled from the agenda since the triumph of neoliberal capitalism over socialism at the beginning of the 1990s. "That space of alternative potentials," he writes, "however unappealing and compromised under Stalinism, at least allowed liberalism's bid for the one universal and necessary path of history to be contested."[78] Eley's line of questioning echoes an issue that Edward Said grapples with in *Culture and Imperialism* (1993): What are the alternatives to imperialism? Cooper concludes, "African states will probably remain stuck within the limitations of the gatekeeper state – with its brittle and heavily guarded sovereignty – unless nation-states in Europe and North America as well as Africa acknowledge a shared responsibility for the past which shaped them and the future to which they aspire."[79] In this respect, the example of South Africa and Mandela's demands in his Rivonia statement is instructive: that the people should have a just share in the whole of the country, including profits from natural resources and human labor, and the right to choose their own government. If these fundamental rights and freedoms were protected within the nation-state, it would create the possibility for achieving meaningful freedom for the majority and would put an end to imperial exploitation in all its guises.

To conclude this chapter, let us consider two novels about war. If the system is perceived as rigged against the majority and the social fabric starts to unravel, one option is migration while the other is armed conflict. The prevalence of narratives about armed conflict in twenty-first-century African fiction and film testifies to these consequences of persistent inequality and corruption. Emmanuel Dongala's striking novel *Johnny chien méchant* (2002; *Johnny Mad Dog*, 2005) represents a generic civil war in sub-Saharan Africa in order to suggest a pattern that is unspecific to one nation, and Nuruddin Farah's feminist novel *Knots* (2007) about a woman returning to reclaim the family home and rebuild it after decades of civil war in Somalia.[80] It is worth noting that these two novels are part of wider field of cultural expression. Mahamat Saleh Haroun's film *Un homme qui crie* (2010) is a fascinating meditation on the effects of globalization in Africa that starts with the din of fighting in the background that slowly overtakes the lives of a father and his son and changes them forever. Newton Aduaka's film *Ezra* (2007) is a compelling portrait from an African point of view on the fate of child soldiers and the challenges of reintegration and reconciliation post-conflict. Kourouma's novel *Allah n'est pas obligé* (2000) was a path-breaking narrative in this genre that effectively conveys the toll taken on young men who long for simple pleasures and basic freedoms. As part of Nocky Djedanoum's 1998 Write Rwanda Project, the Senegalese writer Boris Boubacar Diop offers a retrospective gaze on the genocide in Rwanda in his novel *Murambi. livre des ossements* (2000) and meditates on the existential dilemmas that division, self-interest, corruption, and violent conflict create for ordinary men, women, and children. One of the characteristics of these narratives about conflict, as we will see, is that they are often told from the point of view of African expatriates who left home or represent conflicts in other countries from the outside looking in. A second defining feature of these films and novels is the central importance of masculinity and the gendered nature of violence

Johnny Mad Dog by the Congolese novelist, Emmanuel Dongala, who settled in Massachusetts after fleeing civil war in Brazzaville during the 1990s, is about the rage of the dispossessed when a gatekeeper state fails and war breaks out. This post-national narrative offers an unforgiving portrait of men with guns during a time of war and the existential crisis they create for the survivors caught in the chaos and crossfire. In this and other narratives, armed conflict is explicitly gendered: women are survivors and men are perpetrators. The conventional gender division in narratives of a nation's struggle for liberation and freedom has been that male characters are defined by their instrumental freedoms as activists that can shape the course of history, whereas female characters tend to be defined by the relative degree of their substantive freedoms within the society. During a time of war, these gender conventions get recalibrated because everyone is engaged in an existential battle to survive.

Dongala narrates the survivor's perspective from the point of view of a sixteen-year-old girl called Laokolé who is practical, courageous, and excels in school. Laokolé's father – who devoted his life to building new structures as a mason – is already dead when the drama starts. Her brother, Fofo, gets lost in the shuffle as the children flee from the violence while pushing their mother – who has lost the use of her legs – in a wheelbarrow. The symbolism suggested by Laokolé's family is heart breaking. Children are left unattended and vulnerable without paternal protection and the constructive potential for the father as a mason to help rebuild post-conflict has been eliminated from the start. The mother is a tragic figure, crippled by war and living with the world upside down as her own children must risk their lives to meet her basic needs. As a maternal symbol, a mother who has lost her legs and is pushed in a wheelbarrow by her children is a poignant reflection of the perversions of war. That Laokolé – who is hard-working, intelligent, and ambitious – should have to use a wheelbarrow, not to help her father build a fence or a house, but to try to survive the destructive forces of war by carting her mother through war-torn streets, constitutes a powerful social tableau that anchors the narrative.

In Ferguson's discussion of globalization seen from Africa he argues that spaces and territories are delimited and often have sharp jagged edges. In the conflict zone that Dongala represents in *Johnny Mad Dog* there are havens of humanitarian aid for Western nationals that are rigorously enforced. These razor-wire enclaves of foreign diplomatic protection set up hierarchically ranked spaces that admit people protected by powerful Western nations and exclude, reject, and abandon those who are not. The implicit boundaries that separated French, Canadian, and American employees of multinational corporations from African people who live on the land that is being exploited become explicit in Dongala's novel. During a time of war, the segregation of space is categorical and uncompromising. Once they are on the move, Laokolé and her mother come up against walls with symbolic meaning: those that have been built to keep them out of foreign embassies, and that demarcate a critical line between those who will be protected from violence and those who will not. While on the run an African-American aid worker helps Laokolé at a UN refugee center, which is a rare moment of kindness, but Laokolé also witnesses her childhood friend get killed when a military vehicle runs her over while backing up to rescue a Western woman's dog. Dongala's narrative ultimately shows us that Western administrative definitions of lives worth saving include foreign nationals, their pets, and endangered gorillas rescued by an international organization – but not Laokolé. She mimics a chimp out of despair, but is unable to convince the foreigners that her life matters so, left behind to fend for herself, she just keeps walking and wrestles with her fears of being devoured by animals in the forest or raped and killed in the city. The view of globalization seen from an African perspective that is defined by a neoliberal world order and social regimes that exploit labor, extract resources, and delimit space is operative in Dongala's narrative. He adds to this view of global Africa by making painfully explicit the modalities of social exclusion, spatial segregation, and the patrolled enforcement of enclaves that existed before the war.

We have seen varying degrees of post-feminist awareness in novels and films by men about male-perpetrated violence and abuse of power. Cheick Oumar Sissoko's feminist criticism of dictatorship and patriarchy in *Finzan* and *Guimba* contrasts with Beti's more conventional representation of gender in *Trop de soleil tue l'amour*. Abani's forthright critique of the culture of impunity that men enjoy at the expense of women and children in *Graceland* contrasts with the gender conventions in Thiong'o's *Wizard of the Crow* that ends with activist getting married. In *Johnny Mad Dog,* Dongala offers a feminist critique of masculinity that represents the culture of male violence and abuse of power as a terrain that prepares explosive, unhinged, and uncensored violence perpetrated by men against women during war.

He narrates the perpetrator's experience of war from Johnny Mad Dog's perspective in the broken French of a child soldier. The novelist alternates between the opposite viewpoints of a young woman (Laokolé) who is a survivor and a young man (Johnny) who is a perpetrator of violence to offer contrasting reactions to social disintegration in gendered terms. Johnny Mad Dog has a rudimentary education and hides behind a fake, embattled, and puffed-up sense of his intelligence, virility, and personal power. To reveal the psychology of semi-literate youth who join the ranks of rag-tag military units Dongala explores their adoption of war names. While there is some humor in the different kinds of names the men choose from "Lufua Liwa" (to escape or cheat death) to "Matiti Mabé" (bad grass, strong weed), war names such as "Mad Dog" and "Roaring Tiger" are intended to convey an intimidating ruthlessness, whereas "Mâle-Lourd" (heavy-sex) is a sexual pun that combines heavy artillery and penises. These war names project an image of hyper-masculinity and convey the effect holding an AK-47 has on young men who come to see gang-raping women as a male bonding experience. The novelist provides Johnny's introspection on what these war names mean and on his basic level of education to paint a portrait of a thoroughly mediocre young man who epitomizes the pathos of masculinity during a senseless civil war. In *Johnny Mad Dog* the complete absence of a coherent ideology on either side coexists with adolescent boys feeling deliriously powerful simply because they have guns in their hands. The two protagonists finally meet face-to-face and it is Laokolé's fearlessness that undoes Johnny; he intends to rape or kill her but she prevails and emasculates him by stomping on his genitals. Laokolé's final thoughts are of the future, children, and peace.

Dongala's novel suggests that the most powerful motivations for war stem from the inequalities set up by gatekeeper states. If people's freedoms are confiscated under a repressive dictatorship, once a society is overtaken by violence there is a total deprivation of human freedom worse than imprisonment. Some try to flee while others join the conflict. The fact that the people's substantive freedoms were thwarted by persistent inequality and corruption prior to the conflict are, however, woven into this war narrative. We see this in how Dongala represents the motivations of young men. The ethnic hatred that warlords use to whip up feelings of resentment, fear, and vengeance is not convincing enough to prevent Johnny from having a girlfriend from the "enemy" ethnic group. There is one dramatic scene, however, where the soldiers' resentment makes sense: when they invade Mr. Ibara's home and take turns raping his wife in front of him. The dialogue between the couple and the rapists exposes that the young men feel cheated by the lack of legal opportunities to advance their lives before the war through education and employment. The orgiastic rage they unleash on Mr. and Mrs. Ibara is explained by the fact that Mr. Ibara was a customs official who enjoyed the privilege of getting rich by collecting "rents" on the import/export market as a gatekeeper. Those who collected rents and taxes before the war got rich and enjoyed the freedom to make choices, while others trapped in poverty did not. Otherwise so much of the war seems an endless series of violent clashes between rag-tag militias, desperate civilians fleeing, empty propaganda, and men with guns getting intoxicated with rape, drugs, and alcohol. This scene in which dispossessed youth seek revenge by savagely attacking a customs official who benefitted from the gatekeeping structure stands in stark contrast with the emptiness of ethnic rivalries.

Dongala's perspective as an expatriate is evident in several important ways in *Johnny Mad Dog*. He offers a panoramic, wide-angle perspective on actors during the conflict exploring their relationships with each other and with the international community. The novel represents a web of relations at work from the local to the global. Dongala's sharpest criticism of foreign diplomats, charitable groups, and the international community pinpoints the glaring hypocrisy in Western organizations that are willing to run over a girl to save a pet and justify abandoning a teenaged girl while rescuing gorillas as a matter of adherence to policy. The novel explicitly thematizes how hard it is to understand conflict. Characters must evaluate their own experience of the war in contrast to what foreign journalists report on cable news networks. Laokolé tries to comprehend the interpretations of adults like her mother, who says the reasons for the conflict are essentially political and so should be the solutions, and decides that international news engages in misinformation. Part of Dongala's long-distance view can be seen in his post-national narrative with multiple references to conflict zones including Sierra Leone, Somalia, DRC and Congo-Brazzaville suggesting that civil wars in Africa can be looked at as part of a broader pattern of conflict. A specific geography of place is not an important reference point in *Johnny Mad Dog* and this makes setting the film adaptation in West Africa, rather than the author's native Congo-Brazzaville, appear a matter of choice. This post-national narrative represents the unraveling of a nation as a pattern of violence that can engulf regions and cross borders.[81]

Farah's novel *Knots* (2007) stands out from other literary representations of global Africa as a frankly utopic work about the potential for cultural feminism to revitalize Somali society after decades of civil war. The novel initiates a conversation about how Somalis might live together differently in terms of new possibilities for creative associations and community building in the aftermath of conflict. While the author is interested in Africa's place in the world, the narrative explores issues from the point of view of a Somali woman with a cosmopolitan outlook as part of a conversation *within* Somalia about the future. Although the novel proposes an optimistic vision of what is possible, Farah can hardly be dismissed as a wide-eyed idealist given his chilling account of finding himself with a gun to his head when he was facilitating negotiations between Somali warlords.[82] *Knots* is an expression of ethical devotion to a Somali way of life that was tolerant and open to the world in the days before the migration of political Islamists from Yemen and the Gulf states during the 1980s, and before the chaos that ensued after Mohamed Siad Barré fell from power in 1991.[83]

Knots represents the devastating consequences – social, cultural, political – of years of misrule with poor leadership, what Farah characterizes as incompetent men who have been spoiled as boys growing up and then put in charge of the nation.[84] The turmoil of the present and hopes for a different future are largely seen from Cambara's perspective. She is a middle-aged expatriate who returns to the capital city of Mogadiscio to reclaim her family's home that warlords have overrun and to stage the play *The Eagle and the Chicken* by the Ghanaian writer Ama Ata Aidoo. For Cambara the family home does not evoke conventional associations of domesticity or silent sequestered wives, rather it represents a hub of collective initiative and creative activity. While *Knots* is certainly not the first of Farah's novels to have what he calls a "female central consciousness," what distinguishes Cambara from his previous female protagonists is her status as a transnational feminist with a global network of support that extends from Toronto in Canada to Nairobi in Kenya. As Cambara makes her way around Mogadiscio the cosmopolitan flavor of her cultural point of view permeates the narrative and opens new ways of seeing things that suggests possibilities for progressive change. What Cambara sees reflects what she believes and a culturally distinct point of view. Farah tells the story of her return with a hybrid gaze that brings everything up for reconsideration making careful use of the duality of her expatriate position; she is both a native (of Somali origin and raised as such) and a nonnative (not having lived in the country for many years). Farah chose a close third-person narrator focused primarily from Cambara's perspective, which allows a productive tension to emerge between different visions of Somalia. To some extent her hybrid perspective also decreases the space between insider and outsider, between "us" and "them," by trying to articulate a new way forward without conflict.

The title refers to knots in a woman's veil or headscarf, and the gathering of different strands at one point when tying a knot becomes a trope for how gender identity is entangled within multiple spheres of experience (intimate, religious, political) – hence, the plural noun. While her actions define her sense of self, Cambara is not entirely her own invention and much of the drama that surrounds her complex identity as a cosmopolitan Somali woman stems from the fact that patriarchal social expectations, Islamic customs, and the realities of a failed nation-state constrain her options while she simultaneously benefits from a transnational network of feminist support. Cambara is the inverse of Elvis in *Graceland* insofar as she chooses to return home and reclaim her family's property, precisely because she has not given up on the possibilities for radical transformation and intervention at the national level. At times, her gender identity is abstracted into a political allegory about freedom with descriptions of her veil and headscarf: "She struggles to undo the knotted strings of her veil" and then with the "knots of her head scarf" (*Knots*, 197). Farah develops her sense of vulnerability as a woman in terms of this entanglement: "She feels as if she is in a free fall, the string attaching her to the parachute becoming so entangled that there is no chance of it opening. The intensity of her vulnerability, the unpredictable nature of her volatility surprises her as much as it shocks her" (*Knots*, 309). Thus, her capacity to live free from the social symbolism of the veil with all of its political implications is represented as a precarious, frightening idea.

It is against a backdrop of residual violence and inequality that Farah deliberately proposes a good news story. The way Farah develops Cambara's character inverts the conventional gender roles in nationalist discourse. Her fortitude derives in large measure from her mother, Arda, who made wise financial investments and was in a position to empower her daughter to transcend the difficult circumstances of her life – divorce, the loss of a son – without male protection. Other support and resources come from a transnational feminist network that operates independently from the nation-state. With the temperament and wisdom to change the lives of people around her, Cambara's character represents a much broader attempt to imagine how women who are educated, emancipated, and self-confident have the capacity to redefine the values that will shape Somalia in the future. Her ex-husband, Zaak, who is a "hopeless man in a ruined city" is inert, backward-looking, and the transmitter of rotten patriarchal values, whereas she is a progressive agent for change. Cambara's maternal instincts also contest the status quo. First, her natural attachment to her only biological child, a son named Dalmar, results in a traumatic wound when Dalmar dies in a tragic accident because his father left him unattended while copulating with a mistress. After she discovers the grim reality on the streets of Mogadiscio she decides to informally adopt two boys in need. With the theme of adoption in *Knots* Farah returns to parenting as a means of challenging the patriarchal structure of Somali society. He contrasts Cambara's elective maternal assistance, as she nurtures and protects abandoned children, with warlords who have a clannish investment in bloodlines that has destroyed the kind of Somali culture Farah grew up in as a child. In Somalia one says motherland, not fatherland, so Farah posits a different family trope for imagining the national community in his motherland as he promotes a genealogy of cosmopolitan affiliation as the basis of a new Somali nation, instead of the destructive clan-based politics that have fueled civil war for a generation.[85]

Cambara's values are an amalgam of her upbringing in Somalia in the days before zealots and fundamentalists, what Anthony Appiah calls the "counter-cosmopolitans" in *Cosmopolitanism: Ethics in a World of Strangers* (2006), and the worldly cultural influences and associations that Cambara acquired while living abroad. Her cultural perspective and ethical character are on display when she becomes reacquainted with the new, war-torn Somalia:

> She elects not to acquiesce to the easier options, her thoughts wandering away, her eyes likewise. She sees more ruin everywhere she looks, houses with no roofs, lampposts denuded of cables, windows lacking glass panes: a Mogadiscio raided and destroyed. Looking around from where she is, she sees women in cheap chadors, men in sarongs and flip-flops, their guns slung over their shoulders. She concludes that the city, from her encounter with it in the shape of most of its residents, appears to be dispossessed of its cosmopolitan identity and in its place has begun to put on the clannish, throwaway habits of the vulgar, threadbare semi-pastoralists. Even though she cannot contain her despair, she does not wish to dwell on the consequences of the civil war and the destruction visited on the entirety of the society; she wants to focus on the shopkeeper and his wife, who, according to her husband, is active in the Women for Peace network that Raxma had told her about. *(Knots, 132–3)*

Farah invites us to imagine Somalia before it was "dispossessed of its cosmopolitan identity" by the warlords and their recruits who have the "vulgar" and "threadbare" habits of making enemies out of people who are not like them. While the narrative description registers Cambara's disgust with the cheap ugliness of war and her nostalgia for a motherland that was at peace and proud of its status on the continent and its place in the world, this protagonist has no illusions about simply returning to the past either; "it isn't that she has a wistful desire to return to a hierarchical, male-run taxonomy in which women occupied the lowest rung in the ladder" (*Knots*, 361). The practical and ethical implications of Farah's cultural feminism challenge the place accorded to women in the "high-octane anti-Western rhetoric" characteristic of Islamist movements in the twenty-first century of the kind we find in Somalia where "the woman question" is one of the sources of cultural conflict.[86]

Although *Knots* does not reveal all the sources of conflict that have been feeding the civil war, the narrative explicitly refers to the effects of inequalities that were created with the implementation of neoliberal policies as global capitalism expanded across the continent. There are, here again, signs of the terrain Ferguson presents in *Global Shadows* as characteristic of a neoliberal world order, this time, as seen from Somalia. Farah's description of how Mogadiscio changed as inequality grew and human development declined resembles the capital-intensive enclaves that we have seen in Mora-Kpai's *Arlit* and Nugent's *End of the Rainbow*. In *Knots* residents in the capital retreat behind fences and razor-wire for protection and security:

> It was common enough for people to leave their doors open night and day when she lived in Mogadiscio and you could take peace for granted. Later, with kickbacks and other forms of corruption creating overnight millionaires, the city became flooded with unemployed, the poor, and the migrants from the starving hinterland, and fences went up faster than you could tally the changing death and birth statistics. Sometime later, residents upgraded the fences, putting broken glass, razor blades, and electric wire on top to deter robbers. *(Knots, 112–13)*

Cambara's willingness to return home, to walk the streets alone and to reclaim her family home represents concrete steps to repossess territory that was overrun during the war. Her community-minded efforts seek to overcome the residual segmentation of space that happened during the war and they run counter to the impulse of the rich and guilty who retreat behind barbed wire and walled-in compounds.

In addition to portraying the landscape of inequality that defines the neoliberal landscape in this novel, Farah also contemplates a significant shift that happens in global Africa when war breaks out: the transition from gatekeeping dictators to transnational warlords. As long as a dictator remains in power and is able to keep the gate, a neoliberal social economy can be sustained. However, once the state fails and the gate collapses, then power brokers in Somalia turned themselves into warlords.[87] It will not come as a surprise, at this point, to learn that oil money has been helping to fund the warlords in this country when Cambara stumbles across "pages torn from an American oil-drilling company's document detailing payments to one of Mogadiscio's notorious warlords" (*Knots*, 182). Cooper warned that the one thing worse than a gatekeeper state is a failed state: the complete collapse of state structures and national institutions as we have seen in Somalia as well as in Sierra Leone and the DRC.[88] After the demise of Barré's dictatorship and the failure of the state, access to new technologies of violence changed the calculus for the emerging warlords:

> Anthropologists can celebrate the ability of the Somali clan structure to balance the relative strengths of different kinships, foster equality among males, and settle conflicts within the kinship system itself, but once – following the cynical manipulations of both the United States and the Soviet Union – Somalis got access to AK-47s and truck-mounted artillery, clan conflict took on an altogether different aspect."[89]

While *Knots* acknowledges the transnational flow of commerce and weapons, as we also see in Aduaka's film *Ezra* and Diop's novel *Murambi*, this narrative about post-conflict reconstruction focuses primarily on the possibility for cultural feminism to revitalize a society destroyed by men with guns.

Like Dongala, Farah advances a forthright critique of masculinity in a time of war with an emphasis on the residual effects of violence on survivors. As with our imagination of Somalia yesterday and today, Farah allows a tension to exist between utopic and dystopic themes in the novel. We see this in the coexistence of different forms of masculinity. On the one hand, there are the men in charge who have completely failed the people. Cambara describes Zaak, whose "hick mentality" exemplifies the failures who have been entrusted with running the nation, as "a top-of-the-range loser, typical among the men to whom we've entrusted the fate of the nation for far too long" (*Knots*, 273). And then, there are warlords like Gudcur who beats his pregnant wife Jiijo, enacting the moral depravity of his cohort of men with disdain for women, children, and a peaceful community based on freedom and equality. On the other hand, there are good men who have been sickened as they witness civil war laying waste to the cosmopolitan Somalia of years past. The narrator describes the effects of this "heartbreaking wasteland" on men like Bile, one of a handful of decent men and she falls in love with him, "Cambara decides she is bearing witness to the birth of a terrible ugliness, the start of a gradual falling apart of a giant man who is otherwise famous, from what she has heard, for his inner strength" (*Knots*, 316). Considering Bile's legendary strength it would seem that it is questionable whether *any* man with integrity and honor can survive war-torn Mogadiscio intact. She concludes that even Bile caved into "nihilistic self-assessments confronting the evil manifestations of the darker side of the Somali character in these troubled times" (*Knots*, 317). His mental infertility is an intimate, individual expression of the country's fate "like the darkness of winter descending on the soil of Bile's mind, that nothing will grow on such a soil" (*Knots*, 319). If the prerogatives that patriarchal social structures create for men make life easier for "top-of-the-range losers" like Zaak, decent men with Bile's integrity who embrace progress and are willing to marry women like Cambara must confront the evil they have witnessed and take steps to heal their psyches.

Farah's novel asks us to approach the question of meaningful freedom from the other way around, not as an ongoing struggle to realize the promises of national liberation, but as an attempt to rebuild an inclusive, egalitarian, and just society on the ruins of a failed nation-state. The project *Knots* proposes is rooted in cultural feminism. Cambara exercises her instrumental freedoms by adopting children and raising them with her values, by enlisting the community to stage a cosmopolitan, feminist play and by reclaiming her family home overrun by warlords. She defines her life by making use of her substantive freedoms to get divorced, to travel, and to network with others who support her initiatives. Although Farah offers a utopic vision for national reconstruction, he does make specific recommendations for progressive action that entail key aspects of freedom. These choices, particularly the contrast between doing popular theater engage with the community and waging civil war, have ethical and historical resonance. As we observed in Head's novel *When Rain Clouds Gather*, also inspired by cultural feminism, Farah concludes with the prospect of marriage between Bile and Cambara as the foundation for a productive partnership in addition to the fulfilment of their substantive freedoms as a man and a woman. These various efforts can be seen as an existential struggle for the survival of a Somali national identity.

Finally, *Knots* allows us to circle back to the two analytical questions with which we started this section on film and fiction: Who gets to participate in the global conversation? Can capitalism improve lives? All the narratives we have considered, including *Knots*, have made a point of showing us what globalization looks like from Africa in a way that revises the myth of seamless interconnection and equal access in a flat world. The possibility in *Knots* of enhancing women's freedom by increasing their access to resources – financial assets, transnational networks, and human capital – raises the question of gender and development. The contribution that women like Cambara could make to Somali society has specific ethical implications when considered in relation to Sen's work on the numbers of "missing women" who have perished as a result of insufficient resources being devoted to their well-being – from malnutrition, inadequate medical treatment, and the effects of illiteracy – in predominantly Muslim societies.[90] *Knots* offers a deliberately progressive portrait of what access to resources and opportunities could do to transform the lives of people in cities like Mogadiscio, not only for women and children, but for the whole of society. So, although Farah explicitly acknowledges the landscape of inequality that defines global Africa from the perspective of post-war Somalia, he also posits as Sembène does in *Faat Kiné* (2000) that money in the hands of feminist women can transform patriarchal culture. At the conclusion of *Knots*, the narrator observes the fulfillment of Cambara's dreams through successful collective creativity, the reunion of family and friends, and the promise of romantic love from the mother's point of view. The narrator observes Arda, Cambara's mother and a significant source of the daughter's strength, "Arda looks on from close by, profoundly happy. This is quite evident, despite her self-restraint – her uncontrollable enthusiasm at being home after several years and finding that her daughter has achieved a miracle, through what, if she were a politician, she might call consensus building" (*Knots*, 384). Farah's utopic vision invites us to consider the power of the imagination to recreate beauty and harmony in the wake of devastating civil war.

In this chapter, we have explored the limits of national sovereignty that have resulted from the expansion of neoliberal capitalism in Africa. The emphasis has been on how the concentration of wealth in the hands of global corporations and African gatekeepers destroy the social fabric. Some novels and films show how the deprivation of the people's substantive freedoms through exploitation of labor and resources, and the system being rigged to benefit of the wealthy and powerful can lead to migration and armed conflict – i.e., when people give up on progressive intervention at the national level. We have considered representations of ongoing pillaging and its consequences, including increased public scrutiny in our digital age as a starting point for deconstructing the ideology and discourse of globalization.

This chapter has also allowed us to articulate how this new area of narrative interest represents the ongoing struggle for meaningful freedom with complex, layered narratives that continue to engage with areas previously discussed from within the context of global Africa. The way, for instance, that Dongala and Farah use gender identity to structure their narratives about the struggles nations face today when the expansion of global capital frays the social fabric and armed conflict ensues allows us to appreciate the interconnections in these spheres of experience. The narratives we looked at in this chapter represent the individual's relationship to communities – Elvis in *Graceland*, Cambara in

Knots – at home and abroad with a greater sense of entanglement that happens across different spheres of experience from the intimate self to the transnational or post-national networks in which expatriates operate. An antihegemonic and anticapitalistic discourse has been formulated in the era of global capitalism as a critique of neoliberal policies imposed by the World Bank and the IMF and as a debate about whether economic reforms can increase opportunities and generate shared prosperity, or whether capitalism is by definition anathema to social justice.

It will be useful to summarize the kinds of freedom we have considered in this chapter in the evolving conversation about meaningful freedom in terms of how globalization is seen from African perspectives today:

Instrumental. In *Arlit,* workers in the uranium mine struggle to have their rights represented even as they die of lung cancer and we meet a migrant who is fleeing Cameroon and the absence of instrumental freedoms in that country, which we looked at in the preceding chapter. In *Bamako,* Sissako imagines a tribunal for the people to speak directly to representatives of Western banks in the absence of meaningful sovereignty in Mali. This is a dramatic and symbolic exercise of their right to free speech and the expression of dissidence in the public square. In *Graceland,* Elvis decides to immigrate because there are no good options for intervening productively in national politics. He is fleeing the effects of a spigot economy, but also, more specifically, the deprivation of his instrumental freedoms after he is arrested during Operation Clean the Nation and tortured by agents of the state. In *Wizard of the Crow,* people stand in line to get their basic needs met and are forced underground to mount a resistance against grotesque dictatorship. In *Johnny Mad Dog,* Dongala represents how war constitutes a deprivation of human freedom that is worse than imprisonment and shows how Laokolé's many requests for assistance are declined. In the midst of war and a humanitarian crisis the rights of only whites, their pets, and gorillas are protected by "official policy." In *Knots,* Farah invites us to consider Cambara's freedom of expression in staging a play as a necessary building block in the project of reconstructing a just society in the aftermath of war.

Substantive. In *Arlit,* none of the workers in the uranium mines enjoy substantive freedoms as long as they live in poverty and are sick, but the women who resort to sex work illustrate this kind of deprivation most forcefully. What choices do they have? In *Bamako,* Sissako uses Melé and Chaka to put a human face on the absence of substantive freedoms when people live in poverty, are unemployed, and unable to treat illness. In addition to the repressive political environment that Elvis wants to leave behind, he also chooses to immigrate to the United States in pursuit of life as it should be. In this post-national narrative from an expatriate point of view, Elvis hopes to enjoy self-definition and self-expression as an artist in America. In *Wizard of the Crow*, the people who are surviving dictatorship in the Free Republic of Aburiria enjoy few substantive freedoms; their choices appear over-determined by their servitude to white capitalism, but the novel ends with Kamiti and Nyawira's decision to marry. Their marriage is a joint partnership that will be devoted to progressive activism together in the future. In *Johnny Mad Dog*, Dongala plays around with warlords who keep choosing different names as an absurd attempt at self-definition, which stands in contrast to Laokolé who improves her life through education. Cambara's character is defined by all kinds of choices, most notably her decision to return home and to adopt children to whom she is not related to by blood.

Existential. In *Arlit*, the detail of how mine workers use metal scraps dumped in the desert that are contaminated with radioactivity is a poignant symbol of the scale of dehumanization that defines the landscape of global Africa. It evokes the intangible loss of human dignity when labor is brutally exploited and resources are pillaged under a social regime of labor of the kind that Eley articulates. Sissako concludes his film *Bamako* with men carrying Chaka's coffin into the street, which is a powerful symbol of the community's dispossession. The loss of Chaka's life echoes Diouanna's suicide at the end of *La noire de ...*, which reflects an existential struggle for human dignity. In *Graceland*, Elvis describes life unraveling under the bridge in Maroko and says "nothing prepares you for this." This is another powerful moment of intangible loss that cannot be quantified in dollars or measured in hours. In *Wizard of the Crow*, Kamiti flies around the world in search of new inspiration for black liberation and becomes a wizard to cure the "White Ache" that plagues the leaders in Aburiria. His is a quest to end the alienation of black men in power. In *Johnny Mad Dog*, the image of Laokolé pushing her injured mother in a wheelbarrow in the midst of civil war is a symbol of devastating existential dispossession. Finally, in Farah's novel, the knots in a woman's headscarf are a trope for how gender is entangled in other spheres of experience, most notably religious identity, which reveals the complexity of Cambara's existential struggle to rebuild her community on feminist values.

Notes

1. The Tuareg rebellion of the 1980s and 90s was a popular movement that split into factions with time; UFRA (Union des Forces de la Résistance Armée) was one of the last to lay down its weapons. Participants in the rebellion

have told me that the divisions into factions and Mano Dayak's death, when his airplane was shot down, were the result of French interference. For a description of the various armed factions, see www.ucdp.uu.se/gpdatabase/gpcountry.php?id=118&=.

2. I claim that the rebellion was waged over the issue of uranium, which requires some qualification. One could say that the rebellion was the result of dictatorial regimes marginalizing the ethnic Tuareg and the violent opposition this provoked. One could also say that it was a nationalist movement seeking to establish a Tuareg zone where children could learn to speak Tamashek. Yet, all these crucial issues of language, ethnicity, and national sovereignty were, I believe, exacerbated by the inequality between the north and south of the country and the conditions of exploitation in the uranium-rich Tuareg regions.
3. Frederick Cooper, *Colonialism in Question: Theory, Knowledge, History* (Los Angeles: University of California Press, 2005), p. 104.
4. James Ferguson, *Global Shadows: Africa in the Neoliberal World Order* (Durham, NC: Duke University Press, 2006), p. 35.
5. Ibid., pp. 34–42.
6. The general dispossession of Tuareg nomads living in Niger cannot be separated from their exploitation as a result of the uranium mining industry. There were specific triggers that set off violence, like disputes over which language should be used in primary schools and ethnic persecution such as the massacre at Tchin-Tabaraden in May 1990. For a detailed description of these human rights abuses, see Amnesty International's summary of concerns: http://amnesty.org/en/library/info/AFR43/001/1991/en. In the years since, much has been written by journalists and academics about the Tuareg predicament in Niger and the challenges of weak governance, which seem only to get worse with time.
7. United Nation's Development Index for 2013. International Human Development Report for Niger. http://hdrstats.undp.org/en/countries/profiles/NER.html (consulted July 15, 2013). Reuters reports "Areva Q1 revenue up 12.5 percent on strength in mining." www.reuters.com/article/2013/04/25/areva-results-idUSL6N0DC4VD20130425?type=companyNews, posted April 25, 2013 (consulted July 15, 2013).
8. For a description of Areva's presence in Niger by staff writers at Agence France Presse for Nuclear Power Daily, technology, science and industry, see "Areva, world's 2nd uranium company heavily present in Niger," at www.nuclearpowerdaily.com/reports/Areva_worlds_2nd_uranium_company_heavily_present_in_Niger_999.html (consulted on July 15, 2013). The Africanist historian Gabrielle Hecht has published two books on this topic: *The Radiance of France: Nuclear Power and National Identity after World War II* (Cambridge: MIT Press, 2009) and *Being Nuclear, Africans and the Global Uranium Trade* (Cambridge: MIT Press, 2012).
9. For data on the productivity of Niger's uranium mines from 2005–12 in a global context, see "World Uranium Mining Production," at www.world-nuclear.org/info/Nuclear-Fuel-Cycle/Mining-of-Uranium

/World-Uranium-Mining-Production/, updated July 2013 (consulted July 15, 2013). For specific discussion of France's exploitation of mines in Niger and the dangers they are facing today, see "Niger's Uranium Facilities under Assault," at EconoMonitor: www.economonitor.com/blog/2013/06/nigers-uranium-facilities-under-assault/, posted June 4, 2013 (consulted July 15, 2013).

10. For an account of the state of Niger's uranium industry, I consulted www.world-nuclear.org/info/inf110.html on January 27, 2013. For a description of France's nuclear arsenal, I consulted www.armscontrol.org/factsheets/Nuclearweaponswhohaswhat on January 27, 2013.
11. For an update on the politics of uranium and French influence in Niger, see "Niger's Uranium Coup," at *Toward Freedom: A Progressive Perspective on World Events since 1952*: towardfreedom.com/home/global-news/1882-nigers-uranium-coup, posted March 8, 2010 (consulted July 15, 2013). For documentation of human rights abuses in Niger and the historical persecution of Tuaregs, see reports by Human Rights Watch and Amnesty International for the relevant years, especially starting in 1990. For a fairly thorough review of the factors contributing to Kountché's successful coup overthrowing Hamani Diori in 1974, including ethnic tensions, corruption, a severe drought decimating Tuareg livestock, an international oil crisis and France's growing interest in nuclear energy on favorable terms, see Richard Higgott and Finn Fuglestad, "The 1974 Coup d'Etat in Niger: Toward an Explanation," *The Journal of Modern African Studies*, vol. 13, no. 3 (September, 1975), 383–98. For a direct discussion of French disapproval of Diori's attempt to charge a higher price for uranium in order to deal with Niger's financial crisis to which the drought contributed, see Jibrin Ibrahim, "Political Exclusion, Democratization and Dynamics of Ethnicity in Niger," *Africa Today*, vol. 41, no. 3, Electoral Successes: Harbingers of Hope? (3rd Quarter, 1994), 15–39. Published by: Indiana University Press. Stable URL: www.jstor.org/stable/4187000.
12. To suggest that French administrators engineered an absence of sovereignty may seem like an overstatement to some readers. It is possible to read the political instability in Niger as deriving exclusively from internal problems and poor leadership. While these local factors are no doubt relevant, French military intervention in Niger has contributed to the absence of meaningful sovereignty and benefitted France's nuclear program as a direct result.
13. Ferguson, *Global Shadows*, p. 41.
14. See "Niger's Uranium Facilities under Assault." Lydia Polgreen discusses the different militias that were occupying northern Mali in "Faction Splits from Islamist Group in Northern Mali," *New York Times*, January 24, 2013.
15. Tony Todd, "French special forces 'to protect' Niger uranium mines," *France 24 international news*.www.france24.com/en/20130125-france-niger-uranium-areva-special-forces-mali-security-special-forces, posted January 25, 2013 (consulted July 15, 2013).

16. Ferguson, *Global Shadows*, p. 36.
17. As Geoff Eley puts it (drawing on Fred Cooper and James Ferguson): "In other words, globalization as an actual set of processes affecting the world (as against the idealized claims of the globalizing grand narrative) necessarily presumes and produces, in fact specifically feeds off, dynamics of destabilizing and destructive unevenness and inequality (p. 161)" "Historicizing the Global, Politicizing Capital: Giving the Present a Name," *History Workshop Journal* 63 (Spring 2007), 154–88. Published by Oxford University Press.
18. Eric Schmitt, "Drones in Niger Reflect New U.S. Tack on Terrorism," *New York Times*, July 10, 2013.
19. The volume of scholarship that has been published on this topic since 1998 is impressive, especially as regards: development, political science and mineral-resource extraction. The relationship between coups, political instability and violence, and the uranium industry has been substantially documented.
20. Amartya Sen, *Development as Freedom* (New York, NY: Anchor Books, 2000), p. 14.
21. Ibid., p. 33.
22. Ibid., p. 147.
23. Ibid., p. 148.
24. Ibid., p. 148.
25. Ibid., pp. 174–5.
26. Ibid., p. 152.
27. Ibid., p. 262.
28. Ibid., p. 263.
29. It is necessary to acknowledge that "[g]atekeeper states are thus not 'African' institutions, nor are they 'European' impositions; they emerged out of a peculiar Euro-African history," Frederick Cooper, *Africa since 1940: The Past of the Present* (Cambridge: Cambridge University Press, 2002), p. 160.
30. Cooper, *Africa since 1940*, p. 130.
31. Ibid., p. 130.
32. Ibid., p, 130.
33. Ibid., p. 156.
34. Ibid., p. 156.
35. Ibid., p. 172.
36. Ibid., p. 174.
37. Ibid., p. 160.
38. Sen comments on popular protest in Africa: "Similarly, while political freedom is widely denied in Africa, there have been movements and protests about that fact whenever circumstances have permitted, even though military dictators have given few opportunities in this respect" (*Development as Freedom*, p. 152).
39. Cooper, *Africa since 1940*, p. 183.
40. Sen, *Development as Freedom*, p. 183. While Sen has specifically demonstrated that democracy and transparency can prevent famine, his work also has

broader implications for understanding the role of political sovereignty in creating shared prosperity.

41. Jeffrey D. Sachs, *The End of Poverty. Economic Possibilities for Our Time* (New York, NY: Penguin, 2005), p. 74.
42. Ibid., p. 80.
43. Ibid., p. 189.
44. Ibid., pp. 41–4 and 46–9.
45. Ibid., p. 49.
46. James Ferguson, "Globalizing Africa?," *Global Shadows*, pp. 48–9.
47. Sachs, *End of Poverty*, p. 67. See Sen, *Development as Freedom*, pp. 99–100 and 103 for his discussion of the economic decline in Africa and the metrics that show it.
48. For a full discussion of the development data, please see the Appendix.
49. Eley, "Historicizing the Global," pp. 154–6.
50. Ibid., p. 158.
51. Ibid., p. 161.
52. Ibid., p. 163.
53. Ibid., pp. 161–3.
54. "Bangladesh clothing factory hit by deadly fire," BBC News Asia. October 8, 2013. With review of fire in April in Dhaka. www.bbc.com/news/world-asia-24453165 (consulted June 20, 2014). "Children in Burkina Faso Take on Dirty, Dangerous Work of Digging Up Gold," PBS NewsHour. July 10, 2013. www.pbs.org/newshour/bb/world-july-dec13-burkinafaso_07-10/ (consulted June 20, 14). "South African Platinum workers strike over pay," BBC News Africa. www.bbc.com/news/world-africa-25854482 (consulted June 20, 14).
55. Eley, "Historicizing the Global," p. 165. For Sen's discussion of the dangers of asymmetry in the markets, see Sen, *Development as Freedom*, p. 142.
56. Eley, "Historicizing the Global," p. 165.
57. Mongo Beti, *Main basse sur le Cameroun: autopsie d'une décolonisation* (Paris: Maspero, 1972) and *La France contre l'Afrique: Retour au Cameroun* (Paris: Découverte, 1993).
58. Cordula Meyer, "Tuareg Activist Takes on French Nuclear Company," April 2, 2010. www.globalpolicy.org/security-council/dark-side-of-natural-resources/minerals-in-conflict/48926-tuareg-activist-takes-on-french-nuclear-company.html?tmpl=component (consulted: June 4, 2014).
59. "Niger uranium mining dispute a test case for use of African natural resources," by Mark Tran, January 10, 2014, *The Guardian*. www.theguardian.com/global-development/poverty-matters/2014/jan/10/niger-uranium-mining-dispute-african-natural-resources (consulted June 4, 2014). In May 2014, the French company Areva reached a deal with the government of Niger to increase the taxes paid from 5.5 percent to 12 percent. Areva also announced plans to open another uranium mine in Niger at Imouraren that is expected to double Niger's output of uranium to 9,000 tons a year. See www.mining.com/areva-reaches-uranium-mining-deal-with-niger-delays-project-46579/ (consulted January 4, 2015).

60. Robert Nugent has a background in natural resource management and his work history includes a project for the World Bank in Somalia and two projects for the United Nations in Afghanistan and Cambodia. After 11 years at the UN, he decided to study documentary filmmaking at the Australian Film, Television and Radio School. He founded a company called Visible Impact Assessment, which "evaluates how film can be used by communities to monitor and evaluate change." See www.itvs.org/films/end-of-the-rainbow/filmmaker (consulted June 11, 2014).
61. African filmmakers working with traditional and new audiovisual media and technology are looking to bridge the conventional divide between video and film. Similarly, critics take up this idea and seek to further expand the parameters of debate to deconstruct old dichotomies such as insiders/outsiders and recast notions of authenticity to allow for discussion across borders. My inclusion of Nugent's film obeys similar principles. For more discussion of these developments, see Lindiwe Dovey, "African Film and Video: Pleasure, Politics, Performance," *Journal of African Cultural Studies*, vol. 22, no. 1 (2012), 1–6.
62. ITVS press release for the PBS Global Voices series that aired on August 30, 2009. http://cdn.itvs.org/end_of_the_rainbow-pressrelease.pdf (consulted June 11, 2014).
63. ITVS press release for the PBS Global Voices series that aired on August 30, 2009. http://cdn.itvs.org/end_of_the_rainbow-pressrelease.pdf (consulted June 11, 2014).
64. See, for example: Adélékè Adéèkó, "Power Shift: America in the New Nigerian Imagination." *The Global South*, vol. 2, no. 2 (2008), 10–30.
65. Tejumola Olaniyan, "Of Rations and Rationalities: The World Bank, African Hunger, and Abderrahmane Sissko's *Bamako*," *The Global South*, vol. 2. no. 2, "Africa in a Global Age" (Fall, 2008), 130–8.
66. See Adéèkó, "Power Shift," pp. 10–30. For a discussion of new trends in literary writing by Nigerian authors of the third generation including Abani and Chimamanda Ngozi Adichie in addition to Unoma Azuah, Sefi Atta and Chika Unigwe, see Pius Adesanmi and Chris Dunton's introduction "Everything Good is Raining: Provisional Notes on the Nigerian Novel of the Third Generation," *Research in African Literatures*, vol. 39, no. 2 (Summer 2008), vii–xii. For a discussion of similar trends in West African literature in English, see Tanure Ojaide, "Migration, Globalization, & Recent African Literature," *World Literature Today*, vol. 82, no. 2 (March–April 2008), 43–6. For a more general discussion of new trends in the African novel, see Dominic Thomas, "New voices, emerging themes," *The Cambridge Companion to the African Novel* (Cambridge: Cambridge University Press, 2009), pp. 227–41.
67. Adéèkó, "Power Shift," p. 11.
68. Ibid., p. 18.
69. During his TED talk "On Humanity," Abani makes reference to the South African concept of "ubuntu." www.ted.com/talks/chris_abani_muses_on_humanity (consulted June 20, 2014).
70. See, for example: Adéèkó, "Power Shift," pp. 10–30.
71. For more discussion of Armah's writing, see Chapters 1 and 3.

72. See Helen Nabasuta Mugambi and Tuzyline Jita Allan, eds. *Masculinities in African Literary and Cultural Texts* (Oxfordshire: Ayebia Clarke Publishing Ltd, 2010), which I discuss in Chapter 2.
73. Abani, "On Humanity" TED Talk, February 2008. www.ted.com/talks/chris_abani_muses_on_humanity.
74. Robert Spencer reviews the literature on this topic in *Cosmopolitan Criticism and Postcolonial Literature* (New York, NY: Palgrave, 2011). If the spread of globalization is remaking the world in the image of American capitalism, then cosmopolitanism, for Spencer, is a constructive, if idealistic, reaction to counter this process. He describes such initiatives as the "cosmopolitan democracy project" and mass-based emancipatory forms of global consciousness. While the nation is still recognized in the West, for the moment, as a locus of power, Spencer argues for the need to cultivate post-national institutions that would enable activism beyond, rather than, between nations. He summarizes the positions of the idealists for whom cosmopolitanism means a borderless world (Homi Bhabha, Arjun Appadurai) and those of the "trenchant socialists" for whom the nation-state remains the "indispensable conduit of capitalism" (Timothy Brennan, Benita Parry, Arif Dirlick) and seeks to carve out a space of reconciliation between these different schools of thought.
75. The emergence of non-European writers using European languages in newly independent nations posed critical and theoretical questions for characterizing the formation of these new literary traditions. The question, for instance, of working out a "national model" versus a regional or comparativist model for reading emerging literary forms in European languages whether in Africa, Asia, Latin America or Australia was already a concern in 1989 for the contributors to Bill Ashcroft, Gareth Griffiths and Helen Tiffin, *The Empire Writes Back: Theory and Practice in Post-Colonial Literatures* (New York: Routledge, 1989). The next year, Homi Bhabha sparked more theoretical interest in mapping the relationships between storytelling, cultural narratives of identity and ideas of the "nation" in the volume of essays he edited *Nation and Narration* (1990). Homi Bhabha, *Nation and Narration* (New York: Routledge, 1990). Bhabha's introduction was followed by Ernest Renan's famous lecture "Qu'est-ce qu'une nation?" in English translation. In African literary criticism of this era, Abiola Irele examined nationalism's impact on literature and ideologies of liberation in *The African Experience in Literature and Ideology* (Bloomington, IN: Indiana University Press, 1990) and Richard Bjornson worked out a national model focused on Cameroon in *The African Quest for Freedom and Identity: Cameroonian Writing and the National Experience* (Bloomington, IN: Indiana University Press, 1991). Bjornson opens with three chapters that articulate, in broad terms, the importance of the idea of the nation with respect to identity, literature and colonial culture. He maintains a consistent focus on the political and ideological aspects of nationalism and offers a thoughtful discussion of the emergence of Cameroonian writing as a response to the colonial encounter. What is more, he follows representations of national experience all the way through to the expression of disillusionment in "The Corrupt Society and the Sensitive Self: Literary Anatomies of Contemporary Cameroon." It bears

mentioning that his project – a magisterial treatment of national literature – was completed before gendered critiques of the nation introduced new concepts and opened new directions, so gender identity and the contribution of women's writing gets insufficient attention.

76. In Edward Said's, *Culture and Imperialism* (New York, NY: Knopf, 1993) – who was a Christian of Palestinian origin born in Jerusalem and raised in Cairo – understood better than most literary critics the importance of *territory* in colonial empires. Said opens his chapter "Themes of Resistance Culture" with this: "The slow and often bitterly disputed recovery of geographical territory which is at the heart of decolonization is preceded – as empire had been – by the charting of cultural territory" (Said, *Culture and Imperialism*, p. 209). Charting the cultural territory of anticolonial nationalism was integral to the field of postcolonial studies from the beginning. In addition to Frantz Fanon's *The Wretched of the Earth* (New York, NY: Grove Press, 2005), there were writers such as Albert Memmi who defined the colonial encounter in *The Colonizer and the Colonized* as a relationship that was people to people (in the sense of national communities) and never individual in nature. In French, see Albert Memmi, *Portrait du colonisé* (Paris: Gallimard, 1957). Aimé Césaire drafted his infamous letter to Maurice Thorez announcing his departure from the Communist Party because of his solidarity with anticolonial nationalist movements. See Aimé Césaire, *Lettre à Maurice Thorez* (Paris: Présence Africaine, 1956).
77. See www.ngugiwathiongo.com (consulted June 12, 2014).
78. Eley, "Historicizing the Global," pp. 154–88. Quote from p. 170.
79. Cooper, *Africa since 1940*, p. 187.
80. Jean-Stéphane Sauvaire adapted the novel into a film in 2008 that was set in Liberia and produced by Mathieu Kassovitz. I find the film adaptation to be only marginally successful because the relentless violence is not offset with the thoughtful social commentary in the novel.
81. For Cooper's discussion of this kind of activity, see his section "Other Africas: connections beyond the nation-state," in *Africa since 1940*, pp. 183–7. For James Ferguson's analysis of dynamics that cross national boundaries, see "Transnational Topographies of Power: Beyond 'the State' and 'Civil Society' in the Study of African Politics," *Global Shadows*, pp. 89–112.
82. Interview with Kwame Anthony Appiah, New York Public Library, February 2007.
83. Ibid. Jeffrey Brown of the PBS NewsHour did an interview with Nuruddin Farah the same year.
84. Interview with Kwame Anthony Appiah, New York Public Library, February 2007.
85. For Kwame Anthony Appiah's discussion of cosmopolitanism and our ethical obligation to others, see "Kindness to Strangers," *Cosmopolitanism: Ethics in a World of Strangers* (New York, NY: W. W. Norton & Co., 2006), pp. 155–76.

86. Appiah, *Cosmopolitanism*, p. 82.
87. Cooper, *Africa since 1940*, p. 183.
88. Ibid., p. 186.
89. Ibid., p. 186.
90. Sen, *Development as Freedom* and Nicholas Krystof and Sheryl WuDunn, *Half the Sky: Turning Oppression into Opportunity for Women Worldwide.* (New York, NY: Alfred A. Knopf, 2009).

14. *Translations from the Night*

Jean-Joseph Rabéarivelo

She/ whose eyes are prisms of sleep
and whose lids are heavy with dreams,
she whose feet are planted in the sea
and whose shiny hands appear
full of corals and blocks of shining salt.

She will put them in little heaps beside a misty gulf
and sell them to naked sailors
whose tongues have been cut out,
until the rain begins to fall.

Then she will disappear
and we shall only see
her hair spread by the wind
like a bunch of seaweed unravelling,
and perhaps some tasteless grains of salt.

5 The Spiritual Realm

Okonkwo's Unraveling and Other Responses

> A qui voulait l'entendre, il décrivait l'apocalypse qui accumulait colère sur colère au-dessus de nos pauvres têtes.
>
> *Sony Labou Tansi*

One evening, I went over to my sister-in-law Oumanana's house in her neighborhood Denke Denke named after a famous singer who lived across the street. It was the best reference to give taxi drivers. I went over to pick up my daughter Bitti, who had been playing with her cousins, chasing after cows barefoot down the middle of the street. I had been spending time alone reading Abiola Irele's book *The African Imagination*, drinking a cold Flag in my favorite buvette, and, most likely, smoking a cigarette or two. My brother-in-law Moussa greeted me at the door to the courtyard. He offered me a bowl of cold water. We all settled into comfortable chairs that recline, sitting low to the ground, in the vast courtyard. We ate sliced mangoes and drank green tea that Moussa poured. Standing fans kept the mosquitoes at bay. It was the rainy season.

In a completely unscripted manner we started to have a conversation about religion. Oumanana was translating for Marghnia, my mother-in-law, and Moussa was translating for me. That's how we had our family chat that humid summer evening. Oumanana asked me, presumably on behalf of Marghnia, if I would please ask my husband to pray. I answered, perhaps too bluntly, with a question: "How can I ask him to do something, that I myself don't do?" This was translated by Moussa, an observant Muslim, with a chuckle. What I did not tell them is that my husband Sidi-Amar, when we were sitting together, would lean back in his chair and light a cigarette after the call to prayer while everyone else got up to pray. He and I would exchange glances and chat as we waited for the day's activities to resume. Next, Oumanana asked what I would say if Sidi-Amar asked me to convert to Islam. This time, I did not answer with a question. I said, "I would not." Oumanana was as amused by my frankness as Moussa and informed me that if Sidi asked me three times to convert to Islam, and I said no, he could ask for a divorce. The exchange

Figure 5.1 Sidi-Amar with Tuareg men. Niamey, Niger, 1999
Source: Photo by Phyllis Taoua

that followed was rather long, perhaps lasting as much as an hour or more. I said that I would not convert to Islam under any circumstances because, in my view, organized religions of any faith too often involve men with guns. I explained that I did not believe that a divine presence could ever be found at the end of a gun, and that if God had spoken to us, we would have all heard the same message. Given the mirth and frankness of our mutual exchange, I was emboldened to tell them what Sidi's position was – at least, as he had reported it to me. He considered Islam to be a foreign religion in Niger that was brought on the backs of camels from the Middle East. He also would say emphatically that Islam has no influence on how Tuareg men conduct serious business, like waging war or marrying a woman. Islam, according to what I understood, was primarily for commerce and philosophy in the Sahara.

At the end of the evening, Moussa walked me to the door and thanked me for speaking so frankly with them. He said, "Tonight, we really talked. Thank you." Anyone who has lived in Africa knows that spirituality represents one of the most important spheres of experience in which individuals navigate relationships within their families and kinship communities. When we had this family chat in 2005 I was left with the impression that everyone who participated in it made choices regarding their faith, choices that made the most sense to them as individuals.

Let me begin this final chapter, which is something of an epilogue, by contemplating the meaning of Okonkwo's suicide. One of the most memorable protagonists in African literature, Okonkwo, commits suicide at the end of Nigerian author Chinua Achebe's novel *Things Fall Apart* (1958) when his world starts to unravel. After the narrator establishes what life is like in Umuofia – including gender roles, clan structure, and their harvests – we are introduced to the arrival of white people in the region. They are strangers from another world. Villagers suppose that they must be the same white people they heard stories about, who sold Africans into slavery. No one thought the stories were true. Now, the white people have come on iron horses and speak of Jesu Kristi. After the Christian missionaries get to work setting up their church, the villagers learn that profound changes may be coming. To make sense of this, "The elders consulted their Oracle and it told them that the strange man would break their clan and spread destruction among them" (*Things Fall Apart*, 80).[1] This ominous interpretation of the effects of Christianity in their midst also entails the elders' response to the encroachment of Western modernity on their Igbo way of life, from bicycles to the concept of equality. Okonkwo is the character in this novel who embodies inflexibility. Unable to adapt to this new world, Okonkwo chooses suicide.

As Achebe told Biodun Jeyifo during an interview: "Actually the culture 'betrays' him. He is 'betrayed' because he is doing exactly what the culture preaches. But, you see, the culture is devious and flexible, because if it wasn't, it wouldn't survive" (*Things Fall Apart*, 143). Okonkwo represents a version of Igbo masculinity that cannot adapt to Christian modernity. Without nuance and flexibility, Okonkwo blindly adheres to the customs of his clansmen. Among the many ideas the missionaries teach is the concept of equality. When the villagers are astonished that the white men accept outcasts among them, the head of the congregation, Mr. Kiaga offers a lesson from the evangel. "'Before God,' he said, 'there is no slave or free. We are all children of God and we must receive these our brothers'" (*Things Fall Apart*, 90). The Christian idea of freedom and equality are appealing to many Igbo in Umuofia, which leads to some new converts. Once the white people survive in the Evil Forest, contrary to everyone's predictions of doom, still more Igbo convert to Christianity convinced that their gods have abandoned them. In the relatively short span of seven years, while Okonkwo was exiled from Umuofia, his clansmen changed. "Okonkwo was deeply grieved. And it was not just a personal grief. He mourned for the clan, which he saw breaking up and falling apart, and he mourned for the warlike men of Umuofia, who had so unaccountably become soft like women" (*Things Fall Apart*, 104). Whereas Okonkwo laments the loss of order, of a certain rigid masculinity of social coherence, Igbo culture did, indeed, survive. In "Igbo Culture and History," Don Ohadike remarks how quickly the Igbo people "succumbed to European civilization" and that "the Igbo people were, and still are, often eager to accept change" (*Things Fall Apart*, 256).

In a tragic act of defiance, the Okonkwo hangs himself from a tree. When this is discovered his wise and true friend Obierika is angered at the loss of Okonkwo's life and at the fact that his people will not be able to give him a proper burial because those who take their own lives commit an irreparable offence. Okonkwo's suicide represents the culmination of the central conflict in the novel and takes place in the final scene:

> Then they came to the tree from which Okonkwo's body was dangling, and they stopped dead.
>
> "Perhaps your men can help us bring him down and bury him," said Obierika. "We have sent for strangers from another village to do it for us but they may be a long time coming."
>
> "Why can't you take him down yourselves?" he asked.
>
> "It's against our custom," said one of the men. "It's an abomination for a man to take his own life. It is an offence against the Earth, and a man who commits it will not be buried by his clansmen. His body is evil, and only strangers may touch it. That is why we ask your people to bring him down because you are strangers." *(Things Fall Apart, 117)*

Okonkwo's tragic character represents one way of responding to the encroachment of colonial modernity on the lives of the people of Umuofia. Achebe's archetypal protagonist sees the world around him falling apart and is unable to comprehend or accept the new order that is emerging.

This novelist's paradigmatic tale of colonial dispossession can be read in many ways. Okonkwo can be interpreted as having made the "wrong" choice because he could not adapt to strange circumstances in an inevitably changing world. He can also be seen as having made the "only" choice possible for a proud patriarch in a coherent, traditional society that was unraveling before his eyes. After the ancestors allowed white people who arrived on iron horses to set up a Christian mission in the Evil Forest without calamity striking while the community watched, many skeptics were persuaded to convert. Young people who saw the social opportunities that came with speaking English were the first to convert to Christianity and voluntarily join this version of a "modern" community, while elders who were unable to adjust to a new world felt increasingly useless in their own land. Evaluating different ways of responding to the colonial encounter is the central issue that readers must grapple with as we seek to understand the complex tragedy that leads Okonkwo to hang himself. Achebe carefully portrays how the spiritual world structured communal life in Igboland and gives us an eminently human character who interprets his existence in a way that reflects both his individual character – inflexible, combative, and proud – and the Igbo culture that organized the society in which he had grown to be a man.

Achebe's title was taken from "The Second Coming," a poem by W. B. Yeats:

> Turning and turning in the widening gyre
> The falcon cannot hear the falconer;
> Things fall apart; the center cannot hold;
> Mere anarchy is loosed upon the world.

What critics have observed, including A. G. Stock, is that the metaphor of "things falling apart" suggests a pattern (*Things Fall Apart*, 259). And this pattern is especially compelling because of the conceptual complexity at work in holding together things that cannot stay together. Figuring out the reason for chaos and anarchy "loosed upon the world" invites us to think about change; to think historically about why things must change. It is a rich metaphor that links the past, present, and future and can serve as a guiding principle for thinking about change as a process of unraveling.

Obierika's reaction conveys Okonkwo's suicide as a grave act with profound consequences. Suicide is also rare in African literature and cinema. In this book, we have only come across two other instances of suicide – Diouanna in *La noire de …*, and Chaka in *Bamako*. These, too, were tragic final acts; gestures of refusal and despair. However, if we set ourselves the task of excavating tropes of unraveling in the canon of African literature and cinema there are many texts to work with. We find evidence of explicit intertextual citations of "things falling apart" from Achebe's novel and similar, related metaphors for unraveling. The metaphor of "things falling apart" has several forms: it can convey a knot that will come undone, a center that will not hold, and the social fabric fraying. Given my approach to the meaning of freedom, this evocative metaphor is of particular interest to me for the layers of interconnection it helps us think about.

In this chapter, we will be looking at the spiritual dimension of loss and intangible aspects of existential freedom. To map out the intertextual terrain let us begin with Chimamanda Adichie's novel *Purple Hibiscus* (2003), which we discussed in Chapter 2 in terms of its engagement with the freedom to be and to do in addition to, and following on, the struggle for unfettered national sovereignty. Adichie opens her novel with this phrase, "*Things* started to *fall apart* at home when my brother, Jaja, did not go to communion and Papa flung his heavy missal across the room and broke the figurines on the étagère" (*Hibiscus*, 3; emphasis added). This intertextual citation of Achebe in a major work of twenty-first-century

Nigerian literature is both close to home and rather explicit. The teen-aged girl named Kambili – who narrates the novel in the first person – witnesses her family being torn apart. As we have seen previously, her mother poisons her father who dies a slow, painful death and her brother takes the blame and goes to jail. The reasons her family falls apart are complex and relate specifically to the central dilemma in Achebe's novel. They have to do with the different ways of responding to one of the most challenging aspects of the colonial legacy: *how to respond to the imposition of a foreign faith.*

In his novel *Graceland* (2004) about how the deprivations of freedom in Nigeria lead Elvis to choose migration, Chris Abani similarly employs the rich metaphor of unraveling. After Elvis's mother dies of cancer and his bereft, alcoholic father takes him to Lagos, the young protagonist drops out of school and is left to fend for himself. One afternoon, the narrator observes, "Elvis leaned back and watched life unraveling in the ghetto settlement under the bridge" (*Graceland,* 116). The teenaged boy's life and the lives of everyone else trapped in poverty seem to be "falling apart" before his eyes. In this instance, we have another intertext in twenty-first-century Nigerian literature although the phrasing is allusive and not a direct citation. In *Graceland,* Abani establishes a connection between how oppressive dictatorship deprives people of their instrumental freedoms as citizens and the lack of opportunities for people who are stuck in the slums. This creates an existential sense of dispossession for Elvis who is perpetually frustrated in his pursuit of a meaningful, creative life. The intangible sense of loss Elvis feels does not have an explicitly spiritual connotation, it is existential.

Jean-Joseph Rabéarivelo's poem, "She/whose eyes are prisms of sleep" published in *Traduits de la nuit* (1935; *Translations from Night,* 1975), uses the metaphor of "seaweed unraveling" to similar effect. In the poem, rain is a metaphor for a kind of power that can dissolve everything, which the poet uses to render his subjective experience of colonial dispossession in Madagascar during the 1930s. Thus, "once the rain begins to fall," the female figure disappears into the sea, where she will join the ancestors:

> Then she will disappear
> and we shall only see
> her hair spread by the wind
> like a bunch of seaweed unravelling,
> and perhaps some tasteless grains of salt.

The paradox of "tasteless grains of salt" evokes the absence of flavor and sensual pleasure, which adds to the poet's complex impression of loss as his world unravels. His poem, "She/whose eyes are prisms of sleep," presents a female figure as a symbol for Merina culture, which was a source of pride before the French colonized the island. "She" has her feet planted in the sea as if an island, like Madagascar, surrounded by coral reefs, which are fragile and integral to the survival of the marine ecosystem. The wealth "she" had in hand – coral and blocks of shining salt – were sold to men, "naked sailors" whose "tongues have been cut out." The cutting of the sailors' tongues conveys painful losses: the loss of language, the loss of their voices as citizens, and the loss of sensual pleasure. In his own life, Rabéarivelo resisted giving up the pleasure of writing poetry in his native language, so he produced bilingual editions, and suffered from his family's diminished status after they were dispossessed of their land, wealth, and way of life as a result of the imposition of French colonial rule. Readers of African literature will notice how the metaphor of life "unraveling" like a bunch of seaweed spread by the wind contains within it the idea of tragic disorientation and loss. Yet this metaphor is not an instance of intertextual citation of Achebe's novel. It is an example of how the pattern of things falling apart has been used in African cultural expression to represent the complexity of change that resulted from colonial domination and its existential, intangible dimension.

While these various uses of the metaphor of life unraveling convey different experiences of existential unfreedom, I would like to reflect here on the spiritual dimension. Questions of individual faith and spiritual values that structure societies have surfaced many times in the previous chapters. Kwame Anthony Appiah observed in *Cosmopolitanism: Ethics in a World of Strangers* (2006), "Ghana's atheists could hold their meeting in a phone booth. Almost everybody in Ghana believes not just in a powerful divine creator but in a wide range of other spirits."[2] Appiah's remark suggests, more generally, that spirituality is a pervasive aspect of life for a majority of Africans.

Virtually every African writer has had to formulate his or her own response to Okonkwo's dilemma in *Things Fall Apart*. It is in the spiritual realm that writers and filmmakers grapple with the existential dimension of freedom. They explore ways of understanding the interrelatedness of every sphere of life with a range of viewpoints from a shattered sense of wholeness to cultural syntheses that look to the future with hope. In my view, there have been three primary ways of responding to encroachment of colonial modernity led by missionaries of various faiths: resistance, disorientation, and synthesis.

Conflict and Resistance

Ousmane Sembène's *Ceddo* (1978) represents his most sustained and explicit treatment of religion in Africa in a film that depicts popular resistance to the violent imposition of a foreign faith. *Ceddo* imaginatively recreates the historical past in a Wolof village on the Atlantic coast south of Dakar beginning with the arrival of Catholic missionaries and slave-traders. The plot unfolds in a village where a group of "ceddo" (a Wolof word that means "outsiders") refuse to convert to Islam at a time in the distant past. A standoff ensues between traditional holders of power among the Wolof aristocracy and religious pioneers seeking to grab power, to make money and impose their values. Although Sembène features scenes with Catholic priests and slave-traders early on to frame the question of freedom in a way that encompasses Western imperialism, the drama focuses primarily on the coercive imposition of Islam. It is important to note, however, that not only does Sembène include explicit historical references to the slave trade – unlike the metaphor of Diouanna's slavery in *La noire de* … – he also includes African-American spirituals on the soundtrack to connect the central theme of freedom to the African diaspora.

The ceddo take as their hostage the beautiful princess Dior Yacine, a daughter of the Wolof aristocracy, and keep her outside the village until the end of the film. The ceddo kidnap the princess, who sides with them, in the hope that the king will come to rescue her and refuse to submit to the will of the manipulative, ambitious imam. It is only after the representatives of Islamic power kill the king and subjugate the ceddo population by force – shaving their heads as a public sign of conversion – that the princess returns to the village square and, in a spectacular display of courage, shoots and kills the imam. Her act of bravery challenges one of the premises of patriarchy – that women need male protection – and puts an end to Wolof capitulation to imperial Islam. Sembène creates symbolically charged scenes with close-up shots of slaves being branded with hot irons and African-American spirituals on the soundtrack, which combines powerful elements that evoke pan-African ideals of freedom. In terms of interpreting the decline of traditional African spirituality (as practiced, here, by the Wolof), Mamadou Diouf and others have remarked how Sembène challenges the conventional historical narrative in Senegal of negotiated and selective compromise over years, rather than the violent conquest his film stages.[3]

Ceddo makes a frankly subversive statement that uses a narrative of *longue durée* to bring up for reconsideration what Sembène considered to be an unhealthy arrangement that then-president, Léopold Sédar Senghor, had set up with the Muslim Brotherhood during and after national liberation in Senegal. Sembène's representation of the arrival of Islam at gunpoint and his comparisons with European Christianity and the slave trade establish equivalencies between them. He sets up these analogies, which involve a manipulation of historical time, to take a position in favor of human freedom as an inherent value and against any form of imperialism, including the arrival of Islam in Africa. His unconventional representation of the ceddo's dispossession with panoramic shots of their houses being set on fire at night, is a distillation of imperial history into one dramatic struggle between those who have power and those who do not. This moral vision expresses Sembène's unique blend of pan-African ideas of liberation and Marxist values with a revolutionary's skepticism about any religion.

While this example of conflict and resistance as a model for thinking about African reactions to the imposition of religious values on people by force comes from African cinema, there are several writers who engage in similar ways with these issues. Assia Djebar and Nuruddin Farah, whose works we have examined in previous chapters, come to mind. Djebar's novel *Vaste est la prison* (1995; *So Vast a Prison*, 1999) represents the imposition of patriarchal Islam in the Maghreb as giving rise to social conflict and feminist resistance. In this hybrid text, she explores the ideal of freedom for women with historical reference to the fourth century Tuareg queen and matriarch, Tin Hinan. For Djebar, recovering the precolonial past in Algeria that Tin Hinan symbolizes would provide an alternative historical narrative to the one advanced by the proponents of political Islam in the Maghreb during the late twentieth century. Farah also offers a feminist critique of Islamic patriarchy, but this is within the context of his native Somalia over the past fifty years. He explicitly questions the idea of women's inferiority in religious traditions, including both the Bible and the version of Islam practiced in Somalia in his novel *From a Crooked Rib* (1970). Farah's defense of women's rights as integral to a healthy democracy and his criticism of patriarchal, political Islam as a cultural plague is developed in his later novels with the iconoclastic female character Sholoongo in *Secrets* (1998) and the transnational feminist Cambara in *Knots* (2007).

Disorientation and Apocalypse

Hoscar Hana in Sony Labou Tansi's novel *Le Commencement des douleurs* (1995), written in French with Kikongo inflections and not yet translated into English, stands out as the author's most morally complex character because Hoscar sees himself as both victim and villain. He admits that his actions have caused trouble for himself and his community while he longs for a different set of options. Hoscar has committed an offense against the virginal Banos Maya by giving her an indecent kiss and refusing to marry her afterwards. While the community in Hondo-Noote awaits their marriage, that day never comes; Hoscar agrees to wed and then refuses to follow through and other reasons are given that defer the plot's resolution. The story turns on Hoscar's longing for existential freedom and the capacity to define his life in accordance with his ethical vision of the world.

The novel opens with the phrase "Everything started with a kiss" and the narrator's definition of what this "kiss" means is subsequently elaborated with a play on meanings of the French word "baiser" that includes an idiomatic expression for copulation. We learn that it was a deformed kiss that fractured the foundation of time and the people's very existence (*Commencement*, 22). The origin of the kiss as an offense is attributed to the white man's arrogance. Arthur Banos Maya, the girl's father, is a white plutocrat, and his political influence and social standing in Hondo-Noote are steeped in the region's colonial history (*Commencement*, 25–31). The "kiss" becomes a malediction that afflicts Banos and Hoscar for a wild array of reasons. Eventually, hatred starts fermenting in the people's hearts and they persuade the girl to demand reparations; the people were gossiping about her being bewitched, living under a spell, of damnation, of poisoning by saliva, but Hoscar wants to know why they insist on turning one indecent kiss into the beginning of the end of the world (*Commencement*, 42–3).

The marriage plot in this novel becomes an allegorical way of negotiating the community's political differences in a narrative that develops into a utopic struggle against the dystopic reality in Hondo-Noote. Hoscar refuses to get married without a chastity belt and when Yona Archibald cannot deliver the device in time for the wedding, the people say a demon is behind all of this and is to blame Yona Archibald's American ancestors for wreaking havoc around the world with their money (*Commencement*, 82–3). While the bride files her fingernails and braids her hair in anticipation, the groom has locked himself up in a laboratory where he is trying to invent an island in the middle of the ocean. Hoscar appealed, entreated, and implored the gods, but they have not answered his demand that justice be done; instead, things just got worse (*Commencement*, 96–7). Finally the sky and the earth conspire against Hondo-Noote, unleashing a storm that stained the city in its most intimate regions and uprooted trees from the soil. The wedding was put on hold while the people of Hondo-Noote decided to wage a merciless war for eleven months against stinking beasts, which gave off an abominable odor. Hoscar persists in his dream of creating a virgin island untainted by the history of colonization, freed from the burden of three thousand years of frustrations, humiliations, and perfect negations (*Commencement*, 102–3). Both a symbolic language for the body's cleanliness free from illness and injury (with talk of codpieces and chastity belts) as well as the ideal of a territory free from the stains of colonial history (as in a virgin island in the Pacific Ocean) overlap in this narrative of irreconcilable civil strife. Ultimately, a sense of irreparable offense engulfs the lives of the people of Hondo-Noote as the damned nuptials are never realized because the ancestors have turned their backs on such an incongruous union (*Commencement*, 141–3). The wedding that never happens is an allegory for the national community that never came to fruition, unable to overcome political divisions, and existential rivalries of the past.

Tansi's novels from *La vie et demie* to *Le commencement des douleurs* convey a sense of spiritual disorientation. In the region encompassing both of the Congos, Simon Kimbangou offered a spiritual synthesis that appropriated certain elements from Christianity and blended them with local Congolese traditions. There is evidence in Tansi's writing that he was aware of, and sensitive to, this syncretic spiritual practice. So, to build on what we have already discussed in Chapters 1 and 3, we may say that Tansi's disorientation was not due to the absence of a viable spiritual synthesis, but to his understanding of political power and colonial history. His apocalyptic vision stemmed from his spiritual interpretation of political dispossession. From within his Kongo worldview, being dispossessed of power and dignity was an irreparable offense. In Tansi's oeuvre, the narrative voice in *Le commencement des douleurs* and the character of Hoscar best convey the complexity of this modern dilemma in the Congo.

We have another variation on this theme of disorientation and apocalypse in *Murambi, le livre des ossements* (2000; *Murambi, the Book of Bones*, 2006) where Boubacar Boris Diop contrasts two brothers' reactions to the genocide in Rwanda. Dr. Karekezi secretly helped organize the Hutu's slaughter of Tutsis, while Siméon resisted the violence, but loses his spiritual faith in Imana (creator deity in the Banyarwanda religion) after witnessing such incomprehensible carnage. Near the end of the novel, when the villagers want to pillage Dr. Karekezi's villa in revenge for the loss of their loved ones, their property, and way of life, Siméon asks them not to give into the temptation of interpreting the genocide in terms of moral absolutes, according to which they see themselves as Tutsi victims, and Hutu perpetrators like Dr. Karekezi, as the villains. Siméon explains that ethnocentric interpretations of violence with rigid categories of "victims" and "villains" could lead them down the dangerous path of identities formed in terms of ethnic persecution and eternal victimhood. The danger, in this case, derives from the possibility of an endless perpetuation of cycles of violent retribution.

In addition to Hoscar and Okonkwo, there are many similar characters in the world of African literature. Naana in Ayi Kwei Armah's *Fragments*

(1970) and Fama in Ahmadou Kourouma's novel *Soleils des indépendances* (1968; *Suns of Independence*, 1981) come to mind. In African literature an ethnocentric point of view can sometimes be masculine, old-fashioned, and inflexible. This is the case with Okonkwo's interpretation of Igbo culture and Hoscar's roots in Kongo culture in the aftermath of European colonial rule. Yet in Armah's *Fragments* the character trait of inflexibility is female. Naana is an elderly grandmother and it is through her Akan system of values that she interprets modern society. Within herself, Naana is never able to work out a compromise between her traditional values and modern Ghana. Armah presents Naana's dilemma as something of an epistemological impasse – she can no longer perceive the world around her – so she dies and joins the ancestors. We observe a similar impasse in Kourouma's novel *Soleils des indépendances* (1968; *Suns of Independence*, 1981) with Fama and his Malinké worldview. After national liberation in the République des Ebènes, the last male descendent of the Doumbouya dynasty struggles unsuccessfully to comprehend his diminished status within the new nation-state and modern society. In *Fragments*, as Naana's ability to perceive the world around her fades she passes over to the ancestral realm, whereas Fama appears fatally injured in the end as he attempts to cross the border and return to his ancestral village in *Soleils des indépendances*.

Conversion and Synthesis

Let us now return to Adichie's novel *Purple Hibiscus* and consider how her characters respond to the imposition of a foreign faith and to modern society in the wake of colonial domination. Two siblings, Eugene and Ifeoma, are subjected to a similar set of circumstances; they are raised by the same father who is observant of the Igbo faith and indigenous beliefs; they are subjected to the colonial imposition of a Catholic faith in Nigeria under British rule; they attend Western schools and attain a high level of education; they must navigate the injustices they find in the gatekeeper state where the government is corrupt and repressive. And yet, whereas Eugene completely adopts a colonial mindset and dons the white mask of alienation that leads to his unfortunate self-hatred, his sister Ifeoma achieves a healthy balance between her Catholic faith and Igbo identity. What this contrast shows is that individual self-definition is a choice as far as faith is concerned. Ifeoma's good friend Father Amadi exemplifies the importance of choice for individual behavior; we see Amadi singing Igbo praise songs in church and he will serve as an African missionary in Germany, which is in stark contrast with the white colonial missionaries who cleansed Eugene's hands with boiling water for "sinning against his body" as an adolescent boy. Building on what we discussed in Chapter 2, we can see how Adichie's novel draws a powerful and relevant distinction between the behavior of the faithful and the faith itself, which allows us to examine the manipulation of religion for political purposes that has implications beyond Christianity for the Igbo in Nigeria.

We have seen other variations on this theme of achieving a personal synthesis of faith and African cultural identity with the notable example of Ramatoulaye in Mariama Bâ's novel *Une si longue lettre* (1979; *So Long a Letter*, 1981). While Ramatoulaye is an observant Muslim whose prayers and introspection define the narrative, she also embraces modernity with measured optimism and favors monogamy over polygamy. In Chapter 1, we saw how Ramatoulaye expressed a feminist stance on the question of reciprocal love as the basis for marriage and how she rejected both the practice of arranged marriages, in general, and the specific custom of the levirate, according to which a brother-in-law may inherit his brother's widow against her will, in many Muslim societies. Whereas Ramatoulaye does not choose to divorce her husband when their family unravels after he takes a second wife, her best friend Aïssatou gets divorced when her husband marries Nabou. The different choices that these women make under similar circumstances illustrates a central ethic in the novel: that men and women of faith have options and the choices they make define their lives in accordance with their values as individuals in an expression of their existential freedom. Bâ's novel advances a feminist critique of Senegalese society after independence in large part because of the bad choices men in power made, compromising the goals of national liberation, and destroying the family structure needed to build a "new Africa." In this novel, women lead by example and their choices reveal the corruption of a male-dominated society, which presents ethical issues with implications far beyond Senegal during the 1970s.

In this chapter, we have seen the argument come full circle as we ended with a discussion of Tansi's comprehensive vision as it manifests itself in his novel *Le commencement des douleurs*. Contemplating the meaning of Okonkwo's tragic suicide in Achebe's archetypal novel *Things Fall Apart* served as a starting point for reflecting on the consequences of the encroachment of Western modernity on African communities. This allowed us to set the stage for reviewing three major responses to Okonkwo's dilemma in film and fiction over the years since. These responses were: (1) conflict and resistance, as we see in Sembène's film *Ceddo*; (2) disorientation and apocalypse, as we see in Tansi's novel *Le commencement des douleurs*; and (3) conversion and synthesis, as we see in Adichie's novel *Purple Hibiscus*. A review of works that we have looked at previously, as well as discussion of other canonical texts, has led us to identify and consider the pattern of unraveling as a significant trope for existential dispossession in the spiritual realm. Our discussion in this chapter has allowed us to articulate and reflect on intangible aspects of freedom in film and fiction where existential questions are in the foreground.

In a departure from the format of the conclusions to previous chapters, I would like to offer a different kind of summary in keeping with the spirit of this chapter being the epilogue and to remember one example of intangible, existential longing for freedom from each area of narrative interest that we have considered. The point here is no longer to differentiate between different types of freedom – instrumental, substantive, and existential – but to illustrate the presence of existential, intangible aspects of freedom in every area of narrative interest. This will help us to recall and reiterate the interconnectedness of these spheres of experiences by delineating the existential component of freedom in each:

Chapter 1. **The Self: Unfettering Identity After Independence.** The scene that most vividly portrays Mory's existential longing for wholeness at home is when he holds and contemplates a fragment of the zebus horns at the end of film. This symbol is charged with meaning through an accumulation of references to the effects of capitalist modernity that becomes a mirror of his complex, riven consciousness.

Chapter 2. **Gender: Women's Engagement with Freedom.** In Adichie's *Purple Hibiscus*, existential freedom is the "freedom to be"; the freedom to forge a creative synthesis between Igbo beliefs and Catholicism, and to develop a workable identity free from the kind of colonial alienation that plagued Papa Eugene, as Aunty Ifeoma has done and as Kambili is in the process of working out for herself. It is essentially to enjoy a sense of self free from alienation, which is as rare and beautiful as a purple hibiscus.

Chapter 3. **The Nation: From Liberation to Meaningful Freedom.** In South African narratives about the Truth and Reconciliation Commission, Antjie Krog's account of Lekotse's testimony at the last hearing in the Northern Province stands out. The shepherd who cannot find a language for his existential loss, struggles to adequately convey to the commissioners the extent to which his life was "affected" since the day the police raided his house. Lekotse's intangible dispossession comes from his perception that his place in the world was destroyed. This man's existential battle to resist the violence perpetrated against him relates directly to the cause of Steve Biko's Black Consciousness Movement.

Chapter 4. **Global Africa: Pillaging with Less Impunity in the Era of Neoliberal Capital.** In Jean-Stéphane Sauvaire's film *Johnny Mad Dog*, the image of Laokolé pushing her injured mother in a wheelbarrow in the midst of civil war is a symbol of devastating existential dispossession. As a maternal symbol, a mother pushed in a wheelbarrow by her children is a heartbreaking sign of the perversions of war and the antithesis of nurturing, competent love. That Laokolé should have to use a wheelbarrow – not to help her father build a fence or a house but to try to survive the destructive forces of war by carting her mother through war-torn streets – constitutes a powerful symbol of the consequences of armed conflict.

Chapter 5. **The Spiritual Realm: Okonkwo's Unraveling and Other Responses.** Hoscar Hana dreams of a body without illness and an island without history. He sees himself as both victim and villain, and admits that his actions have caused trouble for himself and his community while he longs for a different set of options. Hoscar dreams of creating a virgin island untainted by the history of colonization, freed from the burden of thousands of years of frustrations, humiliations, and negations. A symbolic language for the body's cleanliness free from illness and injury and the ideal of a territory free from the stains of colonial history overlap in this narrative, which turns on Hoscar's longing for existential freedom and the capacity to define his life in accordance with his ethical vision of the world.

Notes

1. Chinua Achebe, *Things Fall Apart*, Norton Anthology, ed. Francis Abiola Irele, (New York, NY: W. W. Norton & Company, 2008)
2. Kwame Anthony Appiah, *Cosmopolitanism: Ethics in a World of Strangers* (New York, NY: W. W. Norton & Co., 2006), p. 34.
3. Mamadou Diouf, "History and Actuality in Ousmane Sembène's *Ceddo* and Djibril Diop Mambety's *Hyenas*," *African Experiences of Cinema*, eds. I. Bakari and M. Cham, (London: British Film Institute, 1996), pp. 239–51.

Conclusion

We have seen how the ideal of meaningful freedom in Africa today evolved from a complex history of European colonial domination followed by the people's struggle for freedom. We have considered the fact that national liberation movements did not deliver meaningful freedom to a majority of Africans and discussed some of the most important consequences. We observed how the pioneers of African liberation incorporated the ideal of freedom into their discourse of national liberation and promised unity, shared prosperity, and social reconstruction as the fruits of African freedom. While reassessments of nationalism have been underway for a decade or more, articulating a conceptual language for freedom in Africa has been missing until now.

Considering the challenges that remained after independence because of the emergence of gatekeeper states and dictatorships across the continent, I have added to the argument against the equation of liberation with freedom that was commonplace for much of the twentieth century. Because national liberation was presented as a program, and seen by the people as a means of remaking free and independent African societies from the ground up after colonial rule, many artists and activists, in the years since, have engaged with the history and legacy of African liberation movements.

To deal with the confluence of factors that shaped the history of the emergence of freedom as an ideal, my argument draws on scholarship in the social sciences such as history, economics, anthropology, sociology, and philosophy in addition to the United Nation's development data, and complex narratives from African literature and cinema. I argue that to comprehend the meaning of African freedom requires wrestling with layered narratives that represent the world from different African perspectives. I take a pan-African approach and discuss examples from across the continent from north to south and east to west, with an emphasis on countries where cultural production has helped shaped the modern canon such as Senegal, Ghana, Cameroon, and South Africa.

Because my relationship to this material is not purely academic, I include some autobiographical storytelling about experiences I have had to let the reader know where I am coming from. These stories are not meant to be ethnographic; they relate scenes from my life in Africa over the last two decades and the inevitable socialization this entailed for me as a wife and mother.

I organized my textually driven argument around five areas of narrative interest, which evolved from reading Sony Labou Tansi's novels. I argue that these five areas of narrative interest were significant and help us capture what is most essential in the conversation about African freedom that has been evolving since independence. These areas are: (1) introspection and the intimate self; (2) gender relations; (3) the nation and national liberation; (4) the expansion of global capital; and (5) the spiritual realm. I find these areas analytically useful because they are consistently present or they are of major importance. This conceptual framework offers a way of moving beyond the equation of national liberation with freedom by opening up new avenues for a more productive discussion that incorporates multiple, interconnected spheres of experience in the definition of meaningful freedom.

After setting up these areas of narrative interest, I discussed my definition of "meaningful freedom" as having three interdependent kinds of freedom: instrumental (voting, free speech), substantive (choices, self-definition), and existential (intangible, ethical). I argued that these aspects of freedom can be and often are at work within a single work. I show how the language of freedom has been of central importance in canonical works of film and fiction, which had not yet been adequately examined or even acknowledged. Some of the most obvious examples of an explicit engagement with freedom as an idea, theme or structuring metaphor in the modern African canon are: Ayi Kwei Armah's novel, *Beautyful Ones Not Yet Born* (1968), Chimamanda Adichie's novel *Purple Hibiscus* (2007), Ousmane Sembène's films *La noire de ...* (1966; *Black Girl*) and *Ceddo* (1978), Assia Djebar's novel *Vaste est la prison* (1995; *So Vast the Prison*), and Chieck Oumar Sissoko's film *Finzan* (1992). In addition to these modern classics where an engagement with freedom is central, I consider other works that contribute significantly to fleshing out more specific aspects of freedom such as Nuruddin Farah's *Knots* (2007) to explore gender in a trans-national context, and Chris Abani's *Graceland* (2004) to examine how the persistent deprivation of freedoms contributes to migration and a post-national identity. While the chapters are not ordered to offer a chronology or historical argument, I do delineate a genealogy of narrative expression in African literature and cinema, along the way, that coheres around the idea of freedom.

This book took so many years to write because, in larger part, turning away from postcolonial theory had to come first. When I left off reading postcolonial theory a decade ago, articulating an argument like this one would not have been possible. The same ethical urgency that Geoff Eley describes as driving his work as a historian made me turn to the social sciences and primary texts, in addition to facts on the ground, to map out my argument about the ongoing struggle for African freedom after national liberation.

As my choices defined this project, I naturally became aware of the different kinds of books that could be written about African freedom. One could examine attached and unattached freedoms as Tejumola Olaniyan discussed in his intervention at the MLA in 2017 or one could take his distinction (attached/unattached) and consider ethnic affiliation as an obstacle to freedom at a national level in postindependence Africa. One could also write about African freedom with an exclusive interest in slavery, instead of the multifaceted approach I have taken to the ongoing struggle after independence. Finally, one could write a book about freedom in Africa with a focus on diasporic intertexts taking as a point of departure Richard Wright's *Black Power* (1954) and Malcolm X's *February 1965: The Final Speeches* (1992). These are roads I did not take but that have become apparent to me as other productive options going forward in pan-African freedom studies. What is of particular interest, to me, for future research is an audio-visual archive to document the words for and meanings of freedom in African languages.

The fact that much of the conversation about freedom over the past half-century in Africa has been grim, and has often entailed an existential struggle against oppression, should not leave us with an impression of eternal suffering. On the contrary, one hopes that these narratives of the struggle for freedom will have contributed to social progress, pan-African unity, and more prosperity for all the people in the future.

Appendix

The 1990s marked the end of two decades of economic crisis and the question of "whether an expanding world economy at the turn of the new century is bringing about modest improvement or continued malaise in Africa's economies" has been the subject of some debate.[1] Whereas some economic gains were made through the 1970s, many African economies faltered when the global economy contracted as oil prices went up in the mid-1970s. Monetary policy including the devaluation of the CFA franc in 1994 and structural adjustment plans tied to loans from the International Monetary Fund and World Bank initiated during this downturn made matters worse. The fact that a majority of the world's poorest nations with negative growth rates were in sub-Saharan Africa at the turn of the century makes looking at development data relevant to the struggle for meaningful freedom. As Amartya Sen's work helps us see, claims about estimated life expectancy and social inequality can – and should be – evaluated in relation to the development data that is available.[2]

A sample of statistics relative to the countries most important to my discussion of freedom are provided in the tables (Tables A.1–A.4) below. If we look at development indicators since 1990 they show modest progress in some areas and stagnation or decline in others, suggesting that uneven progress is ongoing. Whereas the overall percentage of the population in sub-Saharan Africa living in poverty ($1.90 per day) has declined from 56.5 percent in 1990 to 43 percent in 2012, some countries have made substantial advances and only one country, Cameroon, lost ground. Table A.1 shows data available for the poverty headcount ratio at $1.90 per day (percentage of the population (PPP) by country.

Cameroon has not made substantial progress in alleviating poverty in terms of total percentage of population and ranks near the bottom of the human development scale for countries worldwide (Table A.2). Constraints on democratic freedoms and widespread corruption continue to thwart social progress in Cameroon in contrast to Niger and Senegal where the poverty rate has been cut in half since 1990. In

Table A.1

Country	Year	PPP	Year	PPP	Year	PPP
Cameroon	2000	23.1%	2010	29.3%	2016	24.0%
DRC	1990	—	2010	77.1%	2016	—
Ghana	1990	47.4%	2010	13.6%	2016	—
Guinea	1990	92.3%	2010	35.3%	2016	—
Kenya	1990	23.1%	2000	21.5%	2016	—
Mali	2000	57.9%	2010	49.3%	2016	—
Niger	1990	78.2%	2010	50.3%	2016	45.5%
Nigeria	1990	57.1%	2010	53.5%	2016	—
Rwanda	2000	77%	2010	60.3%	2016	60.4%
Senegal	1990	68.4%	2010	38.0%	2016	—
Somalia	1990	—	2010	—	2016	—
South Africa	1990	29.3%	2010	16.6%	2016	—

Source: The World Bank, Poverty & Inequality data by country https://data.worldbank.org/country

Niger and Senegal, people generally enjoy the benefits of democratic rule although these institutions are fragile and must not be taken for granted, as the situation in neighboring Mali makes clear. South Africa has made significant progress in the years since apartheid ended, but sharp inequality between those who enjoy the largest share of the wealth and those at the bottom of the ladder presents serious challenges as do public health issues with a life expectancy at just 57.7 years, below many other sub-Sahran countries (Table A.2). The World Bank in South Africa identifies this persistent inequality as a key development challenge:

> South Africa remains a dual economy with one of the highest inequality rates in the world, perpetuating both inequality and exclusion. According to Statistics South Africa, the Gini coefficient measuring relative wealth reached 0.65 in 2014 based on expenditure data (excluding taxes), and 0.69 based on income data (including salaries, wages, and social grants). The poorest 20% of the South African population consume less than 3% of total expenditure, while the wealthiest 20% consume 65%. (*www.worldbank.org/en/country/southafrica/overview*)

It is striking that Kenya, Nigeria, and Cameroon – countries with enormous economic potential – have not been able to lift more people out of poverty despite a relatively educated population and better human development (Table A.2) because of corruption, political instability, and violence (Table A.3). Although the percentage of people living in poverty in Niger has been cut in half since 1990, the country still struggles with human development due, in part, to extremely low literacy rates (Table A.2) and the worst gender inequality in the region (Table A.4).

Table A.2

Country	Life Expectancy 2000	Years of Education 2000	Life Expectancy 2016	Years of Education 2016	Ranking worldwide 2016
Cameroon	52.0	7.1	56	10.4	153
DRC	50.0	7.0	59.1	9.8	176
Ghana	57	8.0	61.5	11.5	139
Guinea	51.3	5.1	59.2	8.8	183
Kenya	50.8	8.4	62.2	11.0	146
Mali	48.9	4.6	58.5	8.4	175
Niger	50.7	2.9	61.9	5.4	187
Nigeria	46.6	8.0	53.1	10	152
Rwanda	48.1	7.1	64.7	10.8	159
Senegal	57.8	5.4	66.9	9.5	162
Somalia	50.9	—	—	—	—
South Africa	55.9	13.0	57.7	13.0	119

Source: UN Human Development Report 2016 http://hdr.undp.org/en/countries/; Comparative indicators 1990–2015 http://hdr.undp.org/en/countries/profiles/ZAF

Table A.3

Country	CPI Score 2012	CPI Score 2016	CPI Ranking of 177 2016	WB Political Stability 2005	WB Political Stability 2015
Cameroon	26	26	145	41	14
DRC	21	21	156	1	4
Ghana	45	43	70	53	50
Guinea	24	27	142	15	31
Kenya	27	26	145	12	9
Niger	33	35	101	31	15
Nigeria	27	28	136	6	6
Mali	34	32	116	54	8
Rwanda	53	54	50	19	44
Senegal	36	45	64	40	40
Somalia	8	10	176	0	2
South Africa	43	45	64	41	39

Source: for CPI scores and rankings: Transparency International, the global coalition against corruption http://cpi.transparency.org/cpi2013/results/

Table A.2 provides United Nations Human Development data for 2000 and 2016 relative to two key indicators and 2016 human development rankings worldwide.

These baseline indicators of how the African countries under discussion have done with poverty alleviation and human development since

Table A.4

Human Development Index 2016	Male	Female
Cameroon	.555	.474
DRC	.469	.390
Ghana	.606	.545
Guinea	.464	.364
Kenya	.577	.531
Mali	.491	.385
Niger	.397	.291
Nigeria	.569	.482
Rwanda	.495	.491
Senegal	.523	.464
Somalia	—	—
South Africa	.677	.651

Source: International Human Development Indicators. http://hdr.undp.org/en/countries

1990 show some impressive accomplishments as well as a few instances of decline. While there has been some economic improvement, human development is generally slow to improve. Tables A.3 and A.4 provide information on contributing factors such as corruption, political stability, the absence of violence, and gender inequality in terms of human development. Cameroon, where Paul Biya has been president since 1982, is very corrupt and is no longer as politically stable as it once was, also due to Boko Haram and growing political unrest within the country. Ranked just above the DRC in terms of corruption and political stability, Nigeria is very corrupt and suffering from greater political instability and violence than its neighbors, with an ongoing threat of terrorism from Boko Haram in the north and northeast. Rwanda has been relatively successful in recovering from the genocide with democratic institutions ranking near the top in terms of political stability and the absence of violence. It is interesting to note that Rwanda and South Africa have both made substantial improvements since the 1990s when the two countries appeared to be heading in such opposite directions. Somalia ranks at the bottom with a war-torn country profile that is substantially worse than the DRC, based on the incomplete data available. The political instability in Mali and violence in the northern region since 2012 may reverse the dramatic gains in poverty alleviation between 1990 and 2010. As Table A.4 shows, those countries with the most stability – Rwanda and South Africa – also have the best conditions for girls and women to share prosperity. The data show that increasing access to opportunities for girls and women improves a nation's economy overall.

Table A.3 shows data for corruption and political stability. The first two columns compare data from the Corruption Perceptions Index for 2012 and 2016 (0 = highly corrupt – 100 = very clean); the third column gives 2016 rankings of 177 countries worldwide. The last two columns show World Bank data rating countries on a scale by percentile for political stability and absence of violence (0 = unstable – 100 = very stable).

The CPI ranks 177 countries measuring perceived corruption based on expert assessments and opinion surveys from eleven institutions including the World Bank, African Development Bank, and the World Economic Forum. Corruption is defined as the misuse of public power for private benefit.

Source: World Bank Governance Indicators Report: Data for 2005 and 2015 for "Political Stability and Absence of Violence and Terrorism" http://info.worldbank.org/governance/wgi/index.aspx#reports This data is part of the World Bank's good governance criteria including: corruption, government effectiveness, political stability, regulatory quality, rule of law, voice, and accountability.

Source: http://info.worldbank.org/governance/wgi/index.aspx#doc

Table A.4 shows the 2016 UN Human Development Report's HDI comparing male and female indices.

This index shows the disadvantages women and girls face in terms of access to health care, education, and job opportunities compared with men and boys in every country listed. Data on gender and development still need improvement due to insufficient and unreliable data tracking gender equality and other issues related to women in African countries, partially because of the absence of measurable trajectories over time.[3]

Overall, the trend of modest economic growth with patchy progress in human development continues and a large number of African countries are still ranked at the bottom of human development charts, between 119 and 187, worldwide. We observe, across the board, gains in life expectancy and education, yet gender inequality persists in every country considered. Three countries have been slow to mitigate socioeconomic inequality between the rich and the poor: Cameroon, Kenya, and Nigeria. Only the DRC, Rwanda, and Nigeria have more than half of their population living in poverty. Four countries have made the most progress: Niger, Senegal, Guinea, and South Africa. Political stability and the absence of violence and corruption have been good predictors of economic growth and human development with Rwanda and South Africa serving as the best examples of post-conflict success; and, with Senegal and Ghana showing relatively high stability. This data suggests that when political corruption allows exploitation of resources and labor to continue unfettered, the social fabric can unravel and the chance of violence, political instability, and discrimination against women and girls increases.

Notes

1. Frederick Cooper, *Africa since 1940: The Past of the Present* (Cambridge: Cambridge University Press, 2002), p. 87.
2. In *Global Shadows*, James Ferguson who is also quoted by Geoff Eley and others, claims that, "[Global Africa] features entire countries with estimated life expectancies in the mid-thirties and dropping; warfare seemingly without end; and the steepest inequalities seen in human history" (Ferguson, Global Shadows, pp. 48–9).
3. Claire Griffiths, *Globalizing the Postcolony: Contesting Discourses of Gender and Development in Francophone Africa* (Lanham, MD: Lexington Books, 2011).

Works Cited

Abani, Chris. *Graceland*. New York, NY: Farrar, Straus, Giroux, 2004.
Becoming Abigail. New York, NY: Akashic Books, 2006.
"Chris Abani: On Humanity" (Lecture, TED Talks 2008, Monterey, California, Filmed February 29, 2008, Posted July 2008).
Abrahams, Peter. *Tell Freedom*. London: Faber and Faber Limited, 1954.
Achebe, Chinua. *Things Fall Apart*. New York, NY: Fawcett Crest Books, 1959.
Morning Yet on Creation Day. Garden City, NY: Anchor Books, 1975.
The Trouble with Nigeria. London: Heinemann, 1983.
Adéèkó, Adélékè. "Power Shift: America in the New Nigerian Imagination." *The Global South*, vol. 2, no. 2 (2008): 10–30.
Adichie, Chimamanda Ngozi. *Purple Hibiscus*. Chapel Hill, NC: Algonquin Books, 2003.
Half of a Yellow Sun. New York, NY: Knopf, 2006.
The Thing Around Your Neck. London: Fourth Estate, 2009.
Aidoo, Ama Ata. *The Dilemma of a Ghost*. Essex: Longman, 1964.
Alidou, Ousseina D. and Alamin M. Mazrui. "*Secrets:* Farah's 'Things Fall Apart'." *Research in African Literatures*, vol. 31, no. 1 (2000): 122–8.
Anderson, Benedict. *Imagined Communities: Reflections on the Origin and Spread of Nationalism*. Revised Edition. London; New York, NY: Verso, 1991.
Andrade, Susan Z. *The Nation Writ Small: African Fictions and Feminisims, 1958–1988*. Durham, NC: Duke University Press, 2011.
Appiah, Kwame Anthony. *Cosmopolitanism: Ethics in a World of Strangers*. New York, NY: W. W. Norton & Co., 2006.
"Areva Q1 Revenue Up 12.5 Percent on Strength in Mining." *Reuters*, April 25, 2013. www.reuters/com/article/2013/04/25/areva-results-idUSL6N0DC4VD20130425?type=companyNews (consulted July 15, 2013).
"Areva, World's 2nd Uranium Company Heavily Present in Niger," *Nuclear Power Daily, Technology, Science and Industry*, May 23, 2013, www.nuclearpowerdaily.com/reports.Areva_worlds_2nd_uranium_company_heavily_present_in_Niger_999.html (consulted July 15, 2013).
Armah, Ayi Kwei. *The Beautyful Ones Are Not Yet Born*. Boston, MA: Houghton Mifflin, 1968.
Fragments. London: Heinemann, 1970.
"One Writer's Education," *West Africa* (August 26, 1985): 1752–3.

"Armah's Celebration of Silence: Interview with Dimgba Igwe." *Concord* (Lagos, April 2, 1987).
"Awakening." Filmed in 2008. YouTube Video, 75.31 divided in eight parts. Posted July 15, 2008. www.youtube.com/watch?v=Lv7JZceMCag.
Armes, Roy. *African Filmmaking: North and South of the Sahara*. Edinburgh: Edinburgh University Press, 2006.
Arms Control Association. "Nuclear Weapons: Who Has What at a Glance." *Arms Control Association*, Updated November 2013. www.armscontrol.org/factsheets/Nuclearweaponswhohaswhat (consulted on January 27, 2013).
Arnfred, Signe et al., *African Gender Scholarship: Concepts, Methodologies, and Paradigms*. Dakar, Senegal: Council for the Development of Social Science Research in Africa, 2004.
Ashcroft, Bill, Gareth Griffiths and Helen Tiffin. *The Empire Writes Back: Theory and Practice in Post-Colonial Literatures*. London: Routledge, 1989.
Attenborough, Richard. *Cry Freedom*. Universal Pictures. 1987. Film.
Bâ, Mariama. *So Long a Letter*. London: Virago, 1981. Originally published as *Une si longue lettre*. (Dakar: Nouvelles Editions Africaines, 1979).
Barlet, Olivier. *African Cinemas: Decolonizing the Gaze*. London: Zed Books, 2001. Originally published as *Cinémas d'Afrique Noire* (Paris: L'Harmattan, 1996).
Bensmaïa, Réda. *Experimental Nations, or, The Invention of the Maghreb*. Translated by Alyson Waters. Princeton, NJ: Princeton University Press, 2003.
Berman, Bruce et al., eds. *Ethnicity & Democracy in Africa*. Oxford: James Currey Press, 2004.
Beti, Mongo. *Main basse sur le Cameroun: autopsie d'une décolonisation*. Paris: Maspero, 1972.
La France contre l'Afrique: Retour au Cameroun. Paris: La Découverte, 1993.
L'histoire du fou. Paris: Juillard, 1994.
Trop de soleil tue l'amour. Paris: Juillard, 1999.
Branle-bas en noir et blanc. Paris: Juillard, 2000.
Bhabha, Homi, ed. *Nation and Narration*. London/New York, NY: Routledge, 1993.
Biko, Steve. *I Write What I Like: Selected Writings*. Chicago, IL: The University of Chicago Press, 2002.
Bissek, Philippe. *Mongo Beti à Yaoundé, 1991–2001*. Rouen: Editions des Peuples Noirs, 2005.
Biyaoula, Daniel. *L'Impasse*. Paris: Présence Africaine, 1996.
Bjornson, Richard. *The African Quest for Freedom and Identity: Cameroonian Writing and the National Experience*. Bloomington, IN: Indiana University Press, 1994.
Blakely, Thomas D. et al., eds. *Religion in Africa: Experience and Expression*. London: James Currey, 1994.
Bockie, Simon. *Death and the Invisible Powers: The World of Kongo Belief*. Bloomington, IN: Indiana University Press, 1993.
Boorman, John. *In My Country*. Sony Pictures. 2004. Film.
Brink, André P. *Reinventing a Continent: Writing and Politics of South Africa*. Cambridge, MA: Zoland Books, 1998.

Bureau of Democracy, Human Rights, and Labor with the U.S. Department of State. "Senegal," In 2006 Country Reports on Human Rights Practices. U.S. Department of State, March 6, 2007. www.state.gov/j/drl/rls/hrrpt/2006/78754.htm (consulted October 26, 2011).
Burnet, Jennie. "*Murambi, the Book of Bones*" (Review), *African Studies Review*, vol. 51, no. 3, (2008): 213–14.
Butler, Anthony. *The Idea of the ANC*. Athens, OH: Ohio University Press, 2012.
Césaire, Aimé. *Cahier d'un retour au pays natal* [1939]. Paris: Présence Africaine, 1983.
Discourse on colonialism. New York, NY: Monthly Review Press, 2000. Originally published as *Discours sur le colonialisme* (Paris: Présence Africaine, 1989).
Chapman, Michael. *Southern African Literatures*. London/New York, NY: Longman, 1996.
Chatterjee, Partha. *The Nation and Its Fragments: Colonial and Postcolonial Histories*. Princeton, NJ: Princeton University Press, 1993.
Empire and Nation: Selected Essays. New York, NY: Columbia University Press, 2010.
Clark, Phyllis. "Passionate Engagements: Sony Labou Tansi's Ancestral Shrine," *Research in African Literatures*, vol. 31, no. 3, (Autumn, 2000): 39–68.
Clingman, Stephen. *The Novels of Nadine Gordimer: History from the Inside*. Boston, MA: Allen and Unwin, 1986.
Coetzee, J. M. *Waiting for the Barbarians*. London: Secker and Warburg, 1980.
Cole, Catherine M., et al., eds. *Africa After Gender?* Bloomington, IN: Indiana University Press, 2007.
Conteh-Morgan, John and Irène Assiba d'Almeida, eds. *The Original Explosion that Created Worlds, Essays on Werewere Liking's Art and Writings*. Amsterdam: Rodopi, 2010.
Cooper, Frederick. *Africa since 1940: The Past of the Present*. Cambridge: Cambridge University Press, 2002.
Colonialism in Question: Theory, Knowledge, History. Los Angeles, CA: University of California Press, 2005.
Africa in the World: Capitalism, Empire, Nation-State. Cambridge: Harvard University Press, 2014.
D'Almeida, Irène Assiba. *Francophone African Women Writers: Destroying the Emptiness of Silence*. Gainesville, FL: University Press of Florida, 1994.
Daly, John. "Niger's Uranium Facilities under Assault." *EconoMonitor*, June 4, 2013. Reposted from *Oilprice.com* June 3, 2013. www.economonitor.com/blog/2013/06/nigers-uranium-facilities-under-assault (consulted July 15, 2013).
Dangarembga, Tsitsi. *Nervous Conditions*. London: The Women's Press, 1988.
Davidson, Basil. *Let Freedom Come: Africa in Modern History*. Boston, MA: Little Brown, 1978.
The Black Man's Burden: Africa and the Curse of the Nation-State. New York, NY: Random House, 1992.
Dia, Alioune Touré. "Succès littéraire de Mariama Bâ pour son livre 'Une si longue lettre'," *Amina*, 84 (November 1979): 12–14.
Diouf, Mamadou. "History and Actuality in Ousmane Sembène's *Ceddo* and Djibril Diop Mambety's *Hyenas*," *African Experiences of Cinema*, eds. I. Bakari and M. Cham. London: British Film Institute, 1996, pp. 239–51.

Djebar, Assia. *La Soif*. Paris: Julliard, 1957.
Les Impatients. Paris: Julliard, 1958.
Children of the New World: A Novel of the Algerian War. New York, NY: Feminist Press at the City University of New York, 2005. Originally Published as *Les Enfants du nouveau monde* (Paris: R. Julliard, 1962).
La Nouba des femmes de mont Chenoua. Distributed as *The Nouba of the Women of Mount Chenoua*. New York, NY: Women Make Movies 1978. Film.
La Zerda ou les chants de l'oubli. Algiers: Télévision Algérienne, 1982. Film.
Fantasia: An Algerian Cavalcade. London: Quartet Books, 1985. Originally published as *L'amour, la fantasia* (Paris: Albin Michel, 1985).
So Vast the Prison. New York, NY: Seven Stories Press, 1999. Originally published as *Vaste est la prison* (Paris: Albin Michel, 1995).
Algerian White. New York, NY: Seven Stories Press, 2000. Originally published as *Blanc de l'Algérie* (Paris: Albin Michel, 1995).
Dostoevsky, Fyodor. *Crime and Punishment*. New York, NY: Penguin Books, 1991.
Dovey, Lindiwe. "African Film and Video: Pleasure, Politics, Performance," *Journal of African Cultural Studies*, vol. 22, no. 1 (2010): 1–6.
Dugger, Celia. "Senegal Curbs a Bloody Rite for Girls and Women." *New York Times*, October 18, 2011.
Ekotto, Frieda and Kenneth Harrow, eds, *Rethinking African Cultural Production*. Bloomington, IN: Indiana University Press, 2015.
Eley, Geoff. "Historicizing the Global, Politicizing Capital: Giving the Present a Name." *History Workshop Journal*, vol. 63 (Spring, 2007): 154–88.
Eley, Geoff and Ronald G. Suny, eds., *Becoming National: A Reader*. Oxford: Oxford University Press, 1996.
Ellerson, Beti. "Center for the Study and Research of African Women in Cinema/ Centre pour L'Étude et la Recherche des Femmes Africaines dans le Cinéma." Last modified August 5, 2013, http://africanwomenincinema.org/AFWC/Centre.html.
"African Women in Cinema Blog." *Blogspot*. http://africanwomenincinema.blogspot.com (consulted July 25, 2012).
Elsanhouri, Taghreed. *All about Darfur*. San Francisco, CA: California Newsreel, 2005. Film.
Our Beloved Sudan. Sudan: Taghreed Elsanhouri Films, 2011. Film.
El-Tahri, Jihan. *Cuba: An African Odyssey*. San Francisco, CA: ITVS and Temps Noir, 2008, Film.
Emecheta, Buchi. *The Joys of Motherhood*. New York, NY: G. Braziller, 1980.
Erickson, John. *Islam and Postcolonial Narrative*. Cambridge: Cambridge University Press, 1998.
Fabian, Johannes. *Remembering the Present: Painting and Popular History in Zaire*. Berkeley, CA: University of California Press, 1996.
Fanon, Frantz. *Black Skin, White Masks*. New York, NY: Grove Press, 1967. Originally published as *Peau noire, masques blancs* (Paris: Seuil, 1952).
The Wretched of the Earth. New York, NY: Grove Press, 2005. Originally published as *LesDamnés de la terre* (Paris: Seuil, 1952).
Farah, Nuruddin. *From a Crooked Rib*. London: Heinemann, 1970.
Maps. New York, NY: Pantheon Books, 1986.

Gifts. New York, NY: Penguin Books, 1992.

Secrets. New York, NY: Penguin Books, 1998.

Interview by Kwame Anthony Appiah. Heyman Center for the Humanities, New York: February 21, 2007. Online. http://vimeo.com/44057167 (consulted March 3, 2012).

Knots. New York, NY: Riverhead Books, 2007.

"Fellowships. The McMillan-Stewart Fellowship in Distinguished Filmmaking." http://filmstudycenter.org/fellowships_mcmillan.html (consulted July 25, 2012).

Ferguson, James. *Global Shadows: Africa in the Neoliberal World Order*. Durham, NC: Duke University Press, 2006.

Field, Connie. *Have You Heard from Johannesburg?* 2010. Film.

Folly, Anne-Laure. *Femmes aux Yeux Ouverts,* Distributed in English as *Women with Open Eyes*. San Francisco, CA: California Newsreel, 1993. Film.

Femmes du Niger: Entre intégrisme et démocratie. Distributed in English as *Women of Niger. Between Fundamentalism and Democracy*. New York, NY: Women Make Movies, 1993. Film.

Frankel, Glenn. "When Mandela's, and the World's Fate Changed at Historic Rivonia Trial," *Washington Post*, (December 5, 2013).

Fraser, Robert. *The Novels of Ayi Kwei Armah*. London: Heinemann, 1980.

Gide, André. *The Immoralist.* New York, NY: Knopft, 1970. Originally published as *L'Immoraliste* (Paris: Mercure de France, 1902).

Gikandi, Simon. "Nuruddin Farah and Postcolonial Textuality." World Literature *Today*, 72, no. 4 (1998): 753–8.

Ngũgĩ wa Thiong'o. Cambridge: Cambridge University Press, 2009.

Givanni, June, ed., *Symbolic Narratives/African Cinema. Audiences, Theory and the Moving Image*. London: British Film Institute, 2000.

Gordimer, Nadine. *Occasion for Loving*. New York, NY: Viking Press, 1963.

July's People. New York: Penguin Books, 1982.

Gourevitch, Philip. *We Wish to Inform You That Tomorrow We Will Be Killed with Our Familes: Stories from Rwanda*. New York, NY: Farrar, Straus, Giroux, 1998.

Gramsci, Antonio. *Selections from the Prison Notebooks of Antonio Gramsci*. New York, NY: International Publishers, 1971.

Griffiths, Claire. *Globalizing the Postcolony: Contesting Discourses of Gender and Development in Francophone Africa*. Lanham, MD: Lexington Books, 2011.

Gugler, Josef. *African Film: Re-imagining a Continent.* Bloomington, IN: Indiana University Press, 2003.

Harris, Marvin. *Cows, Pigs, Wars, and Witches, the Riddles of Culture*. New York, NY: Random, 1974.

Head, Bessie. *When Rain Clouds Gather*. London: Heinemann, 1969.

Hemingway, Ernest. *The Sun Also Rises*. New York, NY: Charles Scribner's Sons, 1926.

Higgott, Richard and Finn Fuglestad. "The 1974 Coup d'État in Niger: Toward an Explanation." *The Journal of Modern African Studies*, vol. 13, no. 3 (September, 1975): 383–98.

Hutchinson, John and Anthony D. Smith, eds., *Nationalism*. Oxford: Oxford University Press, 1994.

Ibrahim, Jibrin. "Political Exclusion, Democratization and Dynamics of Ethnicity in Niger." *Africa Today*, vol. 41, no. 3, Electoral Successes: Harbingers of Hope? (3rd Quarter, 1994): 15–39.

Iltis, Tony. "Niger's Uranium Coup." *Toward Freedom, A Progressive Perspective on World Events since 1952*, March 8, 2010. http://towardfreedom.com/home/globalnews/1882-nigers-uranium-coup (consulted July 15, 2013).

Ireland, Corydon. "Soyinka Deplores Decline in Free Expression: Nobelist in Literature Suggests that Christianity and Islam are in the Midst of a Worldwide Religious War." *Harvard University Gazette* (October 12, 2006).

Irele, Francis Abiola. *The African Imagination: Literature in Africa and the Black Diaspora*. New York, NY: Oxford University Press, 2001.

Négritude et condition africaine. Paris: Karthala, 2008.

ed. *Things Fall Apart*. Chinua Achebe. A Norton Critical Edition. New York, NY/London: W. W. Norton & Company, 2008.

Izevbaye, D.S. "Ayi Kwi Armah and the "I" of the beholder," in *Ghanaian Literatures*, ed. Richard K. Priebe (New York, NY: Greenwood Press, 1988): 241–52.

Jebens, Holger, ed. *Cargo, Cult and Cultural Critique*. Honolulu: University of Hawai'i Press, 2004.

Julien, Issac. *Frantz Fanon: Black Skin, White Masks*. San Francisco, CA: California Newsreel, 1996. Film.

Kom, Ambroise. *Mongo Beti parle: Interview réalisée et éditée par Ambroise Kom*. Bayreuth: Bayreuth African Studies 54, 2002.

Remember Mongo Beti. Bayreuth: Bayreuth African Studies 67, 2003.

Kourouma, Ahmadou. *The Suns of Independence*. London: Heinemann, 1981. Originally published as *Les soleils des indépendances* (Paris: Éditions du Seuil, 1970).

Waiting for the Vote of the Wild Animals. Charlottesville, VA: University Press of Virginia, 2001. Originally published as *En attendant le vote de bêtes sauvages* (Paris: Éditions du Seuil, 1998).

Kpaï, Idrissou Mora. *Arlit, deuxième Paris:* Distributed in English as *Arlit, the Second Paris*. San Francisco, CA: California Newsreel, 2005. Film.

Krog, Antjie. *Skull of My Country: Guilt, Sorrow, and the Limits of Forgiveness in the New South Africa*. New York, NY: Three Rivers Press, 1998.

Krystof, Nicholas, Sheryl WuDunn. *Half the Sky: Turning Oppression into Opportunity for Women Worldwide*. New York, NY: Alfred A. Knopf, 2009.

Kuoh-Mukouri, Thérèse. *Rencontres Essentielles*. Paris: L'Harmattan, 1969.

Lacourse, Daniele and Yvan Patry. *Chronicle of a Genocide Foretold*. New York, NY: Icarus Films, 1996.

Lazarus, Neil. *Resistance in Postcolonial African Fiction*. New Haven, CT: Yale University Press, 1990.

Le Sueur, James D., ed. *The Decolonization Reader*. New York, NY: Routledge, 2003.

Liking, Werewere. *It Shall Be of Jasper and Coral: A Misovires Journal and Love Across a Hundred Lives*. trans. Marjolijn De Jager. Charlottesville, VA: University Press of Virginia, 2000. Originally published as *Elle sera de jaspe et de corail*. (Paris: L'Harmattan, 1983).

Interview by Lady Ngo Mang. Lady Vous Écoute. Télésud, Paris: March 19, 2012. Online. www.youtube.com/watch?v=SGlxUKGXI9o

Lonsdale, John. "Moral and Political Argument in Kenya," *Ethnicity and Democracy in Africa*, ed. Bruce Berman et al., Oxford: James Currey Press, 2004, pp. 73–95.

Loomba, Ania. *Colonialism/Postcolonialism*. London: Routledge, 1998.

Lorber, Judith. *Gender Inequality: Feminist Theories and Politics*. New York, NY: Oxford University Press, 2010.

MacGaffey, Wyatt. *Kongo Political Culture: The Conceptual Challenge of the Particular*. Bloomington, IN: Indiana University Press, 2000.

Majumdar, Margaret A., *Postcoloniality: The French Dimension*. New York, NY: Berghahn Books, 2007.

Mamdani, Mahmood. *Citizen and Subject: Contemporary Africa and the Legacy of Late Colonialism*. Princeton, NJ: Princeton University Press, 1996.

Mambéty, Djibril Diop. *Touki-Bouki*. New York, NY: Kino on Video, 1973. Film.

"Interview with Djibril Diop Mambéty," *Adhoua*, January–March 1981, p. 3.

Hyènes. San Francisco, CA: California Newsreel, 1992. Film.

Le Franc. Paris: Médiatheque de Trois Mondes, 1994. Film.

"The Hyena's Last Laugh," Interview with Nwachukwu Frank Ukadike *Transition*, no. 78 (1998): 136–53.

Mandela, Nelson. *Long Walk to Freedom: The Autobiography of Nelson Mandela*. Austin, TX: Holt, Rinehart and Winston, 1995.

Marx, Karl. "Manifesto of the Communist Party." in *The Marx-Engels Reader*, ed. Robert C. Tucker. New York, NY: Norton, 1978 [1848].

Matip, Claire. *Ngonda*. Paris: Bibliothèque du jeune Africain, 1958.

Mbembe, Achille. "The Banality of Power and the Aesthetics of Vulgarity in the Postcolony," *Public Culture*, vol. 4, no. 2 (Spring, 1992): 1–30.

On the Postcolony. Los Angeles, CA: University of California Press, 2001.

McClintock, Anne. *Imperial Leather: Race, Gender and Sexuality in the Colonial Contest*. New York, NY/London: Routledge, 1995.

"'No Longer in a Future Heaven': Gender, Race and Nationalism," in *Dangerous Liaisons: Gender, Nation, & Postcolonial Perspectives*, eds. Anne McClintock, Aamir Mufti and Ella Shohat. Minneapolis, MN: University of Minnesota Press, 1997.

Mignolo, Walter D. *The Darker Side of Western Modernity: Global Futures, Decolonial Options*. Durham, NC: Duke University Press, 2011.

Miller, Christopher. *Theories of Africans: Francophone Literature and Anthropology in Africa*. Chicago, IL: University of Chicago Press, 1990.

Minyuku, Biki, Chief Executive Officer. "Truth and Reconciliation Commission of South Africa Report." Truth and Reconciliation Commission, Department of Justice. 1995. www.justice.gov.za/trc/contacts.html.

Mitchell, Timothy. *Questions of Modernity*. Minneapolis, MN: University of Minnesota Press, 2000.

Mokam, Yvonne-Marie. "L'Oeuvre post retour d'exil de Mongo Beti." PhD dissertation, University of Arizona, 2009.

Moore-Gilbert, Bart. *Postcolonial Theory: Contexts, Practices, Politics*. London: Verso, 1997.

Mortimer, Mildred. "Entretien avec Assia Djebar, Écrivain Algérien." *Research in African Literatures*, vol. 19, no. 2 (1988): 197–205.

Journeys through the African Novel. Portsmouth, NH: Heinemann, 1990.

"Reappropriating the Gaze in Assia Djebar's Fiction and Film." *World Literature Today*, 70, no. 4 (1996): 859–66.

Maghrebian Mosaic: A Literature in Transition. Boulder, CO: L. Rienner, 2001.

Mugambi, Helen Nabasuta, Tuzyline Jita Allan, eds. *Masculinities in African Literary and Cultural Texts.* Banbury: Ayebia Clarke, 2010.

Murphy, David. *Sembene: Imagining Alternatives in Film & Fiction.* Oxford: James Currey, 2000.

"Between Socialism and Sufism: Islam in the Films of Ousmane Sembène and Djibril Diop Mambety." *Third Text*, vol. 24, no. 1 (2010): 53–67.

Murphy, David and Patrick Williams. *Postcolonial African Cinema: Ten Directors.* Manchester: Manchester University Press, 2007.

Mwangi, Evan Maina. *Africa Writes Back to Self: Metafiction, Gender, Sexuality.* Albany, NY: State University of New York Press, 2009.

Nacro, Regina Fanta. *Un Certain Matin.* Paris: Médiathèque des Trois Mondes, 1991. Film.

The Night of Truth. London: British Film Institute, 2004. Originally distributed as *La nuit de la verité* (New York: First Run/Icarus Films, 2004). Film.

Nairn, Tom. "The Maladies of Development," in *Nationalism*, eds. John Hutchinson and Anthony Smith. Oxford: Oxford University Press, 1994, pp. 70–6.

Nandy, Ashis. *The Intimate Enemy: Loss and Recovery of Self under Colonialism.* Delhi: Oxford University Press, 1983.

Ndebele, Njabulo S. *Fools and Other Stories.* Essex: Longman African Classics, 1985.

Nfah-Abbenyi, Juliana Makuchi. *Gender in African Women's Writing: Identity, Sexuality and Difference.* Bloomington, IN: Indiana University Press, 1997.

Ngaboh-Smart, Francis. "Secets and a New Civic Consciousness." *Research in African Literatures*, vol. 31, no. 1 (2000): 129–36.

Beyond Empire and Nation: Postnational Arguments in the Fiction of Nuruddin Farah and B. Kojo Laing. Amsterdam: Rodopi, 2004. PDF e-book.

Niang, Sada. *Littérature et cinéma en Afrique francophone: Ousmane Sembène et Assia Djebar.* Paris: Harmattan, 1996.

Djibril Diop Mambety, un cinéaste à contre-courant. Paris: Harmattan, 2002.

Njendu, Wanjiru M., *Look Again.* Culver City, CA: A Magic Works Production, 2011. Film.

Njoya, Nimu. "*Murambi, the Book of Bones.* (Review)," *Logos*, vol. 5, no. 4 (Winter–Spring 2007): 1–7.

Nottage, Lynn. *Ruined: A Play.* New York, NY: Theater Communications Group, 2009.

Nugent, Robert. *End of the Rainbow.* San Francisco, CA: California Newsreel, 2007. Film.

Nwapa, Flora. *Efuru.* London: Heinemann, 1966.

Nyoni, Rungano. *Mwansa the Great.* UK: Icreatefilms, 2011. Film.

Nzongola-Ntalaja, Georges. "Patrice Lumumba: The Most Important Assassination of the 20th Century" *The Guardian* (January 17, 2011). URL: www.theguardian.com/global-development/poverty-matters/2011/jan/17/patrice-lumumba-50th-anniversary-assassination (consulted August 6, 2014).

O'Brien, Donal B. Cruise. "A Lost Generation? Youth Identity and State Decay in West Africa." in *Postcolonial Identities in Africa*, eds. Richard Werbner and Terrence Ranger. London: Zed Books, 1996: 55–74.

Ogede, Ode. *Ayi Kwei Armah: Radical Iconoclast*. Athens, OH: Ohio University Press, 2000.

Ogot. Grace. *The Promised Land*. Nairobi: East African Publishing House, 1966.

Ojo-Ade, Femi. "Still a Victim? Mariama Bâ's *Une si longue lettre*," *African Literature Today*, vol. 12 (1982): 71–87.

Olaniyan, Tejumola. "Of Rations and Rationalities: The World Bank, African Hunger, and Abderrahmane Sissako's *Bamako*," *The Global South*, vol. 2. no. 2, "Africa in a Global Age," (Fall, 2008): 130–38.

Ollenburger, Jane C., Helen More. *A Sociology of Women: The Intersection of Patriarchy, Capitalism, and Colonization*. Second Edition. Upper Saddle River, NJ: Prentice Hall, 1998.

Ousmane, Sembène. *God's Bits of Wood*. London: Heinemann, 1962. Originally published as *Les bouts de bois de Dieu* (Paris: Le Livre Contemporain, 1960).

La noire de ... Dakar: Doomireew Films, 1966. Distributed in the USA with English subtitles as *Black Girl* by New Yorker Films.

Xala. Dakar: Doomireew Films, 1974. Distributed in the USA by New Yorker Films.

Ceddo. Dakar: Doomireew Films, 1976.

Faat Kiné. Dakar: Doomireew Films, 2000. Distributed in the USA by California Newsreel.

Moolaadé. New York, NY: New Yorker Video, 2004. Film.

Oyewumi, Oyeronke, ed. *African Gender Studies: A Reader*. New York, NY: Palgrave, 2005.

Palmer, Eustace. *An Introduction to the African Novel*. New York, NY: Africana Publishing Corporation, 1972.

Peck, Raoul. *Lumumba: Death of a Prophet*. San Francisco, CA: California Newsreel, 1992. Film.

Pfaff, Françoise. *The Cinema of Ousmane Sembène: A Pioneer of African Film*. Westport, CT: Greenwood Press, 1984.

Polgreen, Lydia. "Faction Splits from Islamist Group in Northern Mali." *New York Times*, January 24, 2013.

Pontecorvo, Gillo. *La Bataille d'Alger*. Distributed in English as *Battle of Algiers*. New York, NY: Criterion Collection, 1966. Film.

Quayson, Ato. *Oxford Street, Accra: City Life and the Itineraries of Transnationalism*. Durham, NC: Duke University Press, 2014.

Renan, Ernest. "What is a Nation?" ("Qu'est-ce qu'une nation?") in Homi Bhabha, ed., *Nation and Narration*. London: Routledge, 1990, pp. 8–22.

Reticker, Gini. *Pray the Devil Back to Hell*. New York, NY: Fork Films, 2008. Film.

Ricard, Alain. *Littératures d'Afrique noire, des langues aux livres*. Paris: Karthala, 1995.

Le Sable de Babel: Traduction et apartheid. Paris: CNRS, 2011.

Sachs, Jeffrey D. *The End of Poverty: Economic Possibilities for Our Time*. New York, NY: Penguin, 2005.

Said, Edward. *Culture and Imperialism*. New York, NY: Knopf, 1993.

Samatar, Said S., "Are There Secrets in *Secrets*?" *Research in African Literatures*, vol. 31, no. 1 (2000): 137–43.

Saro-Wiwa, Ken. *Sozaboy: A Novel in Rotten English.* New York, NY: Longman, 1994.

Sartre, Jean-Paul. "La pensée politique de Patrice Emery Lumumba," *Présence Africaine* (no. 47, juillet-septembre 1963), pp. 1–20.

Schmidt, Elizabeth. "Top Down or Bottom Up? Nationalist Mobilization Reconsidered, with Special Reference to Guinea (French West Africa)." *The American Historical Review*, vol. 110, no. 4 (October, 2005), pp. 975–1014.

Schmitt, Eric. "Drones in Niger Reflect New U.S. Tack on Terrorism." *New York Times*, July 10, 2013.

Sène, Momar Nar. *Djibril Diop Mambety: la caméra au bout du nez.* Paris: Harmattan, 2001.

Sen, Amartya. *Development as Freedom.* New York, NY: Anchor Books, 2000.

Shapiro, Dawn Sinclair. *The Edge of Joy.* Chicago, IL: Woodlawn Avenue Productions, 2011. Film.

Sissako, Abderrahmane. *"Sabriya," Africa Dreaming,* (One of six part series). San Francisco, CA: California Newsreel, 1996. Film.

Waiting for Happiness. New York, NY: New Yorker Video, 2002. Film.

"A screenplay is not a guarantee," *Interview with Kwame Anthony Appiah.* www.africanfilmny.org//network/news/Isissako.html (consulted November 16, 2004). Reprinted in *Through African Eyes: Dialogues with the Directors* (New York: African Film Festival, 2003).

Bamako. New York, NY: New Yorker Video, 2006. Film.

Timbuktu. New York, NY: Cohen Media Group, 2015. Film.

Sissoko, Cheick Oumar. *Finzan.* San Francisco, CA: California Newsreel, 1990. Film.

Guimba, the Tyrant. San Francisco, CA: California Newsreel, 1995. Film.

Smith, Sidonie. *A Poetics of Women's Autobiography.* Bloomington, IN: Indiana University Press, 1987.

Smith, Sidonie and Julia Watson, *De/colonizing the Subject.* Minneapolis, MN: University of Minnesota Press, 1992.

Soyinka, Wole. *The Lion and the Jewel.* London: Oxford University Press, 1959.

The Man Died: Prison Notes of Wole Soyinka. New York, NY: Harper and Row, 1972.

Myth, Literature and the African World. Cambridge: Cambridge University Press, 1976.

Open Sore of A Continent. Oxford: Oxford University Press, 1996.

"Hearts of Darkness, An American Journalist Traces the Authors of Rwanda's Genocide." *New York Times*, October 4, 1998.

Climate of Fear: The Quest for Dignity in a Dehumanized World. New York, NY: Random House, 2005.

You Must Set Forth at Dawn: A Memoir. New York, NY: Random House, 2006.

Spivak, Gayatri. "A Borderless World?" Lecture at the University of Arizona, Tucson, Arizona, January 19, 2012.

Stratton, Florence. *Contemporary African Literature and the Politics of Gender.* London: Routledge, 1994.

Taoua, Phyllis. *Forms of Protest: Anti-Colonialism and Avant-Gardes in Africa, the Caribbean and France.* Portsmouth, NH: Heinemann, 2002.

Tansi, Sony Labou. *Life and a Half.* Bloomington, IN: Indiana University Press, 2011. Originally published as *La vie et demie: roman* (Paris: Éditions du Seuil, 1979).

Le Commencement des douleurs. Paris: Seuil, 1995.

Tcheuyap, Alexie. "Comedy of Power, Power of Comedy: Strategic Transformations in African Cinemas." *Journal of African Cultural Studies*, vol. 22, no. 1 (2010): 25–40.

Teno, Jean-Marie. *Afrique, je te plumerai* Distributed in English as *Africa, I will fleece you.* San Francisco, CA: California Newsreel, 1992. Film.

Clando. San Francisco, CA: California Newsreel, 1996. Film.

The Film Study Center at Harvard University. "Fellows 2006–2007." http://filmstudycenter.org/people_fellows_0607.html#nacro (consulted July 25, 2012).

Thiong'o, Ngũgĩ wa. *A Grain of Wheat*. London: Heinemann, 1967.

Petals of Blood. London: Penguin Books, 1977.

Detained: A Writer's Prison Diary. Portsmouth, NH: Heinemann, 1981.

Devil on the Cross. Translated from Gikuyu by the Author. Portsmouth, NH: Heinemann, 1982.

Matigari. Translated from Gikuyu by Wangui wa Goro. Portsmouth, NH: Heinemann, 1987.

Moving the Centre: The Struggle for Cultural Freedoms. London: James Currey, 1993.

Penpoints, Gunpoints, and Dreams: Towards a Critical Theory of the Arts and the State in Africa. Oxford: Clarendon Press, 1998.

Wizard of the Crow. Translated from Gikuyu by the Author. New York, NY: Pantheon Books, 2006.

Todd, Tony. "French Special Forces 'To Protect' Niger Uranium Mines." *France24* International News posted January 25, 2013. www.france24.com/en/20130125-france-niger-uranium-areva-special-forces-mali-security-special-forces (consulted July 25, 2013).

Ukadike, Nwachukwu Frank. *Black African Cinema*. Berkeley, CA: University of California Press, 1994.

"Djibril Diop Mamety," in *Questioning African Cinema: Conversations with Filmmakers*. Minneapolis, MN: University of Minnesota Press, 2002, pp. 121–31.

United Nations Development Programme. "Niger, Country Profile: Human Development Indicators," In *2013 International Human Development Report-The Rise of the South: Human Progress in a Diverse World*. United Nations Development Programme, 2013. http://hdrstats.undp.org/en/countries/profiles/NER.html. July 15, 203.

Vansina, Jan. *Paths in the Rainforests: Toward a History of Political Tradition in Equatorial Africa*. Madison, WI: University of Wisconsin Press, 1990.

Vieyra, Paulin Soumanou. *Le Cinéma africain des origines à 1973 (tome 1)*. Paris: Présence Africaine, 1975.

Werbner, Richard, ed. *Postcolonial Subjectivities in Afirca*. London: Zed Books, 2002.

Wiesner-Hanks, Merry E. *Gender in History: Global Perspectives*. Second Edition. West Sussex: Wiley-Blackwell, 2012.

World Nuclear Association. "Uranium in Niger." *World Nuclear Association*, Updated July 2013. www.world-nuclear.org/info/inf110.html (consulted July 15, 2013).

"World Uranium Mining Production," *World Nuclear Association*, Updated July 2013, www.world-nuclear.org/info/Nuclear-Fuel-Cycle/Mining-of-Uranium/World-Uranium-Mining-Production (consulted July 15, 2013).

Wright, Derek. *Ayi Kwei Armah's Africa*. London and New York, NY: Hans Zell, 1989.

New Directions in African Fiction. New York, NY: Twayne Publishers, 1997.

"Private and Public Secrets: Family and State in Nuruddin Farah's *Secrets*." *The Journal of Commonwealth Literature*, vol. 39 no. 2 (2004): 7–28.

Zabus, Chantal. *The African Palimpsest: Indigenization of Language in the West African Europhone Novel*. Amsterdam: Rodopi, 1991.

Zakaria, Fareed. *The Future of Freedom: Illiberal Democracy at Home and Abroad*. New York, NY: W.W. Norton, 2003.

The Post-American World. New York, NY: W.W. Norton, 2008.

Index